MIKE BRYAN

Uneasy Rider

The author of nine earlier books and
collaborations about golf, baseball, and
religion, Mike Bryan now lives more or
less in New York City.

UNEASY RIDER

MIKE BRYAN

Uneasy Rider

THE INTERSTATE WAY

OF KNOWLEDGE

VINTAGE DEPARTURES
Vintage Books
A Division of Random House, Inc.
New York

FIRST VINTAGE DEPARTURES EDITION, OCTOBER 1998

The Library of Congress has cataloged the Knopf edition as follows:
Bryan, Mike.
Uneasy rider : the interstate way of knowledge / by Mike Bryan.
p.   cm.
ISBN 0-679-41671-4 (alk. paper)
1. United States—Description and travel. 2. United States—Social life
and customs—1971–.
I. Title.
E169.04.B77   1997
917.304'929—dc20   96-38901
CIP

Vintage ISBN: 0-679-74265-4

Author photograph © Marion Ettlinger
Maps © 1997 by Claudia Carlson
Book design by Dorothy S. Baker

Random House Web address: www.randomhouse.com
Printed in the United States
10   9   8   7   6   5   4   3   2   1

FOR P.

In memory of Don Dalton, Joe Fox, Mary Jones,
Hazel Muhl-Thompson, and Horace Webb

With an host of furious fancies
Whereof I am commander
With a burning speare, and a horse of aire,
To the wildernesse I wander.
By a knight of ghostes and shadowes
I summoned am to tourney
Ten leagues beyond the wide world's end.
Me thinke it is noe journey.

TOM O' BEDLAM'S SONG—

ANONYMOUS LYRIC

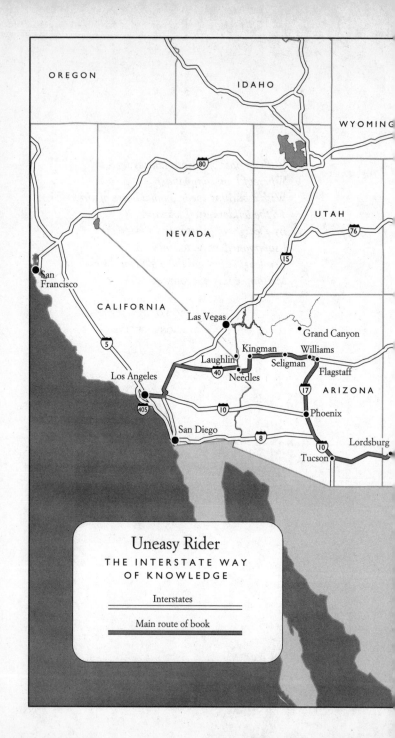

Uneasy Rider

THE INTERSTATE WAY
OF KNOWLEDGE

Interstates

Main route of book

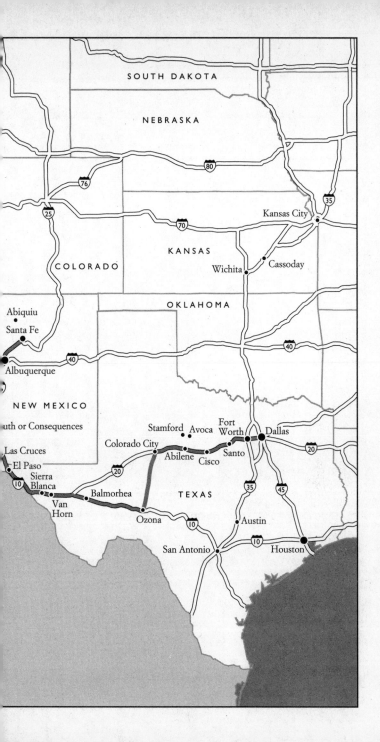

UNEASY RIDER

CHAPTER 1

Open the door to the Brazos River Rattlesnake Ranch sixty miles west of Dallas on I-20 and you see snakes and you smell—what is that smell? I couldn't place it, but I hesitated to ask Jeff Walker, who was manning the operation and had greeted me real friendly-like, and not just because he was new to the job. That's the way most people in Texas are; they can't help it. Jeff had worked as an electronics technician before leaving that company when informed, after eleven years of service, that he'd have to quit dipping his snuff on premises; plus he made only $6-something after all that time. They didn't care about their employees. Although this job with the snakes paid a little less, at least for the moment, it was also a lot less pressure and hassle, and he could dip in peace. I concluded that Jeff has no particular fear of deadly snakes; he invited me to look around for free and then, for a $1 surcharge, to step outside to the petting zoo. While the snakes—most of them—

were in the concrete-walled pits out there, this was fall, the beginning of their hibernation, so I'd have to look pretty closely to find them down in the grass. But some were there, for sure. A few were in these flat boxes stacked around the store, with others in that plastic trash can by the back wall. You never know where the snakes are at the rattlesnake ranch: the owner cannot obtain any kind of liability insurance.

Snake skins, stuffed snakes, freeze-dried snakes, snake meat and oil, snake wallets and key chains and bracelets, snakes in bottles of Jim Beam, snake everything: that's the simplest way to describe the inventory at the ranch. Even canned rattlesnake—a prank, and Jeff said everybody drops that particular item as fast as I did. Western diamondback rattlesnakes, mostly, but also other rattlesnakes, copperheads, bull snakes, et cetera. At the time only three tourists were in the store with me, a couple from Seattle with their young son, and an unusual couple they were, too. Husband and wife were black and white, respectively, and their handsome young son was in-between. Their vehicle out front was a Toyota 4-Runner, they were on the return portion of a round-trip from the Pacific Northwest to Mississippi to visit Dad's family, and they couldn't say they'd seen anything to match this place.

A man walked in carrying a rattling reptile in a gunnysack. The ranch pays $4 the pound except for snakes harvested from the interstate, which might be worth $2 if they're scraped up immediately, in which case the skin can be used for key chains. One long-distance trucker bought a set of tongs from the ranch and uses it to collect what he can when he passes through the desert. He then sells the pulp to the rattlesnake ranch. Jeff Walker told me that rattlesnake meat is mild, sweet, and sells fresh for about $25 the pound wholesale, and you have to buy it in large quantities. The meat doesn't peel off the snake in nice, concise fillets. Snake is like perch in this regard. The employees of the ranch have to *pick* the meat if they're not selling it on the bone. This particular live snake weighed two pounds and measured an ordinary three feet in length. Jeff opened the plastic garbage can and the man started to untie the gunnysack. "Watch out there," Jeff advised calmly, "your sack's got a hole in it." The rest of us stepped back quickly, but the snake successfully joined five or six others at the bottom of the can, rattling all the way. We tourists leaned over and peered down at the suddenly disturbed pile, now swirling and eddying like the silted, sluggish water around the pilings of a pier.

Outside, each of the six snake pits at the ranch is about the size of a backyard swimming pool, with walls five feet high. A few snakes were slithering through the grass. Snapping sharply in the breeze overhead were the American flag and the set of three smaller, tattered flags—advertisements for Ford, Nissan, and Rent-A-Car—that had caught my eye from the interstate. Ranch headquarters is a metal building, one in a series of modest, unrelated structures lining the north side of the interstate for about a mile, separated by stands of mesquite trees and scrub brush. Wrapped around the ranch house is a chain-link pen with a large and restless dog pacing inside; roaming loose is a resplendent peacock. A sign on the fence between the parking lot and the main building reads FEED THE LIVE SNAKES. Surrounding the pits is the fenced petting zoo featuring turkeys, geese, goats, pigs, a new pair of emus, all kinds of semidomesticated creatures, a couple of mules or donkeys, whichever. One of these standing steeds threw his large head up and down, braying loudly, having a ball.

Then ranch owner Bob Popplewell arrived. I took his business suit to be Hart, Schaffner, and Marx, and said so with surprise. Bob laughed. Everybody expects him to sport the hardscrabble look of a veteran rattlesnake wrangler, but one of his other businesses—there are many—is personnel consulting. In this capacity he travels throughout Texas and all over the country. Educated in psychology, sociology, and psychometrics, he has taught college and served as personnel director for Tarrant County (Fort Worth). "Now," he told me matter-of-factly and almost immediately, "I'm hired to fire. And remember, often we're talking kinship and friendship groups in a small community, so the employer wants to remain associated with the person. My specialty is terminating employees for employers who don't want litigation, who have reason to fear litigation, who are too small to have their own personnel director. A one-worker workforce can sue you. As a middle-class employer myself, I'm *hamstrung* compared with the people who work for me. Unemployment breeds conniving, literally. An idle mind is the devil's workshop. If you're a postal employee, you go back with a gun and shoot everybody. If you're a regular person, you sue 'em in some way. So the employer hires an outside hit man to come in and set up the document trail and, if it comes down to it, do the deed and take the heat. So I'm in harm's way. During the summer there are a lot of time-abuse problems. During the spring and summer, I'm nailing people all the time. I stay busy."

The laws are complicated and the repercussions can be expensive if you're firing, say, a pregnant black female or an old white man or a handicapped veteran. So move 'em on in a compassionate, fair, and *legal* way. Not that some of them don't deserve to be canned. Bob is very convincing as he details the decline of the American work ethic over the course of the past twenty years. Look at all the HELP WANTED signs posted at every business up and down the interstate. Restaurants? Perpetual HELP signs; they can't keep people. Employers' expectations have strayed far away from the expectations of their employees. Bob considers the result a veritable chasm. Younger people have a horrible work ethic, or none at all, really. It's the proverbial slacker mentality and then some, in his view: pilfering, sabotage, contempt for rules and regulations regarding time and attendance and application of work effort, no responsibility for materials and supplies. He automatically slips into the jargon And not just your younger workers, either.

Bob is convinced that our society is losing its competitive edge, that we're losing common sense, that we might not be up to the task of moving the nation forward at his own breakneck speed. His attitude regarding this national decline seems to shift between contempt and pity. He sees the education system as a failure, mainly because the students arrive from the nuclear family—if they're lucky enough to have one—unprepared for either academic or economic achievement. Ironically, we could be on our way to fulfilling the otherwise discredited Marxist analysis of the decadent capitalist culture that loses its spine. Bob feels we have become a society of un-reasonable expectations and unearned entitlements. In short, he can sound like an unusually articulate caller to Talk Radio 570 AM, to which I'd been listening while driving west from Dallas, and from which I learned that they're not all complete dittoheads: the voluble talk-show host had just about decided that Anita Hill, not Clarence Thomas, was telling the truth.

Bob will also surprise you. He mentioned his young em-ployee Craig, who would soon move to Arkansas to be with his girlfriend. Craig is a self-proclaimed anarchist with a colorful tattoo of a marijuana plant on his arm. "But ask him what anar-chy means," his boss snorted. "He thinks it means 'no pres-sure, being *free*.' He doesn't know it means the strong would be *free* to stomp the weak."

Just five minutes after I met Bob I thought, *This guy is perfect*. I had stopped by his bizarre ranch because I was out on this interstate because I had decided that the tradition of the great American road book had lost its way on the back roads. I rejected the implied or expressed assumption of virtu-ally all these epics that we've left our authentic culture behind, though it's still out there somewhere on those blue highways, always the blue highways, and the author is setting out in his beat-up vehicle to retrieve this authentic culture for the deraci-nated rest of us. John Steinbeck admitted the bias in *Travels with Charley* and then concluded regarding the four-laners: "These great roads are wonderful for moving goods but not for inspection of a countryside. When we get these thruways across the whole country, as we will and must, it will be pos-sible to drive from New York to California without seeing a single thing."

How wrong can you be and still win the Nobel Prize? I say we see a great deal more on and near the interstates: America as it is and as it is becoming; the real thing, like it or not. To me, the case seems prima facie: are we more likely to tear up I-95 between New York City and Washington, D.C., or to lay down four more lanes into Yosemite? The back-roads journeys purporting to discover the real America are actually running away from the carnivorous beast. What I was doing out on the interstates instead was driving *toward* this culture, *into* this culture as hard and as fast as I could and in as nice a car as I could afford. No quaint vans with the mattress and propane stove in the back for me. Motels and truck-stop food all the way. Stare that beast in the eye. Love thy neighbor. Turn the other cheek. And that's why I was delighted to run almost immediately into Bob Popplewell, whom the snakes might peg as a back-roads sort, but not the personnel consulting nor the cell phone at hand. He's a rattlesnake rancher with twenty-first-century ambitions, the kind of guy who will move the nation forward—if it can still go in that direction, which Bob doubts, information superhighways notwithstanding. He might call it "country" out here in rural North Texas, but no place past which twenty thousand cars and trucks speed daily in the summer is truly country. It's interstate, and it's where an American of his ambitions belongs.

Before I started out, I dutifully plotted a voyage taking me to all of the lower 48 with about twelve thousand miles of interstate travel. The shape of that route on the map looked like a crudely drawn hourglass, just nipping the four states in the corners, dipping into all the Rust, Frost, Corn, Bible, Sun, and Mountain belts in between, logging stints of varying length on Interstates 5, 10, 25, 29, 35, 40, 64, 70, 75, 80, 84, 90, 94, and 95, regretfully omitting only 4, 8, 15, 20, 30, 45, 55, and the myriad loops and spurs and brief connecting segments. Workable, certainly, but then I considered the notion of a story about American mobility and transience and uprootedness that paradoxically sets up a sense of place, albeit a very long and skinny one; a story about interstates that stays mainly *intrastate* somewhere. From Dallas, where my wife and I were staying at the time, these open spaces around Bob Popplewell's place beckoned. The flat farmland of my birth not much farther west beckoned. The idea of the setting sun all the way to the coast beckoned. How about Dallas to L.A. on Interstates 20, 10, 17, 40, and 15?

I liked it. And do these many miles more than once, of course. Back and forth, in different seasons, around and about, and try to have some fun somewhere, too, because we have plenty of the other anyway. On the map, well over a third of those 1,700 centerstripe miles are in Texas. In my story, most of them are. "Tex-as, my Tex-as," the state song goes, and I guess that's right: where I was born, where I grew up, where I left when I had the chance, where I went back to, and where I stay now when I don't stay in New York.

By education and former profession a student of human be-havior, Bob Popplewell believes you see a lot of instructive examples out by the snake pits. In high season—spring and summer—when both snakes and tourists are most active, he sells mice for fifty cents apiece, maybe a dollar, depending on how many mice Bob wants the tourists to feed to the snakes outside in the pits. I asked for a second rendition of this equa-tion. Simplicity itself: when the snakes need more food, he drops the price and visitors buy more mice. Bob has seen men, mainly, but women too, buy dozens of mice and spend hours outside in the heat, flipping the juicy prey one by one into the pit and filming the show on videocam. When the mouse lands in the pit, every snake in the immediate vicinity freezes momentarily, then slides gently toward the little animal. The first to arrive strikes quicker than the eye can see, pumps in the paralyzing venom, and slowly positions its meal lengthwise and headfirst in order to begin ingestion. Two minutes inside the pit, the mouse is gone. People love to watch.

"I've closed up and forgotten people, they stay out there so long."

"Yeah, you have to check outside before you leave." That was Jeff Walker chiming in.

What's going on, in Popplewell's opinion, is what the trade calls psychological transference. People want to establish power over an animal they innately fear. "People really want to prick them," Bob said. "Any way they can."

"*Prick* them?"

"Bother them."

Sometimes Bob isn't real impressed by what he sees out by the pits relating to the complex relationship among snakes and mice and men. Then again, he could be accused of egging us on with the sign taped to the side of the aquarium holding the live mice: TAKE YOUR VIDEO! IT IS EXCITING!

"Part of what I see is fear and fascination," Bob continued. "And these people get into the cruelty of watching the snakes eating the mice. And I see a tendency to take out hostility on animals. A lot of people are actually cruel to the animals in the petting zoo. If you don't watch, they'll throw rocks at them. Out here in the country, people are uninhibited. They do things out here they might not do in the city. A steady stream of college kids, frustrated, in a semistate of depression and stress, come here and this is their liberation. You really have to keep an eye on them. College kids are some of the worst we have."

Bob admitted to a certain skepticism regarding human nature overall. He said, "A lot of people aren't what they appear to be. A lot aren't what they *want* to be. A lot go through life with a front."

Not Bob. He's an entrepreneurial dynamo, a self-confessed carny, a compulsive starter of businesses who understands and even respects any failure except that of trying. He and his wife, Phyllis, who isn't into the snakes at all, try to start at least one new business every year. Bob's latest plan is to become a major player in the turtle trade: 200,000 red-eared, snapper, box, and soft-shelled turtles a year is a plausible goal for the short term, all of them hauled out of nearby lakes during the summer at the request of turtle-plagued farmers and ranchers. A twenty-acre lake can easily produce 1,500 turtles in two days, and the trapping itself is easy. Bob is also preparing to move into the emu market in a big way (five products: meat, hide, oil glands providing hypoallergenic fat for medicines and perfumes, corneas for transplanting into humans, and the carotid artery for heart surgery). He's already into hedgehogs, which are booming as pets. He and Phyllis have a professional writing service named Compose. They're into the coupon collection and sales business, an enterprise that required almost thirty minutes for Bob to explain, but it's a big, big business, no lie. And the Popplewells recently bought a set of eight "900" nationwide phone lines. Naturally enough, one is a person-nel advisory hotline. Another is a snake information line.

A third will conduct polls on behalf of the Sociodynamics Research Center. Another is a self-employment hotline. Bob considers self-employment to be the most secure employment of all in today's downsizing, winner-take-all economy, but take the plunge in a planned, coordinated, and rational fashion. Understand what all the stresses will be. Test yourself before you quit your day job. Make sure you can sell because everything requires selling, even software you bang out in your garage. And, oh, by the way, here's something anybody can sell, a $25 starter kit of rattlesnake souvenirs, $50 retail value. Go test yourself. If you can't sell these, you can't sell squat and shouldn't be any kind of self-employed.

"I have forty-two ideas I think are valid for '900' numbers," Bob stated. "Remember, you're trying to use people's anger, or insult them, or give them pure entertainment, or give them extremely vital information. The placid, devil-may-care person is not going to call a '900' number. *Emotion* must be involved, just like talk radio. I can sit down and spew out literally a thousand ways to make money, I'm not exaggerating."

No one had suggested that he was.

Bob gets along on four hours' sleep, though Phyllis needs slightly more. He travels with suction cup notepads, regular notepads, tape recorders, cell phone, and when he talks about inventing new ways to make money Bob has a way of making anyone who might be more interested in practicing medicine or teaching philosophy or writing books or simply reading books feel not just personally inadequate but socially irresponsible and in some measure to blame for the nation's woes. Since I don't have a job to go to or a clock to punch or a desk to commandeer, I can look back on many weeks, some months, even the scattered year or two and find very little to show for them. While I hope something worthwhile was going on, I'll never be able to prove it. Bob can prove it.

The hired-to-fire business takes about twenty percent of Bob Popplewell's time and the other endeavors, including the "900" numbers, another twenty to thirty percent, which is all to the good because the rattlesnake ranch is struggling on the retail side, where income dropped by half in the first three years of the nineties and hadn't come all the way back. This statistic, Bob knows, is a far truer measure of the national economy than any set of employment or GNP figures. Many people just don't have the disposable income. In fact, Bob can put a sign outside advertising FREE GIFTS INSIDE—usually the cheap little key chain—and his gross for the day won't go up one penny. He sees families come in, look all around at the scores of items, hundreds, if you count the books and jewelry, accept the free key chain, then pool their funds for one insignificant purchase. The sorry-looking flea market to the east doesn't help much either, Bob is convinced, and he's probably right: from the perspective of the motorist flashing past, it does drag down the appearance of the neighborhood. Still, he told me, the worst business should be able to make a living on the interstate. Even in the dead of winter, twelve thousand vehicles pass just fifty yards from the front door, and in the summer almost twice that many. The signs and the generic tattered flags don't have to lure a huge cut of this volume in order to generate decent sales.* Just then, a particularly loud eighteen-wheeler plowed past, eastbound, leading Bob to note the downside to all the vehicular traffic: these semis with overweight loads that, slowly or not, bring to ruin every adjacent building. The vibration is almost subsonic, but it's there, as the protruding nails on any ordinary shingle roof near the interstate clearly attest. The ranch house has a tin roof, but items are constantly falling off the walls, including, not long before I was there the first time, a magnificent set of longhorns, which broke.

No matter what happens to the highway trade, there's always wholesale, mail-order, and specialty orders. Bob gets calls from everywhere inquiring about meat, skins, and whole freeze-dried snakes. He sells a lot of the last and presumes they're used for desktop decoration. He sells to the snake-handling sect in West Virginia. He had just returned home from a round-trip to New York City in his pickup, delivering a thousand rattlesnakes to customers from the Far East. He

---

*Regarding those inappropriate automotive flags, it doesn't matter what Bob flies. He buys them wholesale and hoists them at random as the wind tears them apart at random.

reached behind a counter and produced a small bottle of a dark brown liquid. The dealer in New York City had given him some of this elixir with the label printed in Chinese and English. A deep swig of this snake-based energy potion flushes a person crimson red, induces a sweat, and yields a revved-up energy that makes the highest octane coffee irrelevant for the entire day.

I asked Bob how the rattlesnake population is holding up in light of the strong wholesale demand—thirty thousand snakes a year through his operation alone. Actually, Bob claimed, economic development *helps* snakes because it drives away their real predators: owls, hawks, skunks, raccoons. There's no shortage of rattlesnakes in these parts. He suddenly disappeared into a back room and emerged opening a small glass jar, producing a bright green wet thing the size of a small olive, and declared, with tremendous pleasure, "That's a gall bladder, and I can sell all I can get for two dollars apiece. They're excellent for cholesterol control—if they're poisonous. They must be the bladders of *poisonous* snakes. Regular snakes won't do. The green is the gall itself." Also, snake soup is excellent for Parkinson's Disease, and Popplewell sells it in bulk quantity. Bring snake, water, and spices to a boil.

"What about the snake in the Jim Beam?"

"An aphrodisiac."

I should've known. I picked up one of the videos on the counter by the cash box. "Oh, those are in Wal-Mart and Kmart," Bob explained, turning it over. "See, there's my picture." We were friends by now, so I asked about the smell inside ranch headquarters. He nodded as if he'd been expecting the inquiry. That would be a heady brew of live rattlesnake, live rattlesnake dung, dead rattlesnake, and dead rattlesnake tanning fluids. Now Bob looked over at the couple from Seattle and their son, who were still shopping the displays with amazement. "Have you seen the mongoose?" he called out, pointing toward the long, narrow box with a wire mesh screen at one end. I'd noticed this cagelike contraption earlier. The three visitors walked over tentatively and stopped some distance away. I joined them. Bob stepped to the side of the box and peered inside.

"Take that wire there," he instructed the husband quietly, "and pull it back. He's back inside there. You'll have to pull him into the open."

The guy pulled gingerly; nothing happened.

"Pull it harder; he'll come. But careful, he's fast!" The family eased away. Everyone knows the mongoose is notorious for handling cobras with ease; apparently, a mongoose makes a cat look sluggish. The husband pulled harder and the box popped open with a loud *bang!* and a wad of fake fur sprang out and landed on the floor at his feet. Everybody jumped. The rattlesnake ranch puts you on edge anyway.

That reaction was nothing, Bob laughed. Most folks jump back five feet. Sometimes they get angry, and one woman wet herself. Bob reloaded the device, closed the lid, and set it aside for the next group of Japanese tourists to happen this way. One thing about the Japanese, though, they come with money; the Germans and Scandinavians, too. The family of three departed in good spirits for the long drive up to Puget Sound, and another browser or two stopped by, looked around, and departed. An extended family, surely from some distant point, hurried through, and Bob's quick assessment of these people led him to waive the $1 per capita for the petting zoo. They accepted this kindness without a word, crowded outside as the goats tried to crowd inside, returned five minutes later, and departed without spending a dime. His point driven home, Bob just glanced at me.

Another day I learn how to butcher a rattlesnake. I learn by observation and pick up some religious instruction along the way. First, Bob takes the long-handled pinner of his own devising, lifts the snake from the box by the middle of its body, pins the head gently on the floor, places his boot gently on the midsection, and snaps off the rattle with his free hand.* He then

---

*The number of buttons on the rattle indicates not the age of the snake but the number of moltings, and snakes can molt two or three times a year, depending on conditions. Buttons also break off.

replaces the snake in the box and lifts out another. When all the rattles have been harvested, he lugs the box out back to the slaughtering table beneath the mesquite trees, where he with-draws the snakes one by one with his pinner, lays each on the table, and whacks off the head with his machete. He rolls the heads off into a bucket.

"Don't mess with them," Bob gently reminds me. "They'll nail you." In his thirty years of working with poisonous snakes, Bob has been bitten about a hundred times, but only a few bites were serious. Most poisonous snake bites don't result in the injection of any venom at all. However, in cool weather, the severed head of a rattlesnake can—and will, since it's mad by now—inject venom for up to two hours. Bob demonstrates by using his tongs to pick up a head, grasping it at the severed back. The mouth turns 180 degrees and strikes the tongs, venom pulsing onto the ground. In that same hypothetical cool weather, the decapitated body will coil and strike for a couple of hours, too, but I don't observe this behavior because Bob hands the still-writhing body of each snake to young Craig, the anarchist and soon-to-be-Arkansan. Jeff Walker is off to one side, skinning and butchering the carcass of a goat hanging from a mesquite tree.

Slice the snake up the belly the full length of the body, grasp the skin at the headless end, and pull. A snake peels almost as easily as a banana. Dump the guts in a bucket to be culled later for the pricey gall bladder and other valued items. Lay the white meat into a large cooler for the Korean couple driving out from Fort Worth, who are also buying the butch-ered goat. As the work progresses and blood sometimes splat-ters nastily—Bob is dressed in khakis this particular afternoon, not the business suit—precisely as I'm beginning to wonder about unpleasant dreams approaching fullblown nightmares tonight, he reads my mind: "First night out here, you can have some hell of some bad dreams. Or do this all day . . . I've had bad dreams."

"Am I correct in assuming that not everyone's cut out for this kind of work?"

"This is true."

As it turned out, weeks went by before I had my bad dream

in which the snakes were writhing inside my overcoat and I waked myself and my wife with my flailing. On the other hand, tourists love this tableau. Bob doesn't encourage such kibitzing, but if they want to film the slaughter on their videocams, why not?

The Koreans arrive right on time, a pleasant, shy couple in their midthirties who own a high-rise maintenance company in Fort Worth. They're unusual in that they're driving neither a Lexus nor an Infiniti, standard issue for the Korean businessmen to whom Bob sells so much snake meat, but this ordinary midsized Oldsmobile. And there's a hitch. Bob thought these connoisseurs wanted twenty pounds of live snakes and twenty pounds of skinned, gutted meat on the bone, but the man doesn't want the live snakes. Bob and Phyllis's quick glance betrays a slight annoyance at this waste of time. They're on a deadline this afternoon to put together and deliver the decorations for a political event for Democratic congressman Charlie Stenholm. Now these snakes have to be beheaded, skinned, and bled, and Bob tells me later that this might be for some specific religious purpose.

"What religion?" I ask.

"The Church of the Holy Infinity of the Juxtaposition of the Asian Mind. How's that? Usually, Koreans want at least some of their snakes alive for boiling whole in soups, like lobsters. Japanese want just the meat and Chinese want the meat with the guts. Koreans are unique in wanting the whole snake—the scales, the venom, the guts, the rat hairs in the guts, everything. Nasty, looks like Geritol and tastes like crap. But you're not drinking it because it tastes good. The vitamin potency is unbelievable. You drink a six-ounce vial of this soup and you simply feel good all afternoon. It's a high-yield energy compound."

Not to mention aphrodisiacal qualities. For these purposes, Korean men eat snakes. For these same purposes, Korean women are supposed to eat a certain kind of lizard unobtainable on this continent, so they substitute goat instead. It has to be black, and that's why Jeff leaves a small patch of black hair when he skins it. Anyway, Bob calmly takes the box of live snakes outside by the picnic table under the awning and proceeds to lop off the heads and hand the bodies to his customer to hold by the tail for a few moments while blood courses onto the dirt. The wife stands to the side, not nervously or squeamishly, but not impassively, either. I look over at the interstate, where some of the motorists and passengers are looking back at us. After a couple of snakes, Jeff Walker, now cleaned up after butchering the goat, joins the party and takes over the bleeding job.

Bob had told me beforehand that the many Koreans he deals with have a distinctive way of doing business. "Initially, they will be very polite. When the money is about to change hands, they get very tense. They're rude and blunt. You make three deals with the Koreans: the first one, then they haggle you down; the second one, when they get rude and boisterous and almost call it off; and then the third and final deal. Then when they leave they're just as cordial and polite as when they got here."

As this couple returns inside the building to settle up, I can't wait. Cultural conflict in microcosm! Bob sits down at his desk and works with his calculator, jots figures on a sheet of paper, and stands up to present the Korean couple with their bill of just over $600 for forty pounds of rattlesnake meat and the goat meat. Now something strange happens. This couple doesn't haggle at all. They pay quietly with a combination of cash and a check which Bob accepts without question and then depart with their cooler of snake meat and sack of goat meat in their midsized, inexplicable Oldsmobile.

CHAPTER 2

Because our nation is caught in the grip of a religious revival, with boomers going back to all sorts of churches for all sorts of reasons after years of lying around on Sunday morning, because I'm a longtime kibitzer of the faiths I don't share but sometimes wish I did, and because I had a hunch he would have some interesting notions, I asked the rattlesnake rancher for his views on God. We were sitting at the picnic table next to the highway, eating sandwiches. Bob was quick to answer, and his passion for entrepreneurial independence does indeed yield iconoclastic theological beliefs. "I believe in the deity," Bob replied, "but I'm not a member of a group. Yeah, I'm a Christian in that there is a God, but my Christianity is being fair, doing right, and feeling good about doing both of those. It's sort of a blend of the do-good part of Christianity and the self-reliance of the early democratic American ideal. I'm not focused on the Jesus Christ part and the early biblical stuff."

My friends in the Christian faith smile when they hear this kind of expression of faith, which is often enough. The perceived theological confusion delights them and confirms in their minds the intellectual integrity of their own more rigorous approach. They would also smile if informed that Bob believes in reincarnation, because you'd be hard-pressed to find a more anti-Christian doctrine. Still, Bob would be a straight-ahead Christian according to the fill-in-the-blank polls—one reason this and so much other sociological data must be doubted. Pollsters and pundits alike put way too much faith in straightforward declarations of faith.*

So we have Bob Popplewell on the left wing. For something near his rattlesnake ranch but at the other end of this particular spectrum I recommend the Kendrick Religious Pageant and Diorama, touted by the display at the nearby Santo rest area on I-20 as the largest of its kind in Texas, quite a claim in a state known for prideful extravagance.† On my first pass through the Santo area I proceeded straight from the ranch to the Kendrick place forty miles west, almost to Cisco, and there, less than a mile off the interstate, was a long, two-story concrete bunker, each floor divided into a series of rooms opening onto a field. Most of these rooms were empty, but one on the second floor held three large, high-backed chairs that I decided were the thrones. To the left of the bunker, three crosses on a small mound: Calvary. A long, low, windowless building sat at a right angle to the bunker. In the middle of the field was an unfinished, roofless, eccentrically shaped structure whose cinderblock wall was considerably taller at one end than at the other. At the modest entrance to the site, the tableau of

---

* Preachers know better. They understand full well the distinction between genuine faith and mere wishfulness, including wishfulness for genuine faith. However, they don't scorn the wishfulness. If that's the best you can do, they'll work with it.

† This rest area puzzled me. I could understand the YOU CAN'T AFFORD IT and DON'T MESS WITH TEXAS warning signs, the standard admonitions against DWI and littering, but what about LIVESTOCK NOT ALLOWED ON PARK GRASS? I pulled in at scores of rest areas and roadside parks in the ranching regions of the Southwest and never once saw an animal eating the amenity, or even trying to.

three bargain-basement mannequins—soldier with frayed tunic and spear, Mary Magdalene with her shawl, and Jesus carrying his cross—was losing its struggle with the elements, and I concluded that the Kendrick Religious Pageant and Diorama was facing hard times, or perhaps already abandoned as a failed business venture.

This atmosphere of disintegration and, indirectly, unrequited faith yielded an ever greater poignancy to the figure of the slumping savior. Struggling forward in the unkempt grass and weeds, Jesus appeared to be literally cut off at the knees—a figure out of Goya, a graphic and convincing depiction, accidental or otherwise, of torment on the road to Calvary, here in Texas. It also brought to mind a favorite phrase from Bill Barich's *Laughing in the Hills*, a terrific piece of work about horse racing, the people who live and love that sport, and other matters of import to the author at that time. The title, by the way, has nothing to do with horses; it refers to an imagined coyote that might have killed the sheep whose skull Bill holds in his hands, a coyote now "long gone and ghostly, laughing in the hills." He describes the personal situation which impelled him to initiate a new era at a racetrack in the San Francisco Bay area, and in conclusion writes that his life was—here's that phrase—"knee-deep in ruin." Although the author's circumstances weren't nearly as dire as Jesus', neither do these times in this society easily offer as recompense martyrdom backed by the hope for eternal salvation; so Bill does instead what he and so many of us so often do best. He takes off.

Phil "Shorty" Kendrick has never taken off. The opportunity never came up. After his father was disabled in an industrial accident in Dallas in 1938, Phil's family moved west 140 miles to the tidy stone house eight miles east of Cisco. First they went into the flour business, owning a small mill before the big Baird's refinery put the small operators out of business, then into the dairy business, with seventy head of milking cows, and finally into the egg business, with thirty thousand laying hens, a goodly number. Phil delivered the family eggs to commercial accounts up and down the highway from Abilene to Fort Worth on old Highway 80, now remodeled and occasionally rerouted a mile or two and known from Florence, South Carolina, to slightly west of Pecos, Texas, as I-20. Phil also owned a music store in nearby Eastland. On the side, the family performed throughout the area as a popular gospel quartet, with live radio broadcasts.

Early one morning in 1963, driving east in his egg delivery truck, thinking about nothing in particular but not half-asleep, either, because it was still pitch dark outside and he was and is a careful driver, Phil saw standing in the middle of the roadway in front of him, arms outraised, a vision of Jesus Christ. The figure on the road said, "I have something I want you to do for me." Phil shook his head vigorously and blinked hard, but the figure was still standing there. It then told Phil that he should present an Easter pageant. Before this vision and despite his upbringing in a Christian family, Phil hadn't even known where in the Bible to find the story of Jesus, so on his lunch break that day he went to the Eastland library, where the good book fell open at the Gospel of Matthew. Nor did Phil have any experience in drama whatsoever. But for the last thirty-one years, he had presented that Easter pageant and a good deal more.

So my first impression of the Kendrick Religious Pageant and Diorama had been mistaken, a failure to consider the big difference between incomplete and abandoned. Phil Kendrick's life's work isn't finished, that's all. Back in Dallas, I called up the Pageant and Phil said of course he'd enjoy showing me around and explaining things the next time I was in the area. He didn't care who I was, what I believe or fail to believe, or what I might be writing. Come on out. Although he was fifty-one years old when I finally met him and considerably more than $1 million shy of fulfilling his vision, Phil expressed no doubts that he would be able to do so—he or the board of directors, whom he expects to carry on should he die prematurely. For now, however, the responsibility was Phil's alone, and nothing was getting any easier. His father had passed away, one of his brothers lived in Arizona and wasn't interested in the dioramas, the other brother lived nearby but likewise was no longer keen, his mother was too old and legally blind as well, and donations had dried up "terribly" in the wake of the Bakker and Swaggart scandals, although how anyone could mistake this thrifty Kendrick ministry for being of a kind with those swindles is beyond me. As for the advertising on the interstate, a couple of the signs were still up, but a large one on a nearby hill had been removed when a son with no use for faith inherited his father's land.

The Kendricks own a total of ninety-six acres, and Phil has plans for most of it. He had already staked out the site for Noah's Ark behind the diorama (the windowless building, formerly the main chicken coop). The ship will be 450 feet long, constructed with concrete tilt walls finished to look like logs, and it will house live pairs of many mammals and birds and creeping things. There will also be the Tower of Babel, the Hanging Gardens of Babylon, the Gloryland train, the moat with islands of trees, and the hundred-foot statue of Jesus Christ in the form of Phil's highway vision. You will hike up a stairway in the hollow interior of this statue and look out at the interstate and the countryside through Jesus' eyes as a tape recording reminds you that the Redeemer is looking into and through *your* eyes at all times. The puzzling unfinished structure in the middle of the field will be the cafeteria, now lacking only the floor, ceiling, and equipment. Phil pointed out the cross shape and then explained why the cinderblock wall is taller at one end (the top, twenty-seven feet) than at the other (the bottom, ten feet): this *tilt* will make the building identifiable as a cross from the road.

If this Christian theme park is a tall order, Phil doesn't seem fazed in the least. In the first place, he had successfully mounted his Easter pageant until the spring of 1994, when his cast of performers fell apart on short notice. He had completed the diorama for both the Old and New Testaments, which he would show me shortly. Also, everything happens in good time, and too many times to count Phil has had a sense of being *directed* in his labors, and this has produced conviction and patience sufficient for any related task. Another example of inspiration: uncertain exactly how to convey the stages of the Creation in the diorama, once again driving east along the old highway, Phil had another startling epiphany, this time in the form of a single word which came to mind, a strange word he'd never heard before. He immediately pulled into the local lamp store in Eastwood and asked whether the clerk had ever heard of something called "black light."

"Yes," the clerk said, "it's brand-new."

In the early years, the pageant had to coexist with the chicken farm, so a large hedge was planted to screen the hen house from view if not from hearing. When Phil's mother and father retired from that business and Phil closed his music store, the long shed was enclosed and converted into the small auditorium, museum, diorama, and dormitory, where the beds rent for $5 apiece, plus a $100 surcharge for large groups on retreats or reunions. The sixteen diorama scenes from the New Testament opened in 1975, after five years of planning and construction, primarily by Phil and his father. For over twenty years Phil has given almost every tour through these darkened rooms, charging $2.50 for adults and $2 for children six to eleven. Most of the folks who come through are senior citizens and devout Christians. Phil uses a flashlight to highlight features of each scene to a taped organ accompaniment. The outdated mannequins were donated by JCPenney; other patrons came forward with additional supplies. Phil's mother sewed all the costumes. The baby Jesus is a valuable Bye-Lo porcelain doll. A coursing waterfall highlights the baptism by John the Baptist. The eyes of Jesus delivering the Sermon on the Mount appear to follow the viewer across the room; again, the idea to paint these eyes in this certain way and to position the small spotlight on the floor to illuminate them came to Phil in an unexplained flash. The Last Supper is modeled after da Vinci's fresco, and these and some of the other mannequins in the diorama had to be cut apart and repositioned with plaster of Paris. The mannequins used for Jesus here and in most other scenes are female because, Phil decided, the softer lines more effectively convey people's idea of a nurturing Savior. The Crucifixion scene has light and sound effects which have rendered some people speechless, while others have cried. The last two scenes juxtapose the fiery pits of hell with—at this point in the standard tour, Phil pulls aside a curtain to reveal Jesus in heaven and God holding the Book of Life.

"These two scenes will jolt anyone who's not living right," he said to me.

Four years after the New Testament opened, the wing featuring eight scenes from the Old Testament was ready. The tour here is accompanied by the voice of one of Phil's brothers reading apposite passages from the King James version. Large puffs of cotton, projected slides, and the black lights are used to convey the drama of Genesis 1. The creation of Adam is achieved with a remarkable jerry-rigged device the size of a small closet in which a sheet of sand narrowly encased between two panels of glass slowly slides down on Phil's mechanical cue to reveal the mannequin of Adam, stopping at waist level. After the tour has moved on, the sand is recirculated to the top by a small elevator originally used in the flour mill. I gave Phil the eye after he showed me these inner workings. He shrugged with an embarrassed smile and said, "The Man upstairs designed it. We built it." Later, Phil spotlighted the diaphanous little butterflies that hang by fishing line above the baby Moses hidden in the reeds of the Nile. Just as I was about to ask about the backlit scrolls of the Ten Commandments, Phil answered me first: while they appear to be authentic ancient script, they're just his own arbitrary markings.

The tour of the dioramas completed, Phil showed me some of the old pianos he repairs. This explained the PIANOS FOR SALE sign out front. I met Curley, the fourteen-year-old camel who participates in the pageant and is hauled around by Phil in a modified horse trailer for special appearances a couple of times a week. Finally we walked inside the house to meet the elderly Mrs. Phyllis Kendrick, who immediately announced that she was quite mad at me. If she had had a gun and could see at all, I'd have been dead, or at least shot at, because when I'd first arrived I'd waited outside for Phil, who was a little late returning from Abilene, and Phyllis had had no idea who this potentially violent stranger might be. I apologized and the three of us settled into deep chairs, and Phyllis told me that she came to be terribly scared not just of me but of almost anything because of some medicine she had taken some years back. Her physical and psychological reaction to just four days on that prescription had been immediate and then permanent.

As I was sitting in my car bidding farewell to Phil through the window, he informed me that he'd had his own negative reaction to medicine—specifically, the Prozac prescribed to help him relax and fall asleep despite his painful back. Phil quit taking the drug immediately.

"Prozac?" I exclaimed, perhaps not judiciously. "That's sometimes given for psychological problems."

"Well, I don't have any psychological problems."

Still and all, Phil, in this society, we all do, by definition. Didn't the prescient Goethe foresee that the God-doubting modern world would serve mainly as an outpatient facility, with everyone emotionally unwell?

At the Exxon station at the main interstate intersection in Cisco, ten minutes west of Shorty's diorama, I ran into Jessie Benefield Black. First I spotted the yellow car covered with warning signs, lights on the roof, and carrying all kinds of equipment and paraphernalia in the front seat, the backseat, and, no doubt, the trunk—bells and whistles, literally. Then I took note of this energetic little woman inside the convenience store and immediately intuited the connection: that was her car and that oversized trailer rig just beyond the overpass on the other side of the interstate was her responsibility. Jessie will tell you that and everything else real quick. She's all business out here on the highway. She owns and operates a flag service car company—what some people, but not Jessie, call an escort car company—called B-B Flag Cars out of Herriman, Utah, near Salt Lake City. Time was wasting, that was obvious, but Jessie grudgingly agreed to humor me.

First, what is that strange-looking rig over there?

"That's a chassis off a 120-rock truck, works in the gold mines, the coal mines, the silver mines," Jessie replied. "Coming from the Lucky Mack mine in Riverton, Wyoming, going to Houston to be shipped. That's a combination rig: the truck, then a piece of equipment called the jeep, then his trailer, then another piece of equipment attached to the back end called a booster. Actually, he's got nine axles. He's eighteen foot, six inches wide, and he has to have two cars with him, one in front, the other behind, and you watch him when he goes around corners and make sure he can clear anything on the side. If there's traffic coming, let him know. He can't see behind him, with that width. The one behind lets him know when he's cleared the corner, when he's cleared things on the side of the road. You have to protect the motoring public and make them aware that the load is on the road, and make them aware what they're looking at. They don't realize this thing weighs 160,000 pounds and it can't stop on a dime. They don't realize how big it is. Depending on the wind factor, whether it's raining or not, whether it's snowing or not, how rough the road is, how top-heavy it is, you average from as little as 250 to as many as 500 miles a day. This trip has taken longer than it should have. Ten days so far."

Jessie's words rush at you in a torrent of information, all of it very much to the point. Perhaps it has something to do with battling the pell-mell assault of the big highways, day after day, and of little highways made big by the responsibility, because one of the ironies of the business is that these extremely oversized loads are routed *off* the interstates whenever possible and onto less traveled routes.

"I have two people working for me," Jessie continued. "I'm independent; I've been at it twenty-seven years, a little over twenty on my own. There are lots of us all over the United States. In some parts of the country you have to be certified. I'm certified in Colorado, New Mexico, Utah, Virginia. In other states, anybody could do it but companies won't call you unless you're knowledgeable. This is a word-of-mouth thing. Nobody's going to hire you unless you know what you're doing. It specifies on their oversized permit whether they do or don't have to have an escort. Oversized loads are over eight foot, six inches wide or thirteen-six high or sixty-five foot long or eighty thousand pounds. The combination of those four determines whether you have to have a car or not. You can only run from sunrise to sunset unless it's under special provisions.

I've run a lot of stuff for the government that way. Emergency situations, like equipment for train wrecks.

"We're paid by the mile, but maybe a little more if the load is high since it takes more time and you have to have a little more insight, I think, because you have to have a pole car. That's a vehicle that actually has a high pole on the front to check structures, lines, overpasses, et cetera. If he can't get under it, your job is to know how or where you can get him around it. I work a lot of those, seventeen-and-a-half, eighteen feet high, up and down California.

"You have to figure your cost on the car, what your man-hours are in the car, what your insurance is, what your expenses are. I almost have a photographic memory on figures and numbers. Long years ago I used to work as a bookkeeper. You have to be able to judge how much room it's going to take to get 'em around a corner, depending on if they're wide or long, a single combination or the one we're with now, four different places that thing can bend, got to make sure it can get around. You have to be aware if anything moves, if a chain moves, a block moves. You have to know what you're looking at. The state gives you the route. Every state. It's on their permit. You have to stay on that route. If there's any problem, you have to stop and call. Sometimes you have to leave the route. Specified equipment is CB, overhead lights that rotate something like 160 rpms, fire extinguisher, first-aid kit, extra signs, extra flags, a hard hat, safety vest, and you should go to a flagger's school. I've been to three. In Colorado you have to have a defensive driving course. Best to have a CDL."

The CDL is the Commercial Driver's License.

"Do you enjoy the work?" I asked. Not a brilliant question, I acknowledge, but, finally, and following a withering glance, Jessie replied, "Acclimated by now."

"How many miles have you traveled altogether?" This seemed fair enough.

"I don't know."

"How many days?" This seemed fair enough, too.

"I don't know."

We were at an impasse. I waited. "Never really thought about it," Jessie finally said after a pointed glance at the clock on the wall. She exemplifies that certain kind of can-do contemplation we Americans are also known for in the field of philosophy; she leaves existentialism for the continentals. "Never paid attention to it," she added. "I'd just as soon be out here as at home anymore. I'm out here three fourths, two thirds of the time. Of course you can't run on weekends. *Some* of the states you can, with *some* loads. Colorado up to fourteen foot, Nevada up to fourteen—but not through Las Vegas. On weekends you do your laundry just like anybody else, you go to the beauty shop to get your hair done, put your feet up, and relax. I don't ever turn my regular radio on. This little dog is Cookie, all three pounds of her. My partner up there is Mary. I want somebody that I know they know what they're doing; another thing, common sense, can think on their feet, can make decisions on their feet, because you do have to make decisions. Take that overpass. The first thing I have to do is know whether that overpass will make it. *He's* fifteen-two. It *says* fifteen-six. Maybe it's lower on the other side. When I make that decision I'd better be right. If I'm not sure about a sign, I've got a pole. Most of Texas is pretty good. In New Jersey they don't even give you a route; they only give you a permit and you're responsible for all structures. I think it's the only state like that. That's a different world. I'd rather not work the East Coast. Structures are lower, too. Rather work closer to home."

Rather get going, too. There wasn't much light left. Jessie abruptly excused herself and walked out to her flag car to organize her caravan to Houston by way of Highway 183, down through Rising Star and May and Zephyr.

Closing the books on this stretch of I-20 near the Santo rest area and wrapping up for the moment my consideration of unexpected faiths encountered in unexpected places—including Jessie's, probably, if I'd had time to quiz her—is the ranch with the bold sign on the gate beside the eastbound interstate: NO SMOKING BEYOND THIS POINT. I wanted to meet this anti–Marlboro Man, but when I called Wes Mickle, who Bob

Popplewell told me was the owner, I found myself conversing with Wes's son Stan, the more active partner in the business. Stan said he'd be happy to show me around the 1,500 smoke-free acres of the Valley View Ranch, which happens to be one of the half-dozen premier cutting horse–breeding facilities in the world. This accolade—my own, to be sure; the Mickles would never boast in this way—necessarily follows from the fact that Parker County, Texas, is the unofficial cutting horse capital of the world.

At the designated hour several weeks later I punched in the appropriate code on the locking device by the gate with the NO SMOKING sign and drove slowly up the hill past placid ponds and well-appointed paddocks to the rendezvous site, where I was greeted by young Tammy Mickle, Stan's wife of just five months. When Tammy led me into the palpitation room for introductions, Stan's right arm, wrapped to the shoulder in a rubber sleeve, was all the way up a brown mare's rectum. Nevertheless, the horse was standing relatively quietly in the narrow stall with another man, one of the Mickles' hired hands, a Mexican national with a green card, holding her tail out of the way. Her very young foal balanced itself to her immediate right in a little stall of its own. You cannot take a wet mare away from her foal. She won't allow it. Well, you could *drag* her away with a team of horses, but forget trying to handle her, much less introducing an ultrasound wand in order to check on the status of the next ovulation. Keeping the mare and her foal together is much simpler.

"Hi," Stan Mickle said cheerfully, looking back over his shoulder. "Let me finish up here."

I didn't know where to look. I glanced over at Tammy, who had moved to one side. I think she was tickled about what was probably my all-too-apparent and totally unnecessary embarrassment. Tammy handles the books for the ranch, and she was pregnant with twins. Stan had picked up this important fact from his own ultrasound reading; her obstetrician had initially missed it. An ultrasound on a woman is much easier than an ultrasound on a mare, whose sheer bulk precludes external inspection. It's necessary to go up the posterior end of the gut, and it's necessary to do so frequently, because the timing wants to be just about perfect because a quirky feature of the horse business—cutting horse, quarter horse, and Kentucky Derby thoroughbred—is what's called the "universal birth date." A horse born anytime during 1995 is one year old in 1996. Since horses compete in age groups, the horse born in January of a given year is considerably more mature two or three years later than the horse born in April of that same year. Since the mare's gestation period is eleven months, eleven days—three weeks short of one year—the ideal time for conception is therefore the last week in January, with the foal arriving the first week of the following January. Of course an early delivery on New Year's Eve is an outright disaster, since that horse is officially one year old the following morning and will always be a year behind his or her competitive age group in development.

As Stan continued with his palpitation of White on Right, I chose to study the gray images on the small screen sitting on the desk to his left. He pointed out the reproductive features as they hove into vague view, and I paid close attention. Finished after a minute, maybe two, Stan withdrew his arm, stripped off the rubber glove, tossed it in the trash can, rinsed off the mare and the ultrasound wand, then turned to shake my hand. He was twenty-nine years old and wearing blue jeans, white sneakers, and a Valley View Ranch baseball cap and matching T-shirt. As the handler led the mare and her foal out the door of the palpitation room, Stan entered his notes in the ledger on the counter. On the wall was a magnetic board with a small red or green tag for each of the forty mares currently in house: red for those to be serviced by Freckles Playboy, green for Dual Pep. These were the only two stallions standing stud at that time at the ranch, and they were all that would be necessary. The Mickles specialize in artificial insemination. Their breeding facility is more commonly called a stud farm.

This was in February. Within a month, Stan and his father would be working hard on behalf of two hundred mares. That's why Stan had suggested over the telephone that I drop by as soon as possible. In peak breeding season, what with the dozens of palpitations daily to determine ovulation on all these mares, then more palpitations to check for conception, with either Dual Pep or Playboy standing at stud every day, with all the inseminations to be performed, with all the actual deliveries (a midwife is on duty every night in the foaling barn, ready to alert Stan), with all the embryo transfers performed in concert with neighbor Joe Landers, who happened to walk into the palpitation room while I was there—with all this, the entire Mickle family is just totally busy through the spring and into the summer. After that, the place empties out. Foals, stallions, and pregnant mares are shipped back C.O.D. to their owners all over the country, to be returned early the following year, in most cases, for delivery and more breeding.

After palpitating five or six more mares, Stan took a break and we stepped outside the station to look around. Below us and a quarter-mile to the north was I-20, and Stan pointed to the left and asked if I remembered the terrible crash between the tractor-trailer and the van full of children on Sunday morning, July 3, 1994. I did, and it happened right in front of Valley View Ranch. Stan and Tammy had been working near the front gate when they were rocked by the explosion behind their backs at 9:20 a.m. They turned to see the van, rammed in the rear by the eighteen-wheeler and thrown forward six hundred feet, burst into flames, and they saw two small children running away. They didn't know that twelve children and two adults would die inside the van—all but one of them members of the Funches family on their way from California to a family reunion in Mississippi. Altogether, the state of Texas recorded forty-three traffic deaths that July 3 and surpassed the previous record of forty-two for a twenty-four-hour period. The inferno in front of the ranch made the evening news everywhere. Stan couldn't count the number of emergency vehicles and circling TV helicopters that converged within a matter of minutes. Since July is slack time at the ranch, the family watched the scene the whole day from the deck beside the swimming pool.

To the left near the bottom of the hill sat the lake with elegant swans, stands of handsome live oak trees, and, closer to us up the slope, the private air-conditioned quarters for Dual Pep, Freckles Playboy, and Doluino, a third stallion owned by the Mickles who stands at stud on a much more limited basis. The liver chestnut Dual Pep was pacing in his paddock. This was to be his day in the saddle, and he seemed to know it. Freckles Playboy, the sorrel, was standing placidly on his adjacent turf. Though this was his day off, he was stoking the fires with choice feed grains anyway. Just below us was the birthing barn. To the right were the stables for the mares who will one day join the mothers in the birthing barn. Back to the right, above the multiterraced lawn, were the large two-story house on the hill, the unused and cracked tennis court, and the swimming pool complete with the waterfall.

For this part of Texas, this is a high hill, but not the highest. That would be the next peak behind it, where the prime homesite overlooking the $4 million Canyon West golf course will sell for $75,000. A small medallion driven into the ground verifies that point as the highest in Parker County, at 1,043 feet. Stan and I stepped into his pickup to drive back to the golf course development, of which both he and his father are very proud. They're avid players. Wes Mickle was a junior champion in Arizona, where he began the horse-breeding business and owned the mare Anniversary, who eventually foaled the original Mr. Ed. Wes moved the family to Texas in 1974. As we drove and looked around the ranch, Stan asked if I realized what was missing. I looked around more carefully but finally had to admit I didn't.

"The utility lines."

Indeed, the ranch is cleared of these impediments. There won't be any on the golf course, either. "I *hate* all those lines overhead," Stan said. And there may not be any smoking on the golf course, either. Stan was giving serious consideration to establishing what would probably be the nation's first no-smoking golf club. He and his dad are avid nonsmokers, as the sign on the front gate would suggest, but Wes had doubts about the wisdom of a smokeless nineteenth hole, business-wise. That might be too radical. I told Stan it was, for a fact. The nation isn't ready for it.

Standing on the highest land in the county, Stan pointed out the small herd of cattle grazing in the far southwestern corner of the ranch, distant specks. The pure white ones were Piedmontese. Steaks from these cattle are too lean, but breed a Piedmontese to an Angus, say, and the resulting first-generation steer yields delicious beef that has less cholesterol than a fillet of flounder. Stan was getting into this business. He was already into hay: with the help of a computerized drip system, these pastures were yielding eighteen thousand bales annually. He pointed out the large pile of manure hauled over to the golf course from the stables, ideal for helping the new greens and fairways grow in. Synergy. He pointed out the routing of the eighteen holes at Canyon West. When golfers walk onto the sixteenth green positioned beside the pond below us, they'll trigger a laser beam to activate duck quacking from a speaker hidden by the pond. The laser at the seventeenth green will trigger the unique call of the gamble quail. (The Mickles had tried to establish a covey of these quail, native to Arizona, but they didn't thrive here.) Lasers hidden by other greens as yet unselected will trigger the howl of coyotes, the cackle of turkeys, a variety of other animal sounds. Stan thinks the recorded cacophony at Sea World in San Antonio works great, and he couldn't wait to try the equivalent on his very own golf course. But what will happen when the golfer addressing his tee ball on number four is scared witless by the sudden trumpet of a rogue elephant trampling the third green? I didn't have the heart to ask.

Back at the house on top of the second highest hill in the county, after a brief tour of Future Outlook, the commercial printing business that had taken over the four-car garage, Stan walked me around to the other side of the house to show off something he believes is a "neat deal," though he realizes some people might find it rather bizarre: a fourteen-thousand-pound concrete mausoleum with four crypts. The crushed stone finish matches the house; a carefully engineered venting system assures that the entrance of any kind of bug is almost impossible. Etched into one of the four stainless-steel doors is the name Judy Kay Mickle, Stan's mother, who died of breast cancer in 1994.

He asked me, and not just rhetorically, "When you die, do you want to go twelve miles down the road to be buried with a bunch of strangers? We don't." He noted that private cemeteries, which are not all that unusual, can be a problem should the property be sold to someone who doesn't want another family's cemetery in the backyard—a plausible reaction. But with the mausoleum, it's just a matter of hoisting the big block with a crane and loading it onto a flatbed truck for delivery wherever you like. Not that Stan sees this happening. He and his two sisters, who also live on the property, will someday inherit this ranch and the golf course development from their father. In fact, if the golf club is successful enough and the home sales take off as expected, Stan might phase out the breeding business. In short, the Parker family for which this county was named arrived in this part of Texas first—as it happens, this ranch was part of the original Quanah Parker spread—but the Mickles intend to stay longer.

Stan gestured toward the small pasture down the hillside from the mausoleum with the three stakes scattered across it. "I stand here and hit balls and think about my mother. It's a tribute, really," Stan said. After a pause he added, "One of the most successful things we've done is to keep the family together." As we stood there on that mild winter morning, I found myself in agreement about the mausoleum. As a feature of the landscape, this one is a shock, initially, it's true, but it's also more practical than an immovable private cemetery and it doesn't require permits from any government agency, always a plus in these times. I decided that Stan is correct: the Mickle mausoleum on the tee box of the driving range beside the homestead on the hill above the interstate really is a neat deal.

We returned to the breeding station and palpitation room, where I finally met his father, Wes, who had arrived back at the ranch. Though not very elderly, Wes nevertheless enjoys something of an emeritus status on his ranch: he participates in the breeding activity to the extent that he wants to. Late this morning he was palpitating yet another series of mares. Wes is a trim man with an engaging, intelligent, and very calm demeanor. Perhaps the calmness and the calming quality come from working around horses for most of his life. Often enough, Wes Mickle doesn't even need the ultrasound wand. He can usually judge where matters stand with his sensitive fingers alone. There was definitely no ultrasound capability when he started in the breeding business in Scottsdale. Between palpitations he drew me a diagram of the equine organs, designating where, exactly, he was feeling and what, exactly, for. "I assume that this feels to the horses just the way it feels when a doctor checks me," he said. "Therefore I'm very, very gentle." By the way, he added, you have to be careful not to poke a hole through the delicate lining of the gut. If this happens, the resulting peritonitis can be fatal.

Wes has done as many as sixty palpitations in a single day. Every night during breeding season, he sits down with the records on every horse and makes an assessment regarding what the next few days may hold for her. He could computerize all this, and eventually will, but for now it's an art, it's a science, and it's mainly in his head. Still, Wes told me in what must be the sweetest non sequitur I've ever heard, "It's almost easier to find a world-champion racehorse than to find one that will take care of your little girl who just loves to ride." As he probed and calculated and intuited, Wes followed with a second surprise, one that led to the discussion that aligns him in my mind with Phil Kendrick, and also with Bob Popplewell. Looking over his shoulder, he asked if I'd read *Many Lives, Many Masters*, by Dr. Brian Weiss. I hadn't even heard of it. During his wife's long illness, Wes had read that book and its sequel, *Through Time into Healing*. He had always believed in God but had wanted some details. Dr. Weiss's first book presents the story of a patient who has had dozens of reincarnations over the centuries, according to the author, and Wes found it quite compelling.

First the rattlesnake rancher had declared his interest in reincarnation, now his neighbor at the stud farm: any preconceptions I might have had about what was percolating out here on the interstates were rapidly evaporating, chief among them the notion that the big highways create and convey a homogeneous culture, suburban and absolutely middle-American. Initially, without giving it much thought, I probably bought into this idea. Certainly I rejected the jejune agenda of all the road book writers who strike out on the back roads to find the rare, the poignant, the quaint, the throwback, the eccentric, the forgotten, and the arcane, and I did so on the grounds that these qualities don't have even marginal currency in the culture at large. The interstates figured to be the maw of the real

America, and mine a journey deep into the heart not just of American massness but of its alleged homogeneity and low-end mediocrity as well.

All wrong! Already! These weren't the people I was meeting; not so far. At the same time, I should confess this fact: I'm a pushover. Sure, I'm susceptible to the usual rants about the triumph of bullshit, inanity, and drivel, and I have my moments of cynicism and disdain when I watch the local news—who doesn't?—but I basically can't get behind that stuff in a big way.* Maybe I'm too easy to please, but there you are. I occasionally give our society a hard time, but its citizens, no, not at all, with the exception of the bigots and the blowhards. I've even felt a little sympathy for Richard Nixon's patently ill-equipped and dangerous personality. That's how soft-hearted I can be. Psychiatrists don't believe it's a coincidence that the Western society—ours—that's trying the most desperately to cling to some kind of biblical faith is also the one most enamored, in other quarters, of secular and New Age mental health therapies. I don't think it's a coincidence either. The therapeutic impulse is the secular acknowledgment of—the hope for—the best of all scapegoats, Christianity's "original sin." This secular impulse is a suitably laundered version of what goes on in the confessional or on one's knees—this is obvious enough—but it also issues from genuine pain of many kinds. There are an infinite number of ways for us to be knee-deep in ruin; we've already tried a large number, and invent new ones every day. RN was a master. So I intend to give him and the rest of us a break.

I reminded Wes Mickle, as I had Bob Popplewell, that reincarnation isn't at all a doctrine of orthodox Christianity, and Wes said he understood this and had pondered Dr. Weiss's suggestion that reincarnation *had been* a doctrine in the early church but was dropped from the catechism because it tended to yield, in the wrong minds, a somewhat lackadaisical spirituality. Wes and I continued this conversation during a

---

*Nor would I suggest for a moment that the *quality* of our bullshit, inanity, and drivel surpasses the accomplishments of prior generations. Not at all. What a slur! I wasn't there; I'm sure they, too, were proud of their work.

series of palpitations on dry mares, and then we carried it outside, where Wes interjected a reference to an invention of his, a magnetized device for storing a shop towel under the hood of a vehicle—a perfectly good idea.

For five years Wes had thought about spiritual matters as he nursed his wife through her battle with cancer. During that time he became close friends with Sharon Farr, the mother of Heather Farr, the professional golfer who also died of breast cancer, also in 1994. Heather Farr and Judy Kay Mickle received treatments together at a facility in Arlington, Texas, between Fort Worth and Dallas. This subject—cancer and cancer treatment—is another about which Wes has studied and thought deeply, with strong feelings. He believes the medical establishment is set up to *prevent* finding cures for cancer, in effect, and he would like to write a book about his findings. I explained to him the problem: for purposes of credibility, a major publisher would probably require on the jacket of the book a well-credentialed medical name in oncology, but Wes insists that most of these marquee-value MDs are part of the problem, not part of the solution. So he might have to publish the book himself. I won't be surprised if it happens.

Finally, I asked Wes about the genesis of the smoking phobia at his ranch and learned that it doesn't stem from the family's long acquaintance with cancer. Although he had smoked cigarettes at one time, his opposition goes back many years. Wes is amazed by the way people will ignore the bold sign on the front gate. He has seen the butts on the driveways. He has had individuals actually pull out their pack while standing outside one of the barns talking to him about a favored mare. He relates this to me with astonishment. He tells these people bluntly, "If you want to chew that, I don't mind, but you're not going to smoke it."

CHAPTER 3

When the redesigned Chevrolet Caprice finally rolled out of the factory for ceremonial adulation in 1990, GM's own employees were aghast at the ungainly bulk of the car. This was about as far from state-of-the-art design as the company could have achieved; Detroit had once again gone out of its way to build a loser. Some of the automobile journalists tried to be nice—"the car *does* make a powerful styling statement," according to *Car and Driver*—but the context gave away the sarcasm when another critic quipped in the same issue, "This is one whale of a car." *Motor Trend* noted the difficulty of telling whether the new model was coming or going if it wasn't actually coming or going. The car was embarrassing, and it was resoundingly rejected by retail customers. Sales fell fifty percent over four years; in 1995, Chevrolet announced that the famous nameplate would be decommissioned in 1997.* On the plus side, the Caprice became available to taxi fleets and law enforcement departments nation-wide at even deeper discounts than normal. That's why vehicle #4213, assigned to trooper Martin Hernandez working out of the Abilene office of the Texas Department of Public Safety, is a black-and-white '92 Caprice. Martin appreciates his Chevrolet for its roominess and heavy-duty handling at high speeds. It may not be the sportiest machine on the road, he knows that, but his squad car will catch just about any of the snazzier and more expensive models, and fuel and maintenance costs, which can be high because of all the wear and tear, are on the house and not his concern.

As Martin and I drove off the parking lot of the DPS offices on the south side of Abilene late on a Friday afternoon, a huge storm loomed to the northwest, the precise direction in which we were heading. Our beat for the evening would be I-20 between mile markers 260 and 288, from the east side of Abilene to just the other side of Trent, a small town to the west. Although we motorists usually don't notice, every inter-state in the country is marked every mile by a small vertical pole that measures the distance from some given point. This system is used by dispatchers to direct troopers, sheriffs, ambulances, and wreckers to the scene of the accident, break-down, whatever. These measurements always progress from west to east or from south to north. On I-20, mile zero is the intersection of I-10 and I-20 west of Pecos, Texas, so you don't need the map, just the mile marker pole, to know that Abilene is 286 miles from that spot. Note, however, that the measure-ments always begin anew at every state line. The first marker on I-20 on the Louisiana side of the Texas border is 1, and the marker on the other side of Louisiana reveals that the state is roughly 189 miles wide at the latitude of I-20. Mileage markers tell the observant motorist that the stretch of I-81 in Virginia is 323 miles long, that Texas is roughly 878 miles wide at the lati-

---

*The market has moved overseas, where the Caprice is the unofficial freedom-mobile in the Middle East. For this reason, almost none are available on used-car lots in the States.

tude of I-10, that North Dakota is roughly 350 miles wide at the latitude of I-94, and that Colorado is 299 miles tall at the longitude of I-25.

Martin noted quietly that this approaching storm was bad news for me. Radar isn't trustworthy in heavy rain because of false echoes, so troopers don't even bother. Therefore heavy rain is the speeder's delight if the issue of slippery pavement is set aside. But most drivers don't set that aside, so traffic dissipates and slows down. Less goes on in general. Perhaps dinner and coffee breaks are stretched on both ends. On the other hand, storms move fast and furiously out on this convex tabletop very near the southern limits of the Great Plains. This land feels higher than it is—a couple of thousand feet—because it's steadily lifting up from the coastal plains to the south. That's one reason for the constant wind and the high cirrus clouds and swiftly moving weather fronts: warm air rising up from the Gulf of Mexico to the southeast, the desert to the southwest. Another reason for the wind, especially between spring and early fall, is the dry line that defines the eastern edge of the desert air to the west. This is sometimes called the Marfa line, after the remote southwest Texas town where it so often originates. Almost daily this boundary between air masses shifts hundreds of miles in this direction, bringing the wind, then recedes again with nightfall; in the spring it can spawn incredible thunderstorms here at the southern terminus of tornado alley. This mushroom cloud looming above Martin and me could drop half an inch and be on its way east within twenty minutes. Happens all the time.

As we left the loop around Abilene and climbed onto the interstate, Martin reached forward to finger the radar gun mounted on the left-hand side of the dashboard. Immediately, before I was aware anything was going on, he hit the powerful brakes of the big Caprice, flipped a "U" via the grass median, and we were hauling eastbound at 106 miles per hour, our prey a gray Taurus clocked at eighty-one on the digital readout of the radar unit. The woman driving pulled over immediately as we drafted up behind her, our outboard lights unmistakable in her rearview mirror.* By now the wind was howling and the looming cloud spitted out the first bullets of rain. Martin punched "10-6" into his radio so his dispatcher would know he was busy outside the car and couldn't receive messages over the air. These codes are handy, of course, but they can also cause confusion, because the ones used by state troopers in Texas differ in a few instances from the ones used by the Abilene Police Department. The main discrepancy is "10-10," which means "Negative" for the DPS but "Fight in Progress" for the APD.

Hanging onto his regulation hat and leaning into the wind, Martin delivered the bad news to the driver. Back in the car two minutes later he said, in a tone that indicated a verbatim quote, " 'I didn't know this car could go that fast.' " That one's fairly common. People have said that from behind the wheel of a Camaro, a Riviera, a Land Cruiser, a Thunderbird, and a Corvette, probably. People have said, "I don't understand. My cruise control is set on sixty-five." People have said that the speedometer showed sixty-nine, not seventy-five.† People have claimed to be speeding in order to get to a gas station before they run out. People have actually said, "I wasn't paying attention." And many people have said, "My speedometer doesn't work." You're welcome to try the broken-speedometer excuse or any of the others, but you should understand that if you don't succeed your chances of getting a harmless written warn-

---

*Actually, Martin's cruiser is equipped with four different outboard light systems: the basic, multicolored rotators; wigwags (flashing headlights); takedown (bright lights shining straight ahead); and alley (bright lights shining to each side). There are also three different sirens—wail, yelp, and hi-lo—for the benefit of the tone-deaf motorist, and also one air horn. These cars can really make their presence known and understood.

†This could even be true. In fact, it will be true, to some extent, if the driver has installed oversized wheels, because a car's speedometer measures not miles per hour but the rate of rotation of the wheels, factors into the equation the factory-suggested diameter for those wheels, and computes what the speed *should be*. Wheels with a larger circumference will roll a longer distance for each revolution. The speed of that car might be four or five miles per hour faster than the speedometer indicates.

ing rather than a ticket have plummeted to zero. Troopers look more kindly on drivers who politely hand over the driver's license and proof of insurance and say simply, "Good afternoon, officer."

Within ten minutes this thunderstorm was boiling nicely and the report came in on Martin's radio that a truck had lost the top off its trailer at mile marker 270. High winds. We were west of that point four or five miles, and driving west, and crossing a wet median can be tricky, but Martin pulled off the maneuver and we sped back to the east. Fortunately, the ejected metal top had missed any passing cars. Instead, it had lopped off a light standard designed to break away under any kind of impact and landed on the westbound service road. In the howling wind and rain Martin and I pulled in behind this blown-away cover. The tractor-trailer was parked up ahead. Martin set his overhead lights, radioed for a small wrecker, advised the dispatcher that the highway department should be notified about the downed light standard, and ventured forth to summon the truck driver.

A few minutes later, wearing a faded cowboy hat and seated in the backseat of Martin's patrol car, Juan Rodriguez told us he'd been driving west when he heard a horrible sound above the wind and the rain and the diesel. Suddenly his truck felt lighter and, looking in the rearview mirror, he saw what had happened, proceeded to the next crossover, and looped around. He had been hauling peanuts; the Valencia peanuts from Deaf (pronounced "Deef") Smith County on the New Mexico border are the finest in the world, in my opinion. On this night, fortunately, Juan was running empty. Martin absorbed his story and then reached over to the backseat for a box of forms. He mentioned to me in passing the six hundred different violations, or "arrest titles," that he's authorized to file. For example, there are ten different ways to speed in Texas, including speeding on a beach. You'd think that simply driving a car on a beach would be illegal, but not on most Texas beaches—a fact Yankees are amazed to learn. The form for this "accident event" would take the best part of thirty minutes to fill out as Martin asked and Juan answered questions. Occasionally the dialogue segued without apparent reason into Spanish, then out again within seconds. Truckers have to carry innumerable licenses and permits, and Juan didn't have one of the important ones, so Martin ran a "10-28" on license plate number 669 35Z. A-OK was the response. Martin had no reason to run a "10-29," a deeper search for criminal warrants. After twenty-five minutes the wrecker arrived, and Martin directed that driver to haul the cover off to the side of the service road. The wrecker company would bill the trucking company, the trucking company would send out a flatbed on the morrow to retrieve the cover, Juan Rodriguez would proceed home with the empty rig, and Martin Hernandez and his passenger for the night would repair to the Wes-T-Go Truck Stop to enjoy dinner with trooper Max Shaw, who was working the nearby back roads and had pulled alongside for a brief telephone chat to this effect with Martin, who was ten feet away.

Max and Martin used to team up regularly before cost-saving measures cut back on having two officers in one car. There's no doubt that two officers are better than one when dealing with the public, but the tag team is no guarantee of safety. A few months after I met Martin and Max, thirty-nine-year-old state trooper Troy Merle Hogue was shot and killed by a seventeen-year-old involved in a minor one-car accident on I-20 about seventy-five miles west of Abilene. He was the seventy-fifth Texas state trooper to die on the job in DPS history. His partner and a third lawman, a sheriff's deputy, witnessed the unprovoked slaying.

When the discussion over dinner at Wes-T-Go turned to popular excuses offered by speeding motorists, Max jumped at the opportunity to tell me one of his favorite stories. Seems he had pulled over this young woman doing seventy-eight or whatever, and when he told her where things stood she hesitated, looked over at her passenger, another young woman, then blurted out, "I'm taking my friend to the hospital."

Max is a big man with a deadpan face that does a good job of hiding considerable playfulness. He had been in a particularly frisky mood that afternoon, with some time on his hands.

"Oh, you were?!"

Pause. "Yes."

"What's wrong?"

Longer pause. "Stomach cramps."

Max leaned down and looked across at the passenger, who did look very sick by that point.

"Well, let me go ahead of you and clear the way! We'll get your friend to the emergency room in Anson!"

He jogged back to his cruiser, fired up the lights, and led the way right up to the swinging doors. After the patient was safely in the wheelchair, Max tipped his cap and said, "Hope everything turns out okay. Glad I could help you ladies."

The ladies knew they'd been had, and they knew that Max knew, too. The bill for the emergency room services would cost them appreciably more than any speeding ticket. "I saved a life that night," Max concluded with a grin. Martin then observed that motorists sometimes use their emergency lights as a cover for speeding. This scam seldom, seldom works. When a driver says, "I wasn't paying attention," Max Shaw enjoys replying, "Well, if you're not, who is?! *Someone* in this car needs to be paying attention." Maybe the maximum possible fine will do the trick. The three of us laughed loudly in the restaurant. The waitress delivered my barbecued ribs, which I'd purchased against my better judgment—too heavy, long night ahead—but at Martin's and Max's insistence. Like everyone around Abilene, they swore by the food served up at Wes-T-Go, where the troopers often rendezvous for lunch, dinner, and coffee. By that hour on Friday evening, the cloud had opened up. Beyond the windows, traffic had slowed to a crawl; inside, the conversation meandered. Max mentioned that he enjoys listening to opera in the car, played by a local college station. Martin sometimes listens to opera, too. He had never attended a live performance, of which there are none around here, and Max hadn't been to a performance since his college days in El Paso, where he was a drama major. He served on the board of the 255-seat opera house in nearby Anson, built in 1907 and in need of renovation. But funds were lacking. I asked Max how he had made the transition from drama to highway patrol, and he said, "It's not as far removed as you might think. There's a lot of role-playing here, too."

I made the mistake of asking about speed traps and quotas.

Max resented the terminology. There's no such thing as a speed trap with the DPS, he informed me, although he acknowledged that they might have been imputed in the past to certain rural municipalities that extended their jurisdiction out to the interstate and lowered the speed limit to fifty-five miles per hour for a mile-long section. On the other hand, Texas law does dictate the lower speed limit around cities with populations greater than fifty thousand, including Abilene. Troopers get sick of hearing snide remarks like, "How many of us have you caught in your little speed trap today?" or, at one a.m., "Does this do it for your quota tonight?" Harmless but pointed retaliation is sometimes in order, something like, "Yes, ma'am. Please press hard because this one wins a microwave oven for my wife."

Martin Hernandez, thirty-seven years old, is a native of Abilene and had been on the force here for sixteen years, the only job he'd ever had or ever wanted. Not sheriff's deputy, not city officer. Highway patrol. He doesn't remember the origins of this ambition, but I speculate it might have been Broderick Crawford—in Martin's case, reruns of Broderick's show, because "Highway Patrol" went off the air in 1959, when Martin was a baby. Like the twenty other troopers who operate out of DPS-Abilene, Martin alternated between the day and night shifts on two-week intervals, and by now his wife and young son and daughter were accustomed to the flip-flop.

On an average night, and assuming no time-consuming accident investigation or DWI incidents, he would make between a dozen and twenty stops in his eight-hour shift, five p.m. to two a.m. About half of these encounters would result in just a warning, which isn't reported to the insurance company's computer and doesn't cost a dime. Max Shaw reported the same ratio, and it holds statewide as well: Texas troopers bestow 500,000 tickets and 400,000 warnings annually. These numbers surprised me, because I recall just one warning in all the times I've been stopped. As I learned from Martin and Max and perhaps should have known already, this is because a warning is rare when the speed in question is higher than seventy-five miles an hour, as a matter of policy the slowest I drive on the interstate. As Martin and Max (now seated in the backseat) and I drove slowly west on the interstate after dinner, after the rain had let up and with country tunes playing softly on the radio, I admitted that I drive with a radar detector. "Well," Martin said, "try to hide it if you get stopped, or you're gonna get a ticket for sure." Hiding the detector is standard practice, of course. When Martin and Max were partners, they tried to have some fun with drivers they suspected of this deception. If Martin were standing by the door conversing through the window with the deceitful driver, Max in the patrol car would fire the radar gun. When the hidden detector sounded its alarm, the driver would practically jump through the roof.

"What was that noise?" Martin would ask in all innocence.

"My damn radar detector," in all glumness.

Not a week before my interstate tour with Martin, a speeder had tried to lure him into a debate on the physics of radar measurement. This guy claimed to have a college degree in the Doppler effect, and he was eager to prove that either Martin's device or the laws of physics had worked incorrectly in this instance. Tell it to the judge, Martin advised; and note that he did not say, "Tell it to the jury." With juries, you never know. According to Martin, no lawyer will step foot in the courtroom here in Abilene for less than $150, which is considerably more than most speeding tickets amount to, so the defendant defends him- or herself, the only risk being the extra court costs, usually $35 for a forty-five-minute trial, if the defendant should lose. But often the defendant does not lose. Often she wins because the jury feels sorry for her. Martin gave the example of a recent trial involving a young woman and a stop sign. "She knows she ran the damn stop sign," he said. "This was no rolling stop, either, no California roll. There's a difference between a rolling stop and running the stop sign, and she *ran the stop sign*. But she's real cute. And pregnant. Twenty-three years old. And here's the big, mean police officer. I had been parked probably a hundred yards from the stop sign. She went and took pictures of where I was parked.

Now, in a camera, you take a picture and it will look half a mile away. But the jury doesn't see that. Plus she said she had *measured* my distance at seven-tenths of a mile. Bullshit. I wasn't that damn far. But the jury bought it. They found her innocent. She beat me and the D.A. A soft-hearted jury a lot of times will go for the defendant. But if the jury finds you guilty, it can set your fine." Martin goes to court two to four times a month.

On the highway we received word that a westbound truck had slid off the interstate onto the median, and every available hand was needed to control traffic as wreckers attempted to pull the eighteen-wheeler back onto the highway east of town. Martin raced in that direction, passed the scene and the flashing lights of at least a dozen police and emergency vehicles, and successfully negotiated a U-turn on the soaking median. We pulled up on the inside lane several hundred yards upstream from the truck. Martin set the rotator lights on the roof and got on the radio with the trooper managing the operation up ahead. He also kept a close watch on our rearview mirror because we were at a dead stop on the interstate, with only our flashing lights for protection on a dark night. I turned around to see the traffic for myself, ready to shout a warning.

"There's no safe way to do this," Martin said. "If OSHA took a look at our job, they'd shut us down."

A spirited discussion ensued on the radio under the general heading "What next?" The initial plan had been to shunt all traffic onto the outside lane, then someone proposed completely stopping all westbound traffic. In the backseat, Max declared this a terrible idea anytime and an invitation to disaster on a dark night. For one thing, drunk drivers often gravitate *toward* bright lights; everyone in law enforcement knows this. He and Martin discussed the possibility of going back to the far side of the nearest interchange to the east and diverting all westbound traffic onto the service road, but the highway department doesn't want a lot of truck traffic on those roads, which aren't built for them.

I recalled Martin's remark from earlier in the evening. Almost out of the blue he had said, "A majority of our stress comes from supervisors. You get out here and you do your thing and you always wonder, 'Did I do it right? Are they gonna come down on me for that?' Every year there's more paperwork, but, still, the stressful part is the supervisors. You do something out here in the instant-th of a second. Your decision-making is *right then*. But then you've got these people back on a desk thinking about this situation all day long, or for a week or a month, and they say, 'Well, you should have done it this way.' That's where a lot of your stress comes in." That remark contrasted with the ideas expressed to me by Captain John Marsh, the DPS officer in charge of this entire region of the state, a responsibility stretching southward almost to the Mexican border. It was Captain Marsh who had set up the ride this evening with Martin Hernandez. I'd arrived at the DPS offices a little early and John Marsh was there, perhaps even waiting to meet me to determine if I was indeed the reputable sort. I signed the necessary release forms and we discussed his role and his sergeants' role in the grand scheme of things, which role comes down to the three basic functions: supervision, supervision, and supervision. I didn't get the impression from Captain Marsh that there could be too much supervision.

After long minutes of radio give-and-take regarding this truck mired in the mud, it was suddenly announced that the eighteen-wheeler might be able to get back on the interstate without too much trouble. In fact, the caravan up ahead began to move out almost immediately. Apparently the truck was already back on the road! Problem solved. Turn off the deck lights. Open up the inside lane. Time for coffee at The Kettle. "10-4."

Trooper David Mays was among those who joined the three of us in our booth. Martin and Max had warned me about their associate, the class clown for this DPS region, and he didn't let them down. When David heard that I was born just to the north in Stamford and that my father had grown up in neighboring Avoca, he exclaimed, "Avoca! That's where the family trees grow straight up!"

More backwoods jokes followed, some funny, some not so. At one point Mays kidded me about being a "liberal Democrat," and this was really interesting because that very afternoon I'd been swimming at the local "Y" when the man laboring mightily in the adjacent lane struck up a brief conversation during a much-needed break—for him, that is. I was doing fine, although the water was too warm, as it is at all the refurbished "Y's" around the country, due to all the old paddlers who get cold. Learning that I didn't live in Abilene and was out here in the proverbial heartland working on a book, this swimmer made certain I understood that this is a conservative town, although he assumed I had already figured this out. I had, but only because most places are conservative, certainly so in the Southwest. My main route to and from California on the five interstates crossed fifteen Congressional districts; following the 1994 elections, Republicans held twelve of them; two years later, thirteen. But how did that man know at a glance that I wasn't bedrock conservative, that I must be somewhere left-of-center as the scale is established in Abilene and almost everywhere else? Was there something a little different about my mouth, my chin, my swimsuit, my crow's-feet, my accent, only thirty miles distant?

Then, not ten hours later and without my having said a word either way, here was state trooper David Mays nailing me again. Was I not laughing at the right times—or, worse yet, not at all? No, David had some stuff funny enough even for this yellow-dog Democrat. But he knew. Maybe the tip-off was my admission that I'd lived in Manhattan off and on for years. That idle remark was greeted with the long silence it usually merits, all over the country. Try it; you'll see. People don't understand how you can do it.

What did David Mays know about Martin Hernandez? By Abilene or DPS standards, either one, I'm willing to bet that Martin might be somewhat left-of-center. He agrees, regarding welfare, no additional money for additional children, but stopping all benefits after so many years? "I don't think that will work," he said. "I like the idea some of these politicians spit out about raising the minimum wage. I think that would be good. Raise it enough to where we could get these people out of poverty. How in the world can you expect these people to work if it comes out to fifty cents an hour after child care? It doesn't make any sense. There's no incentive to get off welfare. One thing I do respect Clinton for is that he's the only one that has made an effort. A lot of people do dislike him, but he's brought out these issues like hospitalization for everyone. I think he's doing it for the people. At least he's trying to do something about it. I've always said that. A lot of people don't like Ann Richards. I think she's doing a pretty good job herself. We've never had so many prisons as we do now."

After midnight and nearing the end of our tour of duty, Martin pulled up in front of a truck parked on the side of the highway and walked back to check with the driver. The man had been falling asleep; Martin advised him to return to the truck stop. Cruising the parking lot at Motel 6, we were flagged down by a man complaining that a truck had just run him off the road. Without a license plate number, there was nothing Martin could do. Back on the highway, he suddenly chased and caught a Chevy van. Still wearing his bright yellow slicker under a clearing, starry sky, Martin took time to position his pistol so it protruded visibly through the pocket hole. Then he approached the truck and invited the driver to step out. The rule about approaching every driver and every passenger as a possible adversary, about expecting anything and everything at all times, goes double after midnight. The likelihood that the trooper will wear his bulletproof vest is higher on the night shift. But this man turned out to be a harmless undertaker from Lubbock.

Back in the car, Martin asked if I'd noticed that the interior lights of the patrol car didn't come on when the driver's side door was opened? I sure hadn't. The idea is to make it more difficult for anyone to see at night whether a second trooper is in the car. Martin pointed out the shotgun case bolted to the base of the rear seat. The locked cover is released with a switch on the dashboard. A shell must be in the breach, not in the chamber, of the stored gun; the safety switch must be off. Pump and fire. In his sixteen years with the department, several of those with the driver's license division, Martin had never fired his shotgun, and his pistol just once, in a DWI episode up in Jones County. DWIs are the greatest potential danger the troopers face on any kind of regular basis. The experts testify that an alcoholic gets away with drunk driving two hundred times for every time he's caught, and that lopsided ratio accounts for his anger upon apprehension. Totally unfair! Martin encounters two or three of these drivers a month, usually because they're weaving from lane to lane or traveling very slowly, or both. "If we see weaving in the mirror," Martin explained, "we slow down. If they see us, *they* slow down. They're afraid to pass. We slow down even more. They slow down even more. I've gotten down to twenty-fives miles per hour and they still won't pass. That's when you know something's wrong."

In Texas, .10 blood alcohol is legal intoxication. For commercial operators, .04 will result in a suspension, though not a DWI charge. If a trooper smells any alcohol at all on a trucker's breath, he'll remove him from the truck for a minimum of twenty-four hours. DWIs are cuffed and placed in the front seat of the patrol car, where they're supposed to sit quietly while everyone waits for the tow truck to arrive. The large man up in Jones County surprised Martin with immediate aggression, threw him against the hood of the cruiser, raced for his own pickup, and tried to drive away. Martin and another officer arriving on the scene shot out the tires on the truck—all four of them, plus the spare, in my imagination.

With two drunks, the cruiser gets crowded and the trooper gets nervous. This had happened to Martin about a month before. The first one was running eighty-one miles an hour and taking up both lanes while doing so. It may not be easy to stop such a driver, but Martin succeeded. Riding into Abilene with this inebriate, Martin then spotted a car driving very slowly along the median before pulling onto the highway in the wrong direction. "*That* guy was so bad he scared *this* drunk in the car," Martin exclaimed. "I stopped, ran across the median, got to his door, identified myself, tried to get him out of the car. He started resisting; I managed to get him on the ground. But I didn't have my handcuffs. They were on the other one! Normally, never put anyone in the backseat if you're working alone. But now I had two DWIs. Where was I going to put this second one? I had to put him back there—and without cuffs, too. And he did, he started giving me some trouble on the way in, but fortunately I wasn't too far from the police department."

At 12:30 an armed-robbery bulletin came over the radio: two suspects in a blue Cadillac, possibly heading west on I-20. Martin reversed direction, reached a suitable point on the interstate, and stopped on the shoulder. Lights out, waiting, we discussed felony takedowns, not all that common around here. Martin had been involved in very few. The blue Cadillac didn't appear—just as well—and after fifteen minutes, Martin headed to the house while I drove over to the Ramada Inn across the loop from DPS headquarters, where for $30 over the basic chain rate I rented quite a few more square feet, the credenza, extra chair, bigger mirror in a nicer frame, full breakfast buffet in the morning, and proper bar of soap.

CHAPTER 4

Six hours later I was back at trooper headquarters to rendezvous with John Murphy, my host for this beautiful, warm day now that yesterday's storms had moved off to the east and today's had yet to move in from the west. This tour of duty with another of his state troopers had also been arranged by Captain John Marsh, the boss who believes in all the supervision. Waiting for John, I chatted with the communications coordinator, as I was quickly and not all that cheerfully informed was now the preferred nomenclature. So my earlier reference to "dispatchers" is hereby amended.

John Murphy comes to us straight out of central casting: *GQ*-handsome, short-clipped hair, soft-soled trooper boots, slightly incongruous wire-rimmed eyeglasses. He invited me back to the squad room, where he needed to finish up some paperwork. Desks, file cabinets, and lockers line the walls of this large room, with high school cafeteria tables arranged in a row down the middle. Another trooper was hunkered over his own desk while listening to a subdued broadcast of Click and Clack, the Tappett Brothers, on PBS—and he didn't have a tie on with his brown uniform with the blue-and-red piping. John wore a tie, as had Martin Hernandez and Max Shaw. Why? The tie is mandatory with the long-sleeved shirt, optional with short sleeves; in the summer, the straw hat, in the winter, the felt model. After a few minutes John stowed his papers and pulled up a chair beside me at one of the tables to exchange life stories at his request. I learned these salient points: he was twenty-eight years old, six years on the force after two years working as a roustabout in the oil patch and as a deputy sheriff in Snyder, his hometown about fifty miles to the west, in Scurry County. Out there, John's father knew the location of each and every underground pipeline, but his son didn't take to oil work with the same enthusiasm. Like Martin Hernandez and Max Shaw, not to mention David Mays, John had never been to New York City. He had married for the second time a week before we met.

We followed the basic route out to the interstate to patrol the same twenty-eight-mile stretch Martin Hernandez and I had covered, and just one mile's worth of shaking and pounding in vehicle #4211, John's high-mileage, five-speed, 302cc Mustang, made me appreciate the advantages of Martin's capacious and comparatively plush if embarrassingly ugly Caprice. Cars are assigned to the troopers on a seniority basis; Martin has seniority. The troopers drive them to their homes, where the cars are parked outside in plain view, for the benefit of the whole block or, in John's case, the apartment complex.

Immediately after reaching I-20, John pulled the Mustang off the highway in order to interview a set of three transients, as he referred to them, separated by no more than five hundred yards on the westbound side, almost directly across from the Wes-T-Go Truck Stop. Checking on these men and the occasional woman is optional for the troopers, but they'll do it as often as not. On occasion such an interception will result in a felony takedown. John informed me that I was welcome to join him outside the car when he was talking with the transients or handing out tickets or just warnings, whatever. I stepped out with him as he approached the first subject, a young man with longish blond hair, a beard, one ring in his right nostril, three rings in his left ear, and a long, beautifully carved walking stick. John said good-morning and stationed himself off the pavement on the downstream side of the hitchhiker, so he could talk while keeping an eye on the oncoming traffic. This location and position are called the safety zone. The man said he had come down from Victoria, British Columbia, to join some sort of community in San Cristobal, New Mexico, which he'd read about in a book, and where he'd work for his room and board. John asked for name and I.D., then returned to the car to relay the information to the communications coordinator who would enter it into the computer to search for outstanding warrants and missing persons reports. Meanwhile, I asked this guy where he had spent the previous evening. Beneath an overpass. John returned, handed back the identification, reminded this pilgrim to stay on the *grass*, and to walk *backwards* while facing the traffic, using his right hand to thumb for the ride. Walking beside any road with your back to the traffic is verboten.

We wished this man good luck and coasted the few hundred yards to the next hitchhiker, who had seen us coming, of course. This was a myopic, snaggle-toothed, down-and-out, middle-aged man wearing an unnecessarily heavy coat and backpack. He said he lived in Longview in East Texas and was on his way to Odessa, about 170 miles west on I-20, in order to see his father. He provided John with his driver's license, John called in this name and number, and we bid him adieu.

The third transient was an overweight, scruffy, Willie Nelson look-alike with a hint of meanness thrown in, I thought. Claiming to be on his way to Tucson to work in a sheet metal shop, he said he'd spent almost a month at the Salvation Army in Abilene. Back in the cruiser John informed me that such a lengthy stay would have been an exception to the rules. After a few minutes the report came back on all three of our subjects: on the Generation X-er from British Columbia, nothing at all; on this potentially mean-looking older guy allegedly headed for Tucson, nada; but the harmless-looking dude with thick glasses turned out to have a rap sheet as long as your arm,

charges and convictions including burglary, weapons violations, robbery, and narcotics. Nothing outstanding, however.
Still, John might have chosen to reconvene to ask him for details on recent whereabouts and travels. If a nearby farmhouse
turned up burglarized, there'd be a record of when and where
John had talked with this man. "But this guy didn't act that
way," John concluded. "He wasn't nervous about anything. I
think he's probably okay."

So he walked. When I expressed my surprise about his
long record, John didn't share it. Long ago he had quit judging
people ahead of time. "I'm a lot broader now," he said. "Like
Max Shaw would say, 'You don't know what you're going to
see out here.' *Especially* on the interstate, with so many people
passing through from all over the country. One day I stopped
a guy for speeding, a young man with somebody riding with
him. The driver was real clean-cut, but the passenger looked
about like the third guy we just checked, a really burly guy,
nasty clothes. I had seen the duffel bag in the bed of the
pickup, so I thought this passenger might be a hitchhiker. I
had the driver step outside the car and I asked him if he knew
this man, and he said no, he had felt sorry for the guy, picked
him up, gave him a ride. Sure enough, he was a wanted person
for auto theft and had a rap sheet with like twenty-seven ar-
rests, one of them a homicide. Who knows if the kid who was
driving would have ever made it to his destination if I hadn't
picked him up for speeding? The hitchhiker was pretty cooperative when I arrested him. The kid was really surprised. So
don't pick these guys up. You don't know."

I had always had complete faith in my ability to read the
character of my fellow citizens from a football field away and
to offer rides accordingly, although my powers in this regard
had been tested on I-59 in Alabama about a year earlier. The
guy's car had broken down—or so it appeared: the hood was
up—and he had some kind of shaggy-dog story to go along
with it. I didn't believe a word he said, but in my defense he'd
been close to the hundred-yard limit, and in my rearview mirror at that. When he loped up and leaned in the window on
the passenger side, I realized I was dealing with a dangerous

psychopath, paid no attention to his tale of misfortune, wished him good luck anyway, slipped him twenty—a craven admixture of embarrassment and even a little fear—and kept going for Texas. Touring with John Murphy, I thought about the second of our three transients this morning. I probably would have given that felonious sad sack a lift.

I inquired why any roadside felon would voluntarily provide an inquisitive trooper with his correct name and driver's license or social security number. They just do, often enough. That hitchhiker arrested for auto theft just gave himself up, in effect. On the other hand, John added, "A lot of them will tell you they don't have an I.D. The common story is 'I spent some time in Los Angeles and I got mugged and they stole my wallet and my I.D. I have no identification whatsoever.' So you ask for name and date of birth, and you can run it through the computer. Can't find anything. Then try to get a social security number. If they're *suspected of an offense* I can bring them in, have them fingerprinted, check with the FBI computer. But I can't just take them off the road to do that. I have to take their word on who they are."

We soon encountered an example of this very scam thumbing his way west, wearing a Day-Glo Newport cigarette baseball cap. This uncooperative youth said he had never had a driver's license, didn't know his social security number, and had lost that documentation, anyway. Or maybe it was stolen. And he'd never had a job, either, he said. Disgusted, John and I drove off at a leisurely pace—but not for long, because a white Dodge Shadow with Illinois plates running eighty jolted John's radar out of its torpor. We splashed and bounced across the median, accidentally flipping off John's sunglasses in the process, and red-lined it to the east to catch our first speeder of the day. Eighty must be about top speed for that subcompact, John and I agreed. Finally the car stopped beside a guard rail. John sighed theatrically, detached the small microphone hanging on the dashboard, and through the overhead loudspeaker directed the young woman driving the car to pull *forward* beyond the rail, please. Obviously, the rail would impede an emergency escape from the side of the roadway should some oncoming car or truck swerve in that direction. The safety zone sought by the trooper in every situation excludes any kind of barrier in the vicinity.

Back in the car, John used the identical tone employed by Martin Hernandez to indicate a verbatim quote from a devious driver: " 'Well, what is the speed limit here?' "

Ma'am, in Texas it happens to be exactly what it is in Illinois and in all but four of the states: fifty-five miles per hour in urban areas, sixty-five out in the country.* Before too long, a low-slung, black pickup with a teenager at the wheel hauled ass past us, way over the speed limit, old or new. Following the short chase John reached for his hat and went off for the interview. Again, he unobtrusively positioned the kid between himself (and me) and the oncoming traffic. Generally, John likes to get the men out of the car, where he feels he can carry out his duties much more safely. He doesn't mind asking a woman to join him in the safety zone if she's properly dressed, but not if she's wearing a loose dress, because of the constant buffeting from the traffic speeding past not fifteen feet away.†

After the initial exchange of pleasantries, John looked at this kid carefully and asked if he hadn't stopped him out here before.

"No, sir."

John looked at him again. "Weren't you having trouble with your mother out here one day?"

"Yes, sir."

"Well, I knew you were familiar. How's that going now?"

"We're getting along a lot better."

Back in the cruiser, John filled me in. "About three years

---

*The four states were Delaware, New Jersey, Connecticut, and Hawaii, where the maximum is fifty-five. They stayed at that number even after passage in 1995 of the "pedal to the metal" bill, which lifted federally mandated standards. Most Western states immediately raised their top speed to seventy-five. Texas went to seventy. Montana, "The Autobahn State," has no daylight limit at all other than whatever is "reasonable and proper."

†Troopers suspect truckers of sometimes blasting past as close as they can, maybe trying to blow the hat off. A ticket can be filed against that practice—failure to use due care for pedestrians—but how could you go about assessing it and then making it stick in court?

ago I saw a car pulled over and a lady waving at me. I pulled over and she said she was having all kinds of trouble with her son, this boy. I think he was fourteen at the time, and he had wanted to spend the night over here at Tye High School with his friend, and she wouldn't let him. So he was being really disrespectful, started raising Cain with her, put her on edge, so she just pulled over and waved me down and asked me to talk to him. I spent about an hour on the side of the road talking with him and his mother both. Then I called their preacher to go over and counsel with them.

"I can remember faces, but not names. I go into a restaurant and recognize someone, but I'm afraid to say anything because maybe it's someone I stopped on the highway instead of someone I met at a baseball game."

For the coffee at Wes-T-Go we were joined by another trooper working the back roads around Abilene this Saturday. This man was given to snide remarks about some of his peers on the force, which wasn't very smart because he knew I was writing my book. After ten minutes of this, I acquired a deeper appreciation of Captain Marsh's choice of Martin Hernandez and John Murphy as my interstate nursemaids. I decided he'd intentionally chosen a couple of his younger and more personable troopers, and I was thankful for that. With this hard, older man it might not have worked out worth a damn. On the other hand, who knows? This trooper who seemed like a blowhard might have become a wonderful guy over time, the star of my story. When a family whom both John and the other trooper knew came into the restaurant and the kids swarmed around us, the trooper went out to his cruiser to get some DPS "Junior Trooper" paper badges to hand out, and the kids were ecstatic. He stuck one on my knit shirt, too.

As John and I rolled out of Wes-T-Go, crossed the highway, and started up the entrance ramp heading west, I looked to the right and saw a man in a pickup on the service road cussing us, or so it appeared—and lip-reading "Fuck you! Fuck you!" isn't that difficult.

"What's he so mad about?" I asked John, who had also observed this display and replied, "I don't know, but we're going to find out," jerking the Mustang off the pavement and diving down the incline to the service road. We doubled back a short distance and followed the pickup into the parking lot of some kind of truck service center. The big guy who was driving jumped out hopping mad. Instinct suggested that I stay in the patrol car this time, but the windows were down and I heard "chickenshit," "bullshit," and other denunciations. This guy was hot, while John stayed remarkably cool. But what was the dispute about? I had no idea. After it was all over, John informed me that just as we'd crossed the bridge over I-20 and turned onto the service road, this guy—already pissed off about something—had raced up right behind us before standing on his brakes. John had been pulling off the entrance ramp in order to double back and ticket him for following too closely when we saw the guy yelling at us from his pickup.

Now he was marching around the parking lot, gesticulating. At one point he started to walk off and enter the office. John told him to come back until they had finished their business. The guy glared at me sitting in the car with my tape recorder.

"Is he taping this?"

"I don't know," John replied. "Maybe he is."

"Is that legal?"

"I guess it is."

"Well, I think I'll tape it."

"Be my guest."

That was the gist of the exchange, but I wasn't taping their dispute because my machine doesn't pick up from five feet, much less from fifteen. The guy said he wasn't going to sign the ticket. John calmly explained that a signature was not a plea of guilty. You can call the judge. You can go to court. You can file a complaint. Finally, the man signed and walked up the stairs and into the office. Within moments an older, equally big guy opened the door and came down the stairs toward John. I figured he had to be the younger guy's father, and I was right. He and John shook hands. It turned out that

John had given *him* a ticket not long before. John asked whether his son had some basic problem with law enforcement officers. The father said that if he was in the wrong, he was in the wrong, family or not. *You've got a job to do, I've got a job to do. . . . I never give police officers trouble even if they're giving me trouble—not that they ever do. . . . There are chickenshits in your business like there are chickenshits in my business.* When John finally returned to the car he looked over and said, "You may be called as a witness in this one."

This bubba had been an exceptional case, but all the troopers I met in Abilene were quick to agree about the considerable belligerence they encounter on the highways. Common sense says that any kind of attitude ruins your chances of getting away with a mere warning, but, still, lots of people go ballistic when confronted by a lawman. And maybe not the constituents you'd imagine. Martin Hernandez had been the first but not the last trooper to point out that the worst offenders are your doctors, of course, fat cats in general, certain military personnel, and almost anyone driving a Lexus or other luxury sedan. I thought about the Korean couple at the rattlesnake ranch who had failed to haggle with Bob Popplewell over the price of the snake meat. What if they'd been driving a Lexus or Infiniti instead of their modest Oldsmobile?

Martin Hernandez has had a youth from El Paso boast, "We have money. My parents taught me that laws like this don't apply to me." John Murphy has had people say to him, after he had politely inquired, just as a way to break the ice, where they were heading this evening, "It's none of your business." And Californians, in John's experience, are the worst of the worst. "Really and truly," he said, "they don't have a whole lot of respect for a police officer. I guess with all the stuff they have going on, they could care less what we say to 'em. They're going to do their own thing anyway. I'd rather stop almost any other state than I would someone from California."

And there's another thing: California is one of only eight states that doesn't subscribe to the Nonresident Violator Compact, known in the trade as The Compact. This gets technical, but the bottom line is that motorists from California, Hawaii,

Michigan, Montana, Oregon, Washington, Wisconsin, and Alaska don't have to pay a fine assessed in Texas or any of the Compact states, because their states haven't joined the reciprocal agreement. Therefore, speeders from California and these other states aren't issued a Texas ticket and sent on their way, since they'd never have to pay it. Instead, they must post a cash bond, usually $100, and they tend to get very upset and nasty about the Lone Star State, at which point John says, "Look, all these other states have agreed to be in The Compact, and California didn't. Take it up with your legislature."

This cash bond is a pain in the ass not only for the motorist but also for the state trooper who has to aid the search for a Pulse machine or a means to get the money wired, and who then has to round up a judge willing to accept the bond. John has never actually seen anyone locked up in lieu of covering the bond at the going rate of $50 a day, though he understands it has happened. All things considered, I have to believe that California and other non-Compact drivers receive an inordinate number of warnings in Texas. Send 'em on their way. Get them the hell out of here.

A concluding story about belligerent drivers, related postprandial by John Murphy: "One day about three years ago, near Anson, I stopped a man at about seventy-five miles an hour. He was in his sixties and real disrespectful. He told me, 'Look, I'm going to speed anyway. I've got a job I've got to do. I'm just trying to get to Hamlin. This ticket's not going to slow me down any because I've got to go.' Really rude. All I had asked was where he was going. Anyway, I radioed ahead to the troopers I knew were down the road, and *they* stopped him at, I think, seventy-four miles an hour. This was just three miles down the road. Wrote him a ticket. Five *more* miles down the road he got in a curve and couldn't handle it and had a fatality accident. Two guys with him, they both survived."

Two interpretations present themselves. One, that the guy was asking for it (John's unspoken assessment). The other, that the guy simply had gotten so *angry*.

· · ·

Early in the afternoon, word came over the radio in the 302cc Mustang that the irate driver of the pickup truck had followed through with his threat and phoned in a complaint about trooper John Murphy, who responded to the bulletin with a silent shake of the head. I offered the cheerful reminder that he had a note-taking eyewitness. And then there was his earlier statement regarding his transfer from sheriff's work to the DPS: "Making these traffic stops is a lot more exciting than going out and getting cattle off the roadway." He had to remember this in these times of doubt.

Nor did John have time to mope, because suddenly speeders were coming as hard and fast from every direction as mourning doves in a good late-afternoon hunt. (Yes, we shoot the bird of peace in Texas, and some of us even like the dark, dark meat when it's wrapped in bacon and smoked over coals and served with beer.) The speeders that afternoon would have kept a handful of troopers busy. First, a red Lumina which also failed to have a seat belt on the child in the front seat—a substantial fine, depending on the judge. Next, a pickup with two good ol' boys returning from the big game between Abilene Cooper and Odessa Permian, the latter team the subject of *Friday Night Lights*, the best-selling book about high school football in Texas. Bubba got a warning. Looking carefully at my shirt, one of these guys asked if I was a trooper-in-training or something. I looked down to find my "Junior Trooper" paper badge still in place. In the car, John said he'd wondered about this but figured I must have known, figured I was proud or something, figured people who had lived in New York City must be total dweebs.

Then a couple with Ohio plates, the guy immediately climbing out of his car and walking back briskly toward John's cruiser. Motoring folklore holds that the trooper doesn't like this tactic; stepping out of the car is an aggressive intrusion into an officer's psychic and physical space, and he'd prefer you just stay in the car until invited outside. The theory turns out to be basically correct. Stepping out and waiting passively by the driver's door is okay, but walking toward John might put him on red alert.

In this instance, he didn't seem to mind. The guy was a military pilot from Fort Bliss in El Paso—four years—captain—claiming that because he was military, his expired license was okay. When John assented to that, the flier asked frankly if he could get a warning this time. That often happens, John told me: motorists asking outright. That's chutzpah. I'd never thought of trying. In this case, at twenty-one miles per hour over the limit, the answer was no. But the officer took it well. Next, a black family going to the grocery store in an old sedan, the driver saying something to us about the pills he took for high blood pressure. He explained to John that he used his brother's telephone and provided us with that number. Two teenage girls watched from the backseat with large eyes. Although my unofficial score for the day was seven tickets, one warning, John had assured me that on average he's a fifty-fifty kind of guy, just like the statewide average. "The point is to enforce compliance," he'd said. "Often a warning will do that." Like most troopers, he kept his stack of tickets clasped to the front of his clipboard, his book of warnings clipped to the back. Standing in the safety zone interviewing the motorist, he was prepared to go either way. If ever there were a candidate for a warning, I thought, this was the guy, a family man with high blood pressure who didn't even have his own telephone. I looked at John as pointedly as I dared, but he gave him the works. When this obviously nice man reached out his laborer's hand for his ticket he said, "Thank you, sir, ya'll have a good day. I'll slow down."

The unwritten rule holds firm: without exception, the most polite drivers are those who, by all appearances, can least afford the fine.

Immediately, two speeders coming over the same hill almost at the same time, but just far enough apart that John's radar could draw the distinction. First the Grand Prix, then the pickup with the Harley strapped in the bed. As we roared past the pickup, John's right arm reached across me to point at the driver and then at the side of the road, an unmistakable message. Then we caught the sedan and followed it onto the shoulder while the pickup waited fifty yards back. Tickets, both of 'em, no questions asked, and this time I agreed.

As our Mustang topped a hundred miles per hour in pursuit of another Taurus, lights blazing, an oblivious driver pulled out in front of us in order to pass a still slower vehicle. John calmly hit the brakes and muttered, "Happens all the time," as a vision of the waiver I'd signed for Captain Marsh flashed through my head. The driver, a young woman, completed her passing maneuver and drifted back to the outside lane where she belonged, and I glared as we accelerated past. She didn't even glance over, probably wasn't aware that the law was eight feet away. Now, it has happened that speeders have tried to exploit such delays in pursuit by slipping off the interstate at a conveniently placed exit and attempting to hide among a line of cars parked in front of a convenience store. I myself have fantasized about such a gambit; if the ploy fails, feign ignorance. John assured me that it always does fail, and the scam opens the driver to a second infraction—failure to pull over, in the vernacular—hard on the heels of a guaranteed failure to receive a mere warning. But this yuppie was sitting there waiting for us and couldn't have been nicer while accepting his ticket.

I asked John about the highest speed he'd ever clocked, and this record belonged to a sixteen-year-old girl driving a Buick sedan 116 miles per hour on a back road cutting off the interstate west of Abilene.* "Here, I'll show you the place," John said, turning west. Even in his professionally equipped Mustang, I felt that eighty was fast enough on those bumpy lanes, and he pointed out that the road had been improved since the girl had seized the brass ring. John had felt so strongly about her recklessness that he had called the girl's home, where the mother answered. At first she was suspicious and defensive, as parents almost always are these days. That's part of the whole problem in the schools, I've read and also heard while driving through Des Moines, Iowa, on I-35. The

---

*The department doesn't keep files on the highest speeds ever ticketed, but troopers old enough to remember agree that many more hundred-plus-mph tickets were handed out in the late sixties and seventies, the era of the GTO, the 442, and other muscle cars. A couple per month wasn't uncommon then, while triple-digit speeds are very rare today.

AM program suggested that teachers and administrators get no support from the parents when it comes to discipline because both parents work and feel guilty because they're not *there* for the kid. So they defend Missy automatically, she knows this will be the case, and she runs wild. Eventually John was able to convince this particular working mother that he was calling simply to advise her that if her daughter continued to drive on narrow back roads at remarkable speeds, the next phone call from the DPS would relay a more radical message. The mother ended up expressing her gratitude for John's concern.

Finally, out at Trent, over twenty miles from Abilene, a wide-body pickup rolling east at seventy-nine. Rolling west, John lost valuable time finding both a suitable strip of the median and an opening in the oncoming traffic. (Earlier, in a similar situation, a long line of trucks had allowed a Ford to escape.) When we finally headed in the right direction, the red pickup was far ahead, but John hit every gear skillfully and we were gaining fast. Then the pickup slowed down—the driver had seen us—and unexpectedly dipped onto a luckily adjacent exit ramp. Going considerably faster than the pickup because he was trying to catch up, and still in the passing lane, John had to step on the brakes and dive across two lanes to make the exit, which happened to be in a construction zone featuring a warning sign about uneven pavement ahead. There was a three- or four-inch dropoff onto that ramp, and also a skein of loose gravel everywhere. Traveling about forty miles an hour, I'd guess, maybe a little more, the Mustang's rear end spun out and we were fishtailing toward this, then that, then another sign or pole. Like any accident, this one happened in a flash, and any reconstruction of the details is therefore partly truth and partly fiction, but I know I yelled "Whoa!" or some such when we were aimed directly at the largest of all the signs. Another vision of Captain Marsh's waiver flashed through my head, and John's airbag didn't have a twin on my side. A regular driver, I'm convinced, would already have flipped and rolled or crashed and burned, but John threaded us through the barriers, skidding all the way. We had almost stopped, miraculously undamaged and unharmed, when the right rear of the Mustang clipped a small delineator pole, the very last obstacle in our way. Two seconds later, we were stopped. Up ahead on the service road, the family in the red pickup waited for us, staring back at the accident scene. Meanwhile, on the interstate, all passing eyes were fixed on the embarrassed black-and-white.

John was unhappy. I was happy because I thought he'd done a great job of saving us from a much worse fate, but he was unhappy, with no trace of relief. "This is great," he said sardonically as we got out and inspected the so-called damage. "A 'fleet' and a complaint on the same day." And with a civilian along holding a pencil and a pad as well.

A "fleet" is a traffic accident in a state vehicle. The damage to the Mustang was trivial—a $20 piece of plastic on the bumper and a ding above the wheel well, flaws any lay driver would blow off until he thought about selling the car—but John would have to call this in. While a regular noninjury accident between civilians isn't even written up if it doesn't involve $500 in damages, another trooper would have to drive out and file an official report. John's sergeant would have to be notified and, if available, he'd have to come out to the scene. But for another half-inch, we would've missed that delineator pole and already been sitting at the Wes-T-Go, counting coup, extolling our skillful driving and good luck. Therefore, I figured the driver of the pickup was going to catch an earful from trooper Murphy. After all, he'd started all this by bolting the interstate like a rabbit. Yet John was strangely calm. The driver, Jerry, hustling to Abilene before some important store closed, actually thought he'd been doing the right thing. He told us that even his heavy pickup, at a slower speed, had lost a little traction when it hit that dropoff and the loose gravel. Later discussion among the troopers established that one of the heavier Caprices probably would have handled these problems, too.

Jerry, who worked underground tanks in the oil patch, asked me if I was a trooper out of uniform, for some reason wearing sneakers.

"No. I'm writing a book about the interstate and other things."

"An *author*?"

"Yeah."

Almost without exception, citizens of the world are amazed to meet someone who claims to write books. Some of these people see books around and, should they stop to think about it, which apparently they don't, they'd realize somebody has to write them. But when they actually encounter an individual who labors in this capacity, they're dumbfounded. People would be less surprised if I said I was a retired professional football player, living now on autographs and banquet appearances; maybe I could pass for a former free safety. After the initial astonishment has worn off, their next question is usually, "Have you been published?" A prospective landlord once asked me, "You can make a living doing that?" Often I ask provincials how many copies they think are required for a nonfiction book to sneak onto *The New York Times* best-seller list. Several hundred thousand is the minimum guess, and "Oh . . . half a million" is pretty frequent. When I counter that forty thousand might do the trick, under auspicious stars, they're dumbfounded all over again. And when I look around at a decent turnout for the Rangers at the ballpark in Arlington and realize that just this many readers—no more—might turn that trick for me, it's encouraging *and* dispiriting.

But out at the accident scene on the interstate, Jerry gave me a break. I saw the gleam in his eye before he asked, "You gonna write this up?"

"Probably will."

He seemed really happy to have been thrust into a starring role in this story he will never read, and regarding his speeding ticket he was totally blasé. "What are you gonna do?" he said. "May get another one before I get there."

At last, Greg Arnwine rolled up in his black-and-white, another Mustang. I'd met Greg at lunch. A massive guy, he deserves a Caprice on that basis alone. He did literally unfold as he squeezed out of his coupe. Shortly after Greg started writing up his report, Sergeant Sharp arrived in mufti from the comfort of his home. Him I knew, because Captain Marsh had asked me to confirm with Sharp the specific dates for my DPS assignments. He also deserves some of the credit for selecting Martin Hernandez and John Murphy as my hosts. For half an hour these two peace officers measured distances, took pictures, and drew charts of the yaw marks of the trivial accident. Ridiculous, but it was the rule. I filled out an eyewitness report. And the following morning—Sunday, slowest time of the week on the interstates—John and Greg would return to take pictures from the vantage point of the entrance to the exit ramp, and to take some final measurements. Finally, after more than an hour, the four of us repaired to the Wes-T-Go for coffee, and I saw the young British Columbian hitchhiker whom John and I had interviewed that morning right across the interstate. Seven hours later, not one offer of a ride. Here he was sitting at the counter, drinking a cup, rolling his own.

CHAPTER 5

Driving westbound out of Abilene I glimpsed a hitchhiker wearing Ralph Lauren jeans or, at any rate, designer-type jeans. I checked the rearview, thought about it for a moment, and took the next exit to spin back for closer consideration. This was months prior to my education by John Murphy, I didn't know better, and as things turned out, I'm glad I didn't. The man was standing alongside two luggage bags on the entrance ramp. When I pulled up short on the service road, he walked up quickly. When I asked where he was going, "Phoenix" was his answer. I glanced at his bags still sitting back by the ramp. I looked again at him. These clothes weren't Ralph Lauren, but neither were they camouflage. This was no thief. I explained I'd be turning left at Colorado City, only seventy miles down the line, but seventy miles, he said, were better than nothing.

"Hop in," I said, and he bolted for his bags—"but there's a

catch." He stopped in midstride and looked back with deep suspicion. If I could change my mind, he could change *his* mind. That was the message delivered by that look, and it gave me comfort. "I'm writing a book," I said. "I'll ask you a lot of questions."

"You're writing a book! Well, that's okay."

No, it was perfect. When a well-dressed, articulate hitchhiker is about to tell you how he comes to be a well-dressed, articulate hitchhiker and you're writing a book about highways and I-ways, you're in high cotton, as they say in West Texas, or used to say, back when the cotton actually did get as high as your chest. Bob Smithers, the hitchhiker who was also something of a know-it-all, soon told me there's high cotton no more because the new strains are bred smaller for the sake of mechanical harvesters. Not quite. A county agriculture agent later testified that the plants are smaller not so much for that reason but in order to direct growth into the fruit—the cotton boll—rather than into worthless leafage. The farmer then either uses a defoliant to kill the leaves prior to harvesting or waits until after the first frost. Either way, the harvester leaves in its wake the thin white blanket of cotton Bob and I were discussing as we drove west.

He was going to Phoenix to see his daughter and his grandchildren. "I *was* living in Melbourne, Florida," he said, "but I'm not living anywhere right now. Just gave up my place eight days ago. Work kind of fell off, working in a place called Shooters, which you've probably never heard of. They just laid off a bunch of people because they're getting out of the boat business, basically. I freelanced, had some cards printed up, dropped them off at marinas. After Phoenix I'll be going to see my other daughter in a little town called Folsom, California. You've heard of it?"

Of course: Johnny Cash's famous Folsom Prison Blues.

"Three other kids in California, and my ex-wife. Three grandbabies. I grew up in Texas, got married, my wife was a schoolteacher, we had four kids and lived in Dallas for seventeen years, when I worked for Dresser Industries. My family goes back aways in Texas, one of the original Four Hundred, if you know about Texas history at all."

Bob was off by an even hundred. The Old Three Hundred were those Anglo settlers who received land grants in Stephen F. Austin's first colony in 1822.

"My job at Dresser was to evaluate manufacturing equipment, but they stopped manufacturing, basically. They got into conglomerizing—diversifying. I was making $39,000 in 1983, and they paid us to take extra courses, and I did all those. I started at SMU, but got a degree from UT-Arlington, the extension program, after six and a half years. Got two sabbaticals with pay. It was a good deal. I belonged to the American Society of Mechanical Engineers. Are you familiar with what happened with oil prices in '83? Okay, you know. People walked away from their homes. It was complete chaos. But Texans are basically resilient. After Dresser I took a consulting job with a machinery company. The first two years I actually made more money evaluating tools. That was my forte at Dresser.

"Stayed in Dallas until 1986, when I got a divorce and divided up the assets and she went her way and I went mine. That kind of thing. Divorces picked up then, I had a lot of friends who became alcoholics. It wasn't just my company. It was a lot of them. All the companies were interrelated back then. Of personal friends, I know one who's got a little service station in Montana. Last time I heard of another friend he's living in Hawaii and running a dive shop. I'm just thinking of people on my block. The old barbecues out back went down the tubes. I had piddled until the divorce, keeping the payments up and all that stuff. Since then it's spot jobs and what-have-you. Since '85 I've been scuffling more than anything else."

I asked Bob if he had had any idea this was the way things might turn out.

"No. Lord, no. Thought I'd go back to Dresser. That was the premise they laid on us. But oil field jobs aren't coming back. Why spend money wildcatting and drilling when you can have crude tanked over so much cheaper?" Then I asked Bob how deep the wells were that we're driving past. "About 1,500 to 2,500 feet. They're real shallow out here. Your deep wells are in East Texas and South Texas." Actually, he wasn't quite right about this fact, either. The shallow wells in West

Texas run more like three thousand feet, with the deep wells throughout the state reaching down maybe eight thousand. "What they're trying to do out here now—a truck driver this morning told me about this—is reworking. They'll buy a well they know is no good, okay, and then go out and sell shares in Fort Worth or wherever. They give the buyers this big proposal on reworking the well. You can sell as many shares as you want. You pull the casing, that doesn't cost anything, pour in some concrete, reseal it, put some more casing down, spend maybe $50,000, but you've sold hundreds of thousands worth of shares. Then you send out the news that you didn't hit anything. I heard about that in the Permian Basin years ago. It's big business right now, too, from what I understand." This scam was perhaps inspired by Zero Mostel in *The Producers*, who oversubscribed his Broadway production, confident of a flop, and then was caught flatfooted when "Springtime for Hitler" knocked 'em dead.

"Anyway," Bob concluded, "I went to Florida. I was always a boat person. Sailboats. Rigging, painting, detailing— that's the cleaning of a boat. I'm pretty good on boats, really. A lot of people bring their boats down just to have that stuff done. I had guys come up with hundred-foot yachts didn't know how to get the diesel fuel off their yacht. You've seen that streak—two, usually—down the back. There's a secret how to clean those. If you know your chemicals you can do real well detailing. But I was never making enough money, just enough to pay your rent."

When I asked Bob why he decided to hitchhike to Phoenix, he was offended and snapped, "I didn't *decide* to hitchhike. I financially wasn't able to buy a bus ticket. I left Florida with forty-six dollars in my pocket. It's taken me eight days to get this far. Some days I don't get far. I spent twenty bucks in Fort Worth last night because it got so cold. I had no choice. Never waited over an hour, hour and a half. I didn't think it was going to take me *this* long to get across, but I've only had one good long truck ride so far. I got one truck ride from Ocala, Florida, to Lake Charles, Louisiana. Plus sometimes you can make a few dollars if they've got to load or unload. That's what I was planning on doing. Haven't been too successful on it. I almost had to walk out of Mobile, then caught rides for thirty, thirty, and fifty miles until I got to the other side of Houston, and then I caught a ride all the way to Austin. Then in Austin I stayed in the Salvation Army."

There's a problem here. Bob said he spent a night in Fort Worth *after* a night in Austin, but Fort Worth is almost two hundred miles due north of the state capital—ninety degrees out of the way if Phoenix is the final destination. Why did Bob accept a ride from Austin to Fort Worth? I don't know, and the conundrum didn't strike me at the time, so I didn't ask.

"Independents"—owner-operated trucks—"can pick you up, and near dark, they're tired, they're over their log time and they have to be somewhere, and they want company to talk to 'em. Last night was my first good night's sleep."

I asked Bob whether his kids knew he was hitchhiking out.

"Oh, good Lord, no! They'd have a heart attack. I told 'em I'd be there when I got there. I'm not going to tell them how I came out, no." At this point, Bob asked me not to use his real name in this book; Smithers is not this man's real name. "When I leave Phoenix, hopefully, if everything works out, I'll have a few dollars. I'll work out of a labor pool is what it amounts to and they pay thirty a day." He hasn't had a car in a couple of years. "Kind of local around there"—Melbourne, Florida—"but it's not a problem in Florida, usually. Don't have a car, don't have a bank account. I would like to get back to that situation, but if worse comes to worst, I'm just going to struggle for two years until the investment program kicks in. I've got two more years until I'm fifty-five and can start drawing from my retirement fund. Got screwed out of three years of that. If I could have gotten those, instead of drawing $1,400, I could have drawn about $3,000. I'll draw $1,470 a month. And then I don't think I'll be staying here, to be honest with you. I think I'll be going to the Caribbean.

"I can get by. I found out I can do a lot of things I never thought I could do. I've unloaded 1,300 cases of cucumbers or something. Fifty-two years old, pay you sixty dollars. I've learned how to pour concrete. You never think you're going to be out doing something like this. Hiding my existence from my kids. Putting on false pretenses. They came down, I actually

went and rented a place, a self-contained place with dishes and
TV, $820, because my kids were bringing my grandkids down
to go to Disney World, and so I had to put that show on that
Dad was not broke. Which is a helluva struggle. Actually I was
living in a $120-week motel and splitting the rent with another
guy in the boatyard.

"I don't have a negative attitude toward anything, though.
I gave all that up. I wasn't raised that way. It's not that big a
deal, and it's not because I have any spiritual growth or anything like that. I just realized the only thing you can count on is
change."

We pondered that observation in silence. Renting a
furnished apartment in Florida to hide from your visiting family the fact that you're actually living in a lousy motel, withhold-
ing the fact that you're hitchhiking rides because you can't
afford the bus, yet believing these embarrassing straits are "not
that big a deal": is this the wisdom of the enlightened or the
facade of the defeated?

I asked Bob who'd given him rides.

"I'll give them to you," he replied quickly. "A kid just
picked me up who delivers medical supplies to different doctors out here. He's from Dallas, has a little pickup with a
camper. Had an Army sergeant pick me up coming out of
Austin, I think it was." This may have been the problematic
trip I hadn't picked up on. Did this sergeant give him the ride
to Fort Worth? "Brand-new Cadillac, and he had his sergeant's stripes on. Does ecology studies. Had a lady and her
daughter pick me up, and they tried to get me to go to their
house to have dinner. I didn't like that. I just got out, told 'em
no. That was outside Tallahassee. That was kind of strange.
And I turned down two Mexicans because they had a quart of
beer between their legs. You've got to be semicareful about
what you get in with. I usually talk to the people first, before I
get in. Lot of 'em they tell you about their problems and all
that stuff, mainly. Somebody's mad at his wife or they're going
to split up.

"When I grew up, I don't care what happened, you always
took care of your neighbors. You don't have that now. Our last
family reunion there were eighty-something people. You don't

see that kind of stuff no more. I never ask for anything. I know better than that. I've had cops stop me to I.D. me, make sure I'm not wanted. It's happened twice, once in Alabama, once coming out of Austin, early in the morning. They're basically pretty nice, not giving me any problems, tell me to be careful, which I'm doing anyway."

So the drivers have to be careful with transients, and the transients have to be careful with the drivers. I asked Bob whom he'd voted for in the previous election. It didn't occur to me that this particular hitchhiker would have failed to vote.

"I voted for Ross. I don't like anything Clinton's done. I don't like that damned socialized medicine he's putting in. Why should you go to school for twelve years and make as much as a plumber?"

I suggested that his accounting was a gross exaggeration.

"It's not," he assured me. "I guarantee it's nothing more than socialized medicine."

Here we have the classic illustration why the left wing has rarely been able to play the class card effectively in America, and therefore has never made inroads with the body politic. Here we have, I believe, one of the reasons most of the fans side with the owners in the baseball wars: the owners are owners, they're supposed to be rich, while the players are just *employees*, like the rest of us, and they shouldn't forget it. We Americans are resilient pragmatists, and most of us don't blame our betters for being better. Instead, we appreciate the opportunity to become one of them ourselves. If we fail to match up, it's our own fault, or the government's; and if we try to be what we're not, like the ballplayers, that's unforgivable, too. Many, maybe most, of us are perfectly satisfied with the standard enmities and prejudices, while the fat cats remain sacrosanct. The historian Richard Hofstadter famously delineated the consistent anti-intellectual strain in the American character, while the antirich correlative is confined to sporadic, populist bursts, short-lived and never coincidental with Election Day. I'm sure academics argue that this whole syndrome is yet another manifestation of the frontier legacy, a view of the world bringing together down-but-not-out Bob Smithers and the frenetically entrepreneurial Bob Popplewell at the rattlesnake ranch. And both Bob and Bob have a point. However, none of the above attitudes pertains to the vanquished and embittered minorities, and they may not pertain to Popplewell's young slackers, either. Only time will tell about them.

I liked and respected Bob Smithers, but back home I thought about checking with Dresser Industries and, especially, with UT-Arlington to verify his stories about the job and the degree. That drastically out-of-the-way ride from Austin to Fort Worth, combined with Bob's errors of omniscience, caused me to doubt everything else. As we know, people can spin the most incredible lies and tales, a talent related to our apparently unlimited capacity for fantastic faiths and impossible beliefs. We humans can believe not only just about anything concerning the world, but also just about anything concerning ourselves. Hope, this is called, and I have nothing whatsoever against it; I occasionally slip into the habit myself. So when I had that moment's doubt about Bob's history, I then felt badly about my cynicism. Why would he make all this up? Besides, newspapers daily feature homeless people who, not all that long ago, had enjoyed respectable jobs and circumstances. Some of them are lying, certainly, but *all* of them? I know for a fact it's not so. Just the other day I handed a few coins to a man at a stoplight in Dallas who told me he was now too old to be "hire-able" for construction work. When I asked about social security or disability, he said there was a problem at the welfare agency to which his check was mailed because he lived under a bridge. How much of this was true? I don't know, but he provided some convincing details. I think he had indeed come over from England years before, although people can put on accents, as my wife noted. But if this guy was faking, I say give him credit for an enterprising new wrinkle in his trade. Then the light changed.

Whether or not the story Bob Smithers told me was true in every detail, Bob himself is still out there in the world with his real name, living some totally true story every day. I see nothing wrong in hoping that by now it includes drawing that $1,470 a month pension from Dresser and finally enjoying those mild sea breezes on the leeward shorelines of Anguilla.

Sixty-nine information-packed miles west of Abilene, in

Colorado City, I dropped off my hitchhiker and his luggage at the convenience store, and Bob declined with thanks my offer of a Coke, peanuts, crackers, anything at all. Had I offered him a little money, which I wouldn't have, he would have refused that, and been insulted as well. So I rode off into the sunset after this hour-long encounter with a man I'd never see or hear of again. Never. Almost impossible. And strange, too, I've always thought, to meet someone, share experiences—although in this instance Bob did most of the sharing—and then depart for good. We do this a million times in today's world, but repetition doesn't make the experience any less peculiar, not to me. Today, most of us must meet thousands more people over the course of a lifetime than our great-grandparents, or even our grandparents, ever met. And yet these countless modern connections must serve only to increase our feelings of isolation, rather than to mitigate them, because the connections are so brief and inconsequential and atomized: Gresham's Law once again.

All the haphazard encounters and contingencies dictated by the way we live today scare some people into trying to believe just the opposite, that we're all connected, like AT&T says. We're supposed to be desperately searching for genuine community in the midst of this dehumanizing, isolating materialism, all this getting and spending; searching in order to counter the demeaning, embarrassing, low-end, essentially hollow, ersatz worldwide community foisted on us by the mass marketeers. Not a week goes by without another newspaper or magazine story to this effect. By this analysis, all the churches now filling up with boomers are, first of all, friendly places to hang out.

The highways are implicated, too, and they should be. John Brinckerhoff Jackson, the famed odologist (he coined this term for the student of roads) and vernacularist (he said the future will not have much dignity, but it will have vitality), suggests that the interstate highways are inherently centrifugal, throwing ideas and energy and people outward from the center, disregarding the local and the vernacular—the community—while the back roads and the dead ends are inherently centripetal, pulling things into the community. This characterization makes historical sense, too, because all but two of the great ancient cultures were founded in large measure on superior ground transportation within their borders. The Persian Empire conquered by Alexander the Great had the first interstate system, with all roads leading to Susa; a few centuries later, all roads led to Rome. But not really: all roads led *from* Susa; *from* Rome. The idea behind empire-building and nation-building isn't to bring the hinterlands to the center, but precisely the opposite; the ethos goes out, and only the spoils of conquest and the raw goods come back home. The two great cultures that never got around to building good roads were Egypt, which had the river instead, and the anomalous, sea-faring Greeks, who really did treasure community—the independent city-state—and opposed the homogenization and centralization that necessarily traveled outward with the roads.

I don't doubt that our interstates are bad for community; my doubt is whether all this talk about community is meaningful in the first place. For one thing, yearning for community contradicts devotion to the ethos of the frontier, which we Americans are justly famous for. The frontier is not a community, not initially, and when it does settle down and evolve into one, many folks want to get out and find the next frontier. And this question: if communities were so important to us, why do we move around so much?

I said earlier that my wife and I were staying in Dallas while I traveled the interstates. "Staying"—that's the only word for it. We didn't *live* anywhere, and that was fine, even appropriate, for my interstate purposes. They say that visceral dissatisfaction, inchoate longing, and the resulting rootless transience are the atavistic attitudes and behaviors peculiar to our postfrontier American experience. Europeans don't have these problems, they say, if only because they get all the opposite ones: rampant rootedness, ancient memories, eight-hundred-year-old wars. Maybe so, and maybe my wife and I are exemplars of this peculiar stateside syndrome, although in our defense there are other reasons more mundane why we've had sixteen official mailing addresses and several other fairly lengthy stopovers with understanding friends* in twenty-three years of marriage: bigger place; new job; better town; better place; ownership; better town; bigger place; better place; better borough; green grass, literally; better green grass; different town; different town; different town; disaster. This rootlessness must stem in part from the fact that we have no children. Mix this in with generic, American-style visceral dissatisfaction and inchoate longing and you have this bottom line: three years is the best my wife and I have been able to do anywhere. So we may be extremists, I acknowledge, but we're not alone. Tenacious in this disjointed culture is the notion that some more real and better place and way of life surely exists somewhere at a remove from wherever we happen to be, somewhere on the cultural outskirts. As usual, Tocqueville was right when he wrote 150 years ago, "An American will build a house in which to pass his old age and sell it before the roof is on; he will plant a garden and rent it just as the trees are coming into bearing; he will clear a field and leave others to reap the harvest; he will take up a profession and leave it, settle in one place and soon go off elsewhere with his changing desires." My wife and I are a little different because we go back and forth, back and forth, between Texas and New York City,† but no matter. Americans are prone to pull up stakes and run away. Between 1985 and 1989, almost half of us did so; every year, about twenty percent. The Dallas area is ranked number one in this regard. Just check with the Census Bureau: no one lives where they used to.‡

Most of us are connected to very few people, truly give a damn about even fewer, and that, I believe, is the way we prefer it. *Hello. Nice enough to meet you, I suppose. Goodbye.* The

---

*With one exception, a couple whose kid began stuttering shortly after we arrived.

†The inevitable next time up would be my fifth.

‡This just in: figures for 1993 show a decline in American mobility to the lowest level since 1950. A statistical aberration, or has the great American pastime and, specifically, the postwar migratory period, come to an end? If the latter, experts blame the aging of the population and financial insecurity manifested by smaller, two-income families.

rest is lip service, because the whole community deal begs the one all-important question: community *with whom*? While I enjoy people as much as anyone, that's not the same as wanting all or many of them as close friends. We want very few really close friends and just one really true love. Small towns aren't dying because people prefer to live in them but can't find a job; they're dying because most people don't prefer to live in them. "Northern Exposure": as a TV show, take it or leave it, but either decision sure as hell beats actually living in Cicely, and Cicely is a lot less provincial than real small towns.* We're told that all the joining we Americans do—forty percent belong to support groups—manifests yearning for community. To this I say, Oh, come on, one hour a week is hardly community. In fact, that's why we like these groups: they're *only* one hour a week, which we can live with. The Internet might be the best of all ersatz communities for the modern world, with lots of purported connection but without the messy complications that arise when you actually shake someone's hand: community complete with anonymity, the best kind. Finally, let's see how long this particular religious revival lasts. There have been a bunch over the centuries, and I think this one faces odds every bit as long, and not just because people get tired of communion: they tire of all that obligatory community as well, which becomes stultifying with little effort on anyone's part.

Meanwhile, the cities, even the suburbs, offer guaranteed emancipating isolation. And those militiamen, the total crazies, where do they *invariably* live? My wife and I may be urban drifters—a friend had the nerve to say as much, and to our faces—but that's still better than the kind who hide out on the back roads, plotting revenge. If that's community, they're welcome to it.

---

*But this also just in: from 1990 to 1995, and for the first time in decades, more people moved into than out of rural areas. As recently as 1970, about one in ten Americans lived in towns with populations under 10,000. In 1990, only one in sixteen lived in the official 11,897 small venues. But now the ratio is getting larger again, helped by two unrelated phenomena: better crop prices and modems. If the trend holds for the next thirty years, my thesis is in trouble.

CHAPTER 6

At Colorado City, I hung a left on Highway 163 toward Ozona, almost 120 miles due south on I-10, where my grandmother named Myrtle lived in the nursing home. My route down passed through two tiny dying towns, Sterling City and Barnhart; I encountered maybe two dozen vehicles, one of them the Fed-Ex truck, over two hours on a Tuesday afternoon.* Sparse country, indeed, with Sterling City the only town in this eponymous county. Ozona is the only town in Crockett County, an area almost twice as large as Rhode Island; Sonora, also on I-10, is the only town in Sutton County, abutting Crockett County on the east; and Eldorado is the only town in Schleicher County, also to the east. Many of the resi-

---

*Another time down, another couple of dozen, including the Fed-Ex truck again.

dents living on ranches between these towns still don't have private phone lines; some share eight-household party lines. GTE was busy as I drove past, providing them with cellular phones—cheaper, under the circumstances, than installing fiber optics.

We're now west of the famous 100th meridian, the generally accepted demarcation between east and west on the North American continent, between *more* than twenty inches of rain and *less*, between tall grasses and short, between self-sustaining agriculture and the irrigated version. The meridian falls on the eastern border of the Texas Panhandle and passes a dozen miles west of Stamford, my birthplace, and Abilene. The only proverbially western feature that's still missing at the 100th meridian is a largeness of scale in the landscape. At the latitude of I-10—a third of the way from the equator to the North Pole—this expansion happens about two degrees west of the 100th meridian, or a little west of Ozona, where ridges and mesas lift up abruptly from the surrounding plains. Here, for the first time in its westward journey, sizable cuts are required in order for I-10 to slice through these ancient limestone formations, which once formed the floor of an inland sea and are responsible for the hundreds of caverns that riddle this part of Texas and New Mexico. The Great Plains peter out right around here, in the region known locally as the Edwards Plateau. Dry ranching country, with a little irrigated farming. The traveler who has no affinity for this land—acquired, in my case, during boyhood visits with my grandparents—might look across a particularly flat, barren section around Ozona and dismiss it as God-forsaken territory.

Friends visiting from out of state—from up north somewhere, usually—can be expected to express astonishment at the number of trees we have in Houston or Austin or Dallas, if only because the territory farther west (Ozona is about 350 miles from Dallas, a little farther from Houston) is what they think of as "Texas," and when they think of West Texas they think of *Giant*, which I blame for all the misunderstandings about the geography of the state. That blockbuster was filmed two hundred miles west of Ozona, near Marfa, and during a severe drought. Almost no rain had fallen for four years.

The regional joke was that Baptists had to resort to baptism by sprinkling instead of the normal dunk, Methodists settled for a damp sponge, and Presbyterians took a rain check. That's how dry and sacrilegious it was in West Texas in 1955, and thanks to *Giant* that windblown Dust Bowl became fixed in the world's imagination as representing not just part of the state, but all of it. In fact, a particularly rainy season will produce lush range grasses anywhere out here, parts of deep East Texas happen to be a swampy piney woods best traveled by low-lying watercraft, and Houston is the Bayou City.

On the 100th meridian, mesquite and cedar and various grasses and flowering desert plants are the main vegetation. The ubiquitous mesquite is the ranchers' curse because it hogs scarce water from the grass.* It requires three times as much water as grass requires in order to produce a given biomass; for just one pound of growth, mesquite requires one thousand gallons, while grass takes about three hundred. Mesquite both seems and *is* impossible to eradicate. County agriculture agents who consult with ranchers no longer use that verb. They seek to *manage* the tree instead, but the cattle themselves make this difficult because they eat the beans, and their digestive juices break down the seed coat. Without this scarifying action, the incredibly tough coat, impermeable to water, would degrade much more slowly, over months, even years, depending on conditions. Instead, cattle deposit viable mesquite seed in a warm, moist place in which to live: dung.

Late-twentieth-century mesquite management consists of two lines of attack, both of which amount to your basic scorched-earth policy. The trees can be dug up and burned or hauled away, or they can be sprayed. Digging up proceeds either tree-by-tree or, more spectacularly, by means of an extremely heavy-duty chain-link or wire drag line pulled at maximum tension at ground level between two powerful

---

*The thorns on this tree can be a major problem at some of the roadside stops and rest areas. If a car should for some reason leave the pavement in a recently mowed, mesquite-infested area, the result might very well be four flat tires. And Air Jordans? Wear a pair while walking across a thorny terrain and you'll never do it again.

tractors, yanking from the earth anything in its way. I've been told on good authority—a rancher in the area—that after a large, heavily treed area has been cleared, a nearby creek bed will sometimes spontaneously carry water, quite an illustration of mesquite's thirst. Spraying is more popular than excavating because it's simpler. Prior to the early eighties, an herbicide labeled 2, 4, 5-T was the choice, but its chemical profile is similar to Agent Orange. For starters, it contains dioxin, so it succumbed to the bad publicity and cannot now be manufactured, sold, or transferred (although existing supplies may be, and sometimes are, applied to the land). The herbicides Remedy and Reclaim are the latest popular choices in West Texas, applied either by crop dusters or by exterminators driving four-wheel motorcycles. People are appalled to hear about these massive applications, which can certainly put the water supply at risk, but it's necessary to note the difference between herbicides and insecticides or pesticides. The latter are much, much more toxic.*

Despite Reclaim and Remedy, mesquite seems to thrive down Highway 163 from Colorado City to Ozona. What's more—and this is a genuine puzzle for all concerned—grasslands throughout the west are slowly or not so slowly giving way to woodlands and brushlands of all types. In the debate on why this should be, the leading candidate for chief culprit is the level of CO_2 in the atmosphere; trees and brush plants can handle elevated levels of CO_2 better than grass any day of the week. If this trend continues unabated, as it very well might, the nature of farming and ranching on this continent and throughout the world promises to change fundamentally. Already, some cattle ranchers hereabouts are shifting to other kinds of wildlife management, such as raising exotic deer, sheep, and antelope in order to enhance cash flows.

---

*Within the industry, these chemicals are rated for toxicity on the LD-50 scale, which rates the lethal dose required to kill fifty percent of a given population of small furry mammals. On that scale, huge doses of Reclaim are safer for these mammals than the same amount of table salt, and Remedy scores about the same as aspirin. Meanwhile, the now-prohibited 2, 4, 5-T is almost as nasty for the system as gasoline and many of the pesticides.

Another compounding factor doesn't bode well for the future of ranching: old and absentee ranchers. A younger generation is coming along, but it's comparatively sparse, and the establishment, so to speak, is less susceptible to new thinking and practices. That's the theory, and why shouldn't this apply to ranchers along with everybody else? On top of this, you have all the doctors and lawyers in Houston and Dallas who turn over their million-dollar trophy ranches to a foreman earning a princely $25,000. This basic million-dollar spread would be 2,000 acres, purchased at $200 per acre, plus buildings, animals, and machinery—a considerable operation, given that the median size of a Texas ranch is 320 acres. Would these same professionals dream of delegating any similar investment to a manager pulling down a fraction of their own incomes? How can this dynamic possibly produce the best range management practices? I heard all about it from a county agent.

A draw or gully is a watercourse that seldom carries water, but when it does, watch out. The wide, shallow draws between these low hills of the Edwards Plateau are vulnerable to sudden cloudbursts and the rare sustained rainfall alike, since directly beneath the shallow, inches-deep dirt is a slab of limestone—ten thousand feet thick in some places, although this depth isn't needed to inhibit spectacularly the absorption of water. At the bottom of some of the long and gentle inclines out here, a flood gauge is posted with demarcations up to six feet. A flood at that depth would be a hundred yards wide, at least. Ozona has a rich history of such gully washers. Johnson Draw runs straight through town, about a hundred yards across and twenty feet deep, its flat bottom scarred by dirt bike paths. Out on the interstate, the Dairy Queen has a picture of the scene when a freak tropical storm drove north out of Mexico in June 1954, and Johnson Draw became a powerfully flowing lake. Old-timers and their progeny swear that empty fifty-five-gallon oil drums were filled full in those forty-eight epochal hours. Maybe that story got started by the rancher who said he measured fifty-five inches of rain, three years' worth. In the DQ photograph, Ozona is submerged by maybe twenty-five feet of water pouring down Johnson Draw, which normally is bone-dry. At the time, my father was working for the Texas Company (as of 1960, Texaco) in San Angelo, to the northeast, and he drove down to Ozona to assess the damage to the local filling station. He marked the high-water line on the wood shelves about four feet above the floor. Needless to say, those shelves have since been replaced. A set of impoundments and dams have also been constructed upstream, so a really heavy downpour might now release only a foot of water downstream.

In Ozona, only I-10 and old Highway 290 cross Johnson Draw with a bridge. The regular streets dip down and across and then back up. I loved that rollercoaster while driving around town with my grandfather Bailey Post, after he and my grandmother moved here from Stamford for his job as administrator of the Crockett County Hospital. The weather-beaten sign on the southwest corner of the town square boasts THE BIGGEST LITTLE TOWN IN THE WORLD. What can you say? The town square looks about as it did thirty years before, with the exception of the bank with the clean, modern lines, and the whole town looks almost exactly as it did when the interstate came through in 1979. That fast lane passes seven tenths of a mile to the south of the square, but it has no apparent bearing on life around here except for the short strip of adjacent businesses. The most remarkable sight in town is the row of stately houses on the north side of Highway 290, the main street. These were, and in some cases still are, the "town" residences of major ranchers, and some of these homes *have* changed in the past thirty years. My memory—I'm sure I'm right about this—is of beautifully maintained architecture and gardens up and down the street, and that is no longer the case.

Of my four grandparents, only Myrtle was still alive when I drove into Ozona that Tuesday afternoon. My grandfather Bailey had died fourteen years earlier, while his wife lived on and on and on. She was ninety-five, living in the forty-three-bed county nursing home, an addition to the hospital my grandfather was in charge of back in its heyday, when there were three doctors in town, not just the two. The home is right across Highway 163 from the local country club, where twelve golfers in twelve golf carts were sporting on the nine holes as I drove past. Twice around and the stakes are high, to hear them talk. They play every day: ranchers, oilmen, businessmen, and the like, employees, too, an occasional banker, anyone at all— but men only, by tradition. The women have their own games at their own times. I know some of these guys. One of them was "Horses" Williams, whose wife, Jonesy, had worked in the hospital with my granddad and now visited my grandmother almost every day in the nursing home and did her blue hair.

This home is pleasant and cheerful as such places go, and it would close up shop without Medicaid. Few of the residents can pay their own way. Myrtle Post is one of those, although my father mentioned recently that the income from her savings doesn't quite pay the annual tab of $16,000, so Grandmom's principal is slowly evaporating. Did she know me from Adam that afternoon? I couldn't be sure and hadn't been for several years, but she always did seem to recognize my name when I introduced myself; there was a flutter of recognition, I believe. She smiled and said, "That's good," when I recalled the great times I'd had with her and Bailey out here thirty years before. A lot of them. In answer to almost every question of specific remembrance she smiled and said, "Well, I don't know," but with a lilt and a twinkle in her eye. Maybe that's common with very old people, I don't know, and in any case it's thoroughly enchanting: my grandmother remembers very little, but the *way* in which she fails to remember is distinctly her own. Myrtle is of that generation and upbringing regarding which the word "lady" pertains, not that I necessarily wish the word and its connotations still pertained today. She wouldn't watch the soap operas, which were far too risqué. My favorite story about her was related by my brother and his family. Years ago, after they'd just enjoyed an expensive meal with Myrtle in Houston, they were driving away from the restaurant when my name was mentioned. Myrtle piped up from the backseat, "Well, I was always partial to Mike." Thirty seconds of silence later, she added, "Of course, Bailey was always partial to Nick."

Albert Longoria lived in that nursing home, too. Albert

was ninety years old and, like Myrtle, didn't remember much. Albert is Mexican, of course, with a good deal of Indian blood, too, I believe. Everyone hired to work in the gardens of West Texas thirty years ago was out of Mexico, and the same is true today. I spent hours helping Albert as he manicured the hospital grounds and the lawns and gardens of my grandparents' house just a couple of hundred yards up the hill—never much of a walker and one generation prior to our passion for exercise, Granddad drove his black turtle-backed Chevrolet back and forth—and the landscaping at both places has suffered terribly in the absence of these two men.

Albert's two daughters happened to be visiting him on the same Tuesday afternoon. Jonesy Williams introduced us and they told their father in Spanish that this man standing in front of him was Mr. and Mrs. Post's grandson. Prior to that revelation the old man had been unfocused; now he turned his head slightly and studied me. He must have remembered something, or was trying hard to do so. Like my grandmother, he had not changed in his essence. He was still a man of serious mien, excruciatingly slow and perfect in his labors.

As everyone knows or will learn, it's not easy to say good-bye to someone you love, knowing you may never see her again. I had done that now in Ozona three or four times in recent years. One day I would get the phone call, in Dallas or New York or wherever, but for the time being Myrtle just kept living along, the last of her kind.

Six miles east of town on the interstate is the Circle Bar Ranch complex: truck corral, restaurant, RV park, auto museum, and Best Western motel. When the place opened in 1977, all of Ozona drove out to see this marvel, though for some reason I'd passed up the opportunity on my previous visits over the past fifteen years. Even though my itinerary directed me in the opposite direction, I drove out one night because the Circle Bar is semifamous for its extra-large rooms, VIP suites with two baths and a kitchenette for $65 the night, and especially for the enclosed gardens, swimming pool, patio, and Jacuzzi. Every room opens onto this extravagant greenhouse somewhat larger than a basketball court. Fans high overhead stir the humid air in the middle of this arid plain. The woman sharing the Jacuzzi with me was the wife of a GTE employee from San Angelo, and it was from her that I learned about the telephone party lines on the ranches. Rather than commute daily for over two years, her husband had been living at the Circle Bar four days a week installing the replacement cellular equipment. Many motel rooms in West Texas are rented by the month or even by the year to the employees of large companies, often in the oil field, who foot the bill because no other housing is available. That's why the parking lot at the sold-out Circle Bar may be half-full on Friday and Saturday nights.

The clerk on duty was a stooped and careworn Vietnam veteran who immediately made sure I knew how upset he was about the immigrants from that distant, despised land buying up the crummy motels in these parts. He went into some story about nearly losing it during a fishing-boat confrontation with a "gook" down on the Gulf. He'd had to ask a friend to haul him away from there before something bad happened to that other fellow, like taking a bullet in the chest. Here was a motel clerk who, when confronted by the enemy, was still a veritable lethal weapon.

I didn't pursue the lead. I knew about the trouble between the tightly knit Vietnamese shrimp boat captains and their American competition: bottom-line, the Vietnamese worked too damn hard. This dispute had been out of the news for a couple of years, but that's the way it goes. Even real history happens fast in this culture, then it's over with. Thank you very little. It can't be a coincidence that the only significant exceptions to this rule—Vietnam and the Civil War—were the two wars that we, or a part of we, lost. Still, I had zero interest in this motel clerk's heartburning grievance, nor did I want to listen to him revile all the Indian-owned-and-managed motels throughout the American Southwest (Indians from India, that is), whose ubiquity is made clear by the AMERICAN OWNED signs at some of the *other* motels. Myself, I just wanted the key to my room because I wanted to get back outside for what promised to be one of those gorgeous sunsets unknown in the

East. For these spectacles you need a little bit of altitude (Ozona sits at 2,348 feet), dry air, and the wispy cirrus clouds spawned by those conditions. I made it just in time, and while I sat on the trunk of my car gazing westward and hatching inadequate notes about the day's proceedings, a strange one came to mind: *Hamlet,* Act V, Scene i, in which the irreverent gravedigger introduces our ill-fated hero to the skull of the much-missed Yorick, a man of infinite jest in the court of his slain majesty. Old Albert in the nursing home must have been the source of that allusion, for he was a man of infinite *seriousness*. Then a large American sedan pulled up beside me and a couple in their sixties emerged with their luggage and their toy poodle, maybe their miniature poodle, anyway their *small* poodle, unlike John Steinbeck's Charley, who was a Standard.

Here was conclusive proof of the intriguing interstate axiom I had first heard months earlier from one Jean Stalnaker, the toll taker at the Cassoday exit off the Kansas Turnpike, between Wichita and Topeka. Jean was a very nice lady who formerly had worked at the HoJo's down the pike, and before that as a school bus driver. She had six grown children. Cassoday, the Prairie Chicken Capital of the World, is right on the edge of Chase County, the geographical center of the United States by one measurement, and as such the subject of William Least Heat Moon's *PrairyErth*, subsequent to his more famous *Blue Highways*. Jean had lived in this area for twenty years and, no surprise, hadn't heard of either tome. I took advantage of a rare slow period one morning—at night she'll go as long as thirty minutes without a customer, a good chance to catch up on her reading—and queried her about her job, which is a good one, with sharp uniforms, climate-controlled booths, retirement, hospitalization, instant communication with state troopers, the works. They're inundated with applications, as one might imagine. As a toll taker, you see plenty: how people are in more of a hurry than they used to be, how many of them don't wear much clothing in the summer (laughter here), how they get angrier these days while sitting in a line of only five cars, how so many want to fight—not with Jean, but with fellow passengers. "We've had people shootin' at each other," Jean told me.

Personally, I've never seen gunplay on the highways, but I have witnessed two men in a pickup engage in a fullblown fist-fight while speeding along at sixty-five miles per hour in central Texas—a clear disadvantage for the driver, you'd think, though he seemed to be holding his own. Jean has witnessed several fistfights from her vantage in the booth, and sometimes people *do* want to argue with her. "Not long ago," she said, "I had a lady come in here in the middle of the night and they were mad because the roads were in such a mess. There'd been a lot of construction. These people just sat here and didn't want to pay the toll, didn't think they should *have* to pay the toll to drive on a road in such bad shape. They just cussed and ranted and raved. I get to the point where I just tell people if they don't like the toll road, go another way. Then they say, 'Well, this is the best road to travel on. This is the shortest way to go.' I've had a lot of people say that. Or they say there isn't any other way to get there. No other way to Kansas City? Goodness gracious! I'll give 'em a map and show 'em there's other roads. They don't appreciate that, but you can put up with just so much from people, and then you'll shoot back at them. When they get out of hand you've got to stand up for yourself, because nobody else will do it for you. We have complaint forms but they don't want to mess with them. These people did finally pay and drive on. If they pay their toll and *then* want to argue, I just shut the door.

"I guess the paying public can be extremely rude some-times, but like I tell my kids, 'We're *all* part of the public. It depends on which side of the counter you're on.' I try to re-member that when these people get out of line. It might be me next time. It takes all kinds. Some are nice, some aren't nice, and some never say anything. Of course those might be the nicest of all. That's very true. Once in a while, if it's not busy, somebody'll just sit here and visit, a perfect stranger, asking about the country and what goes on around here."

I asked Jean whether she felt like an eavesdropper. "Yes, you do," she replied. "When people are digging around in their pockets and billfolds I try not to stand here and stare at them. But eventually, if it's there, you'll see it."

Anything. Everything. And one thing Jean has seen enough

of to warrant formulation into this interstate axiom: "The big-ger the car, the smaller the animal. The little cars will have the biggest dogs. This is a rule, really, for some reason or other. I don't know why."

I don't, either, but here on the parking lot outside my room at the Circle Bar was living proof. After carrying a couple of loads of luggage and odds and ends into their motel room, the man returned with his diminutive poodle on a leash.

"Hello." "How ya doin'?" And so on. His name was Love-lady. We were now neighbors. I asked about the dog, almost always the right question.

"Lady, and she shows no partiality."

"She doesn't like anyone or she likes everyone?"

This wasn't the right question. To me it seemed fair—the dog was poised right beside its owner and hadn't given itself away, one way or the other—but Mr. Lovelady was momen-tarily disturbed. Wasn't the answer obvious?

"Oh, she likes everyone."

So I leaned over and held forth my hand. Lady tiptoed over and allowed me to scratch her as her owner explained about the impartiality: "She watches television for fifteen min-utes with me, fifteen minutes with my wife. She sleeps half the night with me, half the night with my wife."

I nodded my approval and recommended the sunset, and Jack took a quick glance in that direction. Being from Roswell, New Mexico, he saw these all the time. What's more, he allowed as how he would have a hard time living again in a humid climate. Nothing could be worse than Alabama, where he once had owned a Ford dealership. He'd lived in Wyoming, too, and that was fine. But New Mexico was perfect. He and his wife traveled all the time and always on the interstates whenever possible. For the convenience.

Suddenly I heard the blare of trumpets proclaiming a profound truth regarding my favorite way of knowledge. For most of us Americans, scenery is what fits on a postcard and wildlife what we can identify through the bug guts on the windshield. Triple-A grudgingly acknowledges that certain malcontents specify "No Interstates" on their Quik-Tik re-quests for vacation routings, but even these good people are making my point. They're what we call the iconoclasts: they don't want to go where they're coming from. They want a vacation. Opposed to this disgruntled minority and the rural folk who actually live along the blue highways and star in all the traditional books about the back roads is that great majority of urban and suburban American dwellers and travelers who, like Mr. and Mrs. Jack Lovelady from Roswell, New Mexico, are perfectly happy with the interstates. They don't really desire a vacation from the tried and the true. They're content to ride from the known to the known *via* the known. This particular fault line in the culture wars broke wide open several years ago when a spokesperson for the malcontents, Russell Baker, wrote about the "high-speed roads" in his column in *The New York Times*. Baker hates them, of course. The editors of *Car and Driver* fired off this angry rebuttal: "How about this? Russell Baker hereafter stays off our interstates, and we'll keep our cars off the noisy, garbage-strewn, mean streets of New York City." They proceeded to defend the safety and the beauty of the interstate system and "the multitude across the nation who live in harmony with their automobiles."

I believe the editors' headcount is about right. I know it is. Jack Lovelady's only complaint is that when he's initially quoted a price at a motel and then asks for his AARP or Triple-A discount, either one, he's always told that the quoted price already includes the discount. "Never fails," he said. "It's a joke." The funniest or strangest or worst thing that had ever happened on all these highway expeditions—he didn't volunteer this piece of information, but I didn't have to pay him for it, either—was when he was passing a truckload of cattle on the way to market and caught a moist one smack on the windshield. And do you want to hear another joke? The EPA, that's a real joke. As it turned out, Jack now owned an Exxon distributorship in Roswell, where one of his ten-thousand-gallon underground tanks had sprung a major leak at one of the welds and a full load of unleaded had escaped into the ground. Couldn't find that fuel to save his life, and he wanted to tell me all about it, and I'm all in favor of letting people do just that whenever possible.

You could put a match to the soil right around Jack's tank

and it would pop a flame, but the bulk of the gasoline had escaped into the caliche rock strata. Even though no amount of money would ever find it, as everyone already knew, EPA regulations nevertheless required expensive measures, including the sinking of wells in order to suck out the vapors. This bureaucratic intrusion was annoying enough, but the kicker for Jack was that the accident had happened in December 1989, and it was almost five years before he received one penny from the Superfund into which he'd been paying one penny per gallon—between $3,500 and $5,000 every month. Furthermore, Jack had asked all around Roswell and hadn't found one person willing to admit they'd voted for Bill Clinton, even though Clinton had carried New Mexico in 1992.*

When Mrs. Lovelady opened the door of the motel room and looked out, Jack surmised it was time he actually walked their dog across the tarmac under the suddenly gray sky. Genuine sunsets in the West last only five or ten minutes, fifteen at the most, as opposed to the manufactured marvels that sometimes glow brilliantly over the Hudson River west of Manhattan for so long it gets disconcerting; you know this can't be real.

An hour later, I saw Mr. and Mrs. Lovelady at dinner in the adjacent "76" restaurant, where the food was surprisingly good for truck-stop food, or so I thought until Brian Trungale informed me that "76" has pretty good food everywhere. The Loveladys were seated at one of the tables in the dining room, but I didn't see any reason to bother them and took my seat instead at the horseshoe-shaped counter. Brian was seated across the angle from me and added that most of the larger truck stops have better food than they used to, that almost all have the salad bar with Bac-Os, and that some even offer a no-smoking section, if only one as laughably ineffectual as the Circle Bar's two booths at the edge of the dining room. Regarding the menu, Brian could recommend everything.

If you can't get good conversation rolling at the counter of a truck-stop restaurant, you have either no talent for it or no interest. On the other hand, you have to be careful because

---

* And again in 1996.

truck stops are notorious hangouts for the millions of under-cover government agents bound and determined to steal our precious First and Second Amendment freedoms. This is the scuttlebutt among trucking's fringe element, Brian assured me, and it wouldn't be in my best interest to be mistaken for an agent. That issue aside, these counter jockeys want to *talk*. They may not wish for an hour-long installment, but they're hard-pressed not to offer commentary on someone else's monologue. Your only job as the moderator is to sidle up and nudge the dialogue in promising directions. And conversing on issues of the day with Brian Trungale is simply a slam dunk. What a superb and informative dinner companion! As a for-mality, I asked what kind of truck he was driving and received in return a lengthy explanation of how Brian's standard chemi-cal rig is designed, in the event of an accident, to break apart at the front and the rear and *leak* before it has a chance to rup-ture in the middle and *explode*. He laid out some of the other safety features, including pop-off valves, assorted fusible links, caps, and the like. Nevertheless, and as Brian well knows, the chemical industry in general and the propane industry in par-ticular have been involved for years in a running battle with critics concerning the safety of the tractor-trailer concept when the trailer is a tanker filled with 9,500 gallons of propane. These critics argue that one-piece trucks are less likely to jack-knife and overturn. Brian says the truck is not the problem. The driver is the problem, and the driver who'd flip his ther-mos bottle (jargon for the regulation two-piece tanker rig) would flip his one-piece bobtail just as fast. Furthermore, the use of bobtails, which have less capacity than two-piece rigs, would require many more trucks on the highway, and that doesn't sound like a safety advance. Industry watchdogs also argue that all tankers should be baffled. The load in a baffled tanker is separated into a series of smaller compartments, and this cuts down on dangerous sloshing. Absolutely correct, Brian agreed, and that sloshing phenomenon explains why truckers refer to a smooth-bore tanker as a shotgun: the way that load slams into your backside on a sudden stop. But there's a catch: the baffled tanker has to be cleaned out compartment-by-compartment, while a smooth bore can be cleaned in one shot in five minutes. For this reason, companies that run a lot of different fuels and chemicals usually run smooth-bore shotguns.

Brian Trungale's rule of thumb is to drive at least five miles per hour under the posted limit for trucks, and with a half-load even slower because that sloshing liquid wants to climb the wall in the turns. Here I thought I had an opportunity to throw Brian an interesting and analogous fact of my own: statistically, a single-engine plane with no engine is better off than a twin-engine with one. But Brian already knew that gliding a crippled single-engine plane is relatively easy—all you need is a runway—while handling the imbalanced thrust from one engine on a twin-engine model requires real expertise, and he knew this because he'd been an airplane mechanic and then a builder of airplanes for nine years before he left his line job with General Dynamics in Fort Worth in 1970 because he was taking home a little under $100 a week and had found a position in Chicago making twice that much *stocking groceries*. Then he earned even more while *driving a uniform delivery truck*. Makes you wonder about the nation's priorities; makes Brian wonder, too.

In the trucking industry, safety must be paramount, and chemical haulers can expect to be singled out. Brian understands this, but still, he suggested, there's a limit. He recently had been stopped coming south on I-39 out of Rockford, Illinois, for a fullblown D.O.T. spot-check. Department of Transportation. The guy checked everything. Brian passed everything. Seven miles down the road he was stopped by another D.O.T. inspector, this time for a burned-out headlamp. Brian pointed out to this well-meaning authority that, first, it was daytime and headlights were not obligatory, and, second, that he'd passed the D.O.T. inspection, including headlights, not fifteen minutes earlier. This second inspector relented. Twenty miles farther down the road, Brian was stopped by *another* D.O.T. inspector who took sympathy when told about the hat trick and waved Brian on immediately.

Brian referred to these individuals as D.O.T. inspectors,

but they're actually state troopers assigned to License and Weights rather than to Highway Patrol. In Texas, they have a different patch on the uniform, and the insignia on their black-and-white cruiser reads License and Weights. Now I knew the answer to the question that had puzzled me for years. Quite a few times I'd blown scot-free past a trooper sitting in the median. Why? He was probably License and Weights, looking for trucks. They often prefer the median to the shoulder for this purpose, and they aren't interested in cars. They usually aren't interested in Brian, either, because he has the common sense to trim his hair, keep the truck clean, maintain all exterior safety features, and never glare with hatred as he drives past. This last point is important. Brian is amazed by the way other truckers invite hassles by glaring with hatred. He's a pragmatic conservative. However, Brian doesn't dislike carrying the chemicals because they're magnets for D.O.T. inspections, or because when they explode they might take out an area with a radius of one third of a mile, with the driver at the epicenter.* No, Brian dislikes the chemicals because lay motorists either don't understand or fail to respect what they see plainly in front of them. Any chemical tank truck is a dangerous hazard, obviously, but motorists will cut you off in a heartbeat. Especially in Houston.

In a prior incarnation, Brian worked in a managerial capacity on the offshore oil rigs. Guys worked under him; back on land he had the use of a company car. When he was laid off during the bust he was lucky to land this job, since many employers don't want to hire a former oil field worker, under the assumption that the new man will quit and return to oil at the first opportunity. Offshore rigs offer some of the best blue-

---

*Nationwide, the industry averages about three explosions a year. Recall the recent disaster on I-287 in White Plains north of New York City, or the one five miles west of the Border Patrol checkpoint near Sierra Blanca, Texas, from which they recovered only some small pieces, or the one a couple of years earlier at that really bad turn on the western edge of Memphis where I-40 makes the hairpin onto the north loop, where trucks of every stripe are always tipping over, and where the authorities have posted a huge warning sign.

collar hourly pay in the world—lawyers' pay, literally. But Brian wangled his current job through a friend, and it's about as good a gig as you could find in the trucking business. At the time, he specialized in long hauls from all the refineries along the upper Texas coast. Other drivers like to stay closer to home, but Brian hadn't had a nine-to-five job in twenty-eight years, so his wife was used to this schedule. She had her own life in his absence. Regular freight haulers may have five, six, seven stops on their way to Seattle; Brian had none. Regular freight haulers have to do their own loading and unloading or hire help; all he had to do was plug in the hose. Regular freight haulers may have to wheel and deal for loads for the return trip; Brian rarely had any load at all. He drove straight to his destination then deadheaded home, often at a leisurely pace. Elapsed time: four to eight days. On one recent trip to the Northwest he had returned by way of the mountain route that he now recommended as the most beautiful in the United States, beginning on U.S. 89 in southern Utah, down through Bryce Canyon on Alternate 89 and U.S. 67 to the north rim of the Grand Canyon, back up to 89 and east across Lake Powell at Glen Canyon Dam, then south on 89 through the Navajo Reservation and the Painted Desert to Flagstaff on I-40.

"I try to make every trip like a vacation," Brian said. "I do a lot of shopping. My boss is real liberal with me."

Many truckers looked harried and unhealthy. Other than carrying a good deal of extra poundage, Brian looked to be the peach of health and happiness. I was surprised to learn he was old enough to have a two-year-old grandson, and I said so. He suggested that the vibration from an idling diesel engine might be part of his secret. Come again? I asked, and he did. In his opinion, that good vibration is a major health benefit in all regards.

"How's that?"

"Haven't you ever taken a nap as a passenger in a car?"

"Many times."

"Wasn't it relaxing?"

"Wonderfully relaxing, but naps always are."

"But the vibration helps. Sleeping four hours up in the truck is as good as eight hours anywhere else."

When he's awake and driving his truck, Brian listens to all the talk radio he can find. It's better than music; it keeps him thinking. He listens to Larry King and Rush Limbaugh and everything in between. Brian implied that Larry King is a liberal.

"Larry King?" I asked. "The guy on television, too? A liberal?" I didn't know. I am (or was, before Robin left) a Mac-Neil-Lehrer man. PBS has to be objective.

"As the day is long," Brian said. "Hey, that's fine, but I'd sooner die than miss Rush: 'Exposing absurdity with absurdity.'"

"That's what he says?"

"That's right."

Rush Limbaugh? Red alert, but Brian recouped his losses by decrying the widespread bias against women and anyone over thirty years of age in his part of South Texas, near Cuero. He once had a landlord who wouldn't talk to Ms. Trungale at all, wouldn't have anything to do with her, judged her incompetent in all respects. Brain expressed only contempt for that attitude. He's no dittohead.

CHAPTER 7

The following morning I asked the new man behind the front desk at the Circle Bar motel, a real fashion plate, whether Tom Mitchell ever made an appearance. He's the rancher whose holdings are blessed with substantial deposits of oil and gas and who splurged during the glory days of the seventies by building this place on I-10 with pocket change. That's the story, at least. Maybe Tom Mitchell sank every penny he had into this spread, and maybe it was all that stood between him and Chapter 11, how should I know? But I doubt it. In these parts, Tom Mitchell is a legend.

"I guess he's here," the clerk replied. "He's here every day."

"Here?" This was like being told by the receptionist at Perot Systems that Ross is down the hall at the Xerox machine, back in five.

"No, around at the shop. You'll see it back there." The

clerk pointed behind him. I got in my car and circled the motel and pulled up in front of the loading bay, where the sign informed all truckers that there was absolutely nothing for them inside. The laundry machines were for motel use only. I didn't see anyone but climbed the stairs anyway, looked around, then stepped over to the air-conditioned office and peered through the little window in the door and saw a man fifty-five, maybe sixty years old, wearing a bright red, oil-stained satin jacket that said FORD RACING, blue jeans encrusted with grease, the cowboy hat of a hardworking man (it takes *time* to produce that deep, deep sweat stain around the brim), and sneakers that didn't fit the rest of the picture except that their color was obscured by the dirt and the grease. The man was just standing there when he caught sight of me. I wasn't a trucker, obviously, so after a moment he opened the door.

When I explained I was looking for Tom Mitchell, he said he *was* Tom Mitchell. On the instant I remembered a conversation with some acquaintance on a previous visit to the nursing home in Ozona. The Circle Bar or something else having to do with Tom Mitchell had come up—maybe the helicopter he used to park next to his house on a hill west of town—and I was told, "Meet him and you'd *never know.*"

Now I knew. After Tom and I shook hands, I gave him a brief rundown on my genealogy in the region, such as it was. He knew my grandparents, of course; I had realized many years earlier that Granddad's position at the hospital automatically made him one of the more prominent citizens in the little town.

Come on, Tom now said, and let me show you my cars. We walked back down the steps to the loading bay and toward the doors of the shop proper. That's when I saw the large painted sign: CIRCLE BAR MOTOR SPORTS. "I've been in mechanics nearly all my life," Tom explained. "I worked on the B-36 in the Air Force. But primarily I'm a rancher, cowboy, whatever you want to call me. The Mitchell ranch started down here on the Pecos, where my dad started out, where my ranch is right now, the one I call my own. We've got three in New Mexico and four in Texas. That's about three hundred sections all together—square miles, that is. All but my home ranch are leased out to individuals. They're making good money now. That's cow country, not sheep, and cows are easier to run, don't have to shear 'em, mark 'em, do all that. I'm still a rancher. I have nothing to do with that over there." He nodded at the two-story motel. Does a man who owns a ranch large enough that it would take an hour to drive around, if in fact you could, also take satisfaction from this interstate kind of spread? "Yeah," Tom replied, "it gives you a feeling of, you know, whatever you want to call it, satisfaction. It's running real good. Have you seen those damn VIP suites? They're super-nice. They got two bathrooms, bedroom, sitting room, kitchenette, more like a little apartment. I built the place about the middle of the boom, about twelve years ago, I guess."

With pocket change from all the oil and gas? I didn't have to ask because Tom's next sentence cleared up any questions in that regard. "I've got quite a bit of production," he admitted. *Production*: I love that aw-shucks, self-deprecating understatement. Production is black gold, Texas tea, cold cash, large green, *mucho* wealth, money. All these and more.

"We just got through renovating, too," Tom continued, "and I bought another one in Fort Stockton just about two or three months ago. Comanche Springs Fina, about half the size of this one, no motel, just restaurant, fuel, convenience store. Built this motel here for all the tourists and RVs. I think the interstate went through Ozona the day we opened. I lease some of it to a group out of Beaumont, and they have about fifteen, eighteen truck stops. Leased on a *percentage* basis; the more they make, the more I make. I've still got an interest as to what goes on. Truck stops make good money. Motels, too. I'd say break-even is probably forty to fifty percent, every day. This one over here runs eighty to ninety percent all the time. I think it's fifty-two, fifty-three rooms. I'm here seven days a week. By myself. I've got to be, somebody's always wanting a question answered over at the truck stop. And my personal business needs a lot of answers. Secretary's always running over here."

Now we were standing in one of the several workshops,

this one equipped with a state-of-the-art lathe, computer milling machine, and a heli-arc welding machine for exotic metals. Tom knows how to run all of them. He did a lot of fabricating for the truck stop right here. Also in this shop are a yellow pickup, blue T-Bird with a white top, and a red Ford—all in mint condition and just the latest of a series of cars and trucks Tom has built over the past fifteen years or so. Others are now displayed in the museum at the front of the Truck Corral. He's been building cars since he was twelve. We stepped over to the pristine Thunderbird and Tom said, "That's not *really* a '55 Thunderbird. It just looks like one. It's a kit from Madison, Wisconsin." I learned all about these kits in the following half-hour. I also learned about the various racing teams Tom has put on the track over the years, how he kind of got burned out on that since it's awfully expensive unless you have a corporate sponsor paying the freight. I asked Tom what had happened with the famous helicopter folks used to talk about in Ozona, and I got a short answer: "I got rid of the helicopter. It's worse than a race car about spending money. We used it to round up with, but a helicopter, for every hour you fly, you've got to work on it two hours. That's the truth. And I didn't work on them. Had a full-time mechanic."

Our tour of the Circle Bar Motor Sports shop completed, I wanted to raise the hood on my 1988 Acura Legend L and ask this Ford aficionado his opinion, even though I thought I knew. Friends and advisers had urged me to drive an American car for this job. I was sympathetic to their point but reminded them that Steinbeck's companion Charley was a French poodle and his pickup was Rocinante, a Spanish surname. These clever rejoinders failed to carry the day, but I still rejected all suggestions that I drive a camper, pickup, or funky hippiemobile rather than my completely paid-off, Japanese-made, basic family sports sedan with good lumbar support. Tom Mitchell glanced at my engine without much interest and remarked, "When you get into this computer and fuel injection, I don't know nothing about it. I mean, I know what it *does*. But the check valves and sensors—I don't know them.

Those engines"—his Ford engines—"have points instead of computers. The All-Pro has an electronic ignition, but that's about all."

What's the main difference regarding quality?

"Well, they"—the Japanese—"have got 'em to where they last longer, and they can run 'em leaner with better fuel mileage, but horsepower-wise they're not near as good. But that's a good little engine"—Tom gestured toward my car as I swelled with pride—"and those twenty-four valves are little bitty, and that's better than a big valve. Watch that front-wheel drive. It goes kind of crazy when you gas it in a corner on a slick pavement. It wants to go straight instead of turn. I think this Japanese stuff is on its way out, because Ford and GM are back now. The sales of these what I call rice-burners are way down. No, if it ain't made in America—well, I was ten years old when they bombed Pearl Harbor. That kind of sticks in the mind, a kid especially."

I take his point, but my father fought over there and didn't express objections to the provenance of this car.

The morning was warm but the much-awaited norther everyone was talking about was poised just beyond the horizon and would be here soon. The Weather Channel reported that the temperature to the northeast in San Angelo was forty-two degrees and falling. At the Circle Bar it was at least twenty degrees warmer with a light breeze still out of the south, and I roamed the generous parking lot because I wanted to catch that first zephyr of cooler air from the opposite direction. On this naked plain, the arrival of a cold front is instantaneous; it's usually short-lived, too, because West Texas will always be on the western side of the fronts that drop south and east from the Pacific Northwest or straight down through Canada from the Arctic. The main thrust of these fronts is always to the east. Therefore, it does get cold out here, but it doesn't stay cold.

That morning, the new air arrived at 11:32 a.m., minutes before I saw something I hadn't expected to see again in this lifetime: a 1962 Ford Ranchero, painted that straightforward tan that on today's models would be burnished to a high finish and hyped as Tahitian Sand or the like. This beaut was complete with a white camper top. I watched from a distance as a happily married couple in their late fifties—anyone could tell they enjoyed a state of assured tranquillity—made trip after trip from their motel room to their car, loading up every available square inch. Picking my spot, I sidled up as the husband was arranging things, his wife back in their room. Out here on the interstate, approaching the wife first is poor strategy.

"A classic," I said, nodding at the car.

The man turned and smiled. I wasn't the first person to say so.

"Yes, and if they'd kept making these there wouldn't be any Toyotas and Datsuns."

Okay, okay, but I didn't want to get into it. Instead I asked, "How many miles?"

"Going on three hundred."

"Original engine?"

"No, rebuilt at two hundred. Worst mistake I ever made."

"Not the same?" A stupid question I wanted to retract, because I knew the everything's-gone-downhill refrain. I met the man's wife and then crossed paths with a trucker and his wife who emerged from their motel room just as I appeared from one direction and a tawny cat holding a squirming mouse loped past from the other. The cat stopped suddenly, looked sharply at the three of us, dropped its doomed prey, readjusted its bite in the flash of a second, then proceeded. This primitive event broke the ice between Eugene Mattingly and myself as his wife went over to their rig. Eugene knew about Don Mattingly—the first baseman—but didn't believe there was any relationship other than the fact that perhaps all the current Mattinglys derive from the original three who supposedly came over on the *Mayflower* and went into the liquor business in the Virginia Commonwealth.

Eugene is a friendly redhead with a beard and a belly, and he's an old hand at the trucking trade: thirty years and counting, three million miles, two and a half million fully documented. Eugene has a bad case of white-line fever. He loves trucking, if not as much as the guy who holds the record: some five million miles. Eugene remembers when trucking was a brotherhood, and he told me, "I did, I ran as a hippie in the seventies, popping, drinking, smoking. But I got the job done and I didn't kill anyone. It used to be a code. That's gone. A lot of jobs opened up when those guys had to leave." Eugene was referring to drivers who couldn't pass muster under the new licensing procedures, adopted a couple of years earlier. "With some of these freight haulers, it's ten days of training and then out on the road." Eugene proceeded to libel two well-known companies, specifying the color of their respective tractors. According to Eugene, the new drivers for these outfits will blast through the parking lot of a truck stop at thirty miles per hour. The same goes for cars, of course.

The Mattinglys had been home in Arkansas two days in ten months. About every tenth day on the road they took a room in a motel. Otherwise it was the queen-sized bed in the sleeper unit. Eugene read my look of amazement. "Hey," he said, pointing at the white Freightliner, "This is our motor home. We save about a third. We have a goal."

By now the cooler air was building and the temperature was dropping rapidly. I noticed Eugene's wife observing us through the window of their cab-over, where she was settled in and ready to go. She didn't look irritated, though. Eugene and I walked around to the passenger side, and Kathy Mattingly was just as friendly as her husband. "Want to see our cat?" she asked, and turned to coax Tommy from beneath the driver's seat. The animal emerged halfway. He looked to be about one generation off the African plain, tops. This cat was a predator, and a large one.

"Would I lose my hand if I reached in there?" I asked.

"You might at that," Eugene said. "He scared the hell out of a colored guy who was cleaning the windshield one day. He got off there fast, wanted to know if that was a bobcat."

There was a certain resemblance. Anyway, it turned out that the Mattinglys and I were both heading west, though their target for the day was a good deal farther than I had in mind. "We've got to make El Paso tonight," Eugene explained. "You've got to have a goal every day in this business and climb over everything to make it. Otherwise, so much little stuff happens you'd never get anywhere." Eugene and I shook hands, he climbed into his cab, the dangerous and stealthy Tommy slipped beneath the seat, everybody waved goodbye, and I retired to the restaurant to consider more carefully the trucker's ideas about goals. Entire books have been written on his two sentences of advice, which are, after all, implicit within the American-style, can-do contemplation at the heart of the interstate way of knowledge: you've got to have a goal every day, climb over everything to make it, don't let the little stuff get in the way, et cetera, et cetera. Bob Popplewell at the rattlesnake ranch would nod his head in vigorous assent. The hitchhiker Bob Smithers might, too. But there's also the contradictory viewpoint which holds that goals are the whole problem, that *seeking* up ahead rather than *seeing* right now is the way of the West (Western civ, that is) and wrong as rain. This contrarian argument, the "Be Here Now" school of Eastern-influenced pop psychology, acquired widespread cachet in the sixties, thanks partly to a book with that title. I pretty much blew it off at the time, then paid more attention in the seventies with *Zen and the Art of Motorcycle Maintenance*—a learned "Be Here Now" treatise in the guise of an eccentric road book. Here's my chance to bring us up to date on how this perspective has played out for me.

The story picks up on May 23, 1992, my forty-fifth birthday and also the day following Johnny Carson's retirement from "The Tonight Show," which I hadn't watched in years and didn't watch that night, either. My wife and I were staying in Dallas in an "executive apartment" near the oft- and deservedly maligned Central Expressway. That was a cloud-covered, dreary morning, and I was heading up I-35 on one of my preliminary interstate trips while my wife was getting ready to meet the movers at the loft we had rented east of downtown in Deep Ellum, the only respectably funky part of town we'd been able to find.

We had lived in and out of New York City for twenty years, as told, but now we were in Dallas, which had seemed okay when I'd lived here for half a year while working on a book; besides, we had good friends here. What I didn't realize was that a *permanent* address in Dallas, Texas, would embarrass the hell out of me. That's how strongly I feel about what happened on November 22, 1963, and about the famous stories of cheering schoolchildren, explained later as their uncomprehending reaction to the announcement that school would let out early. I accept that explanation, but it doesn't make up for the city's well-documented climate of hate in that era.

The tone for that ill-fated trip up I-35 was set early, in the region of Oklahoma known as the Arbuckle Anticline, a former seabed folded into mountains and later eroded by proverbial eons of wind and rain. The mountains are now hills, but the canyons are still canyons, and somewhere in there is the spectacular Turner Falls. I wish I'd found them instead of the Arbuckle Wilderness tourist attraction. Drive down the entrance road, pay my $11.99 (kids only $7.99!), then proceed to the reception center, where, for some reason, my attention was drawn to the family of four, all of whom were female, all four of whom were smokers. Yes! The three-year-old girl wasn't smoking at the time, but she did in the privacy of their home, I know it. There's a train ride and a couple of other attractions at the center. So you do those, walk back out to the parking lot, get in your car, and drive miles and miles of two-lane road across the hills of the so-called wilderness. You stop to feed the wild sheep and deer who poke their heads into your car window to mooch the bagged tidbits bought for $2. Farther on are the two Bengal tigers in a pen the size of the sales floor at the rattlesnake ranch, the pygmy hippos languishing in a putrid yellow pond, the single lion caged by the side of the road. Off to the right in a pen, some wildebeest. The giraffes do have a large area in which to roam, and the sheep and the deer get a pretty fair shake, too, with the free food literally at hand. Otherwise, this is a travesty, and signs tout the Wilderness as the state's number-one tourist attraction. If true, that's sad, or worse. Arbuckle Wilderness is the kind of place that depresses the sunniest disposition, that makes you fear that the nattering nabobs of negativity are correct when they complain we as a culture do not, perhaps by now *cannot*, identify and appreciate the authentic. I've heard naysayers go so far as to assert that the superiority of the authentic to the contrived is no longer axiomatic. You have to prove it, they say, and you should hurry, before supplies run out.

Then, two nights later at the Super 8 in El Dorado, Kansas, not far from Jean Stalnaker's toll booth, everyone I met made a mockery of the chain's motto: "For those whose romance with the road is rekindled with each sunrise . . ." A large man in ill-fitting blue slacks and mailman-type leather shoes didn't understand how to use the telephone in his room and drove away, accompanied by his wife, in an old, yellow, beat-up Pontiac Catalina with no hubcaps and Missouri plates. A sad union, I thought. Then a befuddled husband and wife walked in with their hell-raising little boy. These parents were in their late thirties, and I didn't see the love for their child in their eyes. And when I signed the register and wrote down *Dallas, Texas*, as my address, the bottom fell out. My God, had I somehow ended up living in Dallas, Texas? *Rock* bottom! Finally, the next day, in Cameron, Missouri, the waitress in the truck stop took note of the book I was reading—*America: What Went Wrong*—and said she wanted to read it, and concluded, "Well, what are our options? I'm a conservative, really conservative. I know there are a lot of do-gooders out there, but liberalism is just a bunch of shit, and it makes me mad." She got mad on the spot, really mad; livid—a scary precursor of upcoming national elections.

To top it all off, a few days later in Minneapolis, disaster struck. Literally minutes before I was about to drive out of town on a different route "home," this time down through Madison, Wisconsin, and Memphis, Tennessee, I called Dallas from a café near the repair shop where I was having my driver's side front window replaced. (The car had been vandalized overnight in one of Minneapolis's expensive residential sections.) I could tell from my wife's first words that the new loft in Deep Ellum wasn't working out. In fact, she was in tears. We had been told about one adjacent rock club, but the loft turned out to be sandwiched between several of them. We'd have to break the lease—fortunately, we'd had extensive experience in New York City—and start looking again.

That whole episode with the Deep Ellum loft was the "disaster" listed earlier as the last of the fifteen mundane reasons we had moved. (After all those repetitions, even disaster becomes mundane.) I left the car in Minneapolis, parked exactly where it had been vandalized one night earlier, and flew back to Dallas on the next flight. I was not in a great mood. Mixed in with the anger directly precipitating the crisis soon to be described must also have been a good deal of anger and pain and all the other debilitating emotions still left over from a different chain of events, beginning when we lived in Brooklyn, where the little plot of winter rye beyond the bedroom window of our garden apartment was the "green grass" cited as the reason for our tenth move, and concluding years later, with a miscarriage in Houston.

In the natural history of the world and of this species, a miscarriage is not, it's just not, much of a tragedy. I knew that an estimated thirty percent of all pregnancies, perhaps even fifty percent, suffer the same result, often so early in the term that the woman never even knows. But with us, this was not the case. We knew my wife was pregnant, and the morning we confirmed this I'll always remember as the most joyful in my life—and a personal triumph as well, because I'd been the problem all along, I and my sluggish sperms, and not many of them, either. Apparently you could sit at the microscope and *count* the buggers, one by one. They did come as single spies, not in battalions.

Not promising at all, the doctor had said when he took his seat behind his desk. So this had been the reason for those many months of futility. The evening I discovered this complication, my wife and I decided to see a comedy, I forget the name, in which one of the better lines was the lead guy's rueful remark about shooting blanks. That set the tone for the next two or three years—I lose count, but there were several—of big-science baby-making. The first time I was supposed to jerk off into the jar, no such luck. My johnson started off no bigger than a baby boy's, then got smaller despite my ministrations— a contravention of the laws of both biology and physics, I would have thought, but there it was. And there *I* was, perched on the edge of the couch in my agent's apartment in the Chelsea district of Manhattan, waiting for my wife to call and tell me what time to meet her at the laboratory with the goods.

I can laugh now—and I do, every time I think about it—but at the time? What a nightmare. Meet her *with what*?

When she finally called it was to tell me the appointment had been rescheduled for Monday. What a reprieve. It almost revived my faith in some kind of maliciously playful providence, but that was still the longest weekend of my life because I knew that on Monday my agent's apartment was unavailable. I'd have to use the bathroom stall in the hospital. What were my chances under those conditions? But I pulled it off! If the morning that the pregnancy was confirmed would be the happiest day of my life, that much earlier afternoon hunkered over in the bathroom stall around the corner from the laboratory was a close second. I think every neuron in my head and every nerve in my body fired in perfect rhythm that time. A waste, really, in a way, with no one to share it, but I wasn't brooking any regrets. On the sidewalk fifteen minutes later I was a champion. I was, no kidding, thrilled by the sight of the Empire State Building. Read into that what you will.

Month after month we repeated this procedure, but at least I wasn't plagued by fear and doubt every time I entered the stall; one horrible case of shame and flop sweat was quite enough. I don't think I could have hung in under those circumstances. Still, it wasn't working. Eventually the doctors and the scientists decided to excise the large varicocele from my left testicle. The basic problem with my sperms probably stemmed from a series of high fevers I'd had as a boy. Heat kills sperms. That's the whole reason they hang outside the body: to cool off. In my case, the extra heat from this big lump of blood vessels—the varicocele—wasn't helping matters, and it might have been hurting them. There's also the question whether the lower sperm counts reported in some studies of the male population of the Western world have a more fundamental ecological explanation—insecticides, not herbicides—but even if that were the case, there was no way to correct the situation for my specific benefit. So they did what they could: shaved me like a chicken and cut the lump out. Months after the procedure—the doctors gave us a layoff—motility did go up a little. Not enough, however. After a grand total of two years, maybe more, we decided to take another break, leave town, get the hell out, return to Texas.

Houston was the choice, the first of the three "different towns" in that list of moves, although my wife and I had both grown up there. We immediately went to the top fertility clinic, where they were trying some new things and the doctors wore cowboy boots nevertheless and decorated everything with cowboy memorabilia. Our crack specialist asked whether we minded if he smoked and was surprised at my wife's curt answer. Studying the results of all the requisite tests and the reports of the medical team in New York City, he announced that pregnancy was an astronomical long shot. No shit, Sherlock, but that wasn't why my wife said as we walked out of the building that this man would never be her doctor. Six weeks later—when we were living in an "executive apartment," looking for a townhouse or something—we found out that she was pregnant. That was the wonderful morning alluded to earlier, made even more so because this pregnancy hadn't been engineered by modern medicine. We hadn't stepped foot in the laboratory for months. No, I'm pretty sure that improbable conception was achieved in a motel (I forget which brand) in Lexington, Virginia, on I-81 in the Appalachian Valley. That's how happy my lonely sperms and I were to be getting away from bad times in the Big Apple.

Slightly over two months later, my wife lay on the bed in the clinic at the world-famous medical center in Houston while I stood beside her and we both studied the television screen as the radiologist moved the ultrasound scanner over her lubricated belly and referred jokingly to "the little critter." In retrospect, this turned out to be the best he could do by way of a bedside manner. There the little critter was, without a doubt, several inches long. After several slow, silent passes with his magic wand, stopping for long, long moments to scrutinize the fuzzy picture on the screen, now from this angle, now from that one, now from another, this middle-aged man finally said, his impassive face still locked on the picture, "Well, the first thing we notice is that it's not moving."

Generally speaking, I have a terrible memory, even for

recent events. I don't imagine it's coincidental that several of the clearest images I do retain concern the subject of these paragraphs. Among the chosen few are that scene in the sono-gram room, then in the little sitting room where we were in-vited to stay for as long as we wanted, then driving back to our temporary apartment, then calling my parents and having my father, whom I love dearly and for whom emotional situations are not a strong suit, immediately turn the phone over to my mother. I also remember a later reference by another physician to products of conception.

The following day we were scheduled to move into the townhouse we had leased, and that's what we did. My dad came over to help out. He shook my hand hard and fixed my gaze with his own. He hugged my wife. A couple of months later, my wife and I returned to that same top fertility clinic and this time saw a young woman working the in vitro side of the business. She gave us a lot of figures and percentages—their scoring average, as it were—and I didn't believe them. The parameters chosen to obtain the high success rate were too limiting; the precise phrasing employed was too techni-cal and cautious. I like to believe I have an eye or ear for that kind of thing. "Forget those numbers," I said, point-blank. "They're rigged. The real question is what percentage of cou-ples who walk through the door for the *first* blood test walk out the door with a baby?"

This question she couldn't or wouldn't answer. She said she didn't have those particular figures. I'll bet she didn't, for the simple reason that the number was very low—in the single digits, I learned later, and that would be *optimistic* when deal-ing with sperms as pathetic as my own, even taking into ac-count the intrepid soul that triumphed in the motel in Virginia. I'm aware that recent advances have improved the odds *some-what*, but the clinics are still misrepresenting those numbers shamelessly upward.

We went home. We thought about it. We said no thanks. For my part, I decided that the word "childless" would even-tually lose its sting. After three less-than-splendid years in Houston, we moved back to a sublet duplex in New York City. Eighteen months later we were once again back in

Texas—Dallas, specifically. My wife had retreated to the executive apartment off the Central Expressway after the loft debacle in Deep Ellum, and I was flying home.

By the time I got off the flight from Minneapolis, I was beside myself with anger. This wrath was so deep it was scary. I was like the waitress in the truck stop in Cameron, Missouri. Just about every disappointment in my life—all in all, I'd guess, an average number, no more, and without grading them as to quality—must have become symbolized in my mind by our apparent inability to find not a *home*, forget that impossible dream, but any fucking place at all to live. Lying in bed that night in that executive apartment—some executive!—listening to the low roar emanating from the expressway, I thought for the first time in my life that I might require pills in order to get through the next day. (I realized the night itself was beyond repair.)

I don't know how long I was in this state of near-panic. Half an hour, perhaps. Then I thought about the psychiatrist I'd seen in New York during all the baby-making problems, and about the Indian seer Krishnamurti, whom she had recommended I read. Our problems, Krishnamurti taught, stem from living in contradiction, any kind of contradiction. What is, he said, *is*, and the key to any relatively healthy life is embracing the *given* emotions of every moment clearly, honestly, and completely; no hopes, no fears, no flinching. *Be here now*, in other words, wherever you happen to be. So I decided to just lie on that bed and *see* my anger. I had no idea what I meant when I said this to myself, but I do believe those were my exact unspoken words. Just see the anger. Don't worry about it. Don't be afraid of it. Life goes on. Within moments, deep in the center of my brain or mind or wherever I was peering, a small ball of white light appeared. As I watched—as it seemed to me at the time and still does in my memory—this ball of light literally expanded, slowly, surely, until it was about the size of a baseball, maybe an orange, then burst open. Dissipated. Threw out its contents.

Once it was gone, I knew immediately that this was the most singular thing that had ever happened to me. That ball of white light *was* my anger—there's no doubt about that—and plenty more, too. You can ask my wife, the fact-checker her-self, and she'll verify that as of the following morning, from her perspective, not only was that particular crisis over with, but, also, I rarely get really angry anymore. As I write these words we're still in Dallas, house-sitting, and usually I can laugh at the absurdity of that, too. Something, maybe a lot of things, that had been out of whack in my life simultaneously fell into place in some way I cannot begin to explain, coalesced as that sphere of white light in my brain, and went away. Gone for good. That's how it was. Truly—and I'm not one to say this lightly—those brief moments changed my life, which must have needed it.

Therefore, I can't wholeheartedly embrace trucker Eugene Mattingly's philosophy. Having a goal every day and climbing over everything in order to get there is probably excellent ad-vice for getting your payload down the road on time, for get-ting a raise, for getting elected. But in my experience, this kind of white-line fever—living your life always focused on the fu-ture, on the main chance up ahead—creates problems. I buy the basic "Be Here Now" school of hanging in there with the moment and avoiding the contradictions, even if that's what *I'm O.K., You're O.K.* and John Bradshaw are basically all about as well.

I asked earlier whether it was wise or foolish for the hitch-hiker Bob Smithers to claim that his admittedly embarrassing straits were not that big a deal. I've now answered that ques-tion to my full satisfaction. It's wise.

But what about Davy Crockett? What would the great frontiersman and three-term congressman from Tennessee think? A highlight of the town square in Ozona is the monu-ment to the hero who died at the Alamo on March 6, 1836, and in whose honor this county was named. Etched into the bas relief statue is the phrase for which I suppose Davy's well known: BE SURE YOU ARE RIGHT THEN GO AHEAD. Sounds good, but what if you're sure you're right when in fact you're wrong? At least the defenders of the Alamo paid the price them-selves for their bold decision to fight it out. More commonly, *other* people pay for the zealot's hubris—headlines prove this all too often—so I think you have to be careful with Davy's homespun wisdom. Nor can I get around this irony: he wouldn't have been in Texas at all if he hadn't been defeated for re-election in Tennessee the previous year. The King of the Wild Frontier had enjoyed the role of redneck solon in Washington, D.C. At the Alamo, he was on the rebound.

CHAPTER 8

Of all the places I spent the night on and near the interstates, the cheapest was also by far the nicest: the Ramada Express in Laughlin, Nevada, at $8. However, that was a special break. The marquee out front had announced $10 when I drove up, but between one tour of the little strip and the next, the Ramada management dropped the price $2 and I promptly registered. Sometime that evening the price went back up, because when I opened the curtains at six the following morning the sign again said $10. Forty-five minutes later it was $21, by midmorning back down to $10, then all the way up to $19 by evening. No matter. My rate was guaranteed for as long as I stayed.

This particular Express is organized around a railroad motif, complete with a train that tours the grounds. Across the street, on the banks of the Colorado River, is the Colorado

Belle with its riverboat theme. At the Belle, I saw a defeated couple with their child go inside to register. I started to follow them, then returned outside to look more carefully at the amazing array of items stowed in their old Dodge station wagon. I decided this vehicle with California plates was also their home. Some of the boxes were from the Salvation Army. Down the way at the Hilton I chuckled at the *Love Over 40 Comedy Revue*, with show times at the satiric hours of seven and nine p.m. At the prime-rib buffet at the Express ($5.95, and a perfectly decent cut, too), my waitress, Eva, reported that she gets most of her tips from patrons ages thirty to fifty, then revised her upward limit to sixty, maybe even sixty-five. Eva had moved to Laughlin from Pomona, east of L.A., where she was the manager of a Kentucky Fried Chicken, because she had to get away from the gang crime; she'd already been to quite a few funerals. Nor does KFC offer benefits, unlike the Ramada. There are a great many people from L.A. out here for the jobs. But Las Vegas, of course, is the fastest-growing city in the United States, so even the service jobs aren't that easy to get. Applicants at the Ramada are asked to audition in a game room, where they must dance and display at least a moderately bubbly personality, if not outright effervescence. "Not just anybody can work here," Eva assured me, and three days in town convinced me this was true. I, for one, wouldn't stand a chance. Eva was very happy in this, her first job as a waitress, and along with everyone else she bunked in one of the apartment complexes set up, in effect, for the employees. Across the river in Bullhead City or Kingman, Arizona, rents run a little higher. Eva enjoyed looking at the stars at night, she told me, and after just a few days on the job she had learned to leave work by the back door. At some casinos in Nevada you can draw against your paycheck—one day's pay, say, after three day's work—but not at the Ramada. I respect the company's progressive stance: we may be taking advantage by paying minimum wage and very little more, no matter how long you work here, but we won't openly rob you.

As I opened the curtains that morning I saw the Colorado River—a canal by this point—a few private jets parked at the air strip in Bullhead City, and the Black Mountains, which are indeed dark, if not quite black. This panorama was profoundly *desert*, too, because this region averages four inches of rain a year. That morning I also found out there's no room service; this shows what kind of profit they make every time you go downstairs, if even room service is no match. At the cappuccino cart in the hallway just outside the casino, the lady confirmed Eva's story about the audition in the game room, but she couldn't tell me for whom Nevada had voted in the previous presidential election. *Politics and religion, avoid them:* her motto is more or less the opposite of mine. The elderly lady at the magazine stand, who bore a definite resemblance to my grandmother Myrtle, and who had moved here from California for her now-deceased husband's health, said she thought the answer was Bush (jackpot), but hoped it was Perot. Her greatest surprise in this job had been the number of old men who came in to buy *Penthouse.*

"Aw, give us a break," I said.

"But you're not old."

"Thank you," I said. This lady thus made up for my recent humiliation at the Comfort Inn in Van Horn, Texas. Informed at the front desk there that the price was $36, I commented that this was a lot higher than most rates in that interstate mecca of West Texas. "Well, these rooms are nice and clean," the lady said. "Do you have any discount, AARP or Triple-A?" That was an especially low blow to a guy who never complained when people said, as they were always saying, that I didn't look anywhere near my age. When Dan Quayle came along and people said the same thing about him, I reconsidered, but not for long. I still accepted the remark with gratitude. At the Comfort Inn, I barked an offended response and the abashed clerk said, "Well, I had to ask. You never know." Her associate added that a lot of unqualified-looking guests whipped out their AARP cards, as if that was guaranteed to make me feel better.

"Well, not me. But I am Triple-A."

"Oh, then that's ten percent off. Thirty-two-forty." And this was just one night after Mr. Lovelady with the poodle had told me at the Circle Bar outside Ozona that all these advertised AARP and Triple-A discounts were a joke.

In Laughlin, I asked the nice grandmother at the Ramada Express whether she gambled.

"A little," she said.

"The slots?"

"Poker."

"Poker?"

"*Video* poker."

That's the big game now, as I learned during a casual chat with Bob, Mike, Bill, and Sharon, the idle crew at the one craps table open for business; at 6:30 in the morning, the spotted-owl shift, the casino at the Express was bereft of players. I mentioned video poker and was informed that if they'd had video poker on the *Titanic*, the lifeboats would have been empty. I learned that slot cards—some kind of membership club that gives you a discount while you lose—are called idiot tickets within the trade. I learned that craps is dying because it's too complicated for most suckers, though not a day goes by but what some younger fellow walks up with a computer and a notebook and a system. Schemes for counting cards in blackjack are disallowed in Nevada, but in craps, you're welcome to try anything. In fact, they hope you do, because, pal, this game is two thousand years old and nobody has beaten it yet. I learned that this day shift is strictly penny-ante, and that dealers have a hard time taking it seriously. The real gamblers, such as they are in Laughlin, come out at night, along with all those stars. The mean age of the Laughlin gambler is fifty-eight, and he or she lost $379.21 in fiscal 1994. This "gaming budget" compares unfavorably with Las Vegas, where the average loss was $479.77, but not badly against Reno's, at $408. Total gambling losses for the entire state of Nevada that fiscal year were $6.7232 billion, or $168 for each of the forty million visitors. This average dollar figure is low because the forty million include a few nongamblers, some chump-change players, and, increasingly, youth below legal age.

Mention to veteran casino dealers some friend who says she always wins and they always smile. They wish people did win all the time, because that's when the dealers win, too, with the tips. They can make $40,000 a year, but there's no future in this line of work. It's a job, that's all. A *blue-collar* job at that, and don't you forget it. "Cynical?" I asked. The answer: wouldn't you be if you hadn't had a raise in thirty-four years? I thought this was surely an exaggeration, but it isn't. In the casinos, you start at minimum wage, get a half-dollar raise after six months or a year, and that's probably it. On the other hand, the dealers' tips at certain casinos in Vegas can take the total wage package way above the $40,000 reported to me at the Ramada Express, into six figures. In fact, in the early nineties the IRS got with the dealers and said, in effect, Look, we know you're underreporting, but we'll declare an amnesty if you work with us on setting up a means of accurately pooling and reporting your tips. At Caesar's, say, or the Mirage or the MGM Grand, that official IRS tip calculation might be $200, $300, even $400 for an eight-hour shift. Then you have your high-rollers who sometimes place a $50,000 wager for a favored dealer, and sometimes that wager wins.

Still and all, "a parasite industry," one of the craps crew at the Ramada Express told me.

"Like quite a few others," I said.

"Of course," he replied.

I'd read that sales of the "man-stopper" hollow point bullets were soaring in anticipation of new gun control measures—the Brady Bill—coming out of the nation's capital, so I asked how people felt about the legislation in these parts. Mostly they were scared that before long they wouldn't be able to bear arms legally anymore. When I mentioned the headline about the $43.7 billion price tag on the nation's mental and emotional health, or lack of it, Bill said, sure, he believed it, because after his shift he was going home to drink, take pills, and fall down. Sharon smirked and assured me that Bill was full of it. He reads only the business pages and disdains most forms of recreation. For her part, Sharon is addicted to reading, so I recommended Bill Barich's *Laughing in the Hills* because of the gambling angle. Finally a few gamblers gathered around this table, and soon the empty casino echoed with the triumphant shouts of successful $5 wagers while the last of the big-time spenders tossed $1 white chips at various long-shot options and disdained his mounting losses.

With a stake of $100, I made $36 in thirty minutes playing

your basic bets with help from the crew. Craps can be complicated. Then Bill caught me. "Counting your money!" he whispered, because he didn't want to embarrass me. "That's the worst thing you can do!" Still, I pocketed my profit, dropped a red "fiver" on the team, and strolled away with expenses for the day and night. At breakfast, the young woman seated next to me noted without prompting that she limited herself to losses of $200 a day, then went and did something else—partied, maybe—until the following dawn.

"Gotta go home soon?" I asked.

"Don't have to do anything in this lifetime."

"Gotta make a living?"

"I could make a living out here."

At first I misinterpreted that remark, through nobody's fault but my own. She set me straight and I drove away to see the sights of Laughlin, where the hotels allow RV owners to park free in the lots for a few days—this arrangement is informal, and of course there aren't any electrical or water hookups—or else they can patronize one of the many RV plazas here or across the river in Bullhead City, where dozens of these self-contained neighborhoods bask in the desert sun. Many of the oldsters who pilot these vehicles work at the casinos, not usually as dealers and croupiers, but as store clerks, waiters, change-makers, and roving keno runners. Parked in the lot at the Riverside was a blue-and-white bus with solar panels from the Land of 10,000 Lakes. The Minnesotan inside was cooking dinner and getting ready for his shift, so he didn't have time to talk. He did, however, inform me that the Riverside is one casino that allows its dealers to play while on break. Craps dealers can roll the bones at the very table they work at! This seems ridiculous; we demand legislation. On the other hand, bring in a can of food on Monday through Thursday, December 5 through January 13, and get the second night at the Riverside free.

On that beautiful, mild desert day I drove over the clear, cold desert river. The Arizona side of the Colorado is lined with tidy beach homes, many with moorings for power boats, some with actual ersatz beaches. Buoys bob in the water. A few miles to the south of the bridge I pulled in at the Bullhead RV

Plaza, a pleasant place with 156 hookups, pine trees, showers, pool, Jacuzzi, laundry, and clubhouse with paperback library, color TV, pool table, card tables, and a rack of retail products such as soap, beans, chips, and basic do-it-yourself maintenance items. This park is one hundred percent occupied for the six months of winter, seventy-five percent for the rest of the year. The oldest resident, whom I didn't meet, is an eighty-five-year-old lady from Canada who has someone drive her down in October, back up in May. Thirty, maybe forty percent of these snowbirds leave their trailers in Bullhead City over the summer, and in three or four years that's the *only* way they'll be able to retain their acreage because of all the full-time residents vying for accommodation: "retired" people who need another check, maybe two, from hotel and casino jobs. That's just the way it's going in this country, as Gary Weber sees it.

Gary and his mother run this RV park. On the other hand, I told Gary, the Motel 6 in Bullhead City can get $29.95 for a room versus $8 at the casino hotels across the river because many of the elderly folks don't like the long walks required in the hotels. So quite a few of these retired individuals and couples must not consider the $20-nightly difference critical. Yes, but those are *travelers*, Gary pointed out, not residents. At one of the tables in his RV clubhouse a lively group of grandmothers played bridge and chattered away with no apparent worries about money. That's right, Gary agreed, but plenty of others *are* worried, and their numbers are growing. Then he offered one final thought. He had managed apartments, motels, RV parks, and mobile home parks for thirty years, and they all have their hassles, and the main hassle they have in common is this: "Changing the rules. People don't like change. Maybe that's the reason they don't like Clinton."

The crummiest place I stayed was the Town House Motel in Las Cruces, New Mexico, on Motel Boulevard not far from the conjunction of I-10 and I-25. This was also the second-cheapest place, at $15.95, but I didn't choose it for that reason.

I wanted to see what the crummiest place I could find would be like on the inside. Outside was obvious enough: the kind of place where stray dogs stand in for the roosters in the early morning. Inside was about what I expected, too: the refrigerator was still there, but disconnected, the towels had all the fluff of wrapping paper, and the owner was quick to argue with me the following morning about the heat in my room. I said there hadn't been any; he said there had been.

The owner of the Town House was Indian, and there are, as I've mentioned, many such owners throughout the country. In fact, almost half of the twenty-six thousand "economy hotels" are Indian-owned; an Indian who started with one small motel in North Carolina in 1976 is now president of the 160-motel Knights Inn chain. Of necessity, I conversed with quite a few of these entrepreneurs, and with two at length. In Stamford, Texas, where I was born, the Great Western Inn on the north side of town was owned by Chetan Kakadia, who hailed from several hundred miles north of Bombay in the state of Gujarat. Twenty-five years old, Chetan had purchased this business only a month before I met him. He is an open, friendly talker—unusually so, in my experience; the other Indian motelkeepers were fairly reticent about their standing. They know they're not all that appreciated by the local citizens. They're respected for their entrepreneurial drive and skill, but they'll never *belong*, or not for a long, long time. If not quite black, they're plenty dark enough. Away from the big cities throughout the Southwest, you have your blacks (a few), your Mexicans (loads), and now your Indians and other Asians (more every day, to the point where Patel is a surprisingly common entry in the phone books).

For the previous ten years Chetan had lived with his family in New Orleans, where he and his parents had owned a retail store in the French Quarter and where his brother still owned a bar. Ninety-nine percent of all the businesses in the Quarter are Indian-owned, Chetan told me, and I have since verified the general truth of the statement, if not the precise percentage. The crime problem in New Orleans finally drove him away. Stamford was a radical change, no doubt about it, but

Chetan thought he'd like it out here on the prairie, where there's not much crime. He volunteered that he'd paid about $130,000 for the forty-room Great Western, ten percent down—about what one room costs in Manhattan, with twenty percent down. His immediate plans called for a new parking lot and new carpet in the rooms. If I were Chetan, I'd also do something about the tattered flag and battered flagpole by the roped-off swimming pool, not to mention the shower heads, or at least my shower head, which was chest-high to a child (not that Indians or anyone other than Anglos were responsible for that inaccurate construction).

Chetan and his wife had two small children, his mother and father were joining them in Stamford within the month, and there you have, in Chetan's opinion, the reason why his countrymen own so many motels. As a people, Indians are family oriented and stay together as such. The family is their community, so the small retail business is perfect. Motels are more perfect still because housing comes with the property, right off the reception area. In fact, you know you've stepped into an Indian-owned motel by the smell of the curry wafting in from the kitchen. Some travelers don't like this. I learned all about these sensitivities from J.R. Bhakta, veteran owner of the Daystop Motel in Ozona, and the Comfort Inn as well. The Daystop used to be the Silver Spur; I knew the former owners from visits to my grandparents. When I told J.R. I was working on the interstate book, a cloud immediately settled overhead. Eventually, however, he loosened up, and I felt I could ask him how he felt about the AMERICAN OWNED AND OPERATED signs posted at the other establishments coast-to-coast.

"I'm not insulted," he replied, "although some others are. I take it as a compliment. We must be doing something right."

J.R. has had a few instances in which potential customers walked through the front door, saw him, turned on their heels, and walked away without a word. Other times, potential customers walked through the front door, saw him, turned on their heels, left without a word, then returned thirty minutes later because the other five motels in town were booked solid and he had a room or two left. And once or twice potential customers walked through the front door, saw him, turned on their heels, and left without a word, then returned thirty minutes later because the other five motels in town were booked solid and he had a room or two left, and he politely declined to let them have that room for the night. So J.R. may not be insulted, but he's *something*. And he asked me what that patriotic sign means, anyway, pointing out that many ethnic Indians are American citizens. "But what am I going to do? Put my citizenship papers in the window?" he asked rhetorically, and without a smile. He's right, of course. AMERICAN OWNED signs are flatly a declaration of race, not citizenship.

"And do they only *hire* Americans?" he demanded with a smirk.

He knows the first thing the man or woman walking through the door sees is not-a-white person. He knows he'll never be a full-fledged member of the Ozona business community. He didn't have to confirm this for me, but he did, anyway. On the other hand, J.R. has also had people tell him they won't stay in any motel that makes the AMERICAN OWNED boast.

J.R. has a business degree from Cal-Poly Pomona. He'd been in Ozona for fourteen years, and the longest he had left either of the motels in the hands of employees was five days. Once he did spend a month visiting family and friends in Africa (many of the Indian motel owners came to America by way of Africa), leaving other family members in charge of the business. He reiterated what Chetan Kakadia had told me: this is a family business. He lived with his wife and two children at the Daystop. Basically, you have to want to—or at least be willing to—work twenty-four hours a day. He has a phone on each side of his bed, for convenience. Here he was, working the desk on a Saturday night, and he'd be working it on Sunday morning, too. And the following night. A two-day trip to Dallas to attend an OSHA clinic is a major getaway. (The Occupational Health and Safety Administration hasn't really moved in on the motel industry yet, but if it does, J.R. doesn't intend to complain about the federal government and balk like the rest of us; he's going to adapt and comply.) He has two employees and does almost all of the maintenance work himself. With the rates plumbers charge, he has to. He doesn't foresee ever moving out of Ozona. This cultural isolation is his life; he accepts this. The only reason he can see why Indians would cede the motel business to another ambitious ethnic group is that one day they might become like "real Americans," no longer willing to put in the hours.

I wonder how the folks who don't like the smell of curry would feel if they knew the man behind the front desk was working barefooted. I'm tall and could see this was the case at the Daystop. I didn't care. I liked J.R. Bhakta, and not because I happen to work barefooted myself when I'm typing, not traveling. I liked his chutzpah. I interpreted the white 350 SDL Turbo Mercedes prominently moored beneath the carport out front as a political statement, one I can't afford myself, sometimes decry, but approve of in this special instance.

A mighty fortress is our God, at least on television, even in the Motel 6 in Abilene, where God alone knows what went on last night. At the televised pulpit this Sunday morning was Adrian Rogers, Bible in hand, a wonderful speaker, a tall, elegant man I'd met and heard preach several years earlier in Jacksonville, Florida, at a pastors' conference I was attending for journalistic purposes only. I won't soon forget his depiction in that sermon of the scene on the mountainside when God commands Abraham to sacrifice Isaac, his only begotten son (Genesis 22). As Abraham raises his knife to do the deed, the angel of the Lord calls forth to stop him because God is now convinced of his man's faithfulness. Abraham then sees the ram, its horns caught in the thicket, and slays and sacrifices the animal as the demanded burnt offering. As Adrian Rogers approached the conclusion of the story, he spread his long arms far apart, held them low in front of him, then raised them slowly, slowly upward and closer together as he assured his listeners in stentorian tones, "As Abraham and Isaac had started up one side of that mountain, that ram had started up the other." Only the brain dead could have failed to appreciate that moment. Adrian was great; a chill ran up my spine. But that morning in Abilene Adrian's subject was the more mundane "four spiritual flaws" from Genesis 3, in a sermon entitled "Unmasking

Satan's Lies." I lay there and listened, but without a lot of interest, I have to admit.

As it happened, the cops had pulled up at this very motel just as I was about to register the previous night. Some housewife in town had hired a guy to slash the tires on her husband's car; her husband, the physician. What were the good doctor and his wheels doing here? Your guess is as good as mine, and both are probably correct. Apparently this incident had been just one of a series of harassments-for-hire instigated in recent months by the jealous harridan. Or so the kibitzers out front had it. Then, when I walked into the office, a young guy stormed out the door. He had tried to check in without having—or without showing—the photo I.D. required for security reasons at every Motel 6. This man announced that he was a lawyer in Houston, left his name, and vowed to be back in touch. That meant he'd have to deal with the husband-and-wife management team of Dan and Flora Sherman, who just shook their heads over these contretemps. Not that big a deal. Something's always happening at their place and at every other motel for the simple reason they sell two things that often cause trouble: beds and privacy. Just the night before, right here, four guys had completely trashed their room, scrawling on all the mirrors with Magic Markers, littering the floor with tiny scraps of paper envelopes, plastering the ceiling with wads of toilet paper. Why? Based on vast experience, vandalism for the sheer hell of it was all the Shermans could figure. These visigoths came from Wichita Falls, less than 150 miles to the northeast, but why even attempt to extract the clean-up charges? They wouldn't pay. Only two had paid for their lodging in the first place.

Flora was writing a book on her motel management experiences, and a good deal of it would concern problems among the managers themselves. Motel 6 is unusual among the chains in that all of its locations are company-owned, and its benefits are notoriously good, but stress is still high. Managers have been known to fire pistols at each other. The wife comes home unexpectedly and finds her husband giving the maid a helping hand and then some in room 117. It happens. Everything has happened. At a motel the Shermans had managed in Austin some years earlier, a man had called around to all the other rooms in the motel seeking a certain sexual service. These guests complained to the office, but the phone system didn't provide for the tracing of in-house calls. Then somebody had the brilliant idea of agreeing to the deviate's proposition and headed to room 219 with the ballpeen hammer he always carried on his person. "I'll take care of him," he told the Shermans over the phone. "This guy won't be doing this much longer."

Accompanied by a security man, the Shermans managed to intercept this avenging citizen. On the same night, in the room right next to 219, two men who had engaged the service of a local escort service were so enraged by what they saw when they opened the door they tied this woman up and assaulted her until the screams brought the police. This was a particularly bad motel, what is called a "local" or "hot sheet" or "no-tell motel" in trade parlance, even though it's on I-35. These attract primarily a local clientele, and common sense dictates that most of the activities planned by these patrons are illicit, illegal, or at least rowdy. The best way for a peaceful interstate passerby to spot a "local" is by the number of people lurking around the parking lot, selling dope, probably, or at least drinking beer. Travelers passing through don't spend time on the tarmac except to walk the dog. They want a quiet room, period. The Shermans advise anyone who sees parking lot gatherings to keep driving. In Austin, beefed-up, diligent security measures were finally able to set things straight.

I had also come to know another husband-and-wife team at a motel in Flagstaff, Arizona. I spent worthwhile hours with these people, who were friendly, knowledgeable, full of amazing facts: travelers will lie about having a reservation, if they have to; most carry their own soap (a means that had never, ever occurred to me); elderly widowers are the most likely to be the talkers. This couple had invited me into their living room behind the office and served coffee while telling some of their favorite motel stories. They'd worked and traveled all over the country for many years and were devoted to one another, that much was obvious. So I was stunned when I called the motel some months later to check on my reservations and the *new* manager informed me that his predecessors had split up. The woman was still in town, but her husband had left. At the Motel 6 in Abilene, Mr. and Mrs. Sherman nodded their heads when I told them about my friends. They understood. And Flora was writing down all the hard facts of life in the hospitality industry.

The El Camino Motel in Sierra Blanca, a desert town on I-10 in far West Texas, is yellow with dark red trim and features an awning running the length of both wings; in front of room 14, two hobby horses are frozen in space and time. Two rooms are regularly taken by the UPS drivers who meet at this halfway point, one driving in from Phoenix, the other from San Antonio. They spend the night, switch trailers, and return home the following day. A woman named Holly is the twenty-four-hour-a-day manager here. When you ask for a wake-up call, she apologetically provides you with a small alarm clock. The rooms have real coat hangers you could steal if you wanted to. Best of all, the El Camino surprises you with the soundproof thickness of its walls. This feature alone made me rethink my policy, which had disdained all tired-looking properties; solid walls make up for almost anything else. They don't build them anymore, not in motels; nor solid ceilings.

Holly is on duty from Thursday night until the following Wednesday morning and spends her day and a half off at her home in El Paso. Still, she said, "It's not that hard." She gets along fine, or "as well as could be expected." I sat on the settee across from her small desk. As we conversed in the fading daylight, the cleaning woman came in and handed Holly a copy of *Tough Talk to a Difficult Spouse*, recovered from the room a gentleman had just exchanged for another room. Holly smiled, well aware that this husband was living here because he and his wife were having problems. But the *real* problem today, Holly believes, is that men *and* women alike believe they'll be able to *change* their spouse, and this isn't going to happen. It's not possible. People don't change, not really, and most of us aren't prepared to accept what cannot be changed. And so, when people can't change the spouse, they change spouses.

Holly and I talked about happiness, marital and otherwise. I'd been giving this subject some thought, off and on, following a conversation on a couch in the hallway across from the gift shop at the Wes-T-Go Truck Stop outside Abilene, where the state troopers gather. The large man sitting next to me was a bus driver waiting to ferry the girls basketball team from Hart, Texas, a tiny town in the Panhandle, to a playoff game in some distant place. First he said the girls were okay but their sponsors were rude. Then he told me in no uncertain terms that I could never know the interstates without hitchhiking them, as he'd done while in the service, and he also said that I had to get up to I-40, the mother of them all—because it used to be Route 66. Finally, when I asked if he had his tickets for the big lotto drawing that night, I got the surprise of the day. "What if I won?" he countered quickly. "Would I be any happier? Are their *degrees* of happiness? Of sadness? I've adjusted my standard of living to my income. My home might not strike everyone as a great place, but we're very satisfied with it. We're very satisfied with our standard of living. I'm happy. Can I be *happier*? I'm not sure. Are there *degrees* of happiness? If not, what good would winning the lottery do me?"

From that encounter onward, I looked more favorably on the truckers and bus drivers I saw sitting on couches in truck stops, apparently just idling away their spare time. Holly thought in silence about this man's proposition. I then mentioned a psychiatrist of my acquaintance, a woman in her sixties, sweet and proper and very shy, who one afternoon had flopped back in her easy chair until she was almost prone and concluded, "Sure life is tough. It's *tough*. 'Happy' is a kind of fleeting emotional state, maybe even too intense to be sustained for very long. I use the term very seldom. I prefer words like 'contented' . . . 'satisfied' . . . 'serene.' They're not very popular in our vocabulary, but I sure think they go a long way—further than 'happiness'—in making life livable. But we have a nation of excitement junkies. *Contented?* Who'd want that? Somebody tells me they want an 'exciting' job. Let's see, what would be an exciting job? Jumping out of a plane three times a day, that'd be exciting. But say I want a satisfying job or simply one that I feel good about doing—well, I don't think people talk that way. People think they're supposed to be happy all the time; excited all the time. And when there's so much social reinforcement for those concepts, it's pretty hard to get somebody to change their attitude. And this isn't just with people I see. Lots of people who are functioning okay have a lot of false notions."

Holly spoke again. She told me she had been neither happy nor unhappy since her husband died. Rather, she no longer remembered what happiness was like, it had been so long. In a conversation with a new acquaintance, that kind of remark either opens the gate or slams it shut. I looked at Holly's round face and large, blue, cautious, round eyes, and concluded that she didn't care one way or the other. I could pursue the subject or drop it. Same difference to her. A couple of hours later I chose the former course of action, and this is what I heard.

In 1978, her husband, Otis, a truck driver in his midfifties, left home one morning feeling great and, as usual, laughing about something. His run for the day was out to Tucson and back. As Holly later pieced events together, Otis had felt fine in Willcox, Arizona, on the return leg home, but by the time he got to Bowie, twenty miles farther east, he had to check into a motel in severe pain. He asked the desk clerk to ring him at eight p.m. so he could call home to explain the delay to his wife. When he didn't answer the wake-up call, the desk clerk called the authorities. When Otis didn't answer the door, the officer gained entrance and found the guest dead of a heart attack.

The couple had been married twenty-three and a half years. They had no children. Though her husband had been a truck driver, he was seldom away from home at night. Holly hadn't been to the grocery store without him in more years than she could remember. While she tried to console herself with the fact that Otis had died a quick and relatively easy death, without lingering for years in ill health like so many of her friends' husbands, Holly was utterly devastated. She could not eat. She could not sleep. She could not work. About all she could do was crochet. She stayed home for two years, going through the motions, then shut the house in El Paso, moved to Van Horn, and went to work at a motel. She thought the change would help, but it didn't.

"I had spent twenty-three and a half years learning to be *half* of a *couple*," she told me, "then suddenly I had to learn to be a *whole* person by *myself*." She had no idea how to do this. Returning to El Paso after a year, she reopened the house and took a variety of courses—quilting, hotel management, auto mechanics, and photography, among others—at the community college. The management instructor recruited Holly to work in her hotel. Holly also had her friends, her garden club, and her church. But she still didn't have any sense of how to be that whole person by herself. One evening in November 1984, Holly ate dinner as usual, maybe watched a little TV, went to bed as usual, had no unusual dreams. Nothing special had happened that day, week, month, or year. When she fell asleep she still had no clue what to do with her life, what was left of it. Nevertheless, waking up the following morning, six and a half years after her husband had died, Holly knew she would make it. "Overnight, the weight was lifted," she told me ten years later.

She remembers that experience as clearly as I remember my white-light episode at the executive apartment in Dallas. But what gave Holly's story a little frisson of spookiness I still feel today is the fact that my wife and I had been married almost exactly as long as she and her husband had been when Otis suddenly died in his motel room in Bowie. Who needs these thoughts when they're out on the interstates and occasionally lonely, too? Lying on the bed a few minutes after I left Holly's office, I heard the phone ring in my room. I heard it clearly. But I knew it had not rung.

CHAPTER 9

With its two third-generation motels, three restaurants, one pizza place, three gas stations, two grocery stores, one laundromat, and eight seniors in the graduating class, Sierra Blanca, Texas, might seem inconsequential anywhere, but especially so on the interstate. In 1989, local businesswoman Ruth Love tried to organize a campaign to raise the $32,500 required for two sets of official interstate signs advertising all the local businesses, including her bar. Everyone agreed that this was a town that the interstate really hadn't helped much economically, might even have hurt, but Ruth's campaign fell somewhat short of her goal. In fact, she lost money on a disastrous bingo game and an equally disastrous benefit dance—a story written up in *The New York Times*. Six years later, the unpromising situation remained the same. Sierra Blanca didn't have its interstate signs, and Ruth had given up on her campaign. "These people don't want anything in this town," she told me, embittered. "They just want a dead little town."

Regarding those eight seniors in the high school graduation class, I knew about them only because of my conversation with young Nora Ybarra in the laundromat across the street from the El Camino Motel. The sign in the laundromat, maybe three hundred yards from I-10, asks the last one to leave to please turn out the lights, and represents the reason Nora's parents had moved the family from Fabens, sixty miles to the west, in the outskirts of El Paso. There are no gangs and no drugs and very little crime in Sierra Blanca.

"*No* drugs?"

"Not really."

Nora wants to be some kind of counselor or beautician. Her older sister is a waitress at Michael's Restaurant, where I was headed for dinner, and it was Terry who revealed the size of her graduating class. Terry is single and intends to stay that way, hoping to avoid jealousy of all sorts. The restaurant in which she was employed was empty at 8:30 p.m., and this lack of business struck both of us as strange. I asked about the chicken-fried steak and learned that the football team from Dell City up near the New Mexico border always has the chicken-fried steak when they come down to play the Vaqueros. What a mismatch: Sierra Blanca outnumbers Dell City, 900 to 569.

For a podunk place, Sierra Blanca gets more than its fair share of national coverage, especially in the *Times*. That's because this isolated area on I-10 is where New York City ships part of the famous sludge from its sewage treatment plants. I'd been told previously that the point man on this was the ex-sheriff who handled local public relations for the company. At Michael's Restaurant I saw the sheriff's car, assumed that this current sheriff could hook me up with the former sheriff, and approached him as he sat at a table with his wife and a couple of kids. The man I wanted, the sheriff replied, was Dick Love, who would be in the phone book. (Ruth and Dick Love are unrelated.) In turn, Dick told me that my interstate source was misinformed, that he does some *security* work for the sludge operation, that the man I needed to talk with was Tom Gillane out at the facility itself, and here's that phone number. Two minutes later, Tom Gillane told me that for the foreseeable future all media inquiries had to go through Jon Masters, one of the company's lawyers in Oklahoma City, and here's *that* phone number. Two minutes later Jon Masters got right on the phone and said, "Let me explain our paranoia."

That explanation can be boiled down to five words: Michael Moore and "TV Nation." Love, Gillane, Masters, and a significant but undetermined number of other Sierra Blancans feel that the "TV Nation" segment on their sludge operation was an unconscionable hatchet job. I hadn't seen the nine-minute segment, still haven't, don't care to, not my purview, and it might well have been a hatchet job. After all, that's what Moore does, despite his producers' promises to Gillane and Masters of fair, square coverage. But who could have believed that? Moore doesn't pretend to practice objective journalism, whatever that is. He's an advocate. So is Hugh Kaufman, the renegade EPA official who has attained notoriety as the de facto thorn in the side of his agency, and who appeared on the television show in prosecutorial capacity.

I assured Jon that all I wanted to do was see the sludge, sniff the air, meet some people, and maybe write about it. I had no intention of learning enough science to judge environmental repercussions and the like. My purpose wasn't to dispense publicity good or bad. In short, I didn't intend to sling the mud like they were doing out on their otherwise pristine desert ranchland. And I told Jon I didn't mind passing by him whatever I wrote, not for approval, but for accuracy. Duly agreed, and given his unhappy experience with Michael Moore, Jon seemed helpful and trusting to the point of naïveté. Then I was surprised when he described Hugh Kaufman as a "tree-hugger type." Maybe Hugh is a tree-hugger, but for Jon to be so casual with that pejorative phrase with a reporter of unknown politics is either admirably plainspoken or *dangerously* naive. Anyway, he immediately plugged in his man Tom Gillane for a friendly conference call, and we set up an appointment for the following morning out at New York City's far-removed shithole.

Following the conference call, entirely by accident, I met

the ringleader for the local opposition, a grocer named Bill Addington. I'd made a quick tour around Sierra Blanca, taken in the only remaining adobe county courthouse in the state of Texas, and noted that the old-time water-cooled fans known as swamp coolers are still the air conditioner of choice in this town. I had watched the Vaqueros golf team hit shots on their desert practice range across the road from the classrooms, with orange traffic cones serving as both targets and distance markers. On a small island in the middle of the main intersection in town, I had found the site that commemorates the joining right here in Sierra Blanca of the easterly and westerly sections of the second and southernmost transcontinental railroad in 1881, and on an adjacent plaque I'd read about the "sanguinary" career of the Apache leader Victorio, who "baffled" the United States Army.

Walking back to the motel, I couldn't miss the skull and crossbones and other provocations displayed in the front window of Guerra & Co. General Mdse. Inside this authentic general store that sells a little bit of everything, the entire wall on the right side was devoted to the filing of dozens, maybe hundreds of broadsides and newspaper clippings from around the country, all of them antisludge, usually in a big way. Up at the cash register selling a customer some milk and cookies was Bill Addington himself, a tall chap with long hair, about forty years old and with one single mission in the world, that was obvious. I don't begrudge the fact; with many people, obsession is helpful. Bill told me he had spent $65,000 of his own money fighting the sludge operation—he and his mother, Gloria, that is, who assumed the cash-register duties as Bill led me over to the war room. He warned me, first of all, not to pick up any of the stuff when I went out for my sludge visit, and in exchange for my munificent $5 benefaction he provided me with an extra-large pile of articles, some of them complete with such annotations as "Not True" and "Me," with an arrow pointing at Bill's picture (*The New York Times*, January 25, 1993, in which reporter Roberto Suro notes that the entire population of Hudspeth County, Texas, wouldn't fill the Metropolitan Opera House and unkindly implies, it seems to me, that residents would have to pool resources in order to buy just one ticket for a loge seat at the matinee).

Addington likes to sum up the sludge issue this way: "Why should we be the toilet bowl for New York City?"

Well, that's a nice sound bite, but the answer is pretty obvious and has been since the invention of capitalism and politics. When the EPA decreed that New York City's solid waste could no longer be dumped at sea, an outfit out of Freeport, Long Island, known as Merco Joint Venture won the $168 million, six-year contract to dispose of 225 wet tons of NYC sludge daily, about one fifth of the output, and can you think of a better place to dump it than in the vast, desolate, isolated, and politically inconsequential backyard of a town so poor it can't even afford a sewage system of its own?

Shortly after encountering Bill Addington, I met ex-sheriff Dick Love in Michael's Restaurant. Again, pure accident. Sitting at a table with some other guys, he picked me out the minute I walked in.

"You Mike Bryan?"

"Yeah." I guess it was the pale countenance, plus the notepad glued to my hand. "You must be Dick Love."

We shook hands and I told Dick I'd just met the most notorious grocer in town. I recognized the look he gave me. Maybe he'd thought otherwise initially, but now he knew I was just another media-type dupe, and I got an earful about Bill Addington, his mother, some of his other ancestors, and his rabble-raising friends who were, I should know, a pronounced minority in this town. If I wanted the real story, Dick said, come back about 3:30 and ask the old-timers gathered for coffee how they felt about the shit. Or set up my own personal referendum, which would verify that the great majority of the residents support the project and appreciate the forty-two full-time jobs and the other largesse that's been spread around the community. Of course, Dick didn't put it exactly like that, and neither did Tom Gillane when he let me through the locked and barred front gate at the appointed hour the following morning.

By that time, I was already surprised. I had envisioned

huge black gouts of crap slung across the desert by powerful machines in full view of the passing interstate parade; veritable mountains of shit deserving, soon enough, their own designation as a chain on the maps; stench literally *visible* in that clear desert air. But I hadn't smelled the first foul thing and had seen only the long string of railroad cars and the incongruous architecture of the facility. People drive off I-10 just to ask what these buildings are doing here. The wood-and-stone structure at the site's entrance, the cantilevered rock gardens and beds of cacti, are straight out of Frank Lloyd Wright's desert period. They definitely don't appear to belong to anyone having anything to do with the waste treatment industry.

Tom explained that part of Merco's land is the former Mile High real-estate development, reputed to have had big Hollywood types among its gullible equity holders, the whole thing written off as an $18 million meltdown in 1975. Merco's office on top of the small hill, under a massive wood-shingled roof, had been the sales office for the development. All told, the company bought parts of five ranches for a total of about 128,000 acres, a fair-sized spread of about two hundred square miles, eight times as large as Manhattan; the cost was $5 million and change, or about $40 an acre. The chief landmark of these lands is Sierra Blanca Mountain, at 6,950 feet the third-highest peak in Texas. On the morning I drove up, it was wreathed in thin clouds.

Tom is the on-site manager, a veteran of the industry, a former plumber, and a former resident of Galveston, where I used to be part-owner of a sailboat. Tom and I knew the same funky seafood restaurants on that island, and he'd had a passing acquaintance with my great-uncle, a well-known doctor there. We were playing a game with this conversation, of course, and we both knew it. Tom was trying to size me up and establish any little bit of the "personal history" that might undermine any unfriendly tendencies I might have, and I was trying to loosen him up. He showed me a PR video on the project, "Healing the Land," and dismissed the opposition in language similar to that employed by Dick Love. You have your knee-jerk tree-huggers even out here on the desert, where there aren't any trees. I asked Tom about the stories (in the El

Paso *Times*, June 18, 1992, for one) concerning the testimony in a Brooklyn mob trial by former Lucchese boss Alfonso D'Arco that companies owned by Peter Scalamandre and John Picone, two of Merco's partners, had made $90,000 in construction-related payoffs to the Lucchese family. Merco denied this, and pointed out—logically enough, it seems to me—that *victims* of mob extortion aren't mobsters themselves. Other questions were raised in published reports about influence-peddling in the granting of the New York City sludge contracts, and in the rapid approvals—very rapid: thirty-two days—obtained from state agencies in Texas.

Tom Gillane told me that everyone at Merco was incensed by this Mafia angle. I'm sure they were, but the executives ought to have known these stories would be coming, because the press can't resist anything mob-related. I know I've never been able to. Like most people, I'm mesmerized by these guys.

Tom filled me in on the details of municipal waste treatment. I learned about Class "A" and Class "B" bio-solids ("B" has more bacteria); that fifty percent of all municipal, as opposed to industrial, bio-solids in the United States are applied to the land, somewhere, somehow. The answer to the common question, "If this stuff is so great, why don't they apply it to the land in New York?" is that most of New York State is too inclined (nine degrees is the maximum allowed), too wet, and/or too likely to be snow-covered several months out of the year. And setting aside Empire State versus Big Apple politics, of course. The best land for bio-solids is flat, and the best climate is hot and dry so that the water in the sludge—about seventy percent of the original mass—will evaporate quickly instead of running off. Arizona welcomes New York City sludge. Colorado, too. Texas has 335 other "active" bio-solid sites, which is better than being *radio*active, I suppose, although not one local resident laughed at my joke. Not coincidentally, another part of the public relations problem in Sierra Blanca is the designation of acreage on the nearby Faskin Ranch as the low-level nuclear waste dump for the states of Texas, Maine, and Vermont. Among brochures I picked up at the trailer home that serves as temporary headquarters for that operation are "Radiation in Perspective," "Low-Level Nuclear Waste: Safe, Permanent

Disposal," "Safe Transportation of Low-Level Radioactive Waste," and "Financial Benefits." This convergence of municipal and nuclear facilities near Sierra Blanca tends to make those of a mind that tilts this way anyway—Bill Addington's is a good example—to feel that their area is becoming a target for all manner of volatile refuse for the simple reason that it's so impoverished and politically impotent. Indeed, the residents and politicians of El Paso succeeded in vetoing a low-level site closer to their city. Some Sierra Blancans who approve of, or at least tolerate, the sludge have grave doubts about fissionable isotopes. Holly, for example, my friend at the El Camino, expressed this very opinion.

"Let's go see the sludge," Tom said at last, and we drove out to the active acres in his radio-equipped pickup, in the ceiling of which Tom had mounted a clever spring-loaded device for holding his cowboy hat. I thought this an excellent innovation for state troopers, but suitable only for Martin Hernandez' capacious Caprice; in John Murphy's low-slung Mustang, the hat would block his rearview mirror and half the windshield. With the sludge, the way it works is this: after the 2,100-mile train ride from New York City via El Paso in the locked and numbered containers, the product is dumped into trucks, which then haul it to the designated acres, where it's dumped in a pile on the ground. Bulldozers then scoop up the sludge and load it into the spreaders, two of which are usually in operation at a given work site. These spreaders, which look something like wheat harvesters, then roll out and sling the shit in small wads across the desert, on which the creosote, tar bush, and other stuff have been mowed to within six inches (but leaving the cacti when possible). There are no huge gouts and mountains of sludge because the material is applied at the rate of three dry tons per acre per year—roughly one half of one shipping container per acre per year. A freshly treated site comes out looking like it has a bad rash, with about one salt shaker's worth of sludge per square foot—the analogy used in almost every article ever written about the place.

The odor is noticeable, certainly, although not repulsive. It smells like shit that has been treated with something, which is what it is: artifecal, as it were. I didn't see any of the syringes and other nasty debris alleged by "TV Nation," and I frankly have grave doubts about those charges. They don't make sense, and Merco denies them completely. Anyway, I'm sure the syringes were flushed out in the lawsuit the company filed against the TV show and everyone even remotely involved, including Bill Addington, in which the Pecos jury found for the plaintiffs and hit Sony TriStar Television with $4.5 million and Hugh Kaufman with $500,000 in punitive damages. The appeal is pending, of course.

The city sludge has the texture of very grainy Play-Doh. Tom Gillane scooped up a big handful, and it crumbled between his fingers. Remembering that Bill Addington had claimed thirty diligent washings had failed to remove the smell from one reporter's hands, I fingered my sample carefully. I guess Tom smirked. We returned to the pickup and drove around the rest of the huge Merco property, observing the thick grass growing on the acres treated a year earlier and looking for some of the many deer and antelope. Tom's unspoken point was that the variety of wildlife supported by the land is overwhelming proof of the safety of this nutrient-rich, stabilized sewage. He assured me these desert ungulates could nibble the raw product right out of the railroad car with no ill effect. He showed me the private weather station on site and hundreds of little one-square-foot plots staked out for the $1.6 million research project funded by Merco and staffed by sludge-and-soil experts from Texas Tech University, whose brief is independent and objective research—a statement dismissed by the critics as nothing more than self-serving propaganda. So far, the scientists here have reported no buildup of heavy metals, the main health hazard from bio-solids.

Finally, Tom and I drove up to the abandoned Mile High clubhouse beneath Sierra Blanca peak, now free of clouds and starkly handsome. This clubhouse must have been a great building at one time, with a vast interior beneath its vaulted ceiling, and it's a shame about the nine holes carved onto the slopes beneath it, now overgrown and forlorn.

· · ·

Sludge is gritty; talc is similar in texture, but much finer. As a very soft stone, it is shattered by any kind of blow, and any kind of wind then spreads the dust everywhere. Indeed, every surface in the offices of the talc plant on the other side of Sierra Blanca from the Merco operation is covered with a thin layer of talc dust mixed with regular dust. If the office is dusted early in the morning, it's dusty again by midafternoon. Fortunately, unlike asbestos, say, talc has no known deleterious effect on the tissues of the lungs and other organs.

Although the sign north of the interstate still said Pioneer Talc, the business is now owned by Suzorite Mineral Products, a subsidiary of Zemex. I found this out from the two ladies working in the office when I pulled up after several wrong turns among the labyrinth of roads along which the heavy machinery moves the talc among the railroad cars and crushing mills. Twenty-five people run the whole show here, and a like number the other talc mill two miles farther west. The ore comes from those gashes in the Baylor Mountains to the north, clearly identifiable if you know where to look, but not at all disfiguring from this distance. Sulfur and marble are also mined in this region; copper, uranium, and feldspar probably could be. This talc is used in paints, ceramic tile, wall products, and plastics, though it is not used for talcum powder, which requires a completely different refining process. And not all talc is pure white, by any means. Some is very dark gray, the rest all shades in between.

Informed of the questionable purpose that delivered me to the front door of Suzorite Talc, one of the women said, "That's an interesting hobby." All of us seemed to have time on our hands and the discussion turned to politics and undeserved welfare; corporate welfare (my contribution); the highly popular flat tax; the related fact that most flat tax schemes exclude interest and dividends (my contribution); the earned income tax credit (I was surprised my friends were up on the subject, and I had thought virtually everyone approved of it); state lottery revenue, revealing one reason Ann Richards had lost the recent gubernatorial election (Republicans managed to convince these two and many other voters that the incumbent had promised the money would be dedicated for education, while in fact Richards made quite clear to anyone listening that it would go into the general fund); and dope (four hundred–plus pounds of pot had been found up in the mountains recently).

"I don't like government," I was told by these women, and for the nth time in my travels. Later in the day, when Lee Johnson told me he hated *taxes*, it made for a refreshing change. From the moment I stepped aboard Lee's Newell motor coach, moored at the modest little RV park next to the El Camino Motel in Sierra Blanca, I understood why he has more reason than most people to hate taxes. In all seriousness, this was far and away the nicest one-bedroom apartment in Manhattan I'd ever seen. No wonder the Newell is sometimes called the ultimate land yacht. Other motor coach owners— Prevost owners, mainly—might nominate the Prevost, but based on what I saw of Lee's half-million-dollar machine, and on what he said about the Prevost's new-money glitz appeal, and on the fact that the captain of the "Desert Winds" Prevost parked at an abandoned filling station in Van Horn told me he was too tired to talk—from driving that hunk of junk, I suppose—I'll go with Lee's brand.

The Newell people build only thirty-five coaches every year. About twenty NASCAR drivers and another twenty Indy drivers own Newells. The first thing Jacques Villeneuve did after winning the "500" in 1995 was to buy a Newell, and it cost him about forty percent of his paycheck. I was embarrassed for the other camper homes and trailers parked around Lee's bronze model with the purple double-helix pinstriping. Even the thirty-five-foot Barth berthed next-door looked trivial by comparison. The owner of that one made sure I knew that his machine cost $400,000, but my unspoken response was: don't be so cheap, spring for the extra hundred grand and some real class. As the three of us—Lee, this other owner, and I—stood talking between their two trophies in the declining light, I detected hints of class-struggle in the upper echelons of the RV world.

Lee invited me inside his place and gave me the basic facts: 43 feet in length, 102 inches in width, 500-horsepower 8V92 Detroit diesel power plant that can take the 23-ton coach and whatever it happens to be towing up to 100 miles per hour and about 1,500 miles without a fill-up. No one would be likely to refer to this wheeled palace as an RV, although technically it is one. Of the large motor coaches, only the Newell is built from the ground up on its own chassis. The Prevost's chassis is constructed in Canada, then converted by any one of several companies; likewise, the Barth and the MCI are conversions.

Each Newell is unique. The new owner and the staff get together at the factory in Miami (in the northeast corner of Oklahoma, on I-44) to arrange and appoint the interior. Although they'd owned their coach for only a year, Lee and his wife were already thinking about design changes for their next coach. (Seventy-five percent of Newell sales are to repeat customers.) It's their call, but I couldn't find anything to quarrel with in this one. Nothing. The clean, modern cabinetry (Corian tops), furniture, upholstery, and appliances (Gaggenau range tops) would be declared more than satisfactory by my wife. Levolor blinds for the windows; no drapery or curtains or chintz or cheap wood paneling anywhere in the "European" interior, as it's labeled by Newell.

I had missed Lee's wife, Karen, who had flown out due to an illness in the family. So her husband was driving home by himself, the final leg of a journey that had taken the coach from Texas to Orlando, the Keys, back through Texas on the way to Sun City West and Laughlin, then back to Austin, where Lee had moved when he retired about ten years earlier in order to avoid the Minnesota state income tax. The Johnsons have the house in Austin and the family compound on the lake in Minnesota and the RV space in Naples, Florida (an RV co-op, in effect, with lots selling for $40,000 and renting for $800). Lee affords all this and his two airplanes and, I imagine, other novelties he forgot to mention because, for starters, his grandfather Lee was the first Coca-Cola salesman in Minnesota. That was in 1919. Sixty-five years later, in 1984, his grandson sold the two bottling plants and the four thousand silent salesmen—the Coke machines—and moved his tax base down to Texas, where he dabbled in self-service car washes. This piqued my curiosity. You see so many of these car washes all over the country I figured they must be one hell of a good business, and they are: a large one with, say, seven self-service bays and one automatic bay should gross about $300,000 annually, with expenses only a third of that.

Lee grinned. "I love quarters!" And not just figuratively: he loves the feel of the coin in the palm of his hand, in precisely the same way, I believe, that I love the feel of the "the's" in the preceding clause, and in this one. Each is a tactile pleasure. Lee's a wealthy and relatively young guy—midfifties is my guess—who takes an unassuming, unembarrassed enjoyment in that wealth. The only reason he felt compelled to engage his neighbor for the night in a game of friendly one-upsmanship, Newell versus Barth, was that the Barth guy was so off-base with his own boasting. There's no comparison between the two machines. I would have reacted just as Lee had. In fact, I had brought up the fact that the twenty-kilowatt diesel generator tucked neatly beneath the Newell's elevated front seats serves as the power plant for many of the taxicabs in Europe; that's when the other guy conceded the field and retired inside to join his wife for leftovers. No, Lee is a total pleasure to be around and, I'm certain, a generous host at house parties and other gatherings.

Speaking of Coke, I asked him what the hell they were thinking when they introduced New Coke. Lee, too, had given this conundrum a good deal of thought. Never in a million years could he believe that this was a straightforward, guileless marketing blunder. "If it was a mistake," Lee exclaimed, "why haven't they made any others?" And he wasn't entirely joking. I revealed the same doubts on my part. I don't normally go in for conspiracies, but I read a certain calculated deception in that episode, the company merely pretending to replace Classic Coke with New Coke in order to remind us how much we love the Real Thing. If this was the scam, it worked. After all the hue and outcry, sales soared along with the stock. In April of 1985, before the gambit, Coke stock sold for $66. Ten years later it sold for $60—but after three splits of two-for-one, two-for-one, and three-for-one. Twelve-for-one in all, total, increasing the value of every share by about that ratio. Capitalization had increased from $9 to $75 billion. Lee looks at those numbers and wonders—a blunder? Some blunder.

The Newell he acquired with some of that money carries

325 gallons of diesel fuel, 100 gallons of propane, 167 gallons of fresh water, 167 gallons of gray-and-brown water, a 20-gallon hot water heater, and plenty of Coke; also one remote-control satellite dish, two televisions, and three zones for the air conditioning. Remote control TV serves as the third rearview mirror. The air-cushioned driver's seat adjusts for weight. The plumbing throughout is copper, not PVC. Computerized leveling takes care of a slanted parking space—Mr. Barth has to get out and fool with hydraulic jacks—and Lee levels the corners on the interstate with air bags, not with cheap springs.

Still, I asked, why not the Ritz instead *and*, as though it mattered, save a lot of money? Convenience, privacy, and friendship was Lee's prompt answer. To repeat, the Newell is a more-than-serviceable one-bedroom house on wheels. You skip the packing and unpacking and worrying about what to do with the dachshund who was chewing on Lee's sneaker as we conversed. Folks you meet in RV parks tend to be congenial companions, and genuine friendships are established all the time. Granted, the Rolls-Royce of land yachts can be a minor annoyance in that everyone wants a look inside, but Lee, at least, is spontaneously friendly and happy to oblige. And once you've bought your Newell, he added with a wry grin, expenses are actually moderate, about $1,000 a month.

CHAPTER 10

Sierra Blanca is a modest place with much to be modest about (with the exception of the Newell parked in town for the day) because Van Horn gets all the business, thirty-two miles to the east. Van Horn is, in fact, the paradigm of the interstate mecca, with welcoming signs boasting of seventeen motels, twelve gas stations, four RV parks, and twenty-three restaurants. The lodgings here are almost the only dependable ones on I-10 between Fort Stockton and El Paso, a stretch of 240 miles. The approach into town from the east is a long descent through a slew of five- and six-thousand-foot desert peaks, most of them south of the interstate.* From the apex of the many long highway traverses between these "peaks" you can see vast distances

---

*Altogether, Texas has ninety peaks over a mile high—a semimisleading figure, since all are in West Texas and situated on a surrounding plain more

in the dry air. You can see Van Horn all the way from Plateau, twenty-five miles away, where the wind and the desert have acquired rights to the truck stop, and not all that recently. It was very near Plateau where the Greyhound bus loomed out of the mist on the wrong side of the old Highway 290 on the morning of February 2, 1949, and slammed into the nearly new Cadillac driven by Ben Hogan—the most famous celebrity auto accident in the brief history of American highways until 1956, when Jackson Pollock, drunk, wrapped around a tree on a back road on eastern Long Island and killed himself and a passenger, and then in 1967, when the car in which she was riding near New Orleans ran beneath a truck obscured by mosquito spray, decapitating Jayne Mansfield.

At Plateau, apparently the bus was just beginning to pass a truck, and apparently Ben's lunge to protect his wife, Valerie, in the passenger seat saved his own life, too: the steering wheel was jammed into the front seat. Still, he looked like a hopeless case, and the first attendant on the scene left the great golfer on the side of the highway and tended instead to his wife. Doctors said Hogan would never walk again; eleven months later, he returned to competition. Six months after that, he won the U.S. Open for the second of four times. The movie starring Glenn Ford and Anne Baxter opened the following year.

At dusk, the coalesced lights of the oasis at Van Horn twinkle against the jagged ridge of the mountains directly beyond, and the outline of that ridge is tinged just slightly turquoise by the last lingering light. This otherworldly sight is mesmerizing for thousands of motorists every evening of the year. You do feel almost viscerally connected to your goal through the flowing ribbon of red taillights on this side of the highway, white headlights on the other. Out here, AT&T is right: tired and

---

than two thousand feet in elevation. Most of these ninety don't look much like real mountains. And high is relative, anyway. For example, Mount Everest is no higher than the distance from TriBeCa to the Metropolitan Museum, for those who know Manhattan. These so-called mountains in Texas are about as high above the plain as three World Trade Centers stacked up. That's all.

hungry, we *are* all connected. We're all headed for Van Horn, and at the prime interstate rush hour, five p.m., the traffic can be surprisingly heavy.

At the Chamber of Commerce I met Russ Kuykendahl, the director. He's a friendly transplant from San Angelo who had adapted well to living in a place with no movie, no community park, no roller rink, no bowling alley, nothing but interstate commerce and the funky golf course. This is one reason why the city enjoys one of the highest birth rates in the United States, a provocative fact that made the national news and was passed on by Russ to me, though not, I imagine, to everyone. He told me a few other things about the town, too. The twenty percent of the population that's Anglo owns almost everything, including most of the nice homes, which can be yours for about $60,000. Russ knows of one house that might cost as much as $150,000, a regular mansion. I had already noticed that all the motels and restaurants are on the south side of the railroad, while all of the people who work in these interstate businesses live on the north side of the tracks, where most of the streets are unpaved. A great deal of wealth flows through town every day, but not much puts down roots.

I thought that the five-percent motel tax here would fund almost everything, but Russ informed me that it covers the activities of the Chamber only. Altogether, about half of this area's $12 million revenue comes from tourism and the other half from ranching, mainly, and a little from farming, especially the two large pecan orchards. Farming is down by many thousands of acres since the 1950s, because energy costs have made pumping the aquifers below Van Horn prohibitive for many crops. Pumped or not, these aquifers are unique. Beginning a couple of hundred feet below the surface at the shallowest point and extending to depths of three thousand feet, the set of five known as the Salt Bolson is one of the largest enclosed aquifer regions in North America. "Enclosed" means that very little water runs out. On the other hand, almost no water runs *into* the Salt Bolson, except from the surface, which is a desert. Most aquifers are underground rivers; these are underground lakes. Their recharge capacity is so low they're not considered a renewable resource, and a clue to their presence can be found on the map, which reveals that for many miles in every direction—in Hudspeth, Culberson, and Jeff Davis counties—there are no rivers worth denoting. No rivers, therefore no run-off drainage, therefore plentiful aquifers, because what rainfall there is runs down instead of off and out, and underground water doesn't evaporate.

Someday, when the economics change, the Salt Bolson beneath Van Horn will be invaluable. The city of El Paso has purchased twenty thousand desert acres on top of this water, planning to pump and pipe it 120 miles to the west when the time comes. Someday farming will pick up again, and the dirt streets in Van Horn might get paved, but that won't happen in the foreseeable future. All the tired properties along the main drag, including the Taylor, Sun Valley, and Bell's Seven Kay motels, are likely to remain sleepy for some time. Meanwhile, the attention of the city fathers has turned to water and sewer improvements, and a wind-power turbine project is about to get started north of town, thereby turning a negative into a positive, in Russ Kuykendahl's opinion. He doesn't like the incessant wind. And there's that low-level nuclear waste operation out by Sierra Blanca that will bring a little business, too.

There's also the deal that got away. The town thought it was getting a $1.2 million federal grant to upgrade Broadway, the main street. The idea was to widen each side of the four-lane thoroughfare with an additional lane reserved for the local kids on their bikes and for all the overnight visitors with nothing to do besides watch TV, go out to eat, or go out for a walk. But somehow the $1.2 million became $.2 million, an unfortunate typo that sent the whole project back to the planning stages. Now they're just going to build a few rest areas along Broadway.

On the road, any road, actual or metaphorical road, interstate highway or two-lane blacktop, regardless of your way of knowledge or way of life, you've got to expect some bad times. What I couldn't figure out was why, in my case, these dark hours of the soul kept happening in Van Horn, separated as they were by many months. Example: one night at the Comfort Inn on Broadway I was awakened at three a.m. by what sounded like a metal garbage can being dragged across rough concrete, and powerfully amplified. Parting the curtains of my ground flour suite, I saw nothing and returned to bed. Ten minutes later, the same outrage, the same investigation, the same result. An epigraph came to my groggy mind, the justly famous colloquy between Tom Hagen and Michael Corleone prior to the final bloodbath in *The Godfather, Part II*:

> "Just consider this, Michael, that's all, just consider it. Now, Roth and the Rizottos are on the run. Are they worth it, and are they strong enough? *Is is worth it?* I mean, you've won. You wanna wipe everybody out?"

> "I don't feel I have to wipe *everybody* out, Tom, just my enemies. That's all."

Out of character for me, of course. Ten minutes later, the same deafening and inexplicable racket, for the third time, but now I accepted my fate, rose in fine fettle—in honor of Krishnamurti, perhaps—and peered out once again. Craned right, craned left, then laughed. A guy in a bathrobe was drawing free ice. The dispenser was the source of that racket?! I was standing there listening to the evidence. Finally asleep yet again, I was jolted out of my reveries one last time by the loudest and longest eighteen-wheeler I'd ever heard. I had trucks on the brain; many seconds elapsed before I realized this could not possibly be a truck. It was, in fact, an eastbound express blasting past across the street, behind the Economy Inn; those poor bastards. Another ten minutes and the usual motel departure noises began in earnest—irritated and irritating voices, slammed trunks, slammed doors, revved engines, revved *diesel* engines (a noise resembling the attempt to pulverize marbles in a Cuisinart), a marked increase in plumbing activity on all sides, including above. I called it a night.

On another trip, when the clerk at the Super 8 on the other side of the interstate informed me that my V.I.P. discount was worth $3.95, I turned to the man registering next to me and said in a jocular manner, "Bet you wish you had one." This sourpuss barely managed a wan smile. When I was checking out the following morning, a cowboy-looking guy about sixty years old was checking in, and I overheard him inform the clerk that his stay would be unlimited, a week or two at least, because he and his partner were in town to buy a farm. Okies, they were. Because Russ Kuykendahl had filled me in on the tough local farming forecast, this eavesdropping discovery captured my fancy, but my fancy failed to capture this man's in turn. When I asked how much farms cost around here, he said it depends, anywhere from zero to $350, and more or less turned his back on me and walked away. (This Super 8 happened to be where I saw a graphic demonstration of the power of the prevailing wind; the tilted cypresses along Monterey Bay have nothing on this phenomenon in Van Horn. I had asked for and received a second-story room on the far side of the motel, facing away from the traffic. This also gave me a view over the extra-large parking lot designed to accommodate trucks, and the desert beyond. To the east, the leeward side of the parking lot was festooned with the detritus of the trucking life—hundreds, maybe thousands, of paper and plastic wrappers, containers, and holders blown against the bushes and tumbleweeds and held in place. Really quite a sight. Curiosity aroused, I walked past all the open doors beyond which the TVs were tuned to the same morning soap opera,* down the stairs, and across the parking lot to the edge of the desert, where I carefully toed the evidence. Favorite cigarette: Marlboro and Newport, a tie. Favorite condom: Lifestyles, ribbed. Favorite fountain drink: Big Gulp. Favorite fast food: Big Mac, though this race was rigged since the motel is downwind from the adjacent McDonald's. Favorite non sequitur [or is it a non sequitur, now that Wall Street has captured Main Street by way of the mutual fund]: *Forbes* magazine.)

And then, on the same trip on which I met the unhelpful farmer, a contretemps at, of all places, Chuy's, the Mexi-

---

*All across America, motel cleaning crews watch their favorite shows as they roll their carts from room to room. On weekends, the screens are dark.

can restaurant slotted #12 in the official Visitors Guide's list of twelve reasons to stay in Van Horn, and also, as it happens, where John Madden is customer #1. The overweight ex–Raiders coach and colorful CBS (now Fox) broadcaster mentioned the restaurant on January 25, 1993, on the TV show during which he introduced his All-Madden NFL squad. He said he never misses Chuy's when rolling down on I-10 in his Maddencruiser—a private MCI coach and far and away not the top of the line, according to Lee Johnson, the Newell man. Because Madden doesn't fly and rides everywhere, he had visited Chuy's a dozen times. The John Madden Haul [*sic*] of Fame, in effect John's shrine, is in the second room to the right as you enter the restaurant. Against the far wall is a collection of autographed pictures beneath the big-screen TV. The nearest table for four is reserved in perpetuity for the famous broadcaster, his name emblazoned on the blue director's chair. On the brick wall to the left is a mural of the original restaurant surrounded by cacti and loomed over by mountains beyond which Christ rises to bless the scene with shafts of brilliant light. The entryway is filled with further memorabilia, including another picture of John posing with owners Chuy and Mary Lou Uranga, and one of Jessica Lange posing with the two girls who played her daughters in *Blue Skies*, filmed just to the north of Van Horn, up Highway 54, and for which Lange won the Oscar.

Chuy Uranga was seated in his chair in the lobby when I walked in for dinner, and I asked if his wife was back in the kitchen on this evening. Much of the literature about Chuy's proclaims that she's the main cook, and she is, but on my night she was at church. I'd forgotten it was Sunday. I asked Chuy for a recommendation, and he immediately said #12, the chicken enchiladas with green chile sauce. I inquired about the cheese enchiladas with red chile sauce, the litmus test by which I judge Mexican restaurants. Yes, they're good too, of course, but the owner stood pat on #12. As I debated the choice, he said, "Whatever you like. We'll fix whatever you like." So a combination platter with *both* enchiladas seemed plausible. But, replied Chuy himself, Chuy's doesn't do combinations. There we were, chatting comfortably like longtime acquaintances in the foyer of his famous interstate restaurant, obviously I knew what I was talking about with this cuisine, how hard can it be to take one enchilada from this casserole pan, one from that? I bet I've been to a hundred Mexican restaurants, and combination plates are the mainstay of every last one. But at Chuy's, no way. He must have felt that just one exception, except for John Madden, naturally, would open the door to a flood of special orders from the twenty thousand cars that daily pass on I-10, and he obviously knew that I would be immediately pacified by the chilled glass mug presented with my Carta Blanca and by the #12, which was incredibly excellent. While dining, I considered whether to include enchiladas on the menu of the restaurant I want to open—probably off the interstate, given real-estate prices—which will serve only food that gets better with age, like meat loaf, chili, certain stews and casseroles, and rum cake. The restaurant will be named Used Food and the motto will be either "We Guarantee This Food Is Not Fresh" or "If We Serve Fresh Food, Your Money Back."

At Don's Restaurant and Truck Stop on the south side of the interstate, the waitress at the counter, Lupe, placed a cup of coffee in front of a fairly old man and said, "Morning." He replied, "Glad you just said 'Morning,' 'cause there's nothin' 'good' about it." This is an old one, the kind of quip blowhards believe is both original and clever. I'm certain this particular blowhard had made that statement a thousand times before, maybe in this very restaurant. But Lupe had a surprise waiting for him. "I'm glad to be here," she said, "don't know about you." Not a snap, just a statement. The man didn't say another word. I tried to give Lupe a thumbs-up but failed to catch her eye. Later, I asked her about the competition between Don's and the McDonald's across the street. She said the chain hadn't affected Don's business in the least. "We get a lot of people who are tired of eating there. And the bus station helps, too." All the buses stop in Van Horn. The entire traveling public in this part of the world stops in Van Horn, which receives less than ten inches of rain a year—making it an official desert—and has a growing season of 224 days and is 855 miles from the West Coast, all this from the back of Don's menu. As I enjoyed my huevos rancheros backed up by hash browns, I grew fond of this place. I like Van Horn overall, despite the unpleasantries encountered. Through the window I saw a sharply pressed trucker walking away from his rig in a thirty-five-degree chill, carrying a handsome leather briefcase and either a pool-cue or fly-rod case, I wasn't sure.

To the west of Van Horn on I-10 is the Mountain Time Zone, Sierra Blanca, and, farther on, El Paso. To the east are Plateau, where Ben Hogan crashed; the origination of I-20, which then goes on to Florence, South Carolina; and Balmorhea, sixty-five miles away at the base of the low, rugged Barrilla Mountains. Thus my favorite interstate mecca is framed on either side by my two favorite backwaters.

Throughout the wide-open West, any stand of cotton-woods signifies either a creek bed or a habitation or both. There's no other choice. The size and shape of the stand of trees are often the giveaway: a thin line indicates a creek, a clump indicates a house, a mass indicates a community. The mass of cottonwoods denoting Balmorhea were turning their distinctive, bright yellow the first time I took the exit and drove into town. Altitude: 3,030 feet. Romantic name: just an acronym, in effect, for the last names of the three promoters— Balcom, Morrow, and Rhea—who founded the town in 1906. Decades ago, back before Disney World, when the competition wasn't very stiff, Balmorhea was something of a famous resort, with a wonderful spring-fed swimming hole. Today, it's about as desolate as a town of 765 residents on the interstate can be. Extremely desolate. However, there's no way you can lay all the blame for the stagnant economy on the fact that the interstate bypassed downtown, not according to Billy Lozano. He owned the Exxon station in town and figured the highway cut his gasoline business by only fifteen percent. Despite the cachet it once enjoyed as a spa, Balmorhea was never a boom town, just as Big Bend is the most underutilized of the great national parks. This region of Texas is just too far from any-where, and all the interstates in the world won't bring the world any closer.

Mr. Lozano and I didn't get off to a good start when I asked in perfectly friendly fashion whether his gasoline was au-thentic Exxon or the generic fuel that some dealers have been known to pump under false pretenses. He looked at me care-fully and replied, "I can't pump anything but Exxon gas here."

"Well," I said apologetically, "dealers have been known to use bootlegged stuff."

I started over as I paid up. "How many gallons you pump? Thirty?" By today's standards, thirty thousand is a low number no matter where you are. Thirty was a bad month at the corner service station in Houston where I worked thirty years before. The big mega-stations can serve half a million gallons or more. Nevertheless, Lozano grunted in the negative.

"Twenty?"

"About that. In a really good month."

Still, this wasn't the dealer's main beef, which concerns the lucrative wrecker service he used to have. Billy had been as-signed all the business on I-10 twenty miles in each direction, plus he had the local business in and near Balmorhea. A lucra-tive franchise, no doubt about it. But then some wreckers on I-20, which angles down from the north and intercepts I-10 twenty-one miles west of Balmorhea, pulled some kind of rank with the state troopers in Austin and set up a straight rotation between all the wreckers in this much larger area. Thanks to this new system, Billy no longer enjoyed his monopoly. "So if there's a wreck right *there*"—Billy stabbed a forefinger at the street twelve yards from his desk—"I don't get that business unless it's my turn. Or I might have to drive an hour up I-20 because it *is* my turn. The trooper in that case gets kind of irri-tated, but he understands, too. We're just following orders."

There were two old metal desks in Billy's office, which was also a small store. He was sitting in the chair behind the desk beside the door. Of the three pumps outside, two were self-serve, one full-. Though I neglected to ask Billy what percent-age of his business was full-, I didn't get the impression that he was often called out of that chair to check the oil and the tires.

Sitting on the second desk with her legs swinging freely was a young woman who seemed to belong but had no apparent duties, and she underlined Lozano's disgust with the new wrecking system with a belligerent grunt of her own. I eventually determined she was Billy's daughter. I looked out the window at the static scene and asked, "What do people do for a living around here?" This Exxon station seemed to be it by way of economic activity in Balmorhea.

"Well," Billy responded, "there's farming and ranching, a few cattle yards, the prison up at Pecos"—on I-20, also home of the justifiably world-famous cantaloupes—"and welfare. A lot of them just aren't interested in working."

Six months later, Billy wasn't working here, either. In his stead at the gas station I found Orlando, who'd bought him out and converted from Exxon to Fina. The new owner and I had difficulty conversing, but at the nearby Citgo station, Victor Hernandez told me that Billy had retired from the gas, although he still had the wrecker service. Meanwhile, Victor was contentedly pumping his twenty thousand monthly, thirty in the summer with the RV traffic. As he and I passed the time of day, I couldn't help but notice the steady stream of local residents—so I concluded, since they *walked* up— buying his scratch-off Texas lottery tickets. I was surprised, although I don't know why: there are fifteen thousand other lotto outlets in Texas, and the only requirement for participation other than some degree of solvency is that the business provide retail goods or services. Neiman Marcus could sell lotto tickets if they felt like it. Victor said he sells about $3,000 worth of these instant tickets every month in poor, tiny Balmorhea. Some cost $2, but most just a buck. Some days he sells $300 worth, and his take is five percent of each sale. Free money, practically, but the tickets are almost more trouble for him than they're worth. Victor has to have the cash on hand to pay winners up to $100. The state sets up an automatic weekly withdrawal from his bank. Vendors who commingle their sales of Scratchman and Bluebonnet Bucks with their other retail income, or, worse yet, succumb to the temptation to use the ready cash to satisfy other creditors, well, they're in trouble when the state comes for its ninety-five cents per ticket. If just one automatic withdrawal doesn't go through, your license is suspended or stripped. Victor was trying to be diligent about avoiding these lotto pitfalls and had plans to make his accounting system even more fail-safe. Soon he would use a separate cash register for the scratch games and take that money straight to the bank.

Another problem, he believes, is that some people may be using their income to buy these games instead of gas, and he makes more profit on gas. Victor could be right about misplaced priorities, because the Texas lottery is the second best-selling in the nation and the sixth-best in the world, trailing only Massachusetts and the national games of Spain, France, Italy, and Japan. I asked him for his opinion of Billy Lozano's assertion that many residents of Balmorhea are on welfare because they don't want to work. Victor replied, "I could apply for welfare even though I work seven days a week! I don't make much money here." I asked him about the box of HTA-1000 detergent, Citgo's highly touted fuel additive, I saw on the floor behind the sales counter. Metropolitan dealers would get their gas from the tanker trucks already treated. Victor's gas arrives untreated, and he pours the additive right into the underground tank. In the old days—the late sixties, after I'd graduated from the corner station and was working summers at the Texaco bulk plant in Houston—all the various brand-name gases from reputable refineries were the same, except for the additives. If something happened and Texaco ran low, it just bought some gas from Shell, and vice versa. Even as a part-time employee, I felt badly about this charade. Now I brought up the issue with Victor.

"It's all the same," he said with a dismissive sneer.

"Even with HTA-1000?" I felt obligated to provide him with an out.

"Oh, not then!" Victor's smart. He knew what I was doing.

I'm indebted to Victor for information about the big swimming hole at Balmorhea State Park, which he said was open year-round. For some reason I'd thought this famous pool was another thing of the past, long-closed. The last time through I hadn't even bothered to check it out. Totally wrong again! One of the great swimming holes in the country is indeed open for year-round, seventy-six-degree swimming not three miles south of I-10, technically just outside Balmorhea in Toyahvale, Texas. Originally this oasis was called Mescalero Spring, used by the Apaches of that name for bathing, drinking, and watering crops of corn and peaches. Anglo irrigation was initiated in 1871 by three gentlemen named Miller, Lyles, and Murphy. They had at their disposal in the renamed San Solomon Springs an average of 22 to 26 million gallons of water daily, about 300 gallons every second, flowing from the nearby mountain aquifers at absolutely no charge and mainly through a single fissure in the earth about ten feet across. Today these waters are diverted into a reservoir, then via ninety miles of irrigation canals to fifteen thousand acres of chiles, bell peppers, onions, cotton, cantaloupes, and other cash crops. Meanwhile, ranchers can only look on with jealousy. The midnineties had brought a severe drought to this part of the state. There's a big difference between eight and fourteen inches of rain—seventy-five percent, in fact, which the desert grasses and the animals that eat them understand very well. A good rule of thumb matches the number of inches of rainfall with the number of animals that can be grazed on one section, or 640 acres. In the best of times, a steer out here needs forty or fifty acres all to himself. Lately, the grass had been so thin that some ranchers had shipped out many of their cattle.

The Balmorhea pool was built during the Depression and claims to be the largest spring-fed swimming pool in the world. I took up this question with Tom Johnson, the tall, straightforward, immensely helpful park ranger who had given me leave to evaluate the pool and verify the water temperature before I laid out the $5 admission fee for vehicles entering the park. "But what about Barton Springs in Austin?" I asked when I returned to his little office and bookstore at the park entrance. "That's larger, I know." I should know. I've spent hours swimming in and lolling on the slopes surrounding that famously frigid body of water, in which the year-round temperature of sixty-eight degrees will get your attention every time. Ten minutes refrigerates you sufficiently for several hours in hundred-degree heat.

"I think they mean 'enclosed' pool," Tom said.

"Barton Springs is enclosed."

"I think Barton Springs isn't *completely* enclosed."

We laughed at the fine distinction, but it's accurate. One small section of Barton Springs is bounded by a natural rock outcropping, so I was now willing to acknowledge that the Balmorhea pool is without a doubt the largest completely enclosed spring-fed swimming hole in the entire world. At 62,000 square feet of surface area (larger than a football field, including both end zones), it ought to be. And the water is perfect, clear as a bell, eminently drinkable, twenty-feet deep for most of the length of the longest arm of its L-shape, alive with turtles and fish and, that afternoon, practicing scuba divers from Midland-Odessa getting ready for Oahu, and others from Carlsbad, New Mexico. I crawled slowly above them and flashed the universal A-OK sign, then hovered above the main outlet of the spring itself, a bubbling puddle of sand exactly where Tom had assured me it would be. With thousands of gallons flowing every minute, I expected to feel the surge even at this distance, but it was almost calm. A thousand bathers will show up here on summer holidays, when the adjoining eighteen-unit hotel and campgrounds are full; in the winter the only commotion is provided by javelina hogs rooting around in Tom's front yard. The nearest movie is two hours away, in Odessa;* the nearest skim milk, Tom's choice, forty-five minutes away in Pecos; the nearest cash machine, about which Tom is asked many times a day, at the Conoco truck stop in Van Horn, sixty-eight miles away.

In a specially built branch of the main canal leading from the pool, two endangered fish—the Comanche Springs pupfish and the Pecos mosquito fish—are pampered and protected. Tom led me outside to see if we could spot any of these locally famous creatures, but the water was flowing too swiftly. Two other endangered species in the area are *Phyrnosoma cornutum*, the Texas horned lizard, and *Phrynosoma douglassii hernandesi*, the mountain short-horned lizard. The easiest way to

---

*The old Palace Theater in relatively nearby Marfa, where the whole town had gathered every evening to watch the dailies for *Giant*, closed down decades ago.

distinguish between these two creatures is the arrangement of the spines: a single longitudinal row on the former, two rows on the latter. But the truly interesting point is that you probably won't need to make this identification, because the lizards are disappearing and nobody knows why. When I was growing up in San Angelo and visiting my grandparents in Stamford and Ozona, horned toads, as we called the Texas horned lizard, were everywhere, and fairly easy to catch. Turn them on their backs and rub their bellies and they'd go into a trance. Now they're AWOL, and newspapers periodically carry stories on their mysterious absence. Some observers blame fire ants, a growing problem in Texas and other states, and others blame insecticides targeted at the fire ants. One experiment near Benavides in South Texas starting with twenty lizards outfitted with transmitters on tiny backpacks showed an attrition rate from other causes of forty percent within one year. Three horned toads were run over by cars, two were eaten by roadrunners, one by a loggerhead shrike, one by a wood rat, and the eighth just vanished from the radar screen due to some malfunction or misadventure.

Tom Johnson urged me to drive a few miles south on the road to Fort Davis to a pass in the foothills from where, looking back, I would have a great prospect of the town of Balmorhea, the state park, the swimming pool, the desert, and, winding along in the distance, covered with some kind of little crawling things, the interstate. So I drove those few miles into the hills, was surprised to pass the dive shop along the way, and pulled up by a sidelined camper-trailer with a man and a woman staring under the raised hood. But everything was okay, they thought, they hoped, and they were pleased that I'd stopped to check. They were on their way east somewhere, Florida, I think, and her husband had convinced her that this thirty-mile detour off I-10 to Fort Davis would be worth it. So he'd heard. Did I agree? Definitely. It's a very beautiful area, I promised, without specifically praising the isolated pocket of Eastern Gamma grasses that are greener and lusher than the rest, even during this drought.

When I turned around at the pass, the view looking north across Balmorhea to the interstate was definitely not green. I could understand why some of the ranchers had been shipping out their livestock. What I could not understand, a few minutes later, was how a beekeeper and his hives made any money out here. I had descended the foothills and turned left on farm-to-market road 3078, the brief loop off I-10 that swings through Balmorhea, and I was just noting with surprise the small collection of white boxes set on the other side of a fence when an old van approaching from the opposite direction pulled off the road and parked beside them. I spun around, parked, and introduced myself to Charles Eisler, innkeeper and beekeeper. Charles had moved out here from Galveston about a year earlier and purchased the Country Inn Motel in Balmorhea, the only motel on or near the interstate for a distance of 107 miles. However, the conversation did not linger on that subject since Charles seemed to find the bees far more interesting than the motel and definitely more puzzling. He hadn't determined the ins and outs of the honey trade in this region and was therefore proceeding cautiously, with only a dozen working hives. He wasn't sure why there weren't more commercial beekeepers around—"Do they know something I don't?"—especially considering that choice desert honey commands a tremendous premium in the market: retail price up to $6 a quart versus maybe $3 for regular table honey.*

"These bees here are so docile I could go out there naked. I don't know why," Charles said. They were so docile he was going to move them someplace else. These bees were *completely* docile, he informed me, but most bees are *usually* docile if you, the keeper, are squeaky clean, absolutely clean, no perfume or hair oil, nothing like that. "And no horses!" Charles added with finality. Bees go after horses, though horses understand this and won't go within fifty feet of a hive, while cows will crop the grass right in front of the door. Regarding the premium for fine desert honey, it made sense that the desert would be wonderful feeding grounds after a rainfall, when it explodes in a euphoria of mesquite, creosote, various

---

*In March 1995, Charles told me, the entire honey industry got a boost when the United States retaliated against dumping by the "Red Chinese" by affixing a 140-percent tariff on their stuff.

catclaw, whitebrush, and other blooms. Still, how often does this happen—every other month? Is this enough? No. It's true that bees can be locked in a closet with a sixty-pound supply of honey—a full hive—and do fine for two years. However, the issue isn't what the bees need in order to survive, but what the beekeeper needs. This was Charles's predicament.

In addition to the rainfall-dependent desert flowers and mesquite, there's also some mimosa and, even more plentiful, alfalfa irrigated by the nourishing waters of the Mescalero Spring, as I prefer to call it. Alfalfa is premium foodstuff for bees, and the farmers near Balmorhea fetch eight crops annually. There's only one catch: alfalfa has its highest protein content when it's only about ten percent in bloom, and it reaches ten percent within thirty-six hours of starting to bloom. Naturally, that's when the farmers harvest the crop, and therefore Charles would have only that thirty-six-hour window of opportunity for his bees on a particular pasture, after obtaining permission from the farmer. He was going to give this a try. Months later, I called him for an update. His first experiment with alfalfa had been a great success because heavy rain had hit the region just as the crop came into bloom. The farmer got burned because he couldn't get into the field to harvest, but Charles's bees benefited from the extra days of feeding. This report implied that the problem of sluggishness had been solved, but Charles said, "Halfway." Only half of his insects had picked up the pace; the others were still lagging.

Standing by his hives that afternoon, our conversation concluded, Charles suddenly looked around at the vast desert landscape and at my car and asked me with mild alarm, "Is this your ranch?"

Before World War I, before the automobile finally gained as-
cendency over the horse and the railroad, there were, by the
standards of the day, no more than a few thousand miles of
well-maintained, all-weather macadam roads in the United
States. At least that's what I've decided after reading a variety
of contradictory sources. The other couple of million miles of
dirt, mud, gravel, shell, clay, and plank roads were undepend-
able. Regarding public policy, it wasn't true that the only thing
the country needed was a good five-cent cigar, but roads
weren't high even among the unspoken priorities. As the number of cars grew exponentially from about fifty thousand in
1900 to over five million at the conclusion of the war two
decades later, the inevitable good-roads movement was forced
to look to private funding sources: car companies, tire companies, cement manufacturers, civic associations, agribusiness interests, and the like.

It wasn't until the next world war pulled us out of the Depression that roads and highways were deemed a priority for public funding. The interstate system was sometimes sold as a vital arm of the nation's Cold War defenses, but the pitch wasn't really necessary. Everyone was now a motorist who understood that the proposed 41,000-mile Interstate Highway System, designed to serve ninety percent of the 209 towns larger than fifty thousand and projected to carry twenty percent of all motor traffic as traveled by a projected hundred million vehicles, would be a bargain at $27.5 billion, and almost everyone agreed that the federal government should shoulder ninety percent of that cost with a tax on gasoline. The politics were therefore easy when the National System of Interstate and Defense Highways was created by the series of Federal Aid Highway acts passed by Congress in the late 1940s and 1950s under the leadership, mainly, of President Dwight D. Eisenhower.

For Eisenhower, the hero of D-Day, the necessity of better roads had become his personal conviction thirty years earlier, in 1919, when he participated while a lieutenant colonel in the Army's first transcontinental truck convoy from Washington, D.C., to San Francisco on the Lincoln Highway, parts of which are now I-80. And let me set the record straight on a related point: contrary to popular opinion, the Lincoln was *not* the first transcontinental route to be promoted as one unified highway. That honor goes to the inferior but one-year-older National Old Trails Road, which in 1912 connected Baltimore to Los Angeles, with connecting links to New York and San Francisco, respectively. It was the promotional project, in effect, of the National Old Trails Road Association and the National Old Trails Road Ocean-to-Ocean Highway Association, two booster clubs created by business and civic interests. Despite all the acclaim, both the Lincoln and the National Old Trails transcontinental highways were little more than connected segments of old roads identified with uniform signage and marketed as highways.

The first president of the National Old Trails Road Association was an obscure public official from Kansas City who told a Congressional committee in 1920, "I do not even own an automobile, and would not know what the dickens to do with it if I had one." His successor was also a resident of Kansas City, a functionary of thus-far middling abilities who'd been selling memberships in the Kansas City Automobile Club after losing his re-election bid as judge of Jackson County. This was Harry S Truman, and his most enduring work in this pre-presidential position with the highway group was assisting the Daughters of the American Revolution in their selection and dedication in 1928 and 1929 of the twelve "Madonna of the Trail" monuments along the National Old Trails Road. These heroically proportioned statues honored the pioneering woman of covered wagon times, her babe secure in her arms, her tyke steadfast at her knees. They still stand in Bethesda, Maryland; Washington, Pennsylvania; Wheeling, West Virginia; Springfield, Ohio; Richmond, Indiana; Vandalia, Illinois; Lexington, Missouri; Council Grove, Kansas; Lamar, Colorado; Albuquerque, New Mexico; Springerville, Arizona; and Upland, California.

The National Old Trails Road included portions of the Boonslick Road, Santa Fe Trail, Beale's Wagon Road, and the Old National Road, the first organized highway of any sort on the continent. From his first days in office, George Washington had advocated some kind of pathway through the forests, but Congress didn't pass funds for the National Road until 1806, and contracts weren't let until 1811. Then the War of 1812 intervened. Work finally began three years later, and the first leg of the first American highway was completed after another three years, in 1818. That section of the National Road was named the Cumberland Road and ran a distance of 120 miles from Cumberland, Maryland, to Wheeling, West Virginia, following in part Necomalin's Path, an old Indian trail between the Potomac and Monongahela rivers. Washington's interest in establishing the first national thoroughfare on that route was perhaps nostalgic: in 1753, he had followed a muddy Necomalin's Path on his first western expedition, a provocation considered an opening sally in the last of the French and Indian wars.

Anyway, Ike's journey across the continent in motorized vehicles sixteen decades later did not find a great improvement in conditions. The trip took two months, a labored and eye-opening affair, by all accounts, including the general's own in "Through Darkest America with Truck and Tank," the well-titled chapter in the superbly titled book *At Ease: Stories I Tell to Friends*, a compendium that deserved a better fate than it received: out of print, no plans for reissue. Thirty years later, Eisenhower's presidential exertion on behalf of better roads was a central accomplishment of his administration, and I say that with a straight face. The plan and the legislation reflected the can-do era in which it was conceived. The hubristic spirit that decreed that the West *would have* water, even though it didn't, and proceeded to build dams, viaducts, and irrigation projects on an unprecedented scale—that same spirit envisioned a system of highways grasping the entire land. One thing about the road project: it made a lot more sense, perhaps economically, certainly ecologically, than the watering of the West. The interstate system eventually came to 42,796 miles—the nation's largest public works project, not counting the defense budget. The politics and real-estate manipulations behind the routing decisions can be imagined, and sometimes even known. Some 750,000 parcels of land were claimed by right of eminent domain: 1.6 million acres in all, an area larger than the state of Delaware. The concrete poured would bury Connecticut knee-deep. The signs cost $200 million. I don't know how many people are working on the railroads, but since 1956 an average of forty-five thousand have been employed building and maintaining interstate highways. Most incredibly, our grand total of three million miles of roads cover one full percent of the lower 48's land mass.

The interstate highways were and still are the final word on the subject, the basic answer to the nation's nonrail ground transportation needs until some invention replaces the concept of the automobile and the truck, until it's no longer rubber that meets the road. The total cost of the system has now tripled to $75 billion. It's essentially completed,* but it will

---

*Eighty-six miles in six states and the District of Columbia are under construction or remain tied up in the courts.

never be *finished* because every road eventually wears out. It's true that some Roman thoroughfares of large slabs of cemented stone still carry motorized traffic today, but large slabs of cemented stone aren't suitable for *autostradas* or interstates. They're durable, yes, but too cumbersome, expensive, rough, and impractical in all respects. They're not an option. In 1982, an additional nickel tax on gasoline was approved by Congress, raising the total from four cents to nine and providing $7 billion to the states to repair the system and related infrastructures. Thirty-three states raised their own gasoline tax at the same time, and even in the Reagan era there was no controversy: three quarters of the interstates were approaching their safe-life period of twenty years, and motorists knew it. In Connecticut, for example, the bridge over the Mianus River on I-95 collapsed within a year of the passage of the tax.

During the period of my travels, one of the bigger interstate overhauls in Texas was a 6.7-mile stretch of I-10 between mile markers 31 and 37. This patch of interstate just east of El Paso, west of Sierra Blanca, was over twenty-five years old, so it had done the public treasury proud. Now it was being repaved with (in most sections) thirteen inches of steel-reinforced concrete, and the Zaragoza bridge was being raised four feet, eight inches to meet new clearance standards. Jim McDonald was overseeing the job. Jim was one of the two "rural area engineers" working out of the El Paso district in the state highway department responsible for 790 lane miles* of highway, including all of I-10 east of El Paso to the Brewster County line. This repair job was Jim's biggest by far in 1995 and 1996, requiring 480 working days to complete. That's over two calendar years, calculating 220 working days per year, and there was no good reason that the projection of a November 1996 grand opening shouldn't hold because days lost to bad weather in far West Texas are few; in fact, the contractor, J. D. Abrams Co. out of Austin, gets no "weather days" at all on this job, and will pay a penalty of $2,500 a day for lateness, with no

---

*Highway departments deal in centerline miles and lane miles. Centerline is simply the length of the highway, while lane miles are the centerline miles multiplied by the number of lanes.

compensating reward for early completion. The new surface should last thirty years.

The winning bid: $23 million. By way of comparison, the complete rebuilding and widening of Dallas's Central Expressway, also a nine-mile stretch and next to which my wife and I had an unhappy tenure, will require over ten years and over half a billion dollars—by far the most expensive reconstruction ever in Texas, and one of the largest ever in the country. A single drainage tunnel beneath a depressed section of the new Central cost $30 million, more than this entire resurfacing job on I-10.

On March 2—Texas Independence Day, of course—I met Jim McDonald at his branch office across the street from the airport in El Paso. The bookcase held wide volumes on grouting and bridge-deck joints. A civil engineer, Jim had been with the highway department for twenty-two years since graduating from UT-EP, and he and his whole crew seemed delighted to have been chosen by my nationwide search as a representative highway department team. We rode out to the job in his pickup, since he prefers driving his own vehicle and filing for mileage expenses rather than driving the state vehicle, which he would have to pick up and deliver each day at the central depot. Jim grimaced when I asked if downtown El Paso looks about the same as it did when he was growing up here. "Unfortunately, it does," he said. I asked about the unsightly refinery right in the middle of town, which you can't miss driving in from the east. That's the Chevron operation, he explained, and when it was built decades before, that was the edge of town. And actually the plumes issuing from the stacks are mainly steam and don't pose a real problem for the city. That's at the copper smelting plant on the other side of town, the plumes from which waft right across the city with the prevailing wind. As the day progresses in El Paso, the pollution builds up. The city is one of the EPA's "non-attainment" regions, and thus the gas stations here pump oxygenated gasoline, which is about a nickel more expensive than regular fuel. Another problem is Mexico, where pollution standards of every sort are much less stringent than in the United States, NAFTA or no NAFTA.

The subject turned to roadways, and after just fifteen minutes with Jim I would never look at one the same way again. I learned how to make informed judgments rather than ill-tempered accusations. I learned that asphalt surfacing is considerably cheaper than concrete but has higher maintenance costs. Rutted, wavy, rollercoaster streets and highways are asphalt, almost by definition. Thump-thump-thump streets and highways are concrete—old concrete, in all likelihood, poured in ten-foot sections (thus the thump) and without the reinforcing steel. There are still many rutted, wavy, rollercoaster interstates but fewer and fewer thump-thump-thump highways because concrete is now poured and finished in long, uninterrupted stretches by an awesome train of machinery.

However, even this new technology can go wrong. Jim and I drove over a small section that had been poured only a year before, but the screed used to finish the surface had been incorrectly calibrated. The resulting surface was bumpy, and just six hours after the concrete had been poured it had been too late to do anything about it, short of scooping everything out and starting over, which wasn't going to happen. But should the same problem come up on this new job, the contractor might have to do just that. A profilograph—a bump meter—would profile every inch of the new surface; if the product doesn't meet specifications, the contractor will be penalized financially or required to redo the work.

Most major highways between cities are asphalt. Most city streets are asphalt, too, although you'll notice that intersections have a greater chance of being concrete, because all the stopping and starting and turning are the factors that make asphalt washboard so badly. (You might think that the recycled tires used as an ingredient in much contemporary asphalt might contribute to this bounciness, but apparently this isn't the case.)* If the money's available, it makes sense to use concrete at busy intersections. Jim didn't exactly say so, but I gathered that there might be another reason why asphalt still has a

---

*The same 1995 bill that erased federally mandated speed limits also rescinded EPA regulations mandating the use by states of this "crumb rubber."

large share of the business: politics. No one wants to put the hot-mix plants out of business. A good compromise, a politically correct surface, is HMAC, hot-mix asphaltic concrete, a new cementless material that holds promise and satisfies both constituencies. A new technique is microsurfacing, in which a thin seal of HMAC, just one quarter to three eighths of an inch thick, is used to resurface stretches of roadway when money is extremely tight but something must be done. Sometimes an inch or so of ordinary asphalt will be laid right on top of old asphalt to smooth out the dips and the ruts. This is relatively cheap, and also relatively short-term. Neither new coating will last longer than three years.

Highway engineers have lately focused on the fine aggregates known as the "200s"—those tiny particles in the mix that fall through a sieve with two hundred holes per linear inch, or forty thousand holes per square inch. These 200s have always been considered necessary in order to fill the voids created by the larger rocks in the asphalt, thereby maintaining impermeability, but these minute particles also *shift* under pressure. A new idea is coarse-matrix asphalt without the fine aggregates. But what fills in the spaces between the larger rocks? What gives the asphalt impermeability (because permeable asphalt is no good at all)? That's why there have been successes with coarse-matrix asphalt, Jim said, but failures, too, such as the two-mile stretch on nearby Highway 659. That asphalt was laid down in April of 1994. Two months later it was already "bleeding," with oil flushing out of the surface and creating slick spots. A year later these patches were dry to the touch yet still shiny to the eye; safe but not satisfactory. Another problem with asphalt is the oil. Oil varies. Hot mix made with one oil won't have precisely the same properties as a mix made with different oil. And another uncontrollable problem is that modern highways are designed for loads of eighty thousand pounds, while some of the loaded trucks out here weigh considerably more than that. Whether these loads are specially permitted or simply illegal, they destroy highways, whatever the surface.

Concrete will not wave up like asphalt, but it has an annoying problem of its own: decreased surface friction over time, tending toward slickness. A newly poured concrete surface is therefore "tinned," or scored, and it may be necessary to come back years later and scratch new grooves into the surface. Therefore a concrete highway, old or new, is noisier for the motorist than asphalt. I also learned about compaction, about which I knew a little from my experience as a small-time construction superintendent in Austin in the early seventies, back when I spent my days off at Barton Springs. Concrete and asphalt are materials over which the contractor and the state can maintain decent but not foolproof control, but the same doesn't hold for the ground beneath the pavement. Buckling and rollercoaster roads are caused by movement of these subsurface soils, and the answer for these problems is "compaction effort," which is really the key to a good highway. A wet area like Houston with sandy soils will need maximum compaction effort, including the use of additives to the subsoil to firm it up. A dry area like this stretch of West Texas interstate is much easier to work with. The old asphalt here would be paved over, not dug up, so it would become, in effect, part of both the subsurface and the new calculation. In some sections, the subsurface would also include varying depths of flex base (a quarried mix of rock, caliche, sand, and dirt), old asphalt, new asphalt, and concrete.

Work had begun here in November 1994. By the time of my first visit the following February, both sides were closed, traffic was routed onto the old shoulders, and long stretches looked inactive, work-wise. This appearance of stasis is what makes the occasional motorist call the highway department and complain about delays when there doesn't seem to be any work going on. But work is going on—elsewhere. For example, we passed the crew putting together the steel cages that would reinforce the concrete due to be poured in a couple of months on the eastbound lanes. On the other hand, it's true that the contractor was waiting for the concrete paving machines to arrive on the site, and work on the new concrete mixing plant at the nearby staging ground was somewhat behind schedule. Still, on a job scheduled to require two years, the actual pouring of the concrete should require only fourteen weeks total. The public has to understand this.

Jim's schedule called for completing the eastbound lanes first, moving traffic back onto them, then shifting to the westbound lanes, which had to be closed to traffic all the while anyway, for a variety of reasons, including those dictated by a new computer program out of California. This program factors in volume of traffic, hypothesizes many different scheduling scenarios, and computes comparative delays. In this case, the computer said that dividing up this job between east- and westbound lanes would cause the fewest delays. As Jim explained all this, I considered the situation in New York City when a major avenue is torn up, patched, torn up, patched, and torn up and patched again as the utilities beneath it are replaced *one by one*. The complaints pour in. Why not tear the whole thing up and replace the water, sewage, and gas lines at one time? Spokespersons keep insisting that, contrary to common sense, this isn't the most efficient method. I now suspect California software is the actual culprit.

Jim pointed out the "soil containment measures" mandated by the EPA, easily identified by the black or green plastic screens you see around any construction site requiring earth-moving or excavation. The idea is to keep as much of the soil as possible from running off the site. But Jim swept his arm across the desert landscape and asked, "Out here, where's the water to carry the soil away?" Our loop of the mostly inactive job completed, Jim drove back to the staging area used by J. D. Abrams for both this project and another they had under way around El Paso. This fenced-in area also contained the mobile-home headquarters of the team of four full-time state inspectors who report to Jim McDonald. This seemed like a lot of supervision—even more than that endured by the state troopers in Abilene—but when I met Rocky Rodriguez, an energetic, articulate guy, the chief inspector for the state, he pulled out the blueprints for this job and I understood why all the manpower is required: 351 sheets in all, a stack over two inches thick, a design that took four or five people about six months to generate.* Jim and Rocky directed me to all the

---

*For the Central Expressway in Dallas, the total was over eight thousand sheets of blueprints, a pile about four feet high.

pages devoted to traffic control, page after page, dozens of pages specifying precisely where each cone, chevron, barrier, reflecting sign, and lighted sign must be placed, then moved and replaced as the nature of the work on that particular section of the interstate changed. Sheet number 66 was titled "Typical Layout for Closure of the Outer Traffic Lane and Shoulder for One Work Day or Less." Jim pointed out the thick sheaf of pages devoted to the Horizon Street intersection at mile marker 37, where three truck stops handle a total of four thousand trucks a day. Horizon is a logistical nightmare.

This obsession with traffic control and safety dates back to 1977, when court rulings declared that the state could be sued by motorists and their families for alleged insufficiencies during construction. And within the past five years, Jim added, personal liability had also become a factor. Next, Rocky placed before me the 1,187-page *Standard Specifications for Construction of Highways, Streets, and Bridges*, the industry bible in the state of Texas. Then he presented another book of specifications for this particular job, and it was an inch thick. In concert with the contractors and subcontractors, the four on-site state inspectors spend much of their days parsing these runic texts. Rocky said, "You never find everything you need on one sheet."

J. D. Abrams had submitted its bid broken down item by item, 170 in all. Rocky and his team decide when the contractor is entitled to payment for any completed item. On a $23 million contract, any "change order"—work required above and beyond the original contract—involving more than $500 would require documentation. When I expressed amazement regarding this picayune figure, Jim repeated the operative mantra: "documentation." On this job, maybe twenty change orders had been put through already, with many more to come for the simple reason that the best designers and computer programs in the world can't possibly foresee the myriad contingencies that always arise in the real world.

Jim made sure I noticed the Partnership Agreement signed between the State of Texas and J. D. Abrams, in which item #5 dictates an "enjoyable project." He then explained that the old thinking in the highway department was to have a state guy looking over the contractor's shoulder every time he drove a nail, while the new thinking encourages greater trust, a welcome move from the adversarial to the cooperative: New Age management right here on a highway job.

My father collects and studies maps and so do I. Therefore I admired and appreciated the two maplike critical path management charts pasted on one wall of the Highway Department trailer. CPM is another mantra operative within this and many businesses. On construction jobs, CPM has always been around in one acronym or another to ensure that the trench isn't dug until any heavy machines that need to cross to the other side have already done so. On the CPM charts out here on I-10, each of 247 activities was accounted for, with red bars indicating an especially critical activity. The first job had been the casting of concrete traffic barriers; the last would be the removal of the last of these barriers.

Rocky Rodriguez utilized his cell phone to put in a call to Bobby Hilton, the project manager for J. D. Abrams, who arrived fifteen minutes later in his company pickup and a cloud of dust. He looked like a hardworking James Caan, a wiry dude with a firm grip and blue, can-do eyes. One look at Bobby and you know you're dealing with sheer competence. As a kid growing up in Jasper—deep in the piney woods of East Texas, where they keep hoping the ivory-billed woodpecker, presumed extinct, will prove to be otherwise—Bobby built roads in his front yard. His first paying job was holding the dumb end of the chain on a surveying crew. Soon enough he'd moved to the more intelligent end, then was running the crew, then other crews, then the whole project. This was in and around Houston, mostly, but elsewhere, too. His wife, Courtney, moves with him when necessary. Here in El Paso she had a job working in the office for one of Abrams's suppliers.

"If I had a preference," Bobby told me, slouched even lower in his plastic chair than I was slouched in my own, "it would be these wide open interstate jobs." The opposite kind was his previous assignment for Abrams, a $4 million contract on 1.7 miles of interstate in Houston. A mere $4 million versus $22 million here in El Paso, less than two miles versus nine, yet both were two-year projects? Bobby grimaced. "That one intersection at Airport Road required four phases. Lots of traffic and sequencing hassles." The equivalent hassles on this job in El Paso would be the Horizon intersection and the bridge; the latter would take a year.

On the simplest highway gig, however, "there's never a dull moment," and that's why Bobby likes the work. Already on this job in the wide open spaces a load of rebar steel had arrived with deviations from straightness of more than half an inch, a flaw that would prevent the rebar cages from being wired together with the mandated clearances. The fault lay with the extrusion machine at the steel mill in El Paso; this steel would have to be replaced by the supplier. But Bobby's biggest problem and worst fear is accidents, and there will always be a few. He assumed a management perspective when he said the best you can hope for with accidents is that all your bases are covered, right down to the steel-toed boots. Changing subjects, he said he wished everyone had his knack for visualization, which he believes is a key to construction. "The first thing you have to do is know what you're building," he said. "*Visualize* it. If you can't do that, you're in trouble. We've got some new guys that have a hard time." So I asked about turnover. About five percent, Bobby replied, which is good, even excellent, though it doesn't reflect the thirty percent attrition within the first six weeks for new hires. That's when you get your turnover. Then I asked about pay, which is good, partly because the state sets the minimum wage the contractor can pay for the various crafts employed. And when I asked Bobby about his Spanish, he said it was "fluid enough"—a delightful malapropism, or maybe I misunderstood him.

On my next trip through town, almost a year later, Bobby Hilton was gone, alas, off with his wife and another company on a better job elsewhere in Texas. His replacement had stayed only a few months, so a second new man then came in for him. Supervising engineer Jim McDonald was gone as well, transferred to another sector of the department in El Paso. Net result: the I-10 repair was forty days behind schedule. Plus the repaving job had been extended two miles to the west, between mile markers 30 and 32, so Abrams's new completion date was now April 1997.

The good news was that the concrete paving train was now in action at mile marker 31, and Rocky Rodriguez, my only link with the past, drove me out for a look while informing me about his degree in biology from Texas Tech and his five years in the nightclub business in Lubbock. By now he'd been with the state for seven years; without an engineering degree, Rocky could ascend only one level higher in the bureaucracy, to construction manager, a district-level supervisory position. As we bounced across various unfinished surfaces, he pointed out the welded wire fabric protruding from sections of old, uprooted asphalt. This wire was standard years ago; today all it's good for is several flat tires a week.

Concrete paving trains have been in use on big highway jobs since the 1960s, and they weren't all that different from this latest model. Four machines straddle the new roadway—spreader, paver, drag, and the unit that sprays on the curing compound—each independently diesel powered and separated from the one in front by somewhere between ten and twenty-five yards. All are precisely set up for the width of a particular job (twenty-four feet in this case) and roll along at a rate of about three yards per minute. Nobody sits and nobody rests, not that I saw, and the crew of two dozen men works maybe fourteen hours nonstop. However, since slowdowns are inevitable and breakdowns common enough, two thousand yards in a day is a triumph. Among the slowdown factors on this job is the diverted interstate traffic, because the fifteen or so dump trucks delivering concrete from the plant have to cross this traffic at an unmarked, unregulated, and unsafe "intersection," and rush hour on the temporary eastbound lane begins at three p.m.

The lead machine, the spreader, poses the most problems because it is the most mechanically complicated of the four. Rolling on caterpillar tracks, it uses a conveyor belt to onload the ready-mix from the never-ending stream of trucks and an auger to spread the thick pile of wet cement across the full width of the job. The spreader's tracks are guided straight down the new highway by a sensing device that reads the string stretched by surveyors on small rods staked alongside. Stand beside this device and you can see the huge machine modify its direction ever so slightly as it inches along. The concrete left in its wake is relatively uniform, but lumpy on the surface and marred by occasional holes. These are filled by hand before the paver arrives a few minutes later. Plates on the bottom of the paver smooth the concrete to a uniform depth, and vibrators homogenize the mix and eliminate any voids. Vibration is critical with concrete: too little leaves pockets and air holes; too much separates the mix and brings a watery slurry to the surface. A few days before, Rocky told me, the crew had to dig out a slurried patch and pour it again by hand.

While the spreader's complexities cause the problems, a sudden breakdown by the paver is a real catastrophe. The concrete already spread out will set up before the paver is fixed; the hardened mass and the steel rebar buried within it will have to be cut out and hauled away. Then new cages have to be tied in place and the new ready-mix poured and spread almost by hand. Days and many dollars down the drain. That's just one reason the smaller the gap between the spreader and the paver, the better.

The paver leaves in its wake a flat sheet of concrete thirteen inches deep. Paving manager Dick Cork checks this contracted depth every fifty feet with a yardstick and notes the result on a piece of paper. Earlier in the job, Abrams was fined $23,000 because one section of the new highway was a quarter-inch shy of this mandate. The "slump" of the concrete—roughly, its density—can vary because the loads delivered to the spreader will themselves vary from truck to truck. Therefore Dick may set more vibration on this lane of the new highway, less on that one, then reverse the settings ten yards later. He shouts this explanation above the diesel roar as he paces nonstop along his catwalk on the paver, adjusting the vibrators and the many other controls he doesn't have time to explain. Dick strikes me as a man of no-nonsense demeanor, and he points down at one particular patch and shouts, "This is horseshit mix! I have to run it dry to get it to stand at the edges."

Dick has decades of experience in concrete, and with his talent there are things he can do to tweak a horseshit mix into something more presentable, but there are limits, too, since Rocky and his crew submit daily samples of the hardened concrete to stress tests. It does no good at all for Dick to somehow manipulate his mix into an acceptable-looking roadway that then fails the lab test. If he totally dislikes what he sees coming out of the spreader, he can stop the train in its tracks and get rid of that mix by hand. So far on this job, so good, but he's had to do that elsewhere.

Behind Dick Cork's paver three men work with two straight edges and one "bullfloat" to complete the floating. This is hard work that no machine can accomplish, and it's exactly the same procedure followed on every concrete job that requires a finished surface. If the paving train is proceeding at full speed, such as it is, these men have about ten minutes to finish their work on any given section before the third machine arrives dragging a full-width piece of Astroturf and a rake with tines. This operation imparts just the right texture and scoring to the roadway surface before the fourth and final machine sprays on the curing compound. In this Texas heat, the concrete would harden and be ready for eighty thousand pounds within a week, but the completely refurbished highway is more than just the new surface. Lane lines have to be painted, shoulders graded and perhaps landscaped, barriers installed at entrances and exits, signs mounted—months of work before this new and improved stretch of good road is open and ready for American business and pleasure, an interstate that would make Ike proud.

CHAPTER 12

The ongoing interstate activity at mile marker 102 in West Texas, seventy miles east of the construction job and directly across I-10 from New York City's controversial municipal sludge at Sierra Blanca, is the federally sponsored interdiction of illegal aliens and contraband drugs. But this twenty-four-hour Border Patrol checkpoint is not a secret, and knowledgeable smugglers can easily avoid the confrontation. For instance, they can move their eastbound goods or individuals out of El Paso on Highway 62/180, a two-lane that parallels the interstate about fifty miles to the north and proceeds through Guadalupe Mountains National Park, crosses from Texas into New Mexico, passes the Carlsbad Caverns, and leads from there to points north and east. Or, if they've already visited the caverns—on this continent, I rate them second only to the Grand Canyon in the mind-boggling category—or have no interest in doing so, the pushers can cut to the south at the New Mexico border on back road 652 down to Orla, Texas, and pick up 285 to Pecos on I-20, far beyond the checkpoint. Or they can take I-10 east out of El Paso but loop around the checkpoint by cutting off at Esperanza and proceeding through the desert for thirty miles on back roads and four-wheel-drive tracks.

Given these alternative routes, given what must be the reputation of the checkpoint in this part of the world, you wonder who would try to brazen his or her or their way past this sitting duck. The answer is, all kinds of people. Mennonite farming families with dual citizenship in Mexico and Canada are highly likely to be pulled out of the line for inspection. They fit the profile, or what's left of it, because the profile has been pretty much shattered in recent years as smugglers adapt to the efforts to catch them. The biggest bust ever recorded in Sierra Blanca resulted from intelligence developed about flatbed trucks with false compartments in specially modified undercarriages. One of these rolled into the checkpoint, and half an hour later the agents had recovered 2,300 pounds of marijuana. But only that one time. Frankly, it's a game. The smugglers know it, the Border Patrol knows it, and some lawmen will even use that exact word with the phrase "cat-and-mouse." That's how Mike Jackson described the overall interdiction effort. Mike started out in law enforcement as a cop in El Paso and occasionally worked with Border Patrol agents assigned to that city, and he decided that their work was more interesting than his own. He transferred in 1984, and eleven years later he was in charge of twenty-seven agents and one secretary at the Sierra Blanca station.

Standing beneath the big canopy at the checkpoint, watching an agent send vehicle after vehicle on its way east, Mike told me, "We realize we don't catch all of it, that we do get burned. We do the best we can. When I first started here, it seemed like it was easier to pick out who the smugglers were. But the more smugglers we catch, the more we educate them. We have to testify in open court as to what we picked up on. So now Grandma and Grandpa may have been recruited by some smuggler on the belief we won't pull them over. And when I first started, compartmentalization wasn't that popular. People would just haul it in the truck, and they'd drive up and you could smell the stuff. Now they're smarter; they use sophisticated compartments, and they're hauling smaller amounts, too."

Regarding narcotics, the Border Patrol works under the authority of the Drug Enforcement Administration. Any significant bust at the Sierra Blanca checkpoint is first offered to DEA-El Paso, whose prosecutors might accept it. The factors influencing that decision seem to be the type of drug (heroin and cocaine enjoy a higher priority than marijuana and methamphetamines), the amount, the identity of the suspects, and the existing caseload. DEA prosecutors have been known to scorn a mere two hundred pounds of marijuana. If they do take a case, they drive out and pick up the suspect and the contraband, and they prosecute these cases in the federal court in Pecos. If the DEA declines the case, the Border Patrol calls either the local sheriff or the local Department of Public Safety, either of whom almost always welcomes such an easy collar. These are the numbers: in 1993, the Sierra Blanca station intercepted 236 loads of marijuana totaling 8,641 pounds, plus 265 pounds of cocaine, almost all of it at the checkpoint; in 1994, 195 interdictions totaling 8,025 pounds of pot, and 61.8 pounds of coke; in 1995, 266 pot seizures, for 9,025 pounds, and 531 pounds of coke. The street value of a year's haul is about $30 million.

While these are commendable figures, Mike's squad knows full well that many drug shipments roll right past them, because nothing is holier than a reliable profile and because ten thousand vehicles pass daily through the checkpoint. With only the twenty-seven agents and four dogs assigned to the station—and they, too, work in shifts, just like the people—there's no way that more than a hundred of these cars and trucks can be closely inspected on a given day. The checkpoint doesn't even stop traffic heading west on I-10 toward El Paso; the feeling is that most contraband isn't moving into the city, but out of it.

The U.S. Border Patrol has about 4,500 uniformed agents for the entire nation, and over 4,000 of those are assigned along the Mexican border. Metropolitan Dallas has that many cops. Obviously, the odds favor the drug smugglers, who now serve as middlemen for maybe seventy percent of all shipments out of Colombia. Men and women—illegal aliens, or "undocumented immigrants"—are harder to hide, so fewer smugglers ply this trade. In addition, people can hop out of a truck before reaching the checkpoint and strike out across the desert in order to rendezvous with their ride on the other side. This tends to happen at night, presumably. Sometimes a motorist will tell the checkpoint agent, "Hey, three guys jumped out of a pickup about a mile back and ran off into the desert. Mexican-looking guys." If surplus troops are on hand, they'll be dispatched to locate these individuals. Or maybe this citizen-motorist will say, "Hey, a pickup loaded with guys turned around and drove across the median and sped back toward El Paso. Mexican-looking guys." Brian Trungale, the trucker I met at the Circle Bar outside Ozona, was an eyewitness when a Dodge fifth-wheel pickup suddenly swerved to the side of the road just west of the Sierra Blanca checkpoint, dropped its trailer, jolted across the median, and raced off from whence it came. Brian reported the incident at the checkpoint, and it turned out that men were packed inside the trailer. And once in a blue moon a motorist might tell the agent, "Hey, three guys jumped out of a pickup truck about a mile back and ran off into the desert. Mexican-looking guys," with this motorist *himself* carrying fifty pounds of marijuana and hoping to divert any undue curiosity with the good Samaritan's alarm. This scenario is conjecture on my part, I admit, but any scam that makes so much sense has to happen.

The official figure for illegal aliens "apprehended and located" by the forces at the Sierra Blanca station, mostly at the checkpoint, was 4,712 in 1993, 3,440 in '94, and 2,614 the following year. Given the notoriety of the checkpoint, I asked Mike Jackson why they ever catch anyone. "Some will 'false claim' to U.S. citizenship," he replied, "or maybe they'll present counterfeit documents, or maybe be an imposter with a legitimate document from a cousin or other family member. Usually, the aliens we catch are trying these false claims. Only occasionally are they caught hiding in a truck or under a blanket. And we get a lot who originate in southern California. People in this area know we're here, but a lot coming from California don't. And a lot of people assume that when we speak of 'aliens,' we mean Mexicans, but we catch a large variety from all over the world, maybe people who have come legally as visitors or students and they've overstayed their visa." When this happens, it's a hassle. These people will eventually get matters straightened out, but not before a good deal of lost time and trouble. For example, their automobile, perhaps a rental or lease, might be impounded.

Many of the "wetbacks" intercepted at Sierra Blanca are Mexicans whose level of education and employment status fit neither our concept of that pejorative term nor their own, and in fact are simply people whose paperwork isn't in order, for whatever reason. I met just such a couple one night, pulled off the Greyhound bus and carrying with them a violin, a comparative literature textbook, and Kurt Vonnegut's *Wampeters, Foma & Granfalloons*. The agents at Sierra Blanca once did catch a large number of the other kind of illegal aliens, and that story made the national news. This was early on the morning of July 2, 1987, when the daily Missouri Pacific freight train moving east out of El Paso stopped for inspection, as it does every time, by prior arrangement with the Border Patrol. Men sometimes hide in the wheel wells or hang from the undercarriage, and men and women alike hide in the boxcars. When Stanley Saathof, the former chief of the station, inspected the boxcars about eight a.m. he heard a call for help. Inside one car he found eighteen bodies and the man calling out. The lone survivor, he had used a railroad spike to dig a breathing hole in the wood floor.

The Sierra Blanca checkpoint consists of a small prefabricated office, four adjoining holding pens for detainees, and the covered drive-through where each eastbound vehicle is stopped and a select few are directed to the side for further scrutiny. The canopy was added in 1994; prior to that, the agents worked directly beneath the desert sun. The drive-through area is about thirty yards long. The procedure goes like this: a quarter-mile back, a large sign with blinking lights alerts drivers to the impending obstruction. Everyone is funneled off the interstate by a long line of orange traffic cones, and this single lane of traffic—cars, RVs, semis, and bikers—rolls into the checkpoint and stops, one by one, at the large stop sign. One agent "works the point" at all times, rotating in thirty-minute shifts. This is the agent who decides whether to demand citizenship documentation or to direct a vehicle into "secondary" for a thorough search for narcotics, perhaps with the assistance of a canine colleague. The point agent accompanies this vehicle into secondary, and his position in primary is filled by another agent. Those doing paperwork or taking a break in the office have a sixth sense focused on the cars and trucks outside. If the line stops for any length of time, they'll glance out the window to see what's happening. Three agents are the minimum with which this checkpoint can function. Normally, four are on duty during the day and seven or eight during the prime hours of four p.m. to midnight, plus the dog. If no dog is on hand, there's one on call at home.

The dog doesn't stand with the agent at the point and give every passing car and truck a quick sniff. No animal can work that fast. The dog waits off to the side in his handler's enclosed pickup truck. Some, like Lex, go to sleep. Joe Casteneda, Lex's handler, opened the rear door of his truck and pointed out this fact to me. Lex stirred and looked up, apparently peacefully, and I asked, "Yeah, but what if I reached in there to pet him?" Joe smiled. "Oh, he'd love it. Somebody could pull up and if he was free and I wasn't watching, he'd jump in and ride away with them." But other dogs, like Nora, stay busy barking, and the friendly hand might well come back minus a digit.

Even if the agents had a pack of dogs to work with, instead of just one or two, the traffic would back up to El Paso if each of the ten thousand quotidian vehicles were subjected to animal investigation. Unless and until the agent working the point makes the correct, more-or-less snap judgment and brings the smuggler into secondary, the dog can't do its job. It's the agent who makes the dog and everybody else at the checkpoint look good, and every agent can recite the list of the best busts initiated while he was working the point.

Theoretically, every driver is asked if he or she is an American citizen, but this doesn't always happen. Sometimes a car or truck is waved right through; the driver doesn't even have to roll down the window. The CBS GOLF vans following the pro tour from the West Coast to the East will presumably be waved on through; in any event, I saw it happen one day in late February. In all likelihood, tractor-trailer rigs hauling for one of the reputable major trucking companies will also roll right through, while drivers hauling for certain *other* trucking companies will, with equal certainty, be asked to stretch their legs for a while. An Army convoy operating out of Fort Bliss has an excellent chance of a friendly wave, but it's not automatic. The Maddencruiser has been given free passage any number of times; schoolbuses, too, if they're hauling actual students and not Deadheads. Rock groups and country-western stars are often waved through. (I know, I know, but do you really want to hassle The Tractors, an example chosen only because their bus pulled in while I was working point with Mike Moran. I'd never heard of them, but, as if by rote, their driver handed out autographed photographs and a complimentary CD through the window.)

If the traffic begins to back up onto the interstate proper, therefore posing a hazard, the agent clears the jam by waving through everyone except for the driver and/or vehicle that fits the shattered profile so perfectly that none of the agents I met would give me even a hint of that description. Okay. Adept smugglers must know their odds of breezing through are better during traffic jams. What's to keep them from lingering at the rest area with the tepee motif a mile back, looking for a herd of traffic in early evening, the busiest time on any interstate, then slipping in and very likely getting a free pass at the stop sign? Nothing, and it must happen, but nothing prevents a spare agent from getting into his patrol car at five p.m. and cruising to this rest stop for a quick survey. This also happens, almost daily. And every once in a while the Border Patrol will institute an "enhanced period" for a couple of weeks, when a beefed-up contingent of agents and dogs will direct a much greater flow of vehicles into secondary. That news spreads quickly on truckers' CBs and within a day the El Paso truck stops fill to bursting, and traffic on alternate routes soars. Some of these trucks may be trying to avoid interdiction, but most of them, just delay.

The checkpoint is situated so that neither the structure it-self, the warning sign with blinking lights, nor the traffic cones are visible until you, the driver, come over a slight hill and around a curve—and then it's too late. You're committed. Any attempt to spin around will probably be spotted by the agent working the point or by one of those concerned Americans so worried about our porous borders. At night, once in a rare while a vehicle will turn off its lights, dodge the traffic cones, and try to coast quietly past the Border Patrol on the otherwise empty stretch of I-10 outside the back door. Or maybe he'll try to blow past. But in either event he'll almost certainly be spotted and then hunted down by state troopers.*

Generally speaking, flight from apprehension denotes a stolen vehicle, not drugs, but one night a few years back the classic family of father, mother, teenaged daughter, and some younger kids flipped a "U" when they saw the checkpoint, fled west at a hundred miles per hour *sans* headlights, heaving marijuana out the window until they ran out of gas ten miles away. These were Mexican citizens being paid $8,000 plus the Astrovan they were driving. Then there was the time the el-derly gent blithely motored right through the traffic cones and past the checkpoint at a steady sixty-five. State troopers down the highway couldn't get him to pull over and finally shot out the tires. When this old fellow stepped out, he stretched broadly and looked around at the posse with complete inno-cence. Clueless. Shouldn't be allowed to drive.

---

*After a couple of unfortunate episodes, the Border Patrol decided to leave the high-speed chases to the interstate professionals.

No pistol has ever been fired at the checkpoint itself, not in anyone's living memory, and that goes back to its inauguration in 1975. Only one body has been found, by a new man doing his first inspection in secondary. A notorious episode in Sierra Blanca annals, this stiff in the trunk, but the more interesting corpse story is the time a young couple pulled up at primary in a state of obvious agitation, with a pistol on the seat between them. In Texas, it has always been legal to carry a weapon while hunting or when traveling between counties,* but the agent at the point quite understandably asked a couple of questions of this pair, then decided to take their stories independently and directed their car into secondary. Their scenarios didn't quite jibe, and the ensuing search of the sedan uncovered shovels, rope, gas cans, and a large blue tarp. The pair's claim to be on a hunting trip didn't seem plausible so the agents asked if they could unfurl the tarp. Permission granted, they found a pool of blood. At this point, the woman confessed she'd killed a man (later described as her boyfriend) in Austin and gotten the assistance of this friend riding with her in loading the corpse into the car and hauling it out of there.

Of all the possible places they could have dumped the body in the four hundred vacated miles between Austin and Sierra Blanca, they had chosen the first exit on the other side of this checkpoint. No sooner had they ditched the body off Alaska Road, set it on fire, and started back east than they were guided into the hands of the Border Patrol by those orange traffic cones. That was on October 26, 1984, and new-on-the-job Mike Jackson and his supervisor drove out to recover the remains. If it hadn't been for incredible misjudgment, there's no telling how long the body might have done its bit for the local food chain, which needs all the help it can get. Then again, the retribution of the criminal justice system wasn't all that severe. This woman was indicted for voluntary manslaughter; in Texas, that's "murder with sudden passion." In March the following year, she was sentenced to ten years

---

*In 1995 the state followed the lead of thirty-nine others in passing an even more permissive concealed weapons law.

probation, and was relieved of even that obligation four years later. Her accomplice was not indicted at all. You have to figure the victim was some sort of bad character.

As it happened, one of the first vehicles directed into secondary when I was hanging around the checkpoint was one of those Mennonite extended families—two men, two women, four children, one baby. These were farmers from Chihuahua, Mexico, but their license plates read Alberta, Canada. They passively emerged from their aging Le Sabre and huddled together at one side. They were all very white, as Mennonites almost always are, and they didn't seem the least surprised by this interruption to their journey. Not one of them said a word to any of the agents. The impassive attitude of these travelers impressed me, but not the agents. Some suspects get nervous as hell, others wait quietly. If dope is discovered, some break down; others show no emotion at all. One theory holds that guilty women are more cold-blooded than men. You can stir up a debate on this issue, with corroborating stories on either side. There's also the theory that women are more likely to be carrying their Bible, and that I'm more likely than someone else to mention this.

Nora was the canine assigned to this case. She has the reputation of having an excellent nose—and in her league, "excellent" means phenomenal, because all of these dogs can detect a kilo of cocaine sealed in a PVC pipe, then submerged in a fifty-five-gallon drum of gasoline, or a bale of marijuana buried in the middle of a trailer full to the roof with nuts also harvested in Chihuahua. But Nora's pinpointing talent is a little sloppy, so her handler has to pay very close attention. As Jeff Huite worked his dog around the Mennonites' car, motioning to various parts with a quickly circled finger, Lex's handler Joe Casteneda tutored me in the basics. All of the average-sized and -looking dogs in Sierra Blanca are Belgian Malinois, or, as they're sometimes called, Belgian Sheepdogs or Shepherds. This surprised me, since neither Lex, Nora, nor Jack much resembled one another. But Joe assured me and the books confirm that the Malinois is a breed ideally suited for the work due both to their nose and their energy, if not their uniform appearance. They're working dogs, herding animals with an insatiable curiosity. They're like cats: put them in a car and they really want to know what's hidden under the backseat. A strange yet legal smell might provoke a Malinois to yelps of excitement, which has to be distinguished by the handler from a genuine "alert." The latter would be the first sign to Jeff that Nora has smelled in the Mennonites' sedan one of the five substances for which she has been trained: heroin, cocaine, marijuana, methamphetamine, and *present* but undisclosed human beings (when the act of respiration is the tip-off, presumably).

The dog's alert might be so obvious a display of interest that even I might pick it up, or some movement so slight only her own handler could recognize it. (In the public imagination, the dogs get all the credit, but anyone actually involved will emphasize the role played by their handlers. Once a dog has been selected for the Border Patrol training school in El Paso, she will probably graduate. The same cannot be said for the humans; their training requires six weeks, and some candidates never catch on.) The dog now traces the "scent cone" to the point of highest concentration: the contraband. The next step is the "indication," and it's hard to miss: the dog simply sits down. If the dog *alerts* but then doesn't *indicate*, the handler concludes that drugs *had been* present, but no longer were. The odor of any of the dopes in question lingers for weeks, maybe months. This happens all the time: a car pulls in just reeking of marijuana, but according to the dog, it's clean. Reasonable assumption: the stuff was off-loaded yesterday in El Paso. But what does not happen all the time is what happened on this particular occasion: Nora gave a strong "indication" by sitting down in the trunk of the Mennonites' Le Sabre, but three agents weren't able to find anything untoward in the belongings. Nothing. After four or five minutes the search was terminated and the family invited to return to their car and proceed to Canada—although they were going the wrong way if Alberta, a western province, was their destination. From El Paso, the Mennonites should have gone either west on I-10 or north up I-25. So who knows what they were up to.

What can you do? That was the agents' attitude. These Mexican Albertans had stored illegal contraband in that car, without a doubt, because the dogs make very, very few mistakes. Their handlers feel this strongly and are equally confident in their own ability to find the source if they know roughly where to search. The idea that narcotics could be present but the dog fail to find them strikes both Joe Casteneda and Jeff Huite as laughable. What *can* happen is that the handler fails to detect his dog's detection, or perhaps the dog has a bad-nose day, maybe a cold. But this lethargy is obvious quickly with an energetic Malinois, and she's given the day off.

I was interested in canine and other olfactions? I should call Dr. Larry Myers, neuroscientist and animal behaviorist in the Physiology and Pharmacology Department of the School of Veterinary Medicine at Auburn University—one of the world's leading experts. He consults with the Border Patrol and other law enforcement agencies on their dog training programs and *occasionally* testifies in court cases in which the defense challenges the dog. He doesn't like to, however, because the term "expert witness" can have such negative connotations. Larry gets funding from a long list of sources, including the Defense Department, and when he took my call he was very hopeful about something involving the small set of moths and butterflies that breed and lay their eggs exclusively on *erythroxlum coca*, the most commercially important of the several different coca plants. To leash these insects would be tough, Larry quipped, but what about turning loose a flock—sterilized, of course—inside a warehouse at a major port of entry—Miami, say—to see whether all land on a particular bale of cotton? It's a thought. Or if Larry could isolate the olfactory receptor complexes specific to *erythroxlum coca*, he might be able to harvest these and create a biomedical instrument that would serve beautifully as a durable Geiger counter for cocaine. Such instruments are already in use in many fields, and Larry should know. He founded the Institute for Biological Detection Systems based at Auburn.

I asked Larry about sharks and their phenomenal nose for blood. Yes, he replied, their smell is pretty good, but what sharks are really working with is an extraordinary sensitivity to electrical fields, biological and otherwise. In this regard, they're a match for our best instrumentation, and this sensitivity may explain why they attack shark cages: the electrical field emitted by the steel throws them off. When I asked if dogs have the best olfaction of any animal, Larry said there hadn't been a lot of nose-to-nose competition. Definitive tests would be difficult to set up, monitor, and control, and perhaps not worth the time and effort. Dogs might *not* be the best; cats could be great, but how would we know? Moths and butterflies might be just as good. For some chemicals—hydrogen sulfide, for example—humans are practically as good. We can smell rotten eggs in the range of a few parts, maybe just one part, per billion, and that approaches the range in which dogs operate. *Less* than one part per billion is Larry's rule of thumb for dogs, and maybe even hundreds of parts per quadrillion, but it's difficult to be perfectly accurate when dealing with such minuscule amounts.

Could Lex and Nora find a single seed of marijuana sealed tightly inside an empty cell in the twelve-volt battery of a large, smelly car? Perhaps. How in the world could they identify cocaine sealed inside PVC pipe and suspended inside a tank of gasoline? Here Larry surprised me—deflated me, to be perfectly honest—with his belief that contamination factors into these popular, Disney-esque illustrations of a hound's amazing sense of smell. If the pipe is *one hundred percent* airtight and there's absolutely zero contamination on it or the tank or the car, neither dog could possibly smell what is not there—a molecule of marijuana. But what are the odds of perfect encasement? Incredibly small, Larry suggested, taking into account the IQ of the individual in charge of the shipping-and-receiving department. That's probably why the dogs find a lot of this dope.

In Sierra Blanca, Jeff Huite led Nora back to her mobile doghouse. He and Joe Casteneda had had high hopes for that secondary—a few months earlier, Joe's Lex had sniffed four hundred pounds of marijuana traveling with two other Mennonites—but these compliant farmers drove off, innocent, silent. That kind of acquiescence isn't always the case, as was proved immediately by the individuals in the next two vehicles pulled over: a Toyota pickup carrying three Haitians who said they were moving their stuff to Miami, and a waxed Lincoln driven by a severe, handsome black man. I didn't have to be told (although I was told) that either of these secondaries might be an instance in which the driver complained, "You pulled me over because I'm black." As it turned out, both of these drivers said just that or something close. One of the Haitian passengers didn't have his documentation on hand, and by the time the computer verified his legality several minutes later, he was accusing the Border Patrol of racism. This issue gives agents more grief than any other. It's so ticklish Mike Jackson felt compelled to say to me somewhat defensively, "At least half the people we pull into secondary are Anglo."

The Lincoln was a drug check, and Lex gave an alert at the front passenger door. When told that the dog had shown an interest, the man replied that other dogs at other checkpoints had also shown an interest. Of course. They don't miss. When asked if the agents could check the interior, this man asked whether a search warrant was necessary. The answer was no. At an official checkpoint, the Border Patrol doesn't need the driver's permission to subject the car to an *external* investigation with a dog; this is undisputed case law. An alert from a trained dog then constitutes probable cause for a full search, including the interior, with or without the owner's consent. Defense attorneys have challenged this procedure, of course, but have yet to win. In most instances, this point is moot because the owner generally gives permission, even when he's smuggling drugs.*

Without a dog, the legal situation is different. Without that

---

*I'm no fool or dupe. I'm well aware that the Border Patrol doesn't have a stellar reputation among civil libertarians and others. In some quarters, it has a terrible reputation, right down there with the ATF, and I assume the letter of the law is abused in certain situations. I assume the same is true of the Highway Patrol. I know it's true in the halls of Congress.

court-recognized probable cause, agents must either obtain the driver's consent or "develop" their own rationale for the search, and this improvisational probable cause is quite susceptible to legal challenge. In 1993, our Supreme Court complicated the issue further in a case involving a slow-moving Cadillac pulled over for that reason by Arizona state troopers on I-10 between Tucson and Phoenix. The driver consented to a search, the troopers uncovered 560 pounds of cocaine, and then enticed this courier to complete his delivery at a nearby motel. This impromptu sting caught the husband-and-wife ringleaders and, eventually, the U.S. Customs officer who owned the Cadillac. A lower court ruled that the arresting trooper lacked reasonable suspicion for stopping the Caddy in the first place, thus nullifying the convictions. But the Supreme Court ruled unanimously that the illegality of the search protected only the driver of the car, not "those who are aggrieved solely by the introduction of damaging evidence"—the ringleaders or the Customs agent. Proving once again that the law is, if not a ass, a quirky business.

If consent for a search is withheld, and if the agent is reasonably confident that this delay will pay off, the easiest solution is to call for a dog. This brief detention of sorts has been upheld by the courts. Just the week before my visit to the checkpoint, two agents had pulled a Dodge van into secondary, caught a faint whiff of weed, and called for a dog, who alerted and indicated at the rear of the van. Mike Moran and Lupe Trevino entered under the letter of the law and commenced their search. Initially suspecting the usual hollowed-out side panels, they were surprised and delighted to find they could mash down only a few inches on the rear couch. Beneath that, it was hard. Within fifteen minutes they had taken possession of 94.5 pounds of pot from the two women in the front seat. The three children riding with them were turned over to social welfare workers in El Paso.

On Tuesday morning, the aloof black man driving the Lincoln said, Okay, go inside, even though his approval wasn't necessary, and Lex jumped in and immediately indicated on the floorboard of the front seat, where Joe Casteneda then found a smidgen of a roach. Not worth the bother, and the man was sent on his disgruntled, alienated way. And that's how I learned, to my great surprise, that an insignificant holding of pot—though not of cocaine—might very well be forgiven, in effect, by the Border Patrol. In fact, it can happen half a dozen times a day in Sierra Blanca. "If we presented all the misdemeanors to the prosecutors," Mike Jackson told me, "we'd have to shut down." In Texas, the misdemeanor cutoff for marijuana is four ounces, and no prosecutor wants to fool with a few joints, either, much less with crumbs. Your pot will be confiscated and forwarded to the appropriate authorities, but that's probably the extent of your hassle.

A textbook example of the race problems encountered at the checkpoint is delivered by almost every interstate bus that pulls up. By prior arrangement with Greyhound, these buses, seven a day, drive straight into secondary. If available, a dog is put in the luggage bins underneath while two agents board the bus to ascertain citizenship. The law here is difficult. A United States citizen doesn't have to produce proof of citizenship, and the great majority couldn't do so even if they had to or wanted to, because a driver's license proves nothing. Anybody can obtain one of them. A verbal declaration is all the Border Patrol can ask of U.S. citizens, while noncitizens must have a passport with visa, entry card, or some other documentation. But what happens if a Hispanic traveler speaking poor or no English verbally declares that she's an American citizen nevertheless, and the agent has his doubts? Well, where were you born? Where did you go to elementary school? Who are your parents and where are they now? The agent may ask these and related questions until satisfied the individual is telling the truth. If she isn't, nine times out of ten she'll tire of these evasions and confess. Most people are not good, practiced liars, which is why a too-quick declaration of citizenship might be followed immediately by the question about birthplace. If you hesitate regarding where you were born, you probably weren't born there. Happens *all* the time, but these people are rarely illegal. Maybe they're on a current visa or have the valid green card but mistakenly figure the proclamation of citizenship will be the easiest, quickest way through this checkpoint. American citizens who might not seem to be are well advised to carry a birth certificate or passport in the border areas, even though they aren't legally required to and the rest of us don't. That's just the way it is, and the Border Patrol will tell you as much straight out. And thus the booming trade in *counterfeit* birth certificates.

I asked the first bus driver who pulled in if he'd seen a lot of people yanked away in his thirty years of service, and he replied, "I've seen a lot I'm glad they did." And the fact of the matter is, these eastbound smugglers are overwhelmingly black and Hispanic. That's not racist, every agent says, just the fact. Plenty of white guys and women are smuggling elsewhere, right here in Sierra Blanca, in their cars and trucks, but on the buses coming out of California, the business is black and Hispanic. In order to avoid charges of discrimination, everyone on the cross-country bus is questioned about citizenship, but this indiscrimination merely provides every ethnic group on the bus with an equal opportunity to complain. At least one individual will cause some kind of scene. That's a given. White agents, black agents, brown agents, and Asian agents all catch their fair share of abuse.

In response to the citizenship inquiry, an Anglo guy may snap, "I'm white, aren't I?"

His woman may say, "My hair's blond, isn't it?"

"So was the Norwegian woman's on the last bus. Please, ma'am, are you an American citizen?"

A black man may simply raise his hand to better display his self-evident black American skin. Or he may adopt the sarcastic approach. "No, man. *African.*"

"Well, then, may I see your *African* passport?"

An El Salvadoran or Costa Rican or Panamanian or Peruvian may say, "We're not all illegal Mexicans, you know."

And a Mexican-American may say, "Yes, *third* generation."

And an Asian might say—actually, Asians seldom say anything. Notorious for not carrying documentation, they're also the best ethnic group of all for *having* that documentation. They don't carry it because they're afraid of losing it.

Every Border Patrol agent has a pile of nasty remarks received from bus passengers and motorists alike. People shoot the bird at them all the time. Lupe Trevino has been working the point and been told, "You're a Mexican. How can you ask me if I'm an American citizen?" He's also heard, "You fuckin' Mexican." And the inquiries about citizenship from a black agent of Puerto Rican extraction who spoke an accented English were not much appreciated by a great number of motorists and, especially, I'll wager, by truckers whose radiators sport the confederate flag. That particular agent no longer works at Sierra Blanca. In fact, there are no blacks on the local force, and no women either. None of the agents could tell me how well female Border Patrol agents are accepted by the motoring public because no woman had ever been stationed here. One or two had been expected at various times, then failed the four-month training program at Brunswick, Georgia.

On the highway, motorists who give the state troopers lip *know* their attitude can't possibly help their cause, but they mouth off anyway. The sight of the uniform, the hat, the badge, and the gun sets them off. These checkpoint agents run into the same phenomenon, and you might think the attitude is a guaranteed "secondary," but it's not the case. The agents assume anyone hauling dope will not be that stupid. I wondered whether a nasty attitude might not therefore be a good cover. Mike Jackson believes there's a correlation between any recent negative headlines regarding law enforcement and the attitude of the bus passengers and motorists his agents encounter. "Occasionally we'll get thanked for what we do," Mike added, "but for the most part we're an annoyance to the traveling public. You can say 'Good morning' and you've already made 'em mad. And a lot of people don't feel we have a right to be here. We get a lot of comments from veterans in the military, who tell us right away they shouldn't have to do this."

Veterans? I am naive.

During a slow stretch on the point midmorning, agent Mike Moran added some abuse stories to my list, shrugged, and concluded, "Talk is cheap. This is the United States. As long as they *do* what they're supposed to, I let 'em talk." Mike was raised in Queens Village, New York—an undocumented claim I accepted at face value because he has that borough's seen-it-all attitude. A good guy and a Mets fan, Mike remembers when they could play, back in the eighties with Hojo and Kid and Doc and Straw and Mex. He also confirmed a conclusion I'd already come to. Considering the number of "devout scumbags" whom they confront every day, the agents seem fairly relaxed about their own safety. In secondary, they'll ask you to take your hands from your pockets, and they'll keep an eye on you, but I expected a more forthright diligence, if not quite "hands on the hood, buddy." However, they must be doing something right: as I said, no pistol or gun has been fired in this workplace. A few travelers with an attitude *and* insufficient documentation will get pulled off the buses or out of cars every day, and more than that in the fall as migrant workers head home for the winter. A few drug mules will be collared every week. And, occasionally, a carefully wrapped Christmas gift will have the street value of a diamond from Tiffany's.

"We encounter a lot of different kinds of people here, as you can imagine": that's Mike Jackson's mouthful of truth. For example, there's the guy stuffing the banana in his mouth while approaching the agent at the stop sign. He would be one of the many motorists who believes this is an agricultural checkpoint and intends to eat the forbidden fruit before it's confiscated. Others pull up and say immediately, "I don't have any fruit." In their defense, the warning sign on the interstate says simply, "Inspection Station," and elsewhere on the interstates there are agricultural checkpoints—outside Needles, California, for one, and I've been there myself, stuffing the banana in my mouth as I arrived at the point. And there was the driver who avoided the orange cones and pulled out of the line before entering primary. When the agents walked out to check on things, they found an elderly man in woman's clothing struggling desperately to change into a shirt and slacks. Mike can sometimes even feel a little sorry for the occasional low-level smuggler—not sorry, exactly, but he has actually *believed* one or two who said they'd lost their jobs and had the wife and kids to feed and were hoping to get back on their feet with just this one deal. Once or twice, Mike believed it.

Working the point, the agent engages the driver in a brief conversation regarding citizenship, origination, destination, and cargo, while also scoping out the vehicle, the driver, the passenger, the belongings, always keeping the latest fads in mind. The agent might get close enough to the car or truck to get a good whiff of the inside. With a tractor-trailer rig, he sometimes climbs onto the step to get a better view. He'll be looking for signs of excessive nervousness *or* friendliness, because guiltiness manifests itself both ways. The following story from the nervousness category is famous in the trade:

"Good evening. Where you from?"

"Oh, the shit's in the back."

"What shit?"

"The marijuana."

Usually it's not that simple, but there are clues, too:

▪ The window that can't be rolled down. That's the claim, at least. Possible explanation: the wreaking odor inside of marijuana or marijuana smoke. Unlike heroin and cocaine, which can be smuggled economically in smaller amounts, large amounts of marijuana are the rule, and it's very difficult to hide this smell from the agents, much less from the dogs. For training purposes, Joe Casteneda had with him one morning three cannisters containing samples of the three main drugs in question. He opened the plastic bag with the tarry, black mass of raw heroin in the bottom, worth about $250,000; to my surprise, a powerful vinegary smell poured out. Nevertheless, twenty pounds of pot throws off a more powerful odor than a couple of pounds of well-sealed heroin or cocaine. Coke has very little odor, at least to a human being.

▪ Powerful deodorizers or air fresheners: obvious attempts to mask illegal smells. In fact, these are a red flag, and the agent will almost certainly direct that car to secondary, where the deodorizer won't fool Lex or Nora or Jack at all. I saw one of these cases pulled over, a Ciera reeking of chemical freshener, but to no avail. (If "to no avail" seems to imply a bias in favor of the Border Patrol, I don't intend it. Relieved that this *particular* motorist was innocent, I merely wanted *someone* to be guilty so I might observe the booking process.) People have even tried the old chile powder trick, which works only in the movies—*Cool Hand Luke*, most notably. If the handler feels that his dog is agitated by any such camouflaging smell, that's a large red flag on the situation. I watched the search of an aging Ford Country Squire station wagon with suspiciously fresh air driven by a Mexican national of decidedly nervous demeanor. A likely dopemobile, to be sure, but nada.

• Broken housing on the steering column. This car is almost certainly stolen—or had been once—and will almost automatically get a thorough inspection. I saw one of these pulled over, again to no avail.

• The immediate declaration of American citizenship and concomitant attempt to roll through primary without coming to a stop. I saw a Hispanic male driving a BMW try this with Mike Moran working the point. Mike requested that he stop for just a moment, please, thank you; and when he proceeded to ask where the driver had been born, the man changed his story, acknowledged he was Peruvian, and pulled out a green card. Secondary, of course, but the car was clean.

• No eye contact.

• White guy who says he's from Georgia with Arizona plates and no I.D. Both of these states are marijuana hotbeds. I saw one of these guys pulled over, but he wasn't holding.

• Latinos driving Japanese pickups. Many times, illegal visitors from El Salvador, Guatemala, or Honduras may enter in California and make enough money to buy a little Toyota truck to drive home. In order to get there, they head east out of California bound for Brownsville, Texas, with the idea of remaining in the United States as long as possible because the highways here are better and they don't have to pay off Mexican officials at *their* checkpoints. So I was told.

▪ Truckload of agricultural products or any merchandise coming out of Mexico with American registration. I saw a shipment of kitchen appliances directed to secondary, and then a load of tomatoes.

Also on hand at the checkpoint is a forklift equipped with a cage to lift dog and handler up to the top of any load. If the dog so indicates, the entire load will be, if necessary, disassembled. That February, a crew was installing a hydraulic lift off to one side. The Border Patrol station in Marfa had enjoyed good luck with that lift, which makes it easier for dogs and humans to inspect underneath cars and pickups. Gas tanks are popular hiding places. Drive shafts have come into play.

▪ An early declaration that the vehicle "doesn't belong to me." Save yourself some time in Sierra Blanca and don't blurt out anything like this when the agent asks in his most offhand manner, "This your van?" The disclaimer sounds too much like a preemptive alibi, and secondary is assured. Of course, a similar line is the most common ex post facto explanation for contraband. The two women with the three kids and 94.5 pounds of pot claimed to be driving to Van Horn, where they were supposed to park at a designated restaurant, go inside for lunch, come outside, and find a different vehicle in which they would then drive back to El Paso. The driver assured the agents she hadn't questioned her boyfriend about this unusual arrangement. As Mike Jackson said, "That was not a true story."

▪ Strange vibes emanating from the trunk lid. Agent Rene Tamez has the habit of softly touching this spot on certain vehicles. Looking out the office window, I saw him do this and asked everyone else why. They couldn't say. When Rene came in from his shift, I asked him. "If I told you," he said, "I'd have to kill you." This broke everybody up.

Sometimes the agent will secondary a vehicle and a driver who perfectly illustrates the most clichéd profile imaginable, such as the dude with the long black hair, wearing the Budweiser T-shirt, and driving the Aerostar minivan with all the hiding places. He hopped out of his vehicle and asked whether he fit some kind of profile. "I'm always getting stopped," he said, laughing. We laughed, too, but inspected anyway. Turns out this guy was a professional comedian on his way from California to the Mississippi River, where he had a good-paying riverboat gig. Interesting guy, legal van, and as he walked back to his vehicle I called out, "Hey, what'd the bartender say to the horse?" He turned on a dime, looked at me with disdain, and said, "'Why the long face?'"

The day shift at the checkpoint had warned me about Santos Salinas, who would be working that evening. "A character," one agent said. "Doesn't like anyone—including himself," another said. "Good luck," a third added.

Nonetheless, I found Santos very engaging. Yes, the exterior might be a little gruff, but he was full of charming stories and useful information and pithy opinion. Santos was the agent who told me about the lawyer who called up requesting a receipt for confiscated drugs, since his client's dealer was pressing hard for either his money or his dope, and the mule couldn't deliver either one from jail. And it was Santos who said, "You know, we're not dealing with the boys from Medellín here. I mean, we've caught the same guy *twice*."

We were joined on that Tuesday evening shift by Lee Williams, Juan Guancano, and Charlie Flores, who asked me if my publisher happened to be Simon & Schuster—a step in the right direction, as publishing questions go in the hinterlands. Charlie had been a sound engineer in the music business for eighteen years before deciding he needed steadier work; he remains a considerable fan of John Lennon. Salinas, Guancano, and Flores all grew up in the lower Rio Grande Valley in south Texas—the "Valley," encompassing Brownsville and environs—and no sooner were we inspecting cars than an often-interrupted discussion broke out regarding the preferred terminology along the border. Jim McDonald, the engineer with the highway department, is a Chicano, which, he told me, is the designation of choice among Chicanos on the Texas border. (Formerly, he said with a grimace, the El Paso newspaper used "Latin" as its generic proper noun—not "Latino," just "Latin.") The three agents agreed with Jim about "Chicano," even though *The New York Times* prefers "Hispanic" and the Los Angeles *Times* goes with "Latino." For the local taste in Texas, "Hispanic" is too politely generic and "Latino" too contrived.

I also learned that prior to 1992, Sierra Blanca had been an official hardship posting within the Border Patrol. This fact hadn't come up on the day shift, though now I caught an earful. Live out here and your wife gives up her life, but work out here and live in El Paso and you give up *your* life, with a three-hour daily commute. The following day, I asked Mike Jackson about the hardship business, and he suggested taking these complaints with a grain of salt. He and his wife love living in Sierra Blanca. Once you become accustomed to the peace and quiet, it's great.

Finally, I learned on nightshift that many agents don't much care for this passive checkpoint duty, either. They prefer working "line watch" out in the desert or down by the river, tracking aliens. "This is *inspection* work," Santos told me, "not Border Patrol work." Years ago, Sierra Blanca was a line-watch station only, but in recent years the agency has focused on traffic checkpoints as a better use of money and manpower, because these interdictions are larger and more frequent. Then again, the better the job the Border Patrol does at the checkpoints, the more likely the smugglers are to use alternative means and routes, such as backpacking through the desert, so line watch won't be phased out entirely.

I've mentioned the Mexican couple pulled off the bus with their violin and college-level reading matter. This happened at nine o'clock. They were "European Mexicans," as

Santos labeled them. As such, they are, in Santos's opinion, the worst kind of Mexican national when it comes to arrogance. Worse still in this regard, also in Santos's opinion, are the OTMs, Border Patrol parlance for Hispanics "Other Than Mexicans." Some OTMs are awfully tired of what they perceive to be the knee-jerk assumption that they're Mexican, and illegal, too.

Santos and Juan Guancano worked the paper on the case of these European Mexicans and used Spanish to interview both detainees, although I'd heard each of them speak excellent English. All agents stationed along the Mexican border are required to have at least a working knowledge of Spanish, sufficient to handle searches and incarcerations. Santos assured me that illegal aliens would much rather be interrogated by an Anglo struggling with a second language than by a Chicano who understands not only the words, but also their shadings of tone.

The standard-issue border-crossing card held by each of our two detainees was good for seventy-two hours within a twenty-five-mile radius from the point of validation, but they were en route to Europe. Europe is farther than twenty-five miles away, Santos notified them. The detainees contended that the border officer hadn't asked for their ultimate destination. If he had, they would have told him. "That's your problem, not his problem," Salinas replied to them in English. After another exchange in Spanish, Juan Guancano interrupted and said, in English, "Oh, now your story is getting worse."

I got a quick introduction to the remedies afforded both the detainee and the Border Patrol, in this instance and every other. Do you have the correct documents? No? Then you have two choices. One is "voluntary departure under safeguards," or "VR" (with the "R" standing for "Return," because "VD" has other connotations). You're accompanied to the border and bid farewell. The second alternative is an administrative hearing for purposes of official deportation, with detainment in the meantime. Returning to this country after VR has no repercussions—if caught, you're simply sent back one more time on another VR—but returning after deportation is a felony. Thus, for Mexican citizens, this particular decision is pretty easy. However, VR isn't an option for anyone other than a Mexican national.

These two upper-crust Mexicans would get to Europe sooner or later, as all of us sitting there knew. Talk about a game. They'd take the VR, recross the border to obtain a visa or, conceivably, try the border-passing card once again and avoid this checkpoint. Santos told me that if anything like this inconvenience had happened in Mexico, this pair would have simply slipped the officer a bribe and been on their way. I made some remark to the effect that O.J. Simpson might be able to buy his way out of a murder conviction right here in the United States, and I added that Texas mythology features numerous high-profile defendants who murder a wealthy spouse and beat the rap. "In Mexico," Santos said quickly, "O.J. wouldn't even have come to trial." Everyone present, including our detainees, nodded in agreement.

Suddenly, Santos and the young man got into an intense discussion in my language about the continuing repercussions of the Mexican-American War, which broke out in 1846 upon Texas's annexation by the United States, and it seemed to me that Santos was getting the upper hand. Somehow this debate led to his next remark, directed at me, to the effect that should he, a generic Mexican-American, be seated in an upscale restaurant in Ciudad Juárez, while I and my party of Anglos were seated at an adjacent table, he would wait for service, and wait, and wait, while my group would be treated with extreme courtesy. Mexicans employ the term "pocho" for Mexican-Americans; it means, literally, "to lose its color," and it's a slur.

After more than an hour, the man and woman were led back to the cells. No big deal, of course, since they'd be driven to El Paso and released, but they did look a little cowed at the prospect of cell time. Santos then revealed to me his proposed solution to the whole problem along the international border: charge our neighboring government $200 for each illegal alien sent back home. I immediately pointed out one problem with this plan: the matter of collection. Bill Clinton had just loaned Mexico the famous $20 billion to bail out the peso and, maybe more to the point, American investors. The ensuing discussion produced no clear winner; the night's work, no more detainees and no contraband.

CHAPTER 13

In Luby's Cafeteria in El Paso, where I enjoyed my Thanksgiving repast one fine year, the mother at the next table unloaded the dishes off their trays and arranged the flatware for her two small boys, then said to them and the girl, who was either an older daughter or a much younger sister, "Well, Happy Thanksgiving, everyone . . . isn't this pitiful . . . not really, this is fine."

But it wasn't fine; it *was* pitiful, and their faces agreed. What circumstances compelled them to celebrate their holiday on the cheap at Luby's? The possibilities are as numerous as the sands of the seven seas. A more intrusive reporter might have stepped forward to ask the de facto head of household what series of misfortunes had recently befallen her family, but I wasn't going to do it. But if I *had*, this young mother probably would have answered if she'd been able to maneuver the kids out of the way. In my experience, most people are more than willing to confide in perfect strangers. Bob Smithers, the hitchhiker I carried to Colorado City, is one example. Another is Holly, at the El Camino Motel in Sierra Blanca, with her courageous story. For my own part, my failures in baby-making had been known to only a few of my friends, but I don't mind writing about them in this book. Why shouldn't I? We're *strangers*, so where's the risk? Only true strangers can be counted on not to care, not to pretend otherwise, and most important, to extend the basic milk of human kindness anyway, no strings attached.

Regarding the woman sitting alone with her tray in the far corner of Luby's who kept looking at me as we ate, I thought I knew what brought her to the cafeteria on the holiday: nothing. She was just horribly lonely; this was the cause of the rapacity in her eyes, which I had to avoid because I was deep in consideration of this unrelated question: would term limits be good for those of us in the note-taking classes, too, for political and literary theorists, for philosophers, essayists, and everyone else in the thinking and chattering mode? After twelve years, or even eight, it's certain that you're the rare one who has a new idea. We feel sorry for the mathematicians who are all done with their truly original work by the age of thirty and hang on for decades as teachers, and we assume that chronological age is the barrier, that the gray matter has dried out. But the real problem may be *length of service*. Mathematicians almost always begin their work very young, often in college. Twelve years later, they've thought all they're going to think regarding numbers. The difference between them and the philosophers is that they know they're washed up. Equations don't lie; sentences can and do.

After those proverbial twelve years, or merely eight, what has happened is this: belief has finally crowded out ideas. Krishnamurti finally arrived at his belief about contradiction—a good one, I believe—after years of studiously avoiding all other beliefs. He didn't read books. Other thinkers and professional chatterers hold out as long as they can, too, but then they succumb and any original thought congeals into turgid proclamation, which they publish time and again, shifting things around. Meanwhile, painters, composers, choreogra-

phers, and architects may get better with decades of season-
ing, and often do. Doesn't this settle the debate about how
much these arts have to do with thinking per se? I believe so.
Only poets and novelists remain a problem: some get better;
most don't. But most of the latter weren't all that good to
begin with.

Anyway, once you've selected your Thanksgiving dishes off
the commercial steam table at Luby's,* and especially if you're
in the habit of taking and then developing notes for a living,
these are the kinds of considerations likely to clog the brain
and perhaps depress the mind. Meanwhile, my wife was enjoy-
ing a great holiday feast with friends back in Dallas—and during an exciting ice storm, too, as I saw on television at the
Motel 6 during the broadcast of the annual Thanksgiving Day
game pitting the Cowboys against the Detroit Lions, the one in
which 'boys lineman Leon Lett makes the famous, terrible
blunder of going after Detroit's almost-last-second blocked
field goal. Don't touch the ball or tackle any Lion who does,
and Dallas takes possession. But Leon grabs the ball himself,
then fumbles. Free ball! Detroit falls on it, calls time, sets up
for another icy three-pointer, and wins. I watched from the
mattress in amazement but not disappointment. I hate the
Cowboys. "America's Team"? What short memories we have.

On the bright side that holiday weekend, I had an appointment for lunch the following day with Cormac McCarthy, and
how many people can make that claim? My slight advantage is
that I have the same editor as the famous and elusive novelist
from Tennessee who now lives in El Paso, and when I asked
our editor whether Cormac might be bothered to join me for
coffee, he said give it a shot but call in the morning, when Cormac might pick up. I wanted to meet the novelist for two reasons. First, he writes the most sheerly beautiful sentences of
anyone working in English today. Even if you don't take to
certain of the books, you have to agree with this.† Second, he

---

*Don't get me wrong. This is an excellent chain, as everyone in Texas knows.
†For example, from *All the Pretty Horses*: "Shrouded in the black thunder-
heads the distant lightning glowed mutely like welding seen through foundry

doesn't give a damn whether you agree or not; he doesn't care whether you like his sentences or his books. Does Cormac entertain any notion of writing for the pleasure and satisfaction of his *audience*? He didn't have one to speak of until *All the Pretty Horses*, when he consented to one widely read interview in *The New York Times Magazine*, and then he turned around and wrote an obstreperous sequel. Intentionally, in my opinion. I think he *fought back* with *The Crossing*.* We're always reading about various stars, including writers out on the farthest edge of that constellation, who decide they need to reinvent themselves when the market seems to have lost interest in an earlier incarnation. Cormac isn't about to reinvent himself for God, much less for you and me.

In preparation for my phone call, I worked out a one-sentence introduction into which I squeezed every germane fact and association. Then, the damnedest thing! Nicest guy in the world! Coffee, hell, Cormac said immediately, let's go for some Mexican food. We met at a convenient rendezvous, and when Cormac saw my Japanese courser I discerned surprise and maybe a little disdain. But he recovered quickly and politely invited me to join him in the pickup instead, and we drove to a restaurant down the mountainside from the Spanish architecture of the University of Texas at El Paso, from where we looked farther down toward the high chain-link fence at the Rio Grande (always in the top ten for most polluted river in the country, and number one in 1993); across to Old Mexico, as we called that other country years ago; and beyond to the Juarez Country Club on a distant hill, where Cormac had played golf. Otherwise, I can't say much about either that meal or our conversation. Wouldn't dream of it. This man doesn't want that kind of cheap publicity. Though I will say this: I've finally met someone perhaps even more doubtful than I regarding the future of the well-written word. I don't feel it's an

---

smoke." So far, so good. Then: "As if repairs were under way in some flawed place in the iron dark of the world."

*Or is this wishful thinking? *The Crossing* was well beyond first draft by the time *Horses* was published.

indiscretion to report this much. When I suggested over coffee and flan that in a generation or two there might not be a critical mass of readers who can handle embedded subordinate clauses such as these, Cormac said forget that, there won't be any writers worth the wait.

I recalled this conversation days later in the Singing Wind Book Shop, which Winn Bundy has operated for twenty years out of a wing of her ranch house east of Tucson. Cormac recommended the shop, and as his luncheon companion maybe I enjoyed a certain cachet there. Still I had to wait around to speak with the proprietor while she introduced two young German women to the collection stuffed into the shop's two rooms, and the two rooms took about ten minutes, since the organization on those groaning shelves defies anyone's understanding except, apparently, Winn's own. Then came my turn for the tour, and then I browsed while Winn sat on the floor with her cash box and laboriously sold several books to the foreigners, with whom this shop is very popular. Winn has a great place and, I suspect, a great business. You're not likely to go to the trouble to find it down a back road a few miles off the interstate and then leave empty-handed. Nature titles and Arizoniana are her most popular, and Janice Bowers's *Full Life in a Small Place: And Other Essays from a Desert Garden* might be her biggest seller of all. Covers are more important than they used to be, Winn said, because younger readers—anyone under forty?—need something "more instant" to relate to; likewise, short titles are more appealing than ever, with the exception, I suppose, of *Full Life in a Small Place: And Other Essays from a Desert Garden*.

New Mexico is neither Old Mexico nor plain Mexico. There's ample evidence that many people are confused on this point, which confusion I first encountered while waiting for a Fed-Ex package at a friend's second home north of Taos. When I called to check on the delayed shipment, the clerk said something like, "Let's see, New Mexico . . . so this is international."

I paused, uncomprehending. "No, *New* Mexico."

He paused, also uncomprehending. Then he said, "Yeah, New *Mexico*."

The following day, still waiting for the same package, I called the "800" number again and was routed to the same man at the same substation somewhere in the United States, and we had the same conversation. He didn't understand that New Mexico was one of our fifty states rather than one of Mexico's twenty-two, and I'm not sure I ever convinced him, although I did finally get the package. When I reported the story to my host, this cynical plaintiff's attorney directed me to the back page of the *New Mexico* magazines lying in the wicker basket on the table in front of the fireplace. Every month that page is given over to a column titled "One of Our Fifty Is Missing," true stories about people and businesses all over the country who wonder what kind of customs forms they need for shipments to Santa Fe.*

Leaving El Paso, I drove north up I-10 and crossed the *New* Mexico border at Anthony and learned at the excellent visitors' center that I was traveling along El Camino Real, the oldest historical road in the United States, they claim, a two-thousand-mile route from Mexico City up to Taos. Spanish explorers, including Vásquez de Coronado, rode their New World horses this way, and the trail was officially established in 1598 by Juan de Oñate, the first colonizer and governor of New Mexico. Later it was called the Chihuahua Trail, since it passed through that state of Mexico. If the interstates are used metaphorically as a modern American language, then these old Indian and settlers' trails were the native American tongue. Those hunters, trappers, traders, and ancestral New Agers were the trailblazers for the interstate system, and the same geology that dictated the original routes dictated all subsequent

---

*From the June 1996 issue: informed by the Summer Olympics ticket office in Atlanta that he'd have to contact his "national committee," a volleyball fan in Santa Fe explained the situation and was transferred to a second-level supervisor, who said, "Old Mexico, New Mexico, it doesn't matter. It's still a territory of Mexico and you'll have to contact the Olympic committee office in Mexico City."

roads and highways. As noted earlier, this country's first bona fide road, the National Road, was built on top of Necomalin's Path and the Cumberland Road; on top of that, over a century later, U.S. 40 and, finally, I-70, so a tourist traveling from Pennsylvania to St. Louis today follows a very well-beaten path. Many other interstates follow the paths blazed by Indians and pioneers. I-84 out of Portland tracks the old Oregon Trail to Twin Falls, Idaho. The Mormon Pioneer Trail showed the way for a portion of I-80 in Nebraska and I-70 in Missouri. The traveler on I-80 from Nevada into San Francisco passes the bones of the thirty-four pioneers killed by an early snowfall and subsequently cannibalized just north of Lake Tahoe, less than a day's travel from the Donner party's promised land. My main route between Texas and California utilized portions of the Chihuahua, Butterfield, and Santa Fe trails, among others. Dictated by the land, those early trails and the successive roads and interstates built on top of them therefore encourage a certain geological awareness, especially when there are impediments. I-25 skirts the Rockies to the west. I-15 skirts Utah's Wasatch Range to the east; heading north, you have national forest on your right, desert on your left. In Virginia, I-81 cuts diagonally through a mountain valley, the Shenandoah Trail. Although the information at the Anthony rest area in New Mexico didn't point this out, the reason for the popularity of this particular north-south route is obvious enough: it follows the broad plain of the Rio Grande River. Always, the path of least resistance.

Is it ignorance or naïveté? I thought lush fields of grass and alfalfa were required for productive dairy farming. It hadn't occurred to me that certain desert terrains would be ideal, or that proximity to an interstate and a city would be more valuable than the finest pasturage. Nonetheless, not ten miles north of the New Mexico border, I passed off to the west mile after mile of barns and pens filled with black-and-white cows—dairy cows, I knew that much. Proceeding to the next exit, I crossed over and doubled back via the service road. The first office-looking building yielded no information in a language I could understand, but at the second stop the name "Gonzalez" registered when I asked about "the biggest of these farms," and at the third place I found Gonzalez himself—Joe Gonzalez, a youthful-looking, forty-three-year-old spare-time golfer, friendly talker, and scion of this 185-acre spread. He was wearing sneakers, blue slacks, and a pink knit golf shirt when I stuck my head in his doorway, and he looked momentarily puzzled. While he gets unannounced visitors all the time, they're usually dairymen from Europe or South America. But Joe knows his business and is pleased to inform others as well. His dad, Artemio, was and is pretty much old-school—no bovine somatotropin hormone will be given to any of his cows—and Joe appreciates this, but the old ways don't cut much mustard with the EPA or the IRS or the antidairy neighbors in Doña Ana County, so unlike his old-school father, Joe sees the need for political involvement and public relations.

To illustrate the attitude of some of these neighbors, Joe raised his voice and simpered, " 'Oh, they're smelly. Oh, there's flies. Oh, the lights are too bright. Oh, I moved out to the country and all I smell is cows.' " He shook his head and replied, " 'Well, what do you *think* is out in the country?' I had to go through all that when I went through the county commission to expand this herd. One lady, thank God, got up and said, 'I grew up on a farm. This is what a farm smells like. It brings back good memories to me. These people are good neighbors. They don't bother anybody.' But people said the cows' tails were slappin' 'em in the face. Well, the nearest of those houses is a thousand feet away! I said, 'Lady, that's an awfully long cow tail.' They don't care about how many people we employ, how much money comes and goes through here. 'Oh, no,' they say, 'it's not that kind of county.' "

I'm like Joe. I don't know where his neighbors ever got that idea. Over twenty-five thousand dairy cows, maybe close to thirty thousand, live on the thirteen farms along this three-mile stretch of I-10, and that's just the milking cows, which are joined by thousands of immature cows, young steers, and bulls. Statewide in New Mexico, over one thousand dairy farms gross about $350 million, almost seven times as much as the state's famed chiles. From the interstate down to the Rio Grande River several miles to the west is solid farmland, and farms run all the way along both sides of the river as far north as Albuquerque, well beyond Doña Ana County. Joe's father moved his operation from the Mesilla Valley down south to these sandhills in 1969, and his family feels their cows have seniority.

The lack of neighborly understanding is one thing, but what really saddens Joe is that some of his peers in the dairy and farming business consider him less a dairyman than a businessman. His father's first farm here had only three hundred cows, while the Gonzalezes now have three thousand milking Holsteins, plus one thousand calves. Joe told me, "Their attitude is, 'If you have more than fifty cows, you're not a family farm.' But we *are* a family farm. This place isn't owned by 3M or an insurance company."

Joe feels his detractors are confusing "mom-and-pop" with "family." He and his father have both worked at every last task on the dairy farm. If necessary, both could still take over any given job. Today, Joe runs the dairy operation while Art exercises the veto, dispenses old-school advice, and oversees the thousand acres of farmland along the river. His son didn't really want to reveal the precise acreage because that, too, seems to be a source of jealousy among the neighbors, some of whom started farming (though not dairy farming) years before the Gonzalezes arrived and still work only two hundred or three hundred acres, with most of that leased. Joe doesn't see any reason for undue pride in his own success—clearly he thinks of himself as a family *farmer*—but he doesn't feel like apologizing for growing the *business*, either.

The advantages of this sandhill location for dairy farms include the sandy soil, which provides good drainage, the gentle fall of the land all the way to the river, which also helps drainage, and the adjacent interstate. "The magic of trucking," as Joe puts it. Some of those trucks haul off the 180,000 pounds of milk the Gonzalez cows produce daily; others haul *in* the roughly 250,000 pounds of groceries the cows and calves and steers consume daily—silage and assorted feed grains, primarily, though Joe has also served chile waste from the plant in

Las Cruces, with no ill effects.* Another way to measure all the comings and goings—and Joe does this, reminding his neighbors and the county commissioners when necessary—is to count the $20,000-plus that changes hands daily.

The dairy farms in Doña Ana County are dry-lot farms; there's no pasturing, that is. The Gonzalez family does grow some food down by the river, but most of the green fields up by the interstate are wastewater management fields. The 180,000 pounds of milk that issues daily from the Gonzalez farm amounts to about 21,000 gallons, or seven gallons per cow. In order to accomplish that amazing feat, each cow must drink about twice that much water, some of which comes back onto the ground, and that's why a sandhill is ideal for dairying. Then there's the wastewater produced from washing down the two dairy barns. All this has to be managed carefully.

Joe invited me out of his office and into his pickup in order to show me how he goes about this: Lake Gonzalez, a lagoon almost twice as large as a football field, seventeen feet deep, and lined with three feet of clay. "Open year-round for jet skis," Joe likes to joke, but the operative idea is impermeability, ten-to-the-minus-seventh, something like that, as per the EPA. "Maybe that's overkill," he added, "but it's better to be safe than sorry." This is a food product, after all, and you have to be careful. Some kind of inspector will show up at the farm once or twice a month, but Joe doesn't complain much about the environmental and health regulations they enforce. He does feel that a milk producer such as himself who's obviously making the good faith effort to comply across the board should be given a chance to correct a problem rather than suffer a peremptory punishment, and he's usually given that opportunity. When I mentioned the New York City sludge operation near Sierra Blanca, Joe said he'd heard about it, then asked why, if the stuff is so good, they don't spread it on farms in New York? I repeated the official explanation regarding runoff and permeability factors, and he nodded with a new ap-

---

*In California, cows eat oranges, almonds, beet pulp. In Arizona, they used to feed them cantaloupes and honeydews.

preciation of the complexity of the situation. The last time he had to upgrade his own wastewater system, Joe had no choice but to call in outside experts to help with the contour design, engineering report, topographical maps, other exhibits, and data.

"That cost a little?" I asked.

He looked over sharply. "That cost a bunch."

In addition to milk and wastewater, the cows produce manure, and here the EPA regs "go a little overboard." Joe has to catalog where his manure goes—how much, how often, and where. "People don't realize, or they forget, how many millions and millions of buffalo used to run up and down this whole country. Did those buffalo hold it in? The other day I heard about the millions and millions of passenger pigeons and ducks and geese, and they fertilized as they went. When people say 'get back to nature,' they don't realize how much buffalo shit, duck shit, fish shit, and everything else was in that water. There are fewer animals on United States land now than there were two hundred years ago."

Then again, I don't want to leave the impression that Joe is incensed about the EPA. He doesn't seem like the kind of guy who gets agitated about anything. Besides, regarding the manure, in one respect Joe and his father have most of the other guys beat. The Gonzalez family owns enough farmland to handle their production of maybe fifteen tons a day. The other dairymen have to hope some farmer will haul theirs off, because they have no other use for the stuff and can't sell it; in fact, they're lucky the farmers don't charge them a fee. And the EPA is watching.

These days, Joe is primarily a paperwork man, dealing with suppliers and bankers and the government. A specialized computer program helps out, as does the accounting firm in California that handles most of the dairy farms in New Mexico. The annual payroll for Joe's thirty-plus employees is about $1.2 million. The land is still mortgaged. Even the cows are mortgaged.

"The cows?" I exclaimed.

"Oh, yeah," he said. "It's tough to get out from under. I owe six or seven million to the bank."

That's why some virus or other disease—not the EPA, not the weather, not the price of milk—is the dairyman's greatest fear. To complicate matters, the use of medicines is strictly regulated. Medicine for lactating cows must be isolated from that for nonlactating cows, not just on different shelves but in separate lockers; no antibiotics at all for lactating cows. "And these animals are mortgaged and they're falling over dead?" Joe asked rhetorically. "You've got a problem." Milk samples are pulled at any time by state and federal authorities to check for proscribed medicines, bacteria, protein level, butterfat, somatic cell count, and something called sediment. "I don't even know what that is—dirt, I guess—but they're checking for it," Joe said. It's against the law for Joe to walk into his barn and dip out a gallon of fresh milk for family use, even though this country was raised on unpasteurized milk.

Our tour of the farm completed, Joe and I stood beside one of the pens and he said, "Now, listen. What do you hear?"

After a few moments I said, "Well, I hear the interstate."

"That's right. We've got three thousand milk cows here. You hear any of *them*?"

I didn't. Suddenly it seemed eerily quiet on the Gonzalez dairy farm. "They're happy," Joe continued with genuine satisfaction. "They're contented. A cow moos when something is going on. Why should they moo here? The water's at the end of the pen, shade's in the middle, food at the other end, not too many predators chasing you down and tearing you limb from limb. Hey, life's pretty good here."

The career of his dairy cows may be pleasant enough, I'll give Joe that, but it's also brief. Maybe his (and the bank's) animals don't realize just how limited a life span they have before them. The aggressive dairyman is through with a cow after three lactations, when she's five years old. The problem for this cow is that at five years or even seven or eight years, she's still a perfectly good dairy cow, just not as good as her daughters who are pumping out seventy pounds a day, say, while her own production may have dropped to fifty. Many of Joe Gonzalez' neighbors "beef their cows"—that's one phrase, "go to McDonald's" is another—at fifty pounds, but Joe, who is softhearted, won't let them go until they drop to thirty pounds.

"That's just us," he said sheepishly. He even has a few favorite cows still producing at twelve years. Still, one hundred cows a month go to McDonald's from the Gonzalez farm. This surprised me. Who knew that half the nation's hamburger meat is retired dairy cows? Any prime steaks? Not likely, Joe said. Maybe the flank steak or rump roast from a young one. Obviously, the male calves produced by the dairy cows are castrated and raised for beef. Joe used to ship them out, but now he's experimenting with raising some steers himself, to see how the economics play out.

The famous price support enjoyed by dairymen is a nonfactor here in New Mexico and has been for years, in Joe's view. On the day we spoke, that support was set at $10.10 for one hundred pounds, but the co-op was paying Joe $11.20. Joe also laughs at the benefits received from what he refers to as his contribution to the Gramm-Rudman thing, known in Washington, D.C., as the budget reconciliation assessment. It comes down to this: with the Gramm-Rudman budget contrivances of the eighties, farmers were given a choice between lower price support levels and annual assessments against their earnings, all in the interest of saving about $700 million for the years 1991 to 1995. This was a lose-lose proposition for the dairy farmers, but for complicated accounting reasons the assessments are the better deal. Joe pays five, six, seven thousand dollars a month under this arrangement, and that's just one of the deductions noted on the check he receives from his co-op. There are others for promotion, midmonth advance, hauling, capital retains, and operations, not to mention the adjustments up or down for protein, somatic, and butterfat content. This last adjustment does annoy Joe, because the premium paid for the high butterfat content of his excellent milk has been falling in recent years as the health-conscious nation, unaware of the impact of this decision on dairymen, turns to two-percent and skim.

Joe has a daughter by a previous marriage who lives with her mother in Tucson, without any expressed interest in her father's dairy farm. At any rate, he told me, she doesn't write home and ask, "Dear Dad, How are the cows today?" His son is a part-time college student who wants to attend the Naval

Academy and become a pilot or an engineer. Go for it, Joe told him, or you can always enlist. Oh, no, Joseph Michael demurred, I'm not going in as a grunt. Joe's sister Maria, who works with him in the office, has three daughters; his sister Gloria worked in the office until it was clear there wasn't really enough work for all three of them ("Family is family, but business is *business*!"), and she has a daughter and a son; his sister Iris, a nurse in Las Cruces, has one son and a baby on the way; and his brother, Art Jr., who works on the family farms, has three daughters. Not one of these younger Gonzalezes will pursue a life in dairy farming, not that Joe can see.

Hearing this recitation, I sensed the opportunity to pump Joe for conclusions about dire generational change, declining work habits, and the like—in short, the slacker issue previously introduced by Bob Popplewell at the rattlesnake ranch. While Joe was willing to concede that the idea of working seven days a week, 365 days a year, might have lost some of its romance for the younger set, he thought he had a better explanation for what was going on. "I was working with my dad since I was eight years old. He'd take me out to bring the cows to the barn. He was in a one-man barn, and he could bring my brother and me into the business *with him*. But it's not the same now. I'm busy in here with all the management stuff. Was my son going to hang around the office with me, watch me answer the phone and go to the bank? No. You've got to learn the roots of the business."

Joe could only hand Joseph Michael over to one of the herdsmen and say, "Make sure he works," and that's not an apprenticeship. Therefore, Joe concludes, the main reason this generation of Gonzalez kids is uninterested in dairy farming is that they didn't have the right kind of opportunity to *become* interested in the first place. Without hands-on, family-oriented involvement, a long-hours and unglamorous occupation like dairy farming couldn't possibly compete with, say, jet piloting. In twenty or thirty years, when he retires, Joe Gonzalez will probably have to sell out. Thus the dairy farm that began as an honest-to-god mom-and-pop deal, then became a family farm, then a family enterprise, might indeed end up as something very like agribusiness.

A dozen miles north of Joe's place, I had a decision to make. You don't have many of these on the interstates out west, but the ones you get tend to be big. At Las Cruces, I-10 turns left and proceeds to Los Angeles. The alternative is straight ahead, north on I-25 to Buffalo, Wyoming, and the convergence with I-90. Hang a left at Buffalo, another at Billings, Montana, right at Butte on I-15 to Great Falls, right on Highway 87 to Havre, then east on 2, then south down 240 to Bear's Paw battle-ground, where the immortal Chief Joseph of the Nez Perce handed over his rifle and declared, "I will fight no more forever."

Left or straight? West or north? My official and usual route was west, but one time I did go north. To my left, the stark silhouette of a mountain range at night; underneath, rutted asphalt, which didn't surprise me because New Mexico highways have always had a terrible reputation. Not enough money in the coffers. At the Border Patrol checkpoint south of Truth or Consequences, I was all alone as I glided by the row of orange traffic cones, pulled into primary, and went forward with a scheme concocted to yield a guaranteed detour into secondary and a canine search, if the dog was on duty. I just wanted to experience it. I knew about this checkpoint from Mike Jackson in Sierra Blanca, and had already allowed my beard to produce an unsightly stubble, which it does with ease. Now I reached back for the baseball cap with the phony pony-tail acquired for some such purpose at the airport in Denver. I adopted what I believed was a furtive visage. At the stop sign, I averted my eyes, signified to the agent working the point that my driver's side window wouldn't roll down, and with an intentional yet apparently inadvertent gesture directed his attention to the just-acquired stick of powerful air freshener hanging from the rearview mirror.

But the guy never hesitated. "Go ahead," he said with a dismissive wave of his left hand. How did he know? My respect for the acumen of the Border Patrol agents—high already—was now stratospheric.

Also that night, I saw the sign for Radium Springs and

regretted missing Radium Springs itself, even though it's not related to the Trinity Site. That first atomic explosion was triggered seventy or so miles up ahead and off to the right in the forbidding Jornada del Muerto, not far from the proposed temporary nuclear waste dump on the tribal turf of the Mescalero Apaches. The project manager at the dump was none other than Silas Cochise, a great-grandson of the Chiricahua chief I revere now, as in my youth. Almost no Anglo in that resort area wants anything to do with nuclear waste, but Cochise's forces had won the latest election on this issue. To his eternal credit, Joseph Geronimo, another elder and a grandson of my absolutely favorite Apache chief, opposed the project. In any event, it would be years, if ever, before the first neutron or neuron decayed on tribal lands.

According to the sign, Truth or Consequences, where I spent that night in New Mexico, has seventeen gas stations, nineteen restaurants, twenty-six motels, and fifteen campgrounds—on a par with Van Horn, with more motels but fewer restaurants. And one of these days Ralph Edwards will pass away, bless his soul, and when that happens the town might revert to its real name, Hot Springs, or, better yet, its earliest Anglo name, Geronimo Springs, and once again deserve its place in history as one of the great chief's favorite spas. This new-name business got started in 1950, when Ralph decided that some town in the United States should rename itself in honor of his popular radio program. In return, the star promised to bring in his Hollywood revue on an annual basis. A wacky idea, to be sure, but a significant portion of Hot Springs, New Mexico, happened to be suffering from a serious identity crisis at the time. They had these great hot springs and this wonderful climate—perfect, really, in all four seasons— but nobody had ever heard of the place, which had been "plodding along slowly," to quote the tourist newsletter I picked up at the Chamber of Commerce, and desperately needed something to set it apart from all the other towns named Hot Springs in the country, especially Hot Springs, Arkansas. Citizens understood that there were no fewer than thirty Hot Springs in California alone, although Rand McNally muddies the water here. The index cites only four towns—one each in Montana, South Dakota, Virginia, and, of course, Arkansas—as well as a county in Wyoming, home of the world's largest hot springs at Thermopolis. No Hot Springs at all are listed in California.

Still, this argument helped carry the day overwhelmingly for the new name in 1950. Fourteen years later they had a much closer election, 891 to 762. This election was contested, ballots were impounded, and a third election was held nineteen months later, with Truth or Consequences winning again, 839 to 735. Thirty-one years later, forty-five years after the initial vote, the clerk in Martha's Variety Store said the name's still dorky and she would vote to change it back, but not until Ralph passes on. I heard this opinion all over town, although I'm sure there are plenty of Babbitts to defend the abomination. The fellow handing out the literature at the tourist office dodged my clearly biased query and merely noted that Hollywood can do wonders for your looks. Ralph Edwards still returns to Truth or Consequences the first week in May with an entourage of stars fresh off the set of the reruns of "Hollywood Squares," and he does look remarkably like the man with the receding hairline whose photograph graces the first issue of the Truth or Consequences *Herald*. Still, even speaking as one who's always looking for a nice place to call home, I wouldn't live here. "Dorky" is way too complimentary for this name. Nor am I sure it hasn't backfired, because the passing motorist on I-25 who hasn't read the literature or studied the points of interest on the map wouldn't have a clue about the hot springs—to my knowledge, the only ones located on an interstate highway anywhere in the lower 48.

Truth or Consequences is "nestled," as they always say, in the valley of the Rio Grande, but its valleylike qualities are overwhelmed by the mountainlike competitors. With Turtleback Mountain and a couple of other modest desert peaks looming on various horizons, it's a shock to pull into the modest little town park and find yourself suddenly looking at the famous river, which at this point in its brown flow is about thirty yards wide. To all appearances a natural, free-flowing river, in fact it has just flowed out of Elephant Butte Reservoir to the north and is about to be curtailed by the Caballo

Reservoir to the south. Ted Turner has acquired a large part of the former Spanish land grant on the east side of Elephant Butte and runs some buffalo over there. Bass fishing in both of these lakes is famous, as I learned from the waitress in the Blue Note café, who had left this, her hometown, twenty years earlier and just returned a year before, mainly for the fishing. Nothing had changed during her absence, she assured me, *nothing*, and indeed in my drive around I found nothing to contradict her, except for the Blue Note itself. "It's pretty new," I said, and she said, "It is in *this* town." When I asked about the hot springs, she said she hadn't made it to any of them yet. "There's so much else to do around here!" She and her husband must really like to fish, I decided.

Geronimo Springs, the specific springs in which the chief is supposed to have taken his ease, is now in the middle of town, encased in brickwork, covered by a pavilion, decorated with ceramic pots holding cacti, and lighted at night. Not open for business, alas, bathing-wise, though seven other venues were when I was there. The clerk at the Bath House Motel informed me that several other establishments had recently closed and advised caution because some of the remaining facilities have only a large public pool, and he knew of two cases of female infection and one of a scabieslike outbreak on a man's back. He could confidently recommend only the private tubs at his own place and at the Artesia Bath House and Trailer Court, one street over. Bathhouse *and* trailer court? I sought out the Artesia, and on that splendid late-winter morning I met owner Ellie Martin. She was wearing a Harvard sweatshirt because one of her daughters-in-law is from Boston. Ellie's father had moved here in 1978, then she and her husband moved down from Iowa and bought the Artesia in 1982. Now her husband has passed away, and the place is all hers. Two of Ellie's children also live in Truth or Consequences and help out, mainly on Wednesday, her day off. Ellie lives in the mobile home next to the bathhouse, and both have a front porch with wood trim.

As the name might imply, the Artesia is the sort of place where the snowbird residents of the trailer court sweep the gravel in front of their RVs at 10:30 in the morning as spouses emerge wearing terrycloth bathrobes and hair curlers and walk across to the bathhouse to soak in a private tub. Prices are extremely reasonable to begin with—$3 for a single tub, $6 for a double, $2 apiece for seniors—and residents of the court get a discount off the discount, paying only $1. The thirty-seven hookups at Ellie's two adjacent courts are full throughout the winter. She gets the same people year after year, most because they wouldn't dream of stepping foot in one of the large public pools. I didn't say a word about what I'd heard regarding infections, but the collective memory on the front porch goes much further back anyway. Ellie's clients became committed to the idea of private tubs as soon as Rock Hudson announced he had AIDS, shortly before he died in 1985.

This front porch is the hearth at the Artesia. There's a variety of chairs, including a row of old movie-theater seats with red leather cushions and wooden backs. In this climate, they will be preserved forever. The ambience, if I may call it that, is as cozy and comfortable as you can get after a long soak in the tub on these perfectly warm, dry days. All things considered, I couldn't see any reason to visit any of the other springs in town.

My fellow patrons included two couples from Canada via Texas, the women dressed for church in the middle of the week, and another lady in tiger-skin pants who without explanation squeezed the toe of my sneaker as she walked past. In some context I mentioned to this group the Conrad N. Hilton shrine back in Cisco, Texas, eight miles from "Shorty" Kendrick's religious diorama. This handsome red-brick, two-story building with a portico running most of its length was the first establishment owned by Conrad N. Hilton. The great man came to Cisco during the oil boom of 1919 with $5,000 and every intention of purchasing a bank in order to "launch big ships where the water was deep"—a facetious remark, we may assume, referring to the economic prospects afforded by the oil field and by Cisco's location at the intersection of the north-south rails of the old Texas Central Railroad and the east-west rails of the old Texas and Pacific Railroad. Once he learned that the Mobley Hotel was renting each of its forty rooms in eight-hour shifts and was booked solid twenty-four hours every day, he bought the hotel instead. The rest is history, and you can read and see all about it right there. A grant of $1.2 million from the Conrad N. Hilton Foundation paid for the renovation and conversion of the Mobley into the Conrad N. Hilton Memorial Park and Community Center. On the second floor there's a one-room museum and in another room a large-screen television showing a series of short features on the life and work of Conrad N. Hilton, including his first hotel. A small auditorium in the building is sold out quite a few weekends a year for musicals, some locally produced and cast, others attracting professional talent from all over Texas and, one summer, a director from New York with extensive off-Broadway experience.

I had seen the place with my own eyes, I knew what I was talking about, but I was nevertheless challenged on the porch in front of Ellie's artesian baths. One of the ladies went off to get her book on the subject, and subsequent study revealed that in San Antonio, New Mexico, right up I-25, Conrad had worked in his *father's* hotel, then became his business partner in 1915, and only then moved to Cisco and opened his *own* hotel in 1919.

Ellie surveyed the trailers in front of us, conjured in the recesses of her mind the ones on the other side of the bathhouse, and came up with Michigan, Manitoba, Colorado, Saskatchewan, Texas, Nebraska, California, Montana, Washington, Arizona, North Dakota, and even New Mexico as the home states of these winter residents. One couple from Michigan had been coming since day one, 1982, but this would be their last year. Eight trailers are full-time residents, and some others leave their trailers on a year-round basis, because this is cheaper and more convenient than hauling them back and forth. One trailer belongs to the man I met who builds wooden screens here from April through November and then travels around the world for four months. He can afford this partly because his hookup is only $60 a month. For her winter residents, Ellie will store their trailers over the summer for just $25 a month.

Most of the coaches and trailers at Ellie's place are of the modest variety—no Newells or Prevosts at the Artesia, and I'm not sure they could squeeze in anyway—but there was one

King of the Road, a thirty-four-foot fifth-wheel trailer towed behind a powerful pickup.* Bunk Smith owns this King parked directly in front of the bathhouse. A retired cotton farmer from Spur, Texas, Bunk now lives with his wife, Geneva, at the Artesia in the winter and in Lamesa, Texas, in the summer. Geneva had gone shopping. The Smiths had recently celebrated their fifty-fifth wedding anniversary, and fish less than they used to. Bunk showed me inside the house, which could be acquired secondhand, he guessed, for about $35,000. Inside, the King isn't the Newell, but it's plenty nice, especially with the slide-out section in the living room; some Kings feature a second slide-out in the bedroom. Wood decor and plentiful knickknacks. Bunk opened the sparkling-clean oven and said, "We keep the Christmas gifts in here." So he and Geneva don't eat in very often. And what about all the clothes hanging in the shower? I didn't care to ask.

All day long, folks came and went from the tubs at the Artesia. Most walked up from their coaches and trailers, others pulled up in their cars, perhaps flea market aficionados or shoppers returning from Santa Fe. One day, during a rare blizzard in Truth or Consequences, a Nebraska couple took it upon themselves to count the different state license plates stopping at the Artesia and came up with thirty-six, or maybe it was thirty-eight, plus New Mexico. Almost all the philosophes on the front porch agreed that Truth or Consequences is a dorky name at best. Ellie thinks the change has cost her business, if she needed business.

The eight tubs in her bathhouse run along a central walkway decorated with assorted homilies, instructions, and warnings about blood pressure. A few days before my arrival they had a baptism in #8, with fifteen to twenty onlookers crowded into that small space. My single tub was painted turquoise and white. The water from the springs, 108 degrees on Monday, Ellie said, might have been a little cooler by that Thursday. I

---

*A "trailer" is any domicile towed by a car or pickup; a "motor home" is self-propelled; the Newell class is a "motor coach." Any of the hundreds of makes and models of these formats can be labeled RVs, of which there are nine million in the United States.

was certain. But no matter the temperature, it contains an impressive list of thirty-eight minerals, including lead, and maybe a little extra lead, too, depending on the content of the paint peeling in my tub. A window is set high in the wall, and directly above the tub is a cold-water shower. A two-foot section of PVC pipe fits snugly into the drain hole, serving as both stopper and overflow outlet. One of the full-time Artesia residents swears this water has done more for her arthritis than all the medicines she'd taken for years and years. The discussion on the front porch often turns to these medicinal benefits, and also to organs gone haywire, medicinal teas, potassium, the leaching effects of caffeine on calcium. When I said if this water is good enough for Geronimo, it's good enough for me, everyone nodded. No one has a harsh word to say about Geronimo, not anymore.

Ellie owns three wells: one right in front of the bathhouse, another in the middle of the parking lot, protected from the bumpers by a steel cage, and a third out back. The one in front is sixty-five years old and 211 feet deep, and anyone at all is free to tap it for drinking water. Technically, any well that flows freely is artesian and these three wells are the only true artesians in town, Ellie claimed. Every other bathhouse has to pump the water, and some have to heat it, too. However, there *could be* a great many little artesians, because you can dig a hole in the ground around Truth or Consequences and hot water might bubble forth. That's why it's impossible to grow fruit trees here. The water is good for humans, death for many plants. But even though the springs at the Artesia are truly artesian, their volume does vary considerably. When the Rio Grande drops in the fall, the flow here drops, too, from one hundred gallons per minute to less than half that. The water feeding the hot springs is sucked into the river instead, somehow.

Driving north out of Truth or Consequences, I did find Bob Sundown. People in town had told me about this old goat who for thirty-six years has been riding in a covered wagon all around the West, and who'd been in town yesterday and said he was heading north on the interstate. I found him plodding along ten miles away. I almost missed him, which goes to show my mellow and distracted mood that afternoon. The Artesia will do that for you. A covered wagon pulled by a team of burros is a hard sight to miss on any road, but I was passing the wagon at seventy-five when I woke up to its presence, quickly pulled onto the shoulder, then eased backwards before stopping fifty yards short. I didn't want to start a stampede.

I reached my hand up to the driver's seat and introduced myself as Bob reached down to shake hands, friendly enough. I asked him if "Sundown" was his real surname or just his stage name, so to speak. "Well," he replied, "it was my mother's name, too."

He was seventy-four years old, the same as my father, and had also served in the South Pacific—except in the Marines, not the Navy. In recent years he'd driven his wagon up to the guardhouse at various bases around the country and been given the brush-off until he invoked the name of Colonel So-and-So and said, "You call him and tell him ol' Bob Sundown's out here to see him." Then he'd always get in.

Bob gets up every morning and thinks what a great world this is because the mind can do anything it wants. It can even free him from the noise of the interstate as motorists rip past not eight feet off the port side. Bob had had a heart attack not six weeks before I met him and had survived that encounter with the medical establishment. His dog, Sky, is a fifteen-year-old Scottish Highlander, a beautiful, sweet creature. Bob's wagon, covered with coils of wire, rope, hoses, shovels, and other gear, was made for him by some kids taking one of his survival classes in Flagstaff, Arizona, five or six years before. He has one daughter. His wife died in a car crash. His Coleman lantern is powered by ordinary unleaded fuel because the Coleman fuel sold in the hardware stores is a rip-off at $5. A thirty-gallon oil drum serves nicely as a wood-burning stove. Two of the finest rifles ever made offer protection from thieves. Burros are superior both to horses, which are too flighty, and to donkeys, which are good for a week or two when they're likely to light out across the desert *or* the highway. Yes, Bob sticks to the back roads whenever possible, but the inclines of maybe fifteen degrees around here are too much for his animals. He likes Ronald Reagan, a president who knew which side the bread is buttered on; that peanut vendor was okay; Bush tried, that's about all you can say for him; this draft dodger is a scum-sucking bastard.

So Bob does keep up. He figures war may soon erupt between the people in this country who want freedom and those who don't; and even though he learned a lot of survival skills in the First Marines Recon, he wants to be so far away when it happens that they'll have to pump in the sunlight.* One man gave him two $100 bills, the most he has collected by way of donations from any individual. He has only the one good eye; the left socket is completely grown over. Bob himself is small and grizzled and heading home to Salmon, Idaho. He says he's been written about in *Time*, *Life*, and other places, and I'm taking his word for it. Christianity is the biggest bunch of hooey he's ever heard, although he certainly believes in The Man Upstairs.

I had commenced this roadside conversation with Bob without benefit of either tape recorder or notepad, thinking that the least little sign of transcription would spook the old bird and I'd miss my story entirely, so I'd just talk and listen and make notes from memory in the car. Five seconds after Bob started talking, I groaned. What a mistake. Plant a tape on this talker and run the results verbatim. But then I decided that Bob's a back-roads kind of guy, anyway, really doesn't belong in my interstate book at all, lucky to get this much coverage. And "coverage" it was. Bob has the eye for publicity. He's backwoods and back-roads but by no means backwards.

I donated five bucks and drove on, skipping San Antonio and whatever they might have over there about Conrad N. Hilton and his father. In fact, I skipped almost everything that Friday afternoon and evening, and one of the few places I did visit, the famous migratory fowl refuge at Apache del Bosque, was practically empty except for the snow geese. The mild win-

---

*This was before Oklahoma City; I wonder what he made of that.

ter had already lured the birds of another feather back north. I skipped the Madonna of the Trail statue in Albuquerque—for the good reason that, at the time, I didn't know it was there—and drove straight to the Motel 6 in Santa Fe, registered, and learned that the new European ownership of the "6" chain is phasing out the use of married couples as managers—a major mistake, to my mind. The following night I stayed with friends north of Santa Fe in Abiquiu, the adopted home of Georgia O'Keeffe.* These friends couldn't live more differently from the way my wife and I go about it. Transplanted New Yorkers, they leave the Chama River Valley as seldom as possible and live in the adobe house they built on their land by the river, probably the warmest home I've ever been in, figuratively speaking; and literally, too, given the tremendous insulating properties of adobe. They're both fine painters who don't sell enough pictures to make a living, who work elsewhere and farm and sell organic mushrooms and enjoy a sense of being *here* and belonging *here* that I can only wonder at.

I had vivid and remarkable dreams that night in their home—all the mushrooms we had with dinner, I guess. Early the next morning, one of the dogs barked—probably Ray Charles, the black Lab, a remarkable patriarch who lies so close to the wood-burning stove that his skull becomes hot to the touch—and this caravan of one moved on. Not north toward the Bear's Paw battleground, however, but back east in the general direction of "home."

———

*Abiquiu is *not* Albuquerque misspelled. Even many *New* Mexicans, including the woman working the desk at Apache del Bosque, don't know about Abiquiu and think you're a hick from Texas who can't pronounce Albuquerque.

CHAPTER 14

At the interstate exchange north of Joe Gonzalez' dairy farm, turn west and stay on I-10 in order to visit historic Mesilla, former regional headquarters of the old Butterfield Overland Mail and Stage Line that ran from St. Louis to San Francisco in the late 1850s, a forerunner of the Pony Express. Before the railroad bypassed Mesilla in favor of Las Cruces, four miles to the north, this little settlement was the largest town between San Antonio, Texas, and San Diego. The square here is a very fine old square, overrun with tourists, of course, who buy mostly Tony Hillerman's Navajo mysteries in the quaint bookshop. South of the square is La Posta, the only way station from the Butterfield Trail days still standing with its original adobe walls, now a Mexican restaurant with a large tank of piranhas, cages of tropical birds, and a waiting list of one hour. William H. "Billy the Kid" Bonney, Kit Carson, Pancho Villa, and Douglas MacArthur all slept here. Down the street is the old courthouse where Billy was tried and sentenced to hang for killing Sheriff Brady. Billy was then transported to jail in Lincoln, north of Ruidosa in a valley of the Capitan Mountains, where he escaped after gratuitously violent encounters with lawmen. The Kid was out of control. Several weeks later, on the evening of July 14, 1881, at Fort Sumner, ninety miles northeast of Mesilla on Highway 60/84, he was shot and killed by Pat Garrett, whose job this was.

You can read about Billy the Kid* all over the Southwest, because of the little local museums. Every town has a scattering of residents who are proud enough to commemorate its history in some way, even if by now these caretakers are at least fifty years old. You don't see much of America's youth in such venues. What happens when today's generation passes on? Well, I can't picture the kids taking over. And what about *new* history? What could happen today that would be commemorated a century hence? Maybe *this* will turn out to be the real "end of history" everybody was yammering about several years ago. In the Southwest, the Spanish are long gone, the Mexicans aren't going to invade, at least not officially, and not enough Indians are left to go on the warpath. Texans sometimes talk about splitting into five states, but that isn't going to happen either, though perhaps it could, because the annexation resolution passed by Congress and approved in Texas in 1845 granted the newest state this option. What's to change out here, really, beyond the transformation of the land from ranches to game preserves, as discussed? I believe you could plausibly argue that, as history, the past is more interesting than the present or the future will ever be. You probably could convince me that we'll never replace Billy the Kid and his kind.

West of Mesilla on I-10 is more of the classic basin-and-range geology encountered back in Texas; broad alluvial plains with isolated fault block mountain formations holding gold, silver, lead, zinc, copper, tungsten, and other valuables. There's also a tourist store with lots of rattlesnake stuff, but it's not a patch on Bob Popplewell's. What else? Tumbleweeds

---

*Including the dispute over his actual surname.

stacked against the barbed-wire fence on the north (leeward) side of the interstate; everywhere, trails once ridden by Geronimo, Cochise, Manger Colorado, and Victorio on their swift ponies. Highway 11 at Deming leads south to Pancho Villa State Park, where the original bandito raided Columbus, New Mexico, on March 9, 1916, his last foray into the United States, with John "Black Jack" Pershing in fruitless pursuit.

Twenty-five miles past that exit, I-10 crosses the most un-prepossessing continental divide imaginable, no more than a degree or two of decline in a road that has been rising so gently you don't even realize you're going up until, at 4,585 feet above sea level, you realize you're now coasting oh-so-gradually back down at eighty miles an hour, the speed of choice on this stretch. Close perusal of the map reveals the nearby Rio Grande and Gila rivers as the definition of this divide: the former originating on the eastern slopes of the San Juan Mountains in southern Colorado, flowing south and east to the Gulf of Mexico; while the latter runs down the western slope of the Mimbres Mountains, flowing west to the Pacific.

A few more miles farther west, at the trucker's weigh station at mile marker 23, I met Saturnino Madero, Transportation Motor Inspector #36 for the New Mexico Department of Taxation and Revenue. Saturnino is more commonly known as a port inspector, and he was looking sharp in his sunglasses, white shirt, black pants and tie, a whistle attached to his shoulder epaulette—and with a pistol holstered at his belt, although motor inspectors are not technically law enforcement officers. If Saturnino wants to arrest a thief he calls a cop, just like the rest of us. But he could arrest a thief comfortably enough, since he was a police sergeant in Lordsburg before joining this department, in part because the pay is better at state level.

Saturnino had been working this job for only five months. During a brief break in the line of trucks, he smoked a Winston and sipped his coffee while I explained my purpose, expecting the usual, or at least initial, bureaucratic response. But Saturnino surprised me. He invited me to stand there as long as I wanted as he weighed trucks, interrogated drivers regarding their log books and copious documentation, checked for cracked wheel rims, loose lug nuts, busted air hoses, and other safety violations of which the driver himself might be unaware. When a grandmother pulled through, I suddenly realized that there seem to be more of them than granddads hauling freight these days. So I asked Saturnino. He said, after a long pause to think about it, maybe so.

Normally, the weight limit for trucks in New Mexico is 21,600 pounds per single axle and 34,320 pounds per tandem axle (two adjacent axles). But if the two axles of your rear tandem are separated by anywhere from four to ten feet, they're considered two singles, each of which can carry a specific weight determined by the exact distance between them, for a sum total greater than that allowed for a standard tandem. The same rule applies in all the other states, too, and this is why you see so many tractor-trailer rigs with rear axles separated by a strange-looking distance. "We give 'em maybe fifteen hundred pounds leeway," Saturnino said. That takes into account a calibration factor for the scales, but now I was confused. At the talc plant outside Van Horn, I had run into Don Burleson, the technician for the industrial scales that measure those loads. Don carried with him in his own truck eighteen 500-pound blocks and twenty 50-pounders. He assured me he could calibrate those talc scales to a margin of one tenth of one percent of applied pressure plus or minus one graduation, a graduation being either ten or twenty pounds, depending on the scale. If Don can adjust a 100,000-pound full-length scale to within 100 pounds, why all the leeway here in Lordsburg? I checked around and the answer is threefold: the Lordsburg scale is axle only, not full-length; the trucks are rolling slowly over the scale, in most cases, rather than stopping completely; and commercial transaction is not an issue for Saturnino, whose job is to keep these machines from tearing up the roads.

"Anything over that," Saturnino continued, "and we make 'em adjust the weight with their sliders on the rear tandem, or the fifth wheel can slide forward or backward and that can shift the weight on the steering axle. Or we cite 'em."

The other side of I-10 is the New Mexico port of entry for trucks coming east out of Arizona. Over there, all trucks must stop and have their papers and permits inspected by a civilian inspector. If they don't carry the prepaid fuel permit, they cough up $36 on the spot if they're trucking the width of New Mexico on I-10 with eighty thousand pounds. Only a few states have this port-of-entry system. Others, including Texas, rely on an honor system for fuel tax permits, and also on those roving state troopers assigned to License and Weights. Soon, all the states will achieve the same ends more efficiently with computerized AVI (Automatic Vehicle Identification) systems embedded in the roadways.

Saturnino kept one eye on the digital readout in his little office as each truck slowly pulled in and each axle rolled across the scales set into the pit of the concrete driveway. He also looked for visible safety violations. The average illegal load he sees is about three thousand pounds over, and the fine for anything up to that weight is $41.

"That's not much," I exclaimed.

"No, it's not. Up to five thousand pounds is only $91, I think."

I checked, and Saturnino was correct. A pathetic slap on the wrist, paid by the driver's company. However, as Saturnino pointed out, above six thousand pounds overweight and you can start unloading, which does happen. And any overweight violation also triggers a Level-3 inspection—credentials, permits, log book, safety requirements, the works—profoundly resented by the truckers. But the truth is, when there's a solo inspector on duty—which is usually the case westbound—the truck that simply doesn't stop at the weigh station will probably get away scot-free. It's also easy to take the Lordsburg exit back to the east and skirt the station by driving through town, whose officials and merchants owe a greater allegiance to the truckers' business than to strict enforcement of weights and measures.

This attitude is no surprise, since New Mexico has a long history as an antibypass state. In the early 1960s, when the interstate system was taking shape, state law effectively gave local communities veto power over the routes. Small towns along, primarily, I-40 up to the north feared that the new highways would rob their business, but only in New Mexico did they have statutory leverage in negotiating with the federal agencies for more interchanges and access roads on which to locate or relocate small business enterprises. *Highways, Yes—Bypasses, No* was their rallying cry. In 1964, officials flew in from Washington to see what all the trouble was about, to warn that New Mexico risked losing millions in federal matching funds, and to imply that the state would be a big-time loser if competing interstate routes were completed before I-40. Engineers lobbied for repeal of the antibypass law; so did the Better Highways Association. In 1965, the law was amended to allow unapproved bypassing of towns with populations below five hundred. And the whole law was repealed a year later, although any deals previously negotiated would be honored; Governor Jack Campbell said the legislation had "served its purpose." Maybe so, but three years later the antibypass contagion spread into Arizona, where various towns clamored for, and in some cases got, bonus interchanges. By now, thirty years on, the whole issue is moot. The various markets have made their accommodations with the new facts of life, confirming what the experts had said all along: interstate bypasses often give towns two commercial districts for the price of one, as proved by the experience of Abilene in 1962. Established merchants were fearful when that town became the largest in Texas to lose its downtown highway traffic to a new interstate—I-20, four miles away. Within a year, they were thankful. The loop actually accelerated growth along the old business route: synergy, or something similar. Likewise, Van Horn kept all the business it had before the interstate and added to it. Backwaters such as Balmorhea and Sierra Blanca never had enough going for them in the first place.

Any trucker caught sneaking through Lordsburg in order to avoid Saturnino Madero's weigh station is fined $116, and that must be one reason why the line at the scales sometimes stretches hundreds of yards back to the interstate. But no one honks, ever. I asked Saturnino if anyone had ever tried to bribe him. Never. That's a felony. When a Buick sedan pulled in and tipped the scales at 3,870 pounds total, Saturnino said wryly, "They're usually looking for McDonald's." Tankers hauling liquid fuels and chemicals can also slow things because the famous and sometimes dangerous sloshing often yields an artificially high reading for one axle or another. "You have to stop them completely and wait till the load levels out. But they can be over even then. They're the majority of the fines," Saturnino said just before a tanker rolled through without stopping. He threw the switch for the red light and ran out of the office with his fist in the air—merely a signal to the driver, not a sign of anger. But by that time all the other trucks had rolled forward, giving the tanker no room in which to back up for a better assessment. Nice try, guy, but that's why a loop is built into the station's setup. Saturnino made the looping gesture with his forefinger, indicating to this trucker to drive around and come back through and *stop* this time.

Saturnino waved over a small U-haul truck because the driver wasn't keeping a log book, which is required for any "for hire" shipment of more than 150 miles. This truck was hauling an airplane engine from Florida. The long-haired driver, nonplussed by the delay, sported a T-shirt on which Bart Simpson, his back to the viewer, pissed on a map of the Middle East: "Here's to you, Iraqi dude." This pulled-over patriot was followed shortly by a white truck carrying a New Mexico fuel permit that was incorrectly filled out, raising the possibility that these two drivers might have borrowed it from another truck.

Saturnino was deeply suspicious of these characters, but before either situation was resolved I had thanked him for his time and interest and departed to the west, where signs near the Arizona border warn about dust storms, for good reason. On April 9, 1995, eight people died when twenty-four vehicles, including eight tractor-trailers, stacked up during a zero-visibility, windblown brownout in four separate accidents near Bowie. Up on I-40, signs warn about windstorms, and some of the canyons have wind socks, an effective illustration.

North of Tucson, where I-8 initiates and heads off through the low mountains to the left for San Diego via Yuma, another interstate decision presents itself. Of course, I had heard about this improbably numbered route my whole life—only three interstates are single digits: -4 in Florida, -5 running the length of the West Coast, and this -8 in the Southwest—but I never went that way. I always stayed on I-10 instead, motoring north past all the desert farms and ranches and factories and RV parks, and toward the ominous brown cloud that must be Phoenix and vicinity. Phoenix is important for the odologists—the true road men and women—mainly because of the Deck Tunnel: the ten-lane, half-mile-long excavation that runs beneath the city, a compromise design that finally ended the tenacious opposition to this particular crosstown routing for I-10, known locally as the Papago Freeway. Phoenix was antifreeway, at least until it began choking to death on the traffic that spilled onto city streets from both directions. After three referendums, this posture was finally abandoned. The Deck Tunnel opened on August 10, 1990, to national fanfare, especially fitting because it also marked the official completion of I-10, on which construction had begun thirty-four years earlier with the bridge over the Colorado River at Ehrenberg, not so far away on the California border. Total cost for the entire 2,460 miles from Jacksonville to Los Angeles: about $5 billion, a figure that demonstrates both the ravages of inflation and the complexities of this Phoenix project, because these last twenty miles, including the Deck Tunnel and the soaring interchange with I-17 known as The Stack,* cost $750 million, fifteen percent of the total.

In Phoenix, I faced another decision. Would I follow I-10 west to L.A. or proceed north on the brief I-17 through a hodgepodge of peaks and plateaus, past famous Sedona on a back road to the west, then turn left on I-40 at Flagstaff? As much as I wanted to see the Chuckwalla and Plomosa mountains off the more southerly route, I settled on Flagstaff, the Grand Canyon, and the Aquarius, Hulalapai, and Old Woman mountains instead.

Flagstaff often makes those magazine lists of the best reasonably priced places to live, and somehow it got on my wife's and my list of possible places as well, with the upshot that I

---

*Four levels, eight ramps, eighty-five feet at its highest point, 347 supporting piers, seventy-six thousand cubic yards of concrete, ten million pounds of steel rebar, and twenty-one million pounds of structural steel.

once visited with this specific idea in mind. In the upshot to *that* I realized the problems attendant upon living any-place that's a great place to live. Maybe these havens are fine before the publicity hits, but then the refugees arrive and the towns become insular and self-conscious. On the other hand, I should have understood this already because we'd lived in Austin, where the laid-back uniformity is amazing; high-powered lawyers, street guitarists, engineering professors, em-ployees at McDonald's, and the governor are all implicated. In the early years they said it was too much enervating dope or Lone Star longnecks, but that doesn't wash, because now the town lives on double espressos.

At first, my wife and I were sucked into the scene and even bought a small house near Town Lake, but not even equity could make up for the dearth of difference. If there had been any at all, we might still be living there, free and clear after twenty years; by the time we sold out, our renters had stayed in the house longer than we had. Some of our friends in Austin challenge my analysis of the problem, but others agree: this bustling state capital on I-35 is as homogeneous as any back-roads hamlet—and Austin has half a million people! My wife and I fled to Brooklyn, and for the past fifteen-plus years have lived only in unlisted cities. Dallas, for example, shows up on nobody's list of places to live, and this feature serves the city very well. Big D has absolutely no identity other than the his-torically negative one, circa 1963, and as the home of the Cowboys, who in fact play in suburban Irving. Nonetheless, we stayed there for three years and they were okay, I have to admit, despite my previous grousing. The city leaves you alone. And how does New York City fit in? Gotham is definitely a prized destination and its residents as provincial as they come, but it's so chaotic and foul, and you pay such a premium for the privilege, that the masochism factor eradicates any trace of smugness, at least in our zip code.

About the Grand Canyon, the ultimate destination in the American West, seventy miles up a good road from Flagstaff, the less said the better, and not because some picture's worth a thousand words. I'd seen hundreds of pictures of the Canyon,

I suppose, and read many thousand words, but nothing can prepare you; neither the single picture nor the thousand words can even hint at this jaw-dropping experience. There's nothing to say about the canyon itself, so write instead about the pollution smeared across the sky to the west, or the wonderful geology lessons displayed at various overviews that almost no one studies, or the trucker and his wife absorbing the sight more abundantly than anyone else, especially the tourists, who, first thing, take yet another picture. Write about those aspects, if you're so predisposed, or about the ecstatic children, or their silent, awestruck parents, or teenagers at a loss for words, for once, or senior citizens with their own eternities to contemplate. At the Grand Canyon, most people do finally settle down and lean quietly against the guard rails and stare across the expanses and down into the depths for five, ten, fifteen minutes without saying a word to their families and friends.

Of all the foreigners who crowd the banks of the Grand Canyon and keep the bookshop Cormac McCarthy told me about swarming with summertime business, the Germans are into the whole thing in the biggest way. At checkout counters you can pick up the popular coffee-table book *Route 66: Strasse Der Sehnsucht* (Street of Longing). Apparently the Deutsch can't get too much of Route 66 lore, and that's one reason the I-40 bypass around Williams, Arizona, twenty-five miles west of Flagstaff, has had very little effect on business in town. The bypass opened in 1984, and all it did was pull away the truckers and others who weren't about to stop and shop anyway. I learned this from a local photographer named A.C. "Ace" Emanuel, who had lived in Honolulu until the racism he felt directed toward his Anglo self became oppressive. Now he and his family of five lived in Williams. From August through October, he sold Polaroids to tourists outfitted in chaps and posed before the clapboard storefront he propped against a telephone pole. Five hundred customers in three months, at $9 apiece, mostly foreigners. Ace would get seven or eight sales from every busload of Germans, that much was certain. The Orientals, strangely, aren't into it as much; the Koreans haven't even heard of John Wayne.

Just about the same national preferences hold at the Harley shop west of Williams near Seligman, after you drop precipitously out of the San Francisco Mountains. This is the only authorized outlet between Albuquerque and Kingman, a span of 450 big-time tourist-country miles, and I was told you've never seen so many pale men named Wolfgang or Bernhard buying black T-shirts. This was the first time I'd seen the Harley-Davidson bike and motor clothes catalog, which makes Patagonia look cheap, although it doesn't carry—not that I could find—the recycled-paper claim. The shop owner was busy when I walked in, so he handed me over to his son, whose level of interest in my cause was minimal. But I persisted and learned that the jukebox costs $7,995, that you can obtain a Harley-Davidson credit card, and that their biggest-selling bike is the Heritage Softail Classic with skirted fenders, Fat Bob tank, and fishtail muffler. At $17,500, that was "a smokin' deal," according to the waitress at Mike and Ronda's restaurant in Williams. At my instigation, this young woman had guessed twenty grand as she looked over my shoulder at lunch. Also at Mike and Ronda's, I was told that the forecasts issuing out of Phoenix almost always predict worse weather for the Flagstaff-Williams region than it actually gets. Fred, fellow diner and my source for this intelligence, regards this forecasting as a shrewd plot to draw tourists southward to Phoenix. Dirty tricks everywhere you look: all the roads hereabouts are political, too.

Williams is also a jumping-off point for the Canyon. To show you how frenzied things are in the summer around here, I can report that the couple who run the Super 8 had to turn away 168 customers in one day—a NO VACANCY record. You'll be in trouble if you're driving this stretch of the highway in the summer without reservations, even though the supply in the Grand Canyon jurisdiction is about 8,100 rooms. Gouging's not unheard of, like the motels that triple their price to $125 per person. Super 8's central headquarters received a letter of complaint from a traveler who'd been told to "take it or leave it" by whoever was on duty at the Williams branch; at issue was the price quoted by the desk clerk, slightly higher than the one listed in the published directory, which the po-

tential customer held in his hand. Co-manager Patty O'Neal
was really upset by this accusation. She tracked the customer
down by phone, wanting to know which clerk had intimidated
him. When the man said he didn't want to get anybody in
trouble, Patty said that employee ought to be.

"I live in Kingman, Arizona, and I sell janitorial supplies and
my territory runs from Seligman, which is ninety-one miles east
of Kingman, to about Needles, California, which is about
sixty-eight miles west. But the bulk of my business comes from
the casinos in Laughlin, Nevada."

"Where should I stay?"

"I like the Ramada Express. That will cost you about ten
dollars. The casinos right now are starving. This is the week
after Thanksgiving. On Monday, you could get two nights for
sixteen."

"These are nice hotels?"

"These are top-class casinos."

Of everyone I met on or near the interstates, Bruce
Bollinger takes the cake. I ran into this youthful, bearded,
totally straight-ahead salesman at the Mobil Mini-Mart in
Seligman. He's totally beyond reproach. That much was immediately obvious. Furthermore, he's a living reproach to anyone
not beyond reproach (Patty O'Neal also comes to mind in this
regard). Without at least a minimal number of these stalwarts,
the country grinds to a halt. When Bruce steered me to the
Ramada Express in Laughlin and I dubiously queried him regarding the quality of any hotel with a $10 room, he empha-
sized the words "top-class casinos" and fixed me with his eyes.
Twenty minutes later, seated in a booth at the Copper Cart in
Seligman, he told me he'd sold some floor wax to these people
but hadn't liked the way they used the product and hadn't sold
them anything since. Account closed. I should look inside
the OK Saloon down the street if I wanted to see the proper
way to use the product, and Bruce thought I might very well
want to.

Curious where such integrity might be cultured these days,

I asked Bruce for some background. "Originally I'm from Baltimore and in 1976 somebody made me a deal I couldn't refuse. He moved me and my family out to Las Vegas. We went broke in about three months."

Bruce paused.

"How?" I said helpfully.

"Let's skip that part. It was legitimate. Well, we were going to manufacture and wholesale donuts to the casinos. It sounded like a great idea until we realized the casinos have their own bakeries and don't want to buy from outsiders. It was just a stupid mistake by a kid right out of high school. But Baltimore, when I left, was a sloppy, dirty town, and I was ready to get out"—I could believe it, because Bruce is the opposite of sloppy or dirty—"and the idea of trying something new was too good to pass up. You live and learn. We went broke, so I went to driving a truck. This is the third janitorial company I've been with. This can be a retirement company for me. I'm married a second time and I have a twenty-year-old son, who was born a month before we"—Bruce and the young man's mother—"graduated from high school, an eighteen-year-old daughter, and a sixteen-year-old step-daughter.

"I played as a truck driver for a while, small in-town deliveries, and was involved in a near-accident when I drove off the road. I was shaken up quite a bit and decided I didn't want to drive anymore. I walked in to my boss and said, 'Listen, I don't mind working for you. I like the company. But I'm not going to drive anymore, I want a job as a salesman.'"

"You prefer sales?" I asked.

"I make three times what I made as a driver, yeah. But I put in a lot more hours. My office is in my living room. Most people quit at the end of the day. When I go home at night, that's when I enter my orders into the computer and fax them up to Las Vegas. Most of the supplies are delivered by National Sanitary's own trucks. I think we're twenty-nine states"—eighteen, in fact—"and our farthest-east company is in Toledo, Ohio, and we're constantly buying more places."

To no one's surprise, Bruce adopts the corporate "we" effortlessly. I usually find this usage disspiriting—I've had one job that called for it, and wasn't able to comply—but with

Bruce, it seemed appropriate and necessary. Six years before our conversation at the Copper Cart, he had moved his family across the Hoover Dam from Vegas to Kingman, which is a much nicer place to raise a family, in Bruce's opinion, mainly because he doesn't have to worry about "murders, rapes, kids disappearing on the streets." However, he admitted, "living in Kingman is actually a little more expensive because everything has to be trucked in. We don't manufacture anything in Kingman. And unfortunately, the wages are actually a little lower. When we moved in, I think we paid about $68,000 for a three-bedroom, 1,700-square-foot house. You can't find that in cities. I think we made a really good choice. My wife has opened a small accounting company, working for a number of customers. It's really neat because she's taken over my books, and I haven't been audited. As a salesman, I get audited quite often. So she must be doing something right."

The only comparison between driving a truck and selling wax is the driving part of the salesmanship. Bruce works out of a purple Aerostar, and the travel is his least favorite part of the job, although from end to end his route is only 160 miles. This run from Kingman out to Peach Springs and Seligman is a once-a-month gig, worth between one and two thousand dollars in business. "I couldn't come out here twice a month and only write one thousand dollars each time," Bruce said. "In Needles, I have a sales rep who handles Needles, Lake Havasu, Parker, and Blythe. He actually has maybe two hundred straight miles of territory. I work with him once a month."

For Bruce, the real money is in Kingman and Laughlin, which split the lion's share just about evenly. Kingman, with about fifteen thousand residents, has the interstate, but Laughlin, with only a third as many residents, has the hotel casinos. The interstate is good, but the hotel casinos are better; the best, in fact: nine accounts in Laughlin yield just about the same gross revenue as two hundred accounts in Kingman. As Bruce explained, "I think there's eleven casinos in Laughlin. I do business with nine of them. It's nothing for a casino to say, 'Okay, Bruce, I need a hundred cases of this stuff on this week's truck. And I need a hundred cases next week, and the week after.' Among the big casino hotels, the Ramada, the

Belle, and the Edgewater fluctuate as to number one, two, and three. One month one will be top dog, the next month another. I have, in the Laughlin marketplace, about six competitors. Now, interestingly enough, a gentleman by the name of Ronny Laughlin owns a janitorial supply house. The son of the founder of the town. So you can imagine he's got a real good foothold. He probably does six times the business I do. He's got five salesmen. His warehouse is directly across the river. I have a little business in every one. *The question is*, Who has the best mix of benefits for the customer?"

By contrast, Kingman is what Bruce calls a "combination" town, with hotels, truck stops, college, hospital, and airport. "And by the way," he added, "if you stop at the airport you'll learn a lot of the history about the Army–Air Force training center from the World War II era. I do suggest that you stop in and spend some time in Kingman. It was the home of the Camel Corps back in the 1800s. If you'll remember, the Army experimented with camels back then. That's where they were. A lot of people will be happy to talk to you about what made Kingman what it is. There's a very nice museum. Andy Devine—Jingles*—from the Western movies grew up there. You can listen to a lot of old stories as to some of the troubles he got into as a boy."

Bruce's catalog from National Sanitary lists eight thousand products for sale, of which he has personally sold three thousand, everything from toilet bowl cleaner to parking lot sweepers. He told me, "I am not often affected by the economy. Two things: I refuse to let it affect me mentally—I keep going out and knocking on doors; that means that if somebody else is slipping, then *his* customer will soon be *my* customer; if there's a downturn, that's somebody else's problem—and the gaming community has not really seen an effect from the economy. They complain every year. They have a cycle. It's always dead the week after Thanksgiving. It's always dead April fifteenth. It's always dead the second or third week in January. I work to

---

*Devine was the character actor who played the three-hundred-pound sidekick Jingles on "Wild Bill Hickok."

mellow out those highs and lows. When the casinos are down I go calling on my industry. When industry is down I call on the hospital. When the hospital is having a slow time I go call on the colleges."

Still, Bruce admitted, it does get frustrating when you bust your ass and still don't get the account. What about restaurants, I asked.

" 'Restaurants' is handled more by the companies that service the dish machines. I'm in janitorial, and my company chooses not to mess with dish machines. They require parts, inventory. I can make more money calling on customers that buy juice, which is floor wax, stripper, hand soap, disinfectants for the hospitals and classrooms and such as that. 'Bruce, go on back, tell me what I need, and send it to me next week.' I have a number of customers who do that with me. I don't overstock my customers and I don't *understock* them. My goal is to always have one and a half weeks' stock on hand. God forbid a truck driver has a flat tire, is involved in an accident, something—I don't want my customer running out of toilet paper."

Obligatory laughter, after which I asked how much toilet paper Bruce sells at the Mobil Mini-Mart, for example, knowing he won't sell toilet paper here at the Copper Cart.

"Six cases a week."

"Six *cases*?"

Bruce nodded and agreed with my inflection. "For a place that size, I think that's extravagant. It's not right. I sell ten or so cases a week to a place the size of the Flying J, a large truck stop in Kingman. That's with six jumbo rolls in each case. The advantage of the jumbo roll is it takes less labor to change every time it rolls out. The household roll has three hundred and fifty sheets, these jumbo rolls have about twenty thousand. If your employees are ringing up sales instead of changing toilet paper, you're making money."

Bruce said that with a straight face. If he isn't getting a handsome bonus every year from National Sanitary, something's wrong with that cheap outfit. And what can he do about Laughlin? If it weren't for Ronny with the right last name, Bruce would've taken over that casino town, too.

The inroads he *has* made across the river are remarkable, considering.

Alas, Bruce Bollinger had no more leisure in which to inform and humor me. He was heading west in his Aerostar. Lingering beside my car outside the Copper Cart, I watched four cowboys enter the restaurant with their spurs literally jingling. I noted in the local newspaper that the Brady Bill would do nothing but provoke the sale of handguns. I gazed up at the cliffs to the north and at the high cirrus clouds overhead—a high-plains setting exactly 5,280 feet above sea level, according to the Chamber's publication, and reminiscent of certain parts of Texas and the thirteen other states which can claim Western-style vistas. I was dawdling outside because as Bruce and I were conversing in our booth, I couldn't help overhearing clauses of conversation between a young man and a young woman, both of whom were aimless travelers, or so I gathered. I thought I had to find out. Killing more time, I tried to guess who was driving the Geo Metro, who the Nissan Maxima. But when the two finally emerged from the restaurant, I was astonished to see Kyle head for the Metro, Laura for the Maxima. It goes to show you never know.

Kyle was a freelance photographer and journalist shooting an assignment on I-40 for—honest to god—a German car magazine. At the time, he didn't have a "real home." The Metro was a drive-away, and when he picked it up in L.A. steel belting was showing through the tread on one tire and the crankcase was two quarts low on oil. Laura was a ballet and jazz dancer moving to San Francisco, probably, from New York City, where she'd had a great river-view apartment and had turned down a job at the new Harley restaurant on 55th Street. She had bought this Maxima for $500 the day before she left, and somewhat abashedly acknowledged that she was on a "quest." Kyle and Laura were taken with my own interstate misadventures, of course, and then asked if I'd ever been published. In this manner the three of us lounged beside our cars with the doors already open, chatting about books— Laura had read both *Blue Highways* and *Travels with Charley*—and journeys and other forms of beneficial aimlessness. Then I told them about the salesman of janitorial supplies.

Yeah, they said, it takes all kinds.

No, it doesn't, I answered. It takes *Bruce's* kind.

According to hobbyists, about eighty percent of the original 2,400-mile slab of Route 66 is still drivable if you can find it along the route from Chicago to Santa Monica via St. Louis (I-55), Tulsa (I-44), and Flagstaff (I-40). One of the more substantial and least elusive lengths of the old landmark swerves north out of Seligman, Arizona, beneath the Aubrey Cliffs, briefly intersects the Hulalapai Indian Reservation at Peach Springs, where Bruce Bollinger sells supplies to the school district, then loops back through Truxton, Valentine, and Hackberry before rejoining the interstate near Kingman, fifty-five miles to the west. Though it's a beautiful drive, on this particular trip I hewed to the interstate. I passed Laura in her Nissan Maxima, waved, and dropped down from a high plateau to Kingman, at the base of the Hulalapai Mountains. At the time, as Bruce had noted, the town was known mainly as the birthplace of Andy Devine—the eponymous boulevard is a prominent exit off I-40—but it would shortly register in the public imagination as the most recent residence of Timothy J. McVeigh, of Oklahoma City notoriety. I wouldn't have stopped anyway.

I could probably pretend that Laughlin, Nevada, is on the interstate, but I won't. At Kingman, I-40 takes a sharp left and loops down and around to Needles, California. If you instead go straight on Highway 68 out of Kingman, traverse the jagged backbone of the Black Mountains, wind down a series of switchbacks to Bullhead City on the Arizona side of the Colorado River, cross that now-tamed waterway at an altitude of five hundred feet, picking up an hour thanks to the Pacific Time Zone, you emerge after twenty-six miles into the bright lights of Laughlin's modest strip. This town is like Las Vegas was twenty-five years ago, Bruce Bollinger had told me.

"Actually," he amended, "it's probably bigger than Vegas was twenty-five, thirty years ago. Laughlin is a much friendlier town. I started my sales career in Vegas in about 1980. That town has changed a lot. I watch my words here. It's become unionized and the people don't care. Laughlin is nonunion, and the people are there to serve the customer. It's not so much, 'I only got to work eight hours and I'm gone.' "

That attitude would never cut it with Bruce, obviously, but Laughlin *is* different. It's also amazingly inexpensive and full of snowbirds from everywhere and Los Angelenos beyond the need for high-rolling or the pretense of it, and who like the smaller-town flavor. It's not on the interstate but it's certainly *of* the interstates, and I felt justified staying there. I was told that the original plan for I-40 *did* go through town, but that the Vegas boys on I-15 spread $3 million around in order to move the highway south—out of Nevada altogether—because they didn't want strong casino competition on any interstate less than one hundred miles away. However, and as much as we all enjoy *Chinatown* conspiracies, the original map for the interstate system clearly shows that Laughlin was bypassed from the start. Moreover, Laughlin was no more than a minor fishing camp on the Colorado prior to 1968, when Don Laughlin opened the first casino.

Later, I found out that this gerrymandering allegation about I-40 actually gets things exactly backwards. In the early 1960s, an attempt was made to shift the route *out* of Needles and *into* Nevada—Searchlight, specifically, not Laughlin. The new routing would have been shorter and $30 million cheaper, but alarmed civic leaders in Needles campaigned hard against it, claiming a potential loss of twenty-four of twenty-nine gas stations, ten of nineteen cafés, ten of fourteen wholesalers, most retailers, and one-third of the 1,067 extant jobs. I cite these figures from the February 3, 1966, issue of the Los Angeles *Times*, which also stated: "The bypass would make Las Vegas thirty-two miles closer for east-west traffic but this never publicly entered the controversy as an issue." That implies Las Vegas would have *welcomed* the closer traffic, but perhaps those powers feared a new gambling mecca in Searchlight, just as they were incorrectly alleged to have feared the new mecca in Laughlin. In any event, Nevada politicians did join their confederates from California in opposing the new routing, which was rescinded "'after a thorough study.'" *Chinatown* after all.

One final point: the nonexistent conspiracy against Laughlin nevertheless extends all the way to the cartographers at Rand McNally. On their map of Arizona, Laughlin isn't even designated directly across the river in adjacent Nevada, while tiny, insignificant places in Utah, New Mexico, California, elsewhere in Nevada, and even in Mexico *are* designated. On the map of Southern California, Laughlin is missing but we get Michoacan, Baja California, and Pahrump, Nevada. Something is very wrong here: Laughlin is the second-largest concentration of casinos in Nevada; ten thousand visitors pour in on a summer holiday.

As reported, I stayed at the Ramada Express, but my favorite casino in Laughlin was soon the Regency, a little hole-in-the-wall cavalierly dismissed by Bruce Bollinger as just a casino, no hotel at all. That's not to say that Bruce doesn't call on the Regency; he does, of course, and I'll bet he sells them plenty of stuff for the restrooms. The only one of the original casinos still in business, it's short on glitz and doesn't go out of its way to attract the gambling tourist. Instead, I was told, the Regency is where the locals go to lose their money. In the back, beneath lazily turning ceiling fans, is a dance floor ten feet square. Standing there is Fred, a retired tool-and-die maker from the Los Angeles area who needed something to do after a year of retirement, and the only guard I saw in Laughlin packing a pistol. Fred assured me that the funky-looking Regency nevertheless makes plenty of money for its owner, an individual, mainly because people are stupid.

"How's that?"

"With the dealer showing a face card, they split two tens. I walk away from that table."

Fred also informed me that, without question, the short-order grill here turns out the best food on the strip. In fact, he added and the cook verified, it's the only place in town where you can get food cooked to order and served fresh. I paid $1.25 for my delicious short stack. The man seated next to me, employed as a dealer elsewhere, explained how he'd just won and lost $5,200 in twenty-four hours, starting with a $20 stake. He was now trying to bum $2 for a pack of cigarettes. There must be a certain pride in being a significant loser. To have this attitude, I guess you have to buy into the identity of the sub-culture, whatever it might be—skiing and river-running come to mind—where the eventual big crack-up is a given going in and any disaster short of death is grist for gloating. Gamblers are the same breed of cat. Casino professionals can't hide their disdain for us penny-ante types, just as double-diamond skiers snicker as their chairlift passes above the green slopes and kayakers do as they maneuver around the big oar boats. If that's all you're capable of, why bother?

One night I was walking away from the Regency black-jack table after another quick and inexplicable sequence of losses—I played the hands right; I didn't split any pair of tens with the dealer showing royalty—when this dealer, an attractive woman of undetermined age, chided me gently for not putting up a fight. Or maybe she was remarking obliquely on the scene at her table ten minutes earlier, when a gambler in a satin jacket and yours truly were her only customers. We both were losing and he was drunk. As he lost, he drank and talked. The talking I didn't mind, in theory, because I also find this helpful, but as this man's list of hatreds mounted, so did my annoyance. He hated Yankees—all Yankees, not just *the* Yankees. He also hated bureaucrats, and he despised the Brady Bill, of course. He hated so much stuff that finally I looked over and said, "And you probably hate yourself." He turned his head and looked at me. Our dealer looked at me. I pictured the entire casino looking at me. But I wasn't worried, because I'd already gauged his size, the twerp.

Finally he said, "Yeah, I probably do." When he asked where I was from, he simply couldn't believe the answer; we Texans are supposed to be so friendly and polite. Then he left. The way I look at it, I saved him some money.

Ten minutes later I decided to do the same and rolled out onto the 140-mile stretch of I-40 between Needles and Barstow, straight through the Mohave Desert and maybe the longest interstate run without a gas station. This stretch also holds the honor of being the only interstate construction for which the nuclear option was entertained. In the early 1960s, District 8 engineers explored the feasibility of employing twenty-two tactical devices to clear a 10,940-foot path through the Bristol Mountains. A meeting on this proposal attracted representatives of the Atomic Energy Commission, the Lawrence Livermore Laboratory, and the Santa Fe Railroad, seeking a shorter route for its tracks. Project Carryall was also seen as a feasible validation of JFK's Project Plowshare, which sought peaceful uses for atomic energy, and as a way to save $8 million (not counting the cost of the ordnance, a figure that is still classified). The bombs would range from twenty to two hundred kilotons; the resulting dust cloud, a projected two miles high and seven miles in diameter, might have necessitated the temporary closing of nearby roads, including Route 66, due to reduced visibility, and work on the new trench would have been delayed until the radiation returned to safe levels, and no one could testify exactly how long that might be. Otherwise, this project was green-lighted at every stage until the Nuclear Test-Ban Treaty was signed in August 1963.

At the westbound rest area in the Mohave I met a maintenance man named Alexander, a New Yorker who used to live right around the corner from James Cagney. He and the famous actor sometimes went to the same restaurant on First Avenue and 77th Street, and it was my impression that these were the most gratifying moments of his life. As we talked, I observed the coterie of American Indians selling jewelry displayed on a blanket and asked Alexander about the watchful behavior of one particular elder, a lookout, perhaps. That's exactly what he was, Alexander confirmed. Selling goods at any rest area on the interstates is illegal, so these Indians play a cat-and-mouse game with lawmen. They can make $1,000 on a good day, Alexander said, but one of these days they'd get caught by an airborne unit.

I sauntered over to this illegal commercial district and was pleasantly surprised when my questions weren't immediately rebuffed by these Navajos from Arizona. Once a week they drive three hundred miles one way to set up shop right here. There are usually ten to fifteen in the group, many of them related, and they sleep in Needles. Their leader frankly admitted he was watching for the black-and-white Camaros driven by California state troopers. His fines have helped pay for those Camaros over the years—thirty or so fines in ten years, at $1,100 each. Under the circumstances, I decided it would be counterproductive to ask his name.

"So the cops *know* you're here, right?"

"Not unless someone tells them."

"Well, nobody's going to do that."

He looked at me the way you'd look at a fool who knows nothing about the history of the North American continent. "Yes they are. Prejudiced white people who don't like Indians. Been that way ever since Custer." His subsequent explanation of the ongoing territorial dispute between the Navajos and the Hopi in northern Arizona also focused on the deceitful machinations of the white man. Thirty percent of his jewelry business here at the I-40 rest stop is from wholesalers who drive all the way from New Orleans, mainly to buy an entire blanket of jewelry for resale at much higher prices on Bourbon Street. Truly, the white man always has something up his sleeve, and this native entrepreneur made no attempt to hide his bitterness.

"But what about the casino near Lake Havasu?" I asked. I understood this to be an Indian operation.

"One half white," he corrected me.

There are exactly fifty of these interstate rest areas along my main route between Texas and California, twenty-five in each direction, and there are no better interstate vantage points, and the employees are consistently entertaining. Near Fort Stockton in West Texas, Lalo Ybarra called over to me one afternoon as I loitered in front of the handsome signboard concerning the Chihuahuan Desert, where we were. He was sitting on the limestone ledge outside the pristine restrooms, mop in hand. Lalo worked for the company that held the concession of the highway. An elderly man, he had previously worked in the construction trades and, before that, in sheep shearing. With a frank gaze he assured me he had been an excellent sheep shearer. I realized I might even have watched him work, because my grandparents' ranching friends around Ozona sometimes invited us out for the harvest.

Lalo was born sixty-five miles south of that rest area in Sanderson, not far from the Rio Grande River and about as isolated as any community in this country. You might have to go into Nevada to meet its match. I don't know this from personal knowledge, but I do know how to interpret blank areas on the map, and the one around Sanderson reaches an inch or two in every direction. Sanderson . . . sheep shearing . . . Mexican-American with limited command of English: I'll admit that I pictured an entire life spent in a landscape bereft not only of PBS but of FM radio as well. This was true in that Lalo had never visited the three of his five daughters who lived in Arizona, Michigan, and New York, but he had spent fifteen of his best years working sheep ranches around Redding and Eureka, in California.

Then Lalo giggled. "You know—all those earthquakes. But it was Bigfoot that scared me! He was supposed to be up near there. Somebody saw his footprint." He held his hands three feet apart, grinning with bad teeth. As I departed, Lalo said, "Come back and we'll talk some more," and he looked around for another traveler who might enjoy hearing about this fearsome creature.

Months later I did stop at his rest area, but Lalo wasn't around. Instead I saw a trucker take a leak next to his rig, not fifty yards from the clean restroom.

At the westbound rest area on I-10 west of Deming, New Mexico, my attention was drawn to a Chevette with its hood up and a sign in the front window asking for money. A man and a woman sat in the front; tires, coolers, and other accoutrements filled the back. The proprietor of a Sea Breeze motor home out of the earthquake capital of the world, Hollister, California—on the western edge of the San Joaquin Valley directly across from Monterey Bay—informed me that the rest stops in Wyoming, of all places, are full of these interstate panhandlers. He advised giving food, not money. For fifteen minutes I watched this couple as dozens of resting motorists passed to and fro, and not one gave them food or money. Then the man got out of his car and stood in front of the open hood, looking down in a posture of inconsolable affliction and deprivation, something out of the Blue Period. If you're completely open to it, if you really let it, this world will break your heart in twain, but I've never liked those paintings and I'm sure Picasso later regretted ever painting them, and I irrationally and heartlessly turned against these two beleaguered people and drove off to the west.

For alfresco education of consistently high quality, these rest areas and historical markers are unsurpassed. At Lalo Ybarra's place in West Texas, I learned that the chief "indicator" plant for the Chihuahuan Desert that reaches up from Mexico into West Texas, southern New Mexico, and Arizona is agave lechuguilla, the cactus with the tall, thin stalk and the white fluff on top. The famous saguaro cactus, emblem of all Western deserts with its sentinel-like posture, is actually the indicator for only the Sonoran Desert, which is restricted to the lower and even more arid regions of Arizona and Southern California. In Arizona, at the Texas Canyon stop on I-10 just across the border from Saturnino Madera's weigh station, I read that the local Apaches had been without a doubt "the most fierce, brutal, and cunning of all Indian tribes"—a remarkably politically incorrect series of adjectives, I thought, right around the corner from Cochise's favorite stronghold in the Dragoon Mountains. But the Indians get equal time on I-35, south of the Oklahoma border, where the historical plaque about the Kiowa Raid of 1868 concludes: "Indian raids such as this one were in retaliation for loss of hunting grounds to settlers." In the 1800s, that part of north-central Texas was inhabited mainly by the peaceful Wichitas. The warlike Kiowa and Comanches held forth to the north and west, mainly, though they sometimes made it down this far. The Comanches in particular didn't appreciate Texans, as they proved any number of times, but in January 1868, it was some two hundred Kiowa braves, led by Chief Big Tree, who raided the settlers of the Willa Walla, Clear, and Blocker Creek valleys, burning homes, killing thirteen people, scalping one woman, capturing others and their children. Losses would have been more severe were it not for the Paul Revere–services of one George Masoner, who warned the settlers, and also for the powerful blizzard that cut short the attack.

As I compiled my notes at that rest area on I-35, an extended family of Asian extraction, ten people in all, pulled up in their GMC van and Toyota pickup, piled out with their cooler loaded with Pepsi-Cola and Bud Dry, then proceeded to study the state map also on display. I don't know whether they consulted the legend and learned that only two of Texas's hundreds of lakes are natural lakes, but I doubt it. They certainly didn't walk ten yards over to read the historical plaque. Many other travelers came and went that morning—every imaginable kind of American—and none of them stopped to read it, either.

The big cities are the magnets of the interstates. Just to slow down as you approach the metropolis is hard enough; to stop short of the goal is almost impossible. That's always been the case with me, no matter how alluring and informative the rest area, and so it was on the noon I first approached Los Angeles from the east. Besides, the highway is downhill all the way from the pass west of Needles to the pass between the San Gabriel and San Bernardino mountains, the northeast corner of the L.A. Basin. At one point that afternoon, a truck impeded my progress by weaving back and forth. I thought maybe the driver was falling asleep, and when I finally had the chance to pull around him, weaving back and forth myself in a genuinely friendly message, he gave me the jerk-off in return. On the radio I was listening to a discussion of the appropriateness of broadcasting Rush Limbaugh on Armed Forces Radio (inappropriate, in my opinion). Then, on the same channel, during a discussion of puppy mills, I learned that only one out of twenty dogs, one out of forty-two cats, will ever find a permanent home, and that seventeen million of the rest are put out of their misery every year. Fully ninety percent of the animals impounded in January and subsequently gassed are purebreds; though it took a while, I finally figured out why: unwanted Christmas gifts.

I turned toward my cousin's house in Claremont, off Route 66, where the eucalyptus trees soared overhead and the sunshine filtering through the awful pollution bathed skateboarders and bicyclists and bleached blondes alike with a wonderful light. Now I felt better. At my cousin's place I was somewhere, at last; home, almost, it seemed like, or close enough.

CHAPTER 15

No sooner had my father stepped into my Japanese sports sedan at Love Field in Dallas than he reported with a tinge of resentment that his arrival gate had been the farthest from the terminal; no sooner had we driven past Dealey Plaza than he revealed that his golf handicap had soared five strokes in the past twelve months; and no sooner had we turned right at the intersection with I-20 than he acknowledged that only in the past year had he realized he was now an old man, *considered* himself an old man. In eight months he would be seventy-five. Of course, it was no coincidence that only in the past year or two had I realized I was no longer a young man, hadn't been for quite a few years, in fact, was now indisputably middle-aged and *considered* myself as such, no matter how often people assured me I looked ten years younger. The initial tip-off to this bracing new fact of life was the bewildering realization that young women were now looking right through me.

I saw them clearly, but somehow they flat missed my youthful-looking self. In just over two years, I'd be fifty.

Dad told me the latest joke from the links, in which an old codger is telling the rest of his foursome about his new wife. She can't cook, this hacker says, doesn't have any money, and isn't much to look at, but she *can* drive at night! Apparently this line elicits guffaws of knee-slapping laughter from the elderly set, though my own laughter was tinged with bitterness because the joke revealed an unwelcome parallel between my father's recognition of old age and my own simultaneous, belated recognition of middle age: the reading glasses, three sets of them, one pair on the desk, an auxiliary pair stashed in the car, the main ones on or near my person. So we were off to a great start on this fine February on our way west to Stamford, north of Abilene, where my father grew up and where I was born. Then we'd drive the twenty-five miles to Abilene, go out for dinner at Wes-T-Go Truck Stop, then he'd fly home to Houston and I'd get back on I-20, where I belonged, and keep going.

Passing Dealey Plaza, I asked Dad where he'd been when he heard the news of the assassination, and I could have guessed his answer: working in his office in the Texas Company Building on Rusk Street in downtown Houston, erected in 1913, now boarded up along with just about that entire side of town. I was walking down a covered walkway between the classroom building and the cafeteria at my high school, where my conscientious teacher later went ahead with the chemistry lesson. My mother had just returned to the car after shopping with a friend at an art gallery in the Montrose area. The girl who would become my wife was purchasing her official junior high school pictures in Houston; John Connally's niece Gail was in her ninth-grade class. My father-in-law was having lunch at the Houston Club downtown, and when one of the other businessmen at the table made a disparaging remark about John Kennedy following the television bulletin, one of the *other* men, a lawyer and not necessarily a Democrat, either, got very angry. My sister-in-law remembers running back to her dormitory from a literature class at the University of Texas in Austin after the professor had been unable to continue his lecture, and the Mexican-American cobbler who owned a small shop near the campus hanging out his small American flag. She knew what this gesture must mean. "He died?" she asked, the man said, "Yes," and the two of them, crying, went inside to watch on TV. My brother had just woken from a nap in his incredibly dingy, windowless basement apartment in Baltimore when his roommate at Johns Hopkins rushed in with the news.

On the following Sunday morning, my parents had gone to church while I stayed home to watch the coverage live, as I'd been doing for most of the previous forty-four hours. I can see the chair I was sitting on when Ruby shot Oswald. I can see myself jumping up with excitement when the broadcaster exclaimed, "He's been shot! He's been shot! Lee Oswald has been shot!" Moments later, my brother and some friends were standing outside the Capitol Rotunda watching the arrival of the horse-drawn caisson, which was passing *directly* in front of them when they overheard on another man's prototype transistor radio the bulletin about this second murder, and my brother clearly recalls the sardonic reflection that crossed his mind at that moment: *Isn't it great to be from Texas?*

By itself, Dealey Plaza seems to me sufficient proof of my proposition that on and near the interstates we see America as it is and as it is becoming. Take the Reunion Square exit, loop back under I-35E, and emerge from the famous triple underpass into the middle of modern American history. The most cursory visit lends credence to the closely related notions that evil truly is banal, that mankind can be that way, too, and that life does indeed go on—although we should have the decency to acknowledge that the last truism reflects the perspective of the living only; the dead may have a different idea. Spend enough time at Dealey Plaza and it grows on you as an entirely appropriate site for one of the many Crimes of the Century.

My father and I drove on by, but I knew the place well anyway. Over a period of several years, I had become something of an habitué. For me, it's a powerful place, ground zero for the sixties—my personal favorite among all the eras of mankind—and not a bad touchstone for the nineties, either. In 1960, I was thirteen years old and obsessed with the presidential campaign. Those who hated John Kennedy were irrelevant, except for the fact that they could vote. Neither imaginative nor creative, they were the silent majority for the good reason that they had nothing to say. Hold jobs, make money, stay married, raise kids, cast ballots for Richard Nixon: that was about it. Even at that age I couldn't understand how anyone could prefer Nixon to JFK—my God, the inherent qualities of the two men were written on every feature of their faces—even though my parents were two of the few Democratic votes on our suburban block in Houston. Today, could there be a defining tragedy equivalent to the Kennedy assassination? I don't think so. Not even another assassination. The back of the wooden fence at the top of the grassy knoll at Dealey Plaza is covered with graffiti, most of it respectful, some flippant,* but more thoughtful reflections are found in the visitors' book in the Sixth Floor Museum. I can't imagine such a heartfelt set of messages regarding any other discrete public event in our lifetimes, with the possible exception of those left at the Vietnam Memorial. We're still picking up the pieces from thirty years ago, and there's nothing left to shatter. This new era was born denuded of hope; an entire new generation doesn't seem to care.

Who remembers where they were when they heard about the attempts on Ford, on Reagan? No one I've ever asked.

The thirtieth anniversary of the assassination had fallen eighteen months before this trip with my father. A contingent of television trucks with their telltale antennae and satellite dishes had triple-parked for the dedication of the site as a National Historic Landmark, one of 2,146. In an effort to spruce things up for the ceremony, the grounds crew had rolled out strips of fresh sod along the top and bottom of the grassy knoll, where the plaque would be placed, and then spray-

---

*A recent addition: "O.J. Did It."

painted them a flagrantly fake green—a nice touch if they were thinking of the down-home sense of the place as a whole. Anniversaries aside, Dealey Plaza gives every appearance of being an unimportant civic site on the western edge of downtown Dallas, defined by small-town brick buildings that haven't changed much since that November day, skipped by the bulldozers of development that are busier out in the suburbs anyway.

Still, Dealey Plaza is said to be the second-largest tourist attraction in North Texas, after Six Flags Over Texas, the amusement park. This could even be true, given the dearth of competition, which includes, just two blocks away, the Kennedy Memorial, a boxlike, off-white concrete structure erected around a low stone slab, designed by Philip Johnson and shunned by the public. Dealey Plaza can be swarming while the memorial is forlornly empty, and I can think of several reasons for this discrepancy. In the first place, many visitors don't know about the memorial, situated at a remove from the main action. Moreover, at the memorial, your mood is necessarily introverted, because there's nothing else to do, while the teeming plaza takes us away from ourselves. Finally, the subject at the memorial is the man himself, his presidency, and our nation; at the plaza, assassination.

On any reasonably nice day in Dallas, anywhere from dozens to hundreds of men, women, and children are scattered beneath the live oak trees at Dealey Plaza, listening with much gravity to the purveyors of conspiracy theories and assorted provocations. These vendors pay about $2 wholesale for their publications and peddle them for as much as $5. Occasionally—especially on anniversaries—freelancers will show up to market their particular points of view. One man previews his videotaped conspiracy theory on a small television set powered by a noisy gasoline generator. The tourists look carefully in the direction of the grassy knoll, study the ledge on which Abraham Zapruder was standing with his movie camera, and, of course, stare up toward one of the most famous windows in the world. Among their number will be many foreigners, who seem to be as entranced by the assassination as Americans, maybe more so. The Japanese are devoted JFK buffs, naturally.

Major conventions guarantee an especially good turnout. Weekends are always busy; also the Monday after a Cowboys home game. But the greatest boon for Dealey Plaza was, without a doubt, Oliver Stone's movie *JFK*. The crowds drawn here by that outlandish confection are still coming, and for many of these people the word "plaza" must conjure images of scale and monumentality that don't pertain at this one. Surprise at the diminutive scale is almost universal (as it is at the Alamo in San Antonio, the other world-famous iconographic tourist attraction in Texas). The shot from the sixth-floor window looks close enough for a BB gun. The only institutional features are the three modest pergolas, two on the Houston Avenue side, with the single flagpole below each of them, and another atop the grassy knoll, but these have nothing to do with the assassination. The Works Project Administration erected them in 1934, although any visitor who fails to read the plaques might think otherwise.

The Saturday before the anniversary, I was milling around in a large and building crowd when a tour bus pulled up on the east side of the plaza and Candy Thompson stepped off with her group. Candy was a recent convert to the conspiracy cause, although to exactly which version I couldn't make out as I listened to her devastating critique of both the pristine- and single-bullet hypotheses. She told us how, right before filming began on *JFK*, she'd received a phone call from the Mansion at Turtle Creek, one of Dallas's best hotels and restaurants. The concierge wanted to know if Candy could escort Kevin Costner on a private tour of the assassination site. For *that* she made time, she coyly told her listeners, and our uncontrolled laughter drew disapproving glares from passersby.

Across from Candy at the bottom of the grassy knoll, Dan Stevens held forth before a dozen attentive adults. A young couple walked up, and the man politely interrupted to ask which building was the Texas Schoolbook Depository. When the rest of us laughed knowingly, he said, "Sorry, I don't know everything." On the contrary, bub, around here, if you don't know that, you don't know anything. The depository is that orange brick building to the left as you look up the rise toward Houston Street, the sixth floor's the sixth floor, and the sixth-floor window is that one on the far right with the boxes stacked haphazardly behind it; behind you, that's the grassy knoll from where the second gunman fired what was actually the fatal shot, and right there, not twenty feet from where your girlfriend is drinking her Classic Coke, is where that bullet struck the *front* of the head of the President of the United States.

Dan Stevens is acknowledged by everyone working the plaza to be the best informed of any of them concerning the assassination. He's definitely the best talker, in my experience, which included a number of exchanges and one long conversation in a nearby pub. He can rattle off names, spin scenarios, and summarize theories with the best of them. Only from him did I learn that Jack Ruby, who spent the last nine years of his life in the city jail on the east side of Dealey Plaza and whose official cause of death was listed as stroke, had actually died of intestinal cancer, probably caused by intestinal cancer cells injected into him. Dan is thirty-seven years old and has led quite a life, including, bottom-line, periods of residing on or perilously close to the streets. When we first met, he was bunking with friends (I know the feeling) and had lost his driver's license due to some DWIs. But Dan is nobody's tenth-grade dropout. It was Dan who explained to me, correctly, the distinction between the peristyles and the pergolas framing Dealey Plaza. He's well versed in the theories of Ayn Rand, whose *Atlas Shrugged* he has read seven times, and he asserts that many of his legal problems stem from his rejection of the psycho-epistemology of Alcoholics Anonymous, falsely based as it is on the primacy of consciousness, as opposed to the psycho-epistemology of Rand's Objectivism, correctly based on the primacy of existence. *Atlas Shrugged* was big in my high school, but that was a long time ago, and I read it only once, so I asked the waitress for more coffee as my companion shifted into second gear.

He explained that the name by which he's known in conspiracy circles worldwide isn't his real one, and he'd like to keep it that way in anything I might write about him. Like the pseudonymous hitchhiker Bob Smithers, whom I transported from Abilene to Colorado City, the pseudonymous Dan

Stevens expressed a rapprochement with his present reversals of fortune. "When I first ran out of money and was pretty much ostracized by the stable middle- or upper-middle-class society I come from—I think my family is somewhat ashamed of me—it was very frightening for a while, having to deal with things on a day-to-day basis, and actually having to place some degree of trust in transients and vagrants. But after a while I got to where I could accept a lower standard of living and be happy with it. Not totally happy, but fundamentally happy with myself. When I was first on the way down, I felt like a failure. But I found out I hadn't failed myself, but that society has failed me." Then he had immediately amended that statement: "I don't blame society. I blame myself for my actions. I don't mean to blame any problem I have on anyone else, other than that society was portrayed as ideal to me. And it's not ideal. To the extent I was expected to comply to ideal standards, I do blame society. But outside that, no. Self-esteem can't be a function of what I am in other people's eyes. I have a very high estimate of myself now. I do. Even though I'm on the lower end of the financial scale, what I've learned, my life experiences, nobody can take those away from me. I'm not happy with where I am now, I'm not happy with the way things have turned out, but I do maintain a happiness for being *me*. This is life, it goes on and on and on, and nobody can see the future."

This conspiracy salesman frankly acknowledges that he has always been drawn to social and political ideas that are somewhere out on one fringe or the other—nor, perhaps, does it much matter which one. As a conspiracist, he tends to see wheels within wheels within the eye of that pyramid on the back of the dollar bill. Still, he resents the anti-intellectual connotations of the "conspiracy buff" label. He does in fact belong to one of the famous Texas militias, but he rejects any relationship between his group and domestic terrorism in Oklahoma City and elsewhere. He's writing a book about the assassination, of course. He considers Oliver Stone's movie about ninety percent accurate, and he helped coach Kevin Costner.

"A jerk?" I asked, for this was the star's emerging reputation.

"Oh, no," Dan replied, "Kevin's a real nice guy."

Ron Rice wouldn't know. One of Dan's friends in the workplace, Ron told me that he, too, had been a consultant on *JFK*, although he hadn't had much to do with Costner. On the other hand, he had given the rock band Steely Dan a two-hour guided tour, for which he was tipped $155. Ron showed me his replica of the pristine bullet, manufactured and marketed by a buff in the Midwest. He said he'd written his own assassination book, *Knight to King-3*, coming out soon from a publisher he wouldn't identify for reasons that remained unclear. Dan Stevens told me that *Knight to King-3* is the figment of Ron's overly active imagination, and intuition leads me to side with Dan, but I'm open to eventual correction, and I have no opinion whatever on Ron's assertion that he had nearly lined up the financial backing to open a JFK Center in Japan.

I can confirm that Ron is an effective salesman for whom the pitch is everything. One of his best lines: "Truth has no age. Truth has no anniversary." For a really good day, all he has to do is to convince just two members of any Japanese busload to buy the product, since everyone else will immediately follow suit. But it's tough to get those iconoclasts to break free of the reluctant group—kind of a catch-22. Other nationalities can be a difficult sale as well, but we Americans are the worst, perhaps because we have the least money. Scandinavians are the best. An effective salesman, Ron can also be a contentious personality, by his own admission. About Kevin Costner's personal guide Candy Thompson, he told me simply, "Oh, she's a joke." He'd made a few other enemies at the plaza as well, and taken a particular dislike to a new guy selling a "collector's item" titled the "Question Mark." The man's name was Sam Jenkins, a part-time artist, *he* said, a frequenter of the titty bars on Harry Hines Boulevard, *Ron* said, as well as a scam artist whose assassination material was worthless trash. In return, Sam said that Ron is lacking in the social graces. One day I happened to be nearby when the acrimony between the two escalated into a public shouting match: "You're nothing but an ex–cab driver!" "You're nothing but an alcoholic!" On another day, Ron challenged the snaggle-toothed young man Sam had just employed as his sales assistant—a dispute I inadvertently caused by divulging that the new man was telling potential customers that part of the proceeds from their purchase would go toward research. Ron bristled. He'll readily admit that the conspiracy game is all about making a buck, but he genuinely resents those who fail to demonstrate some finesse while doing so. Now he hollered across the sidewalk, "Research?! *What* research?" When his rival took offense, Ron upped the ante with more insinuations. The man proposed a fistfight, and Ron said fine. J.T., a licensed nurse's assistant who never in her life would've believed that she'd be selling hotdogs on the street for a living, told the two of them to knock it off, and they were happy to oblige. J.T. had already seen her fair share of these altercations, the kind of behavior that has led local reporters to refer to the conspiracy vendors as "the rats of Dealey Plaza."

One afternoon I caught Dan Stevens at the top of his game, preaching to a sizable crowd beneath the large live oak at the edge of the grassy knoll. "Feel free to look at it, folks," he said about his publication. "But I would appreciate it if you'd pay me if you decide you want it. Take a look at the list in the back. That's every eyewitness who heard shots fired from the grassy knoll. Seventy-six of them." When this group broke up, Dan sold several copies, and he was approached by three men of serious demeanor, in town for a convention of the Promise Keepers, that fast-growing group of Christian men founded by the former head football coach at the University of Colorado. It's usually portrayed as a latently right-wing outfit, but at one early point it was accused of heresy because of its implicit endorsement of Robert Hicks's *The Masculine Journey*, an allegedly New Age, drumming-in-the-woods sort of book charged with enshrining men's essentially phallic nature, with urging us to worship with our phallus, and with suggesting that Jesus himself might have been tempted to lust after Mary Magdalene and was almost certainly tempted to engage in homosexual acts. Incendiary ideas, certainly, though an evan-

gelical friend replied under challenge that there's nothing inherently wrong with acknowledging his temptation to hetero-
sexual lust, which had to be the case, in fact, because Jesus
Christ was man as well as God. Another friend likened the distinction between temptation and actual lust to the difference
between admiring a beautiful babe and driving around the
block for a second look. But the Son of God and homosexu-
ality? Even as benign titillation, that will never do.

I read about this Hicks book and controversy in the Dal-
las/Fort Worth *Heritage*—specifically, the post–Oklahoma
City bombing issue headlined "Where Was God?" The persis-
tence of this question down the ages has always puzzled me,
because the answer seems self-evident: wherever He's always
been. Anyway, I knew nothing about the book when I met
these three Promise Keepers, and had no cause to elicit their
opinions. Instead we talked about the assassination. One allowed that he, too, had worshiped the fallen president, and he
was certain that JFK, a confirmed Cold Warrior, would have
nuked the Cong to kingdom come and would be, right now,
a retired, seventy-three-year-old Reagan Democrat, at worst,
more likely a true Republican. I disagreed. As another in-
tensely studied his copy of *Case Reopened*, he demanded,
"How come you never hear this kind of stuff?!" His friends
nodded. Like the large majority of Dealey Plaza visitors who
make their opinion known to the vendors, these Promise
Keepers implicitly accept the notion of some kind of unspeci-
fied conspiracy against JFK, for the classic reason that you
can't trust the government. Sometimes you can't, it's true, but
I think there's more going on as well, another basic principle
that history and ordinary experience have taught us with heart-
breaking regularity, and which I've already mentioned glanc-
ingly because it seems so essential in understanding people and
politics and everything else, whether on the interstates or the
Internet: people can and do believe anything. It's our chief talent. To take a historical example, Abraham Lincoln, in his Second Inaugural Address, said about the Union and the
Confederacy: "Both read the same Bible and pray to the same
God, and each invokes His aid against the other. . . . The

prayers of both could not be answered. That of neither has been answered fully." Still, those opposing armies and their people prayed to the bitter end, each believing that the one God would hear and answer their prayers; when the South eventually reaped only devastation from the Civil War and those wasted prayers, it *still* believed. In fact, that region believes more fervently today than any other, and not because it has finally accepted defeat as divine retribution. This might be a logical conclusion—the only one, I believe—but, of course, belief has nothing to do with logic.

Any belief, even the most revolutionary, necessarily becomes conservative sooner or later. It's not interested in listening, thinking, or, least of all, changing. We believe whatever we believe because we do, for whatever set of probably unknowable reasons or for none at all. It's that simple, that complex. We can even fervently believe something with one part of our mind and know with another that it's absolutely impossible. Angels, for example, who don't exist: we know this, but polls indicate we believe they do. Or we can believe that Orenthal James Simpson wasn't guilty of murdering his wife and her friend, if that's our gut-level preference. No amount of forensic corroboration will convince disbelievers that a single bullet ricocheted and tumbled and shattered assorted bones in both John Kennedy and John Connally in the precise manner required by the official single-bullet explanation. There are problems with this hypothesis, even I know that, but investigations and tests prove to anyone with an open mind that the scenario is at least possible. The enhancements of the Zapruder footage demonstrate a blink-of-the-eye *forward* movement of 2.3 inches before the famous backwards recoil. This critical finding was dismissed by the naysayers. Nor are they bothered by the fact that every single one of the dozens of supposed conspirators have held up for thirty years under the guilt and pressure; that we haven't heard a single death-bed confession in over three decades. An absolutely damning fact, absolutely ignored.

Conspiracy buffs aren't interested in changing their minds, and neither are the rest of us. We're not built this way. We're assured that the human brain is the most complex structure in the known universe, an assessment that serves mainly as a monument to our egos—as well as, perhaps, a comment on the cosmos. Certainly the details of our physical composition and comportment are intricate beyond our comprehension, but why then does a poll of 1,250 Americans peg the rest of us so accurately? You can make too much of this demographic success, certainly, but at the same time you have to make *something* of it. All the major religions contend that we're fundamentally flawed, but they do so in ways that leave our egos intact: it wasn't our fault, there's a way to get right, to break free, there's salvation, whatever. In this psychological essence, big-time religions are all the same, and cleverly so. Nevertheless, the deeper truth may be that we're just not quite as fancy as we're cracked up to be, although I don't expect this idea to catch on anytime soon.

Another idea about the conspiracy theories holds that they spring from our desire to make the explanation of the assassination equal in weight to the evil and repercussions of the deed itself; so profound a loss requires an equally profound provenance. Otherwise . . . well, otherwise we'd have yet another reason not to believe in God or in anything else. A wicked conspiracy involving some combination of the CIA, the FBI, the Mafia, the Soviet Union, generic Cold War zealots including, of course, anti-Castro Cuban refugees, the Trilateral Commission, the Council on Foreign Relations, the Bureau of Alcohol, Tobacco, and Firearms (a recent addition), and even powerful Texas oil interests would balance the scales somewhat, while a lone nut with a high-powered mail-order rifle and the motivation to change the course of history is just too frightening and nihilistic.

William Manchester gave wide currency to this psychological explanation, then Norman Mailer picked up on it, and I'm sympathetic. Evil this banal *is* difficult to accept. However, the notion of balancing requires you to ignore the long list of lone-nut assassins who have already changed the course of history, or tried to, in many nations over many centuries, among them François Ravaillac (Henry III); Jacques Clement (Henry IV);

Richard Lawrence (Andrew Jackson);* Charles J. Guiteau (James Garfield); Carl Weiss (Huey Long, disputed); Lee Harvey Oswald; James Earl Ray (Martin Luther King, Jr.); Sirhan B. Sirhan (RFK); Lynette "Squeaky" Fromme (Gerald Ford); Sara Jane Moore (Ford again just eighteen days later); and John Hinckley (Ronald Reagan).

In *The Godfather, Part II*, Tom Hagen exclaims that the Corleone family's hit men won't be able to get Hyman Roth when he enters the country in Miami. "Mike," Tom sputters, "that's impossible! They'll turn him over directly to Internal Revenue, Customs, and half the FBI. It would be like trying to kill the president!" Michael Corleone looks at his step-brother with loving disdain before taking a bite from his orange and replying, "Tom, you know, you surprise me. If anything in this life is certain, if history has taught us anything, it's that you can kill anyone." Though set in 1958, this sequel was released in 1974 following a decade of assassinations, with more failed attempts to come. Michael then turns to Rocco, who says thoughtfully between bites of what appears to be focaccia, "Difficult. Not impossible, but difficult."

Just so. It's a little late for comforting symmetry in this fallen world.

A woman approached Dan Stevens and said she'd been working in a nearby dress shop on the day of the assassination. She now lived in Laughlin, Nevada, was employed by one of the casinos there—the Ramada Express, in fact, where I had stayed—and was in Dallas to visit relatives. She told Dan and a couple of us bystanders that on that November day she was left alone in the dress shop when her co-workers went to the plaza to see the president and his wife. Within moments of the

---

*A particularly instructive episode: elaborate conspiracy theories began circulating immediately following Lawrence's attempt on Jackson on January 30, 1835—the first attempt ever on an American president—but few were credible and none were even halfway proved.

shooting, she saw men running past the shop carrying rifles. More significantly, a group of black women immediately paraded past with signs reading THEY SHOT OUR PRESIDENT.

She had two questions for the resident expert. Is there anything on the record about armed peace officers on the street at that time? Not to Dan's knowledge. And how could those black women have prepared their professionally lettered signs so quickly? Dan didn't have a clue, but he told the lady that everyone in Dallas in 1963 understood that the KKK operated out of ———'s office. Here Dan accused a former law enforcement official, a charge I haven't been able to verify, although his general point is beyond dispute: the KKK and Dallas indeed have a long history. The main texts are *Big D* and *Hood, Bonnet, and Little Brown Jug*, the former by Southern Methodist University professor Darwin Payne, the latter by Norman D. Brown at the University of Texas in Austin. In the 1920s, there was a Klan Day at the Texas State Fair, and the grounds were segregated, of course. The Klan controlled city politics. Jesse Curry and Will Fritz, the Police Chief and Captain of Detectives, respectively, in 1963, had been members in their youths. R.L. Thorton, mayor from 1953 to 1962, had belonged in the twenties; but this banker, widely known as Mr. Dallas, later led the local desegregation movement in the sixties, on grounds of economic necessity. Thirty years later, in 1995, Ron Kirk was elected mayor of Dallas, without a runoff and with the support of Roger Staubach and most of the downtown political establishment. Texans were surprised: Houston, not Dallas, was supposed to be the first to elect a black mayor.

The woman confiding in Dan at Dealey Plaza explained that she hadn't told her story immediately after the assassination for fear of reprisal, nor would she reveal her name now. In fact, she and her family abruptly walked away. Though it seemed even to me that her testimony, if credible at all, might be an important contribution to the endless investigation, Dan had listened impassively and shown no particular surprise or excitement. In the three years working the plaza, he'd heard plenty of wacky stuff. Plus this witness's credibility had gone way down when she mentioned in passing that she had attended high school in Dallas with Jack Ruby. Everyone knows the man who shot Oswald completed only the sixth grade, despite his claims of an eighth-grade education. Furthermore, he acquired this excellent schooling in Chicago.

CHAPTER 16

My father and I followed Highway 180 from Dallas out to Stamford. This road cuts north off I-20 east of Stan and Wes Mickle's horse breeding ranch and Bob Popplewell's rattlesnake ranch, then follows a roughly parallel route twenty-odd miles to the north. This was the original thoroughfare in these parts, indicated by the fact that the towns it passes through—Weatherford, Mineral Wells, and Breckenridge—are larger than any on the adjacent interstate. Also, there are five county seats on 180 en route to the Abilene region, while I-20 can claim only two.

Twenty years had elapsed since Dad last drove this road. In 1975, while living in Houston, he had been in Dallas on business when his mother died in Stamford. When I began this book, he started lobbying long and hard to accompany me on this trip, for a host of reasons. He has a passion for traveling by car, and always wants to drive; he wanted to see and show me some of the old places; he didn't know when, if ever, he would be out this way again; and, I suspect, he simply wanted to spend some time with me. For my part, I thought I might find some loose ends of metaphor regarding the old pre-interstate way of life out on the old two-lane highway, and I simply wanted to spend some time with him. Two or three days alone, just the two of us, with neither brother nor mother nor relatives along, no hunting or golfing or other friends? Amazing. I don't believe it had happened before.

Dad had been in Dallas when his mother died because he was a land man for Texaco, acquiring possible service station sites along the stretch of residential developments and commercial strips that now define the interstate between Dallas and Fort Worth. Between them, the major oil companies bought practically every corner of every available intersection on the new interstates throughout the country in the fifties, sixties, and seventies, operating under the assumption that all would become prime gas-pumping sites. In fact, the opposite has happened. Twenty-five years ago, 100 million vehicles in America filled up their tanks at 236,000 stations. Today, with twice as many rigs, there are fewer than 100,000 stations. The self-service mega-outlets have taken over. Few and far between are the small, full-service neighborhood stations like the one I worked at as a kid in Houston—Texaco, of course—where the owner sipped vodka straight from the chilled bottle under the mistaken impression that no one would smell this particular vapor on his breath, and where his foreman, Oliver Gayfield, took me under his wing in matters of changing oil and balancing wheels and having the right attitude about everything. Oliver was calm and patient almost to a fault. While the rest of us were annoyed when a smoking car pulled in minutes before we were about to roll down the doors of the three work bays, he didn't blink before raising the hood and setting to work. Oliver was the first black man I knew; it must have been my experience working with him that first fixed my stubborn resistance to the charms of the Old and the New

South.* In my memory, Oliver was the first black person I'd ever *met*, but could this possibly be true? Well, yes. There were no black kids in any of the schools I went to. No black kids or parents in any of the neighborhoods I lived in. As my father recalls, no black men or women worked in any of the Texaco offices in the early 1960s, so he didn't have any black friends over for the Saturday-night barbecues. And at that time, we had never had a maid.

A fool, even a kid, could easily discern the discrepancy between the integrity of Oliver Gayfield—I've never met a better person, period—and the racial politics I wrongly assumed were exclusively Southern. On the other hand, I realize how dangerous it is to rely on personal experience as an explanation, reason, or excuse for subsequent attitudes, because what happens if that initial experience is a bad one? But such judgments are part of our nature, obviously, along with our propensity for believing rather than thinking, and I was lucky to work with someone of Oliver Gayfield's practically perfect nature, as I understood it at the time. Not many years later, after I had shifted to the Texaco warehouse on the other side of town for my summer job at union scale and therefore had lost touch with Oliver, and after I'd acquired a broader perspective on the issues, the idea arose that Oliver might have been just highly skilled and practiced in presenting himself to white folks—an Uncle Tom. Today, I believe he was both practical minded and practically perfect.

On I-20, Dad thought he recognized a station site he'd acquired twenty years earlier, but no gas station was there. We motored past Fort Worth, emerged from the Metroplex, saw our first grazing steers, exclaimed on the beautiful day, cut off the interstate at Highway 180, and drove into Weatherford, where I put a penny in the parking meter on the town square; a

---

*Granted, where I was born and raised and am now writing is technically part of the South, because it was part of the Confederacy. However, Texas was, is, and always will be, first and foremost, Texas—not a fact that necessarily makes my heart swell with pride, because I'm not very patriotic, but at least it's less than fully Southern, I believe.

penny buys twelve minutes, a nickel a full hour. The town is otherwise unremarkable and Dad was more interested in reaching Mineral Wells anyway, which in his day was a regionally famous spa and watering hole, with four hundred active wells. Today there's just the one, as we learned from Sherry Holland, who since 1994 is the owner of Zephyr Water Company. Sherry's well is 110 feet deep and rich in bicarbonate of soda and lithium. In the early days, this water played a major role in the healing of a crazy woman and therefore became known as "crazy water," giving its name to the Crazy Water Hotel. Dad was particularly interested in seeing what had become of this old establishment and its more famous and magnificent limestone competition, the Baker. The answer is that the fifteen-story Baker, a rococo building with Italianate touches, is abandoned and looks that way on the northeast corner of the main intersection in Mineral Wells, while the six-story Crazy Water is a retirement home.

With the trained eye of the real-estate practitioner, Dad surmised this fact the moment he saw that the old building was still in working condition. What other economic fate was feasible in the 1990s in a town whose population was 14,870? None at all. Today, the Howard Johnson's and the Days Inn are more than sufficient for local hostelry needs. If it weren't for the old folks, the Crazy Water wouldn't have any folks at all. My father knew this had to be the case, but just to make sure, we parked and walked up the steps. And there they were, old folks sitting at a large table in the clean but ill-lit and sparsely appointed lobby, playing cards. Others were in the cafeteria off to the left for their very early lunch, and others still were up in their rooms, probably. One card player much younger than the others—a woman in her forties, a disability client in some category, I assumed—looked at me carefully with an expression that said, I know everyone here and their children, too, and I don't know you. I looked back with the expression that said, You're right. The nice lady behind the reception desk took her own look at Dad and me and figured she might have a candidate and his son in the market for one of the two single rooms available at the time. Two out of 196 total. $500 a month for a single, $635 for a double, $710 for a suite,

$845 for a double suite, everything included: she announced her prices before we'd exchanged a civil word.

"Really?" That's my father's all-purpose exclamation, and it suited this revelation, because a nice retirement room in Houston costs almost twice that much. That's why the Crazy Water is booked solid. However, it would never become the return address for the likes of Bob Bryan, not if he could help it. My father is scared to death of ending up in any old folks home. Who the hell wouldn't be? That's his attitude, expressed with the rare if mild curse and the not-quite-so-rare-nor-mild sneer. The lady hadn't realized we were just browsing, not shopping.

Beyond the lobby and down the hallway past the cafeteria is the enclosed pavilion which was the centerpiece of the Crazy Water in its heyday. W. Lee "Pappy" O'Daniel and his Light Crust Doughboys started their career right here. Texas's famous singing governor between 1939 and 1941, Pappy quit in order to enter the Senate after beating Lyndon Baines Johnson in a special election.* The movie director D. W. Griffith must have stopped at the Crazy Water, too, for some reason, because his picture was pinned on a bulletin board. Across the concrete dance floor from the bandstand was the long bar where the mineral waters used to be drawn. A faded shuffleboard was painted on the floor, and an old Model A was parked in one corner. My father obliged with a couple of stories about fooling around with Model A's as a boy, after they'd been supplanted by Model T's.

At the suggestion of our friend at the reception counter, we took the left-hand elevator to the penthouse floor, turned to the left, and stepped onto the rooftop garden, which provided a fine view of the entire town of Mineral Wells. From up there, it looked exactly like all the other old, bypassed, hanging-on towns around the country. Mineral Wells is doomed to these

---

*The loser of this election acquired the ironic nickname "Landslide Lyndon" after his subsequent victory in 1948, pilfered with the help of the most famous 202 votes in American political history. But since he'd *lost* that prior election to O'Daniel by just 1,323 votes, some of them tarnished, too, LBJ probably thought he was just getting even.

dimensions. The only sign of metropolitan life was the vapor trail overhead.

Mineral Wells is near the eastern edge of Palo Pinto County, a cartographer's set of six lines (the northern boundary has a jog in it) that also serves as the rough delineation of a pocket of isolated hills labeled the Palo Pinto Hills on the old maps. My father remembers those maps, although they've been replaced in his library by dozens of newer ones. As we drove into the eastern edge of the hills—none more than a few hundred feet above the surrounding ranchland—Bob broke out the Xeroxes he'd made from the complete set of 254 official Texas county maps, collected in a book I'd given him several years earlier. Glancing up at some tiny little place west of Mineral Wells, he said it had looked just about the same sixty years ago. Then we passed two new $200,000 houses, with only the white wood fence to keep steers out of the backyard. Crossing the Brazos River, we saw off to the north a vast collection of many hundreds of trailer homes and RVs all parked in long, neat rows on what appeared to be the tarmac of an abandoned airport, complete with large hangars. What the hell?

For several years, at almost every opportunity, my father had expressed his curiosity regarding what, *exactly*, I did when I abruptly dropped everything else and headed out for a stint on the highways. I was fairly certain that he was fairly certain that it wasn't anything he would properly call work. Anyway, here was an opportunity to show him what I did for my wages, off and on, so I spun around and drove onto the grounds of the Federal Emergency Management Agency—a small sign provided this information—in order to find someone to whom I could address a series of incisive questions. The man who fit this description was removing supplies from the trunk of his car in front of what appeared to be the office when the Bryans *père et fils* pulled up.

Facts gleaned: the Dempsey Strategic Storage Center is where thousands of RVs and mobile homes are received, refurbished, then driven or shipped out to disaster areas nation-wide. This is one of two such depots; the other's in Kentucky. On hand at this time were two thousand mobile homes and two hundred RVs, but there's always a steady flow of housing in and out, becoming a torrent following a disaster such as Hurricane Andrew on the east coast of Florida in 1992. And why was this operation isolated out here, way off an inter-state? I didn't have to ask. The answer: one of those powerful politicians voters all over the country are sick of re-electing year after year.

As it turned out, Dad didn't seem all that interested by either the strategic depot or my interrogatory skills, so we drove on. A few miles to the west, the Palo Pinto Hills ended rather abruptly and the mesquite and the cactus began to take over. Outside Breckenridge, the next significant town, the sign advised that the next McDonald's was 120 miles far-ther up the road. That's one way to say you're now approach-ing West Texas.

Among the famous limestone courthouses in Texas is the one in Shackelford County, built in 1883. The town is Albany, about thirty miles northeast of Abilene, and you should be sure to visit the Old Jail Art Center, unsurprisingly housed in the old jail, which predates the courthouse by five years. Closed on Mondays, admission free, donations welcome, this museum is nothing you'd expect to find out here. The most prized paint-ings are the Modigliani and the Klee, the former valued at something up to $1 million, the latter at somewhat less. "Really?" Dad said to Joeliene Magoto, the young museum director who'd moved here with her husband, Michael, from Illinois. Michael had a ceramics studio on the main street and, at the time, a large, very beautiful urn on display at the mu-seum. My father wasn't surprised so much by the numbers attributed to the Modigliani and the Klee—he knows what trophy art is worth these days, at least on paper—as by hear-ing those numbers here in Albany. This sophisticated collec-tion is even more unexpected than the Kimball Museum of Art, back in Fort Worth. Just inside the front gate of the Old Jail Art Center, beneath large nonbearing Bradford pear trees, the patio features some nice abstract sculptures, including a granite windmill, and a rough-hewn woman with swinging dugs. Inside the spare, modern galleries are a collection of pre-Columbian figurines; Chinese terra-cotta tomb figures; a nineteenth-century Buddhist prayerbook from Cambodia; drawings by Braque, Ernst, Nevelson, Matta, and Rouault; lithographs by modernists of even higher standing, including Matisse; and usually a special show. The absence of cowboy art disconcerts some visitors, who have a point: what else should a museum out here be expected to display?

Albany's population is about two thousand; the whole of Shackelford County, slightly over three thousand. A compound question immediately presents itself: which way to the big ranch with the considerable oil-and-gas production, and who is or was the iconoclastic owner, because some such figure is the only explanation for this establishment? In short, who's the Tom Mitchell in this area, who's the rancher who couldn't build a first-class truck stop like the Circle Bar Truck Corral because the interstate doesn't go through Albany or anywhere in Shackelford County, and who therefore donated his collection and created this museum instead?

I put the issue to Joeliene in not quite so many words and learned that I was all wrong. While there was an important ranching family, the Nails, the Old Jail Art Center really is a community endeavor; there never was the huge endowment I envisioned, from the Nails or anyone else. Four private collections donated in 1980 are the heart of the museum's permanent collection, and there was a $2 million fund drive under way to benefit the permanent endowment and to build yet another extension, the Local History and Learning Center. Joeliene had every reason to believe this goal would be achieved. Early that Tuesday afternoon, my father and I were the only visitors, considerably outnumbered by the staff and docents—but not by the security guards, of whom we saw not one. However, Joeliene directed us to the three maps—state, national, global—that bristled with pins designating the homes of museum visitors.

· · ·

Not to be confused with the Brazos River, which we had crossed near Mineral Wells, is the Clear Fork of the Brazos River, which runs through the nothing town of Lueders, Texas, twenty-three miles west of Albany. Lueders is on Highway 6, which cuts off 180 and continues on to Stamford, twenty miles to the northwest. Dad emphasized to me that right *here*, on the *west* side of the Clear Fork of the Brazos River, and contrary to expectations, perhaps, is where farming begins in this little part of the state. Something different about the soil and terrain, he said; something better, something deeper, although that depth can vary greatly, six inches on one farm, three feet on another, and the only way to tell from the surface is by color: the shallower dirt is also lighter, almost red; the deeper dirt is dark brown.

Before 1900, soil depth didn't matter, because there wasn't any farming here. But in 1900, the Missouri-Kansas-Texas Railroad, known simply as the Katy, extended the line from Albany to Stamford and opened up these parts to markets that farmers, more than ranchers, required. Homesteaders on these new trains came in from the east, acquired the land for next to nothing, and commenced to grow cotton, mainly, and feed grains. Within a matter of ten years, ranchland became farming country. There's no irrigation in this part of Texas, but this doesn't mean that sufficient rain can be confidently expected. We were twenty miles on the rainy side of the 100th meridian, but wet weather systems often get confused regarding their whereabouts and don't make it this far west. *Average* rainfall here is twenty-three inches, sometimes considerably less, and it's very spotty. What's worse, cotton requires water in the key months of June and July; if early summer is bone dry, thirty inches of rain spread over the remaining ten months won't yield a bumper crop. If the farmers could irrigate this land, they might, but the Seymour Aquifer doesn't have the volume for the job. So dry-land farming it is.

As we drove past fields of harvested cotton, my father said, "My grandmother and grandfather came out from Waxahachie, Texas, when the railroad came through and homesteaded the 320 acres in the place I'll show you. That's where I was born. Granddad later bought another 120 acres two or

three miles from there. Those were the Bryans. The Hines"—
the maternal side of his family—"settled about the same time
in Avoca, and it's possible their house is still there. We'll see."

In one minute I'd learned more genealogy than I had
picked up in the previous forty-eight years; or maybe I'd forgotten, also highly possible. In any event, issues of ancestry
have never been a priority in my immediate family, for whatever reason; and maybe we've missed something, because
somewhere Dad had picked up one intriguing and informative
fact about one forebear and now passed it along to me. His
maternal grandmother had been a Williams before she had
married into the Hines family, and her family had come to
Texas from Virginia, where they had a large cotton . . . planta-
tion, I suppose you'd have to call it. The maternal wing of that
family had come, in turn, from Belgium as the Verhaydens,
and the reason they had come to the United States was that the
Battle of Waterloo was fought on their farm—among others,
of course—on June 18, 1815. That battle killed twelve thousand soldiers, wounded forty thousand others, effectively
ended Napoleon's career, and induced the victorious Duke of
Wellington to write famously, "Next to a battle lost, the greatest misery is a battle gained." More to the point, it temporarily
ruined the battlefield for peacetime agriculture. Disgusted, my
forebears the Verhaydens got up and sailed west. So it is written somewhere.

"We're going to stop here," my father said abruptly as we
approached the Clear Fork.

"Right here?"

"Across the river."

He directed me onto a dirt road fifty yards past this modest
stream, and we followed it past the Baptist Encampment re-
treat and then down a rutted incline to the Lueders city park.
Until the swimming pool in Stamford was built in 1934, this
was the only place to swim in the whole region. My father
hadn't been here for at least fifty-five years, but he remembered the rope swing hanging over the water from the thick
branch of the oak tree—if not the same rope, surely the same
tree. Be careful jumping off because there couldn't be more
than five or six feet of water in the Clear Fork in the best of

times. As a major vacation instead of just a day trip to the swimming hole, families would make arrangements with one of the landowners upriver and pitch camp on that riverbank for a week of freshwater angling.

"And that was *it* for vacations," Dad said with finality. He and my mother have vacationed all over the United States and Europe, have been on cruises here and there, and went to Hawaii for their fiftieth wedding anniversary. But the Depression is still the defining experience for him and his generation, and I suppose that's why he has so little patience for the complaining that goes on nowadays. He *remembers*. It's as simple as that. He has almost no time for the nightly news, the politicians, the pundits, the pollsters, all of whom invite his wrath, mild though it might be. He disdains the general lack of historical perspective. We have no idea what we're talking about. He adheres instead to a Panglossian faith in progress and better times ahead. When I sometimes ask, during dinner discussions, "In which countries?" or "For whom?" he resists the insinuation. My father enjoys restaurants because he can marvel at all the choices on the menu; the food itself is secondary. He acknowledges as much, and I think this attitude also goes back to the Depression, when the Bryans and the Hineses and almost everyone else around Lueders and Avoca and Stamford were hardworking farmers and tradesmen, poor in everything except land, maybe, which wasn't worth much, either, and there wasn't much they could do but make the best of it or leave.

And leave they did, at least in my family. My father counted up nineteen Bryans and twelve Hineses who lived around Avoca and Stamford at that time. Now there are none.

I referred to Lueders as a nothing town, which is true enough; it's not listed in my Rand McNally index, and the population of 511, according to the sign, must include all the nearby farm families, their pets, and some of the stock. But once upon a time Lueders had its own oil refinery. That shows how things have changed in this country: thirty years ago we had all the neighborhood filling stations; thirty years before that, neighborhood refineries. Likewise, there used to be six cotton gins in Stamford alone; now there's one. There used to be a farmhouse every half-mile in any direction, because a farm of 160 acres was the norm. Now more of them are 400 or 500 acres, with some up to 3,000 or 4,000 acres, because much more farmland is required to produce the same profit, factoring in inflation. To justify the deluxe $100,000 tractor, you need at least 1,000 acres. Basic modern economics, the same reason I-20 to the south has replaced Highway 180 as the region's major east-west route. And thank God for basic modern economics, my father feels, and for Keynes, specifically. The standard wage for an itinerant laborer used to be $1 a day plus meals and a pile of hay in the barn for a bed. Dad remembers, and not fondly.

Seven miles west of Lueders is Avoca, not much of a town, either, but a word wonderfully evocative for me. "Avoca" *sounds* country. State trooper and class clown David Mays joked that the family trees here grow straight up, no branching. Funny, I guess, although my father was born on a nearby farm. As we drove into town, Dad alerted me to the fact that there are now two Avocas, the old one on a dirt road about three tenths of a mile to the south of the new one, which sprang up alongside the asphalt highway that came through in the twenties. When the two hamlets add up their populations, the total comes to a few hundred. Tilled farmland comes right up to the back doors of some of these modest homes; a few steers are penned behind others. The well-maintained Methodist Church, built in 1906, is outfitted with a relatively new belfry, with two bells from old railroad engines. This congregation has its roots in the old-time brush-arbor camp meeting in nearby Avo, Texas, which has now disappeared from both map and memory. Another old church is off in the country north of Avoca, the handsome Bethel Evangelical Lutheran Church in Ericksdahl, dedicated in 1907, visible from miles away in certain directions and sometimes referred to as the Chartres of Jones County.

We cruised the streets of Avoca in search of Uncle Roy's house. He was my grandmother Corene's brother, a highly respected member of the Avoca community—involved in cattle, trucking, and so on—until he succumbed to alcohol. Even then, Dad recalled, people understood what had happened.

"And don't put much family in the book," he interjected. Then, suddenly, "This is it." I stopped in front of a house with a fairly new red-brick facade. Could the wiring be the same as Dad had helped the Baptist minister install sixty years ago, before building codes? Surely not. Next, Dad instructed me to cross the highway and proceed north on that dirt road in search of the original Hines home, where his mother had grown up, and which he thought might still be standing. And so it was, if barely, on the west side of the road. I gave it another few years, tops. Right here, for the first time, I learned that I was nearly an heir to a fabulously wealthy oilman. An oil company—Dad doesn't know which one—had leased the Hines property for drilling, then brought in a modest well nearby; but for some reason it was decided that the Hines property wasn't a good enough risk. No one since has taken the risk, either, so who knows. The current owners of this cotton farm could be sitting on a lake of the stuff.

My father didn't go into this, but I happen to know that this same Mr. Hines disapproved of my grandfather as a suitor for his daughter and went out to the barn whenever Henry came over to court Corene. When they eloped at the age of seventeen or eighteen, Mr. Hines went out to the barn for a long, long time. Eventually, however, my great-grandfather came to approve of his son-in-law, and in the end preferred him to everyone else.

We drove past the tottering old Hines home toward California Creek, where my father and his chums used to ride their bikes to look for arrowheads at an old Indian campground. We crossed the creek on a narrow wood bridge, turned around, and drove back to have a look at the house my great-grandfather built in 1928, maybe 1929, when he bought additional acreage. This was a good farmhouse, complete with barn and storage buildings and fecund garden, and it was a big deal for my father and his sister, Mary, to sit on the new front porch and watch the daily freight and passenger trains charge up the tracks from the east. The homestead is still there, occupied, solid-looking, painted white, of course, but the train is history. Even the tracks have been removed. When my great-grandfather moved here, my grandfather and his family of four moved into the main farmhouse on the original 320 acres. My father was eight or nine years old. Three or four years later, in 1932, Henry Bryan moved his family into Stamford, eight miles away, for the simple reason that it was hard to support four people on a farm during the Depression. Not that it was any easier in town. Dad doesn't remember—and maybe never knew—exactly what happened to that original farm, whether it was leased for a while or sold immediately. When the Bryans sold the second farm in the early fifties, they got top dollar, around $250 an acre. Now it would go for $400, conceivably $500 in an inflated market with wet weather guaranteed in writing for the following decade. Obviously, this degree of appreciation doesn't come remotely close to keeping up with inflation.

"What did Granddad do in town?" I asked.

"Anything he could find."

Over the years, I've learned that terse statements from my father signal strong subterranean emotions that will stay exactly where they are.

"What did you want to do?"

"Get out of here. There had to be something better."

Happily, there was. In 1938—the pits of the Depression in Texas—my father went off to the university in Austin. As a Boy Scout, he'd ridden to Ruidoso, New Mexico, three hundred miles distant, on an open-bed truck; otherwise, nowhere. He came home from the university in the summers to work on his grandfather's farm. They grew cotton and enough feed grain for the animals. He worked the whole summer in exchange for school tuition of $50 a year. That was poor pay, I quickly calculated, even by the depressed standards of the day, but Dad just shrugged at this observation. He worked with horses and mules, too, because his grandfather despised tractors. Some of the neighboring farmers did not, however, and sometimes you could hear them plowing in the moonlight. Dad also remembers hauling the cotton trailer to the gin and struggling to control his animals, who were terrified by the noise of the big suction tube used, as it still is, to pull the raw material into the dryer.

Dad guided me down a different road on which, in 1929 or

1930, he had set up a stand to sell soft drinks to the mule skin-
ners hauling gravel from California Creek to spread over the
dirt surface. It's still a gravel road today. As we coasted slowly
along between the fields, he judged that his little business must
have sat right about . . . here. We stopped for a moment and
listened to the crickets. And somewhere around here was the
holding pond for the Stamford water supply, which had to be
pumped up from another holding pond to the east at Lueders,
which in turn had to be pumped up from a defunct lake the
name of which no one I found could remember. From this
pond in Avoca the water could finally flow *down* to the last of
the holding ponds just outside Stamford, where my father and
I arrived late that afternoon.

CHAPTER 17

The home I remember as my grandparents' is the tidy place at 804 Hudson Street, a little frame house with two bedrooms, carport, grandkids bunked everywhere, and, in my memory, the huge swamp-cooler blowing like mad in the living room and creating, right in the middle of a hot, dry semidesert, a cool, damp place to live. But Dad assured me that this was only the last of quite a few Bryan domiciles. Two of them were on the other side of the main Stamford thoroughfare, where the bumpy streets are still the original brick, and my father pointed them out to me. They look poorly today, as Dad assured me they looked back then. There were other houses, too, since the family moved every year or so for a while.

My father also reminded me about the house at the corner of the Avoca highway and Wells Street, the yellow, two-story frame residence on the lower floor of which my mother, brother, and I lived in the early fifties while he was off in the

Korean War. A naval supply officer based primarily at Sasebo, Japan, north of Nagasaki, he saw the actual war once a month when his ship steamed into Korean waters in order to qualify all aboard for combat pay. Over forty years later, he was reluctant to release this compromising information for publication, but I convinced him that it must have been S.O.P. at the time, old news for war buffs and unsurprising now for the rest of us cynics. We drove past the local Carnegie Library, originally funded by an endowment from Andrew himself, whose essay "The Gospel of Wealth" argued that the wealthy are merely trustees, enjoined to use their money for the public good. Carnegie did so to the tune of $350 million. Legend has it that Stamford was in line for benefaction because of the influence of the Swenson family. Originally from Sweden, these folks were major players in this part of the state, while another wing of the family lived in New York City and probably hung out with the famous magnate. Perhaps, but it was probably just the luck of the draw—the very large draw, because Carnegie endowed about 2,799 other libraries.

We checked in at the Great Western Motel and then, assuming that the Cliff House restaurant across the street didn't serve beer or wine, we sat on the two chairs in Dad's room and drank a Pearl apiece. Early in this book, I enumerated the fifteen mundane reasons my wife and I had moved in twenty-three years of marriage. At the Great Western I learned there may be a genetic component to this behavior, perhaps even a Lamarckian component, although that specific doctrine of acquired inheritance lacks for any credibility today. My parents had lived in the same house in Houston for thirty-eight years, but before that had moved even more than I have. I'd known about some of these places, but by no means all of them. As the truth began to emerge, I grilled my father closely. Starting in Stamford, where I was born shortly after World War II, they moved almost immediately to San Antonio, then to Houston, to Key West for naval training, back to Stamford, then back to Houston, penultimately to San Angelo, and finally to Houston for the third and last time: eighteen houses total by the time I was ten years old, in 1957. And there had been a good deal of shifting around before I was born, what with the war and all. In fact, my father didn't see his first son until the summer of 1945, when my older brother, Nick, was almost eighteen months old. Sailors and officers on the U.S.S. *Charette* normally got mail every two or three weeks at sea, but in the winter of 1944, when Nick was born, they waited three months. When the pouch finally arrived, my father ripped open the most likely-looking envelope and out fell a book of matches inscribed IT'S A BOY!

My parents moved for the following reasons, not all of them mundane: job transfer; better place; landlord took back the better place; job transfer; ownership; war; better motel with kitchenette; better place (conch house); different war; better apartment; different war concluded; job transfer; better place; landlord took back *this* better place; ownership; job transfer; ownership.

Most of Stamford is in Jones County, which is dry, but, as it turned out, the Cliff House restaurant is barely across the county line in the portion of Haskell County that's wet. The liquor situation in Texas is nothing if not byzantine; an interstate highway even figures into the story. It's a little-known fact that the Twenty-first Amendment to the Constitution, the legal means for repealing the Eighteenth Amendment, or Prohibition, granted the individual states the authority to regulate all alcoholic beverages. Eighteen of them eventually adopted some form of "controlled" or "semicontrolled" system in which the state itself was retailer, wholesaler, or both. In the other thirty-two "license" states, all retailing and wholesaling functions are in private hands but are closely regulated and highly taxed by the state; nationwide, taxation accounts for forty-two percent of the retail cost of a bottle of scotch. Texas is one of the "license" states, and incorporates the concept of "local option" in its regulations. Three levels of jurisdiction—municipality, precinct, and county—are empowered to vote the seven alternative local options, listed here in order of ascending wetness: completely dry; beer off-premises only; beer on- and off-; beer and wine off- only; beer and wine on- and off-; all alcoholic beverages off- only; completely wet. For any given address, the legal status of alcohol is established by the most recent election in the *lowest* jurisdiction. So a municipal vote overrules the precinct vote, which in turn overrules the county vote. This is why counties can offer varying degrees of wetness. Dallas County, for example, is dry, but the city, like all cities everywhere, is wet. When I was a grandkid visiting my grandparents in Stamford, people drove to Impact, an artificial but legal and wet entity at the edge of Abilene, in Taylor County. Impact was wet. And my grandparents' friends Mutt and Bertha Dyer, who came over on Sunday night to play canasta and "84," owned a small liquor store they ran out of a trailer home in a wet precinct in Haskell County.

The Wholesale Beer Distributors of Texas publishes a helpful reference map. Large areas of South and West Texas are mostly green; they're pretty wet. Large areas of East and North Texas are white—dry—but with splotches of green. I-10, which runs through Houston, San Antonio, and El Paso, is considered the main demarcation between the two major zones, with more green areas leaking north of that line than white areas leaking south. Of the 254 counties in Texas, only 37 are totally wet, and they're outnumbered by the 53 counties that are bone dry. If you do much traveling around the state and like to drink, the map comes in handy.

My father and I could theoretically have bought our beers at the Cliff House, except that the Cliff House doesn't serve beer anyway because, our waitress said, "there are too many churchgoers." She was, of course, referring to one denomination of churchgoers in particular, the infamously, if not always actually, teetotaling Southern Baptists.

The following morning Dad and I paid a call on C.E. Bunkley at his pharmacy on the west side of the town square. Sure, C.E. remembered me from almost forty years earlier, when I'd come into this same store with my grandfather Bailey, the administrator of the Stamford hospital before he and my grandmother Myrtle moved down to Ozona. C.E. had been in this store for forty-eight years and wanted to make it fifty as a matter of principle. Then he would retire. Maybe he'll be able to sell the business, but probably not. What young pharmacist is likely to move to Stamford and try to compete with Wal-Mart? C.E. can't think of one, and neither can I. You have to believe that loyalty and old-times'-sake considerations keep his pharmacy alive, because there is no way he can match Wal-Mart's prices. On the other hand, the increase in the sheer number of prescription medications has been a big plus. C.E. now stocks well over a thousand drugs, over twice as many as when he started this business immediately following World War II. Back then, however, his malpractice insurance cost him nothing because nobody had ever heard of such a thing. Recently he had raised his coverage from $300,000 to $1 million. He had also acquired an "800" number for the use of doctors in Abilene.

All in all, business is good at the back of the store. The problem's up front, where a young woman sells batteries and shampoos and fountain pens. This counter is not a money-maker at all. The long soda fountain along the left-hand wall where I had enjoyed many a milkshake has been discontinued, although a few old-timers do still come in for coffee at three o'clock.

Forty years ago, the whole square was booming. I remember coming to the bustling post office, in the center of the square where the courthouse presides in county seats (Anson, in the case of Jones County). I remember visiting my grandmother Corene at the Strauss dry-goods store on the northeast corner, where she clerked in the fabric department, rolling out long sheets of material for her many friends and neighbors. (This Strauss family also produced the most illustrious figure to come out of this region: Robert "Bobby" Strauss, Democratic kingpin and former Ambassador to Russia.) Now the square has "cleared out," as C.E. put it—four, maybe five years ago, when the Wal-Mart opened up. Over half the storefronts were empty when my father and I came through town, and they're likely to remain that way, although a new Dollar Store was moving in right next to Bunkley's pharmacy, and the old theater on the south side, the Grand, had reopened to good business. At the moment, *Nell* was showing. Admission on Monday night is $2, and the theater might well sell out those four hundred–plus seats. Regular adult admission is only $4.

It's not only kids who say the darnedest things. Standing in front of this theater looking at the marquee, my father asked with disdain, "Why would anyone pay four dollars to go to a movie?" This statement seems to imply that he prefers to let the movies come to him at home on tape and television, but this isn't the case, either. I'm willing to bet he has never watched an entire movie on tape or television in his life—and to the best of his memory, I'm right. He doesn't watch the thing other than for golf tournaments and the occasional ball-game. He will go to the dollar cinema several times a year. His dismissive remark in Stamford reminded me of the time he demanded to know why I or anyone else would have any interest whatsoever in reading about something *that never happened*— that is, a novel. My father reads newspapers, magazines, menus, maps, biography, and history.

From the square we drove to the cemetery north of town to visit the Bryan plot. It's not much of a cemetery, and Dad has never understood why they chose this location on a small rise, exposed to persistent winds, with soil too poor for the most basic grasses, much less for blooming flowers. But I guess that *is* the reason. Why waste any good land for this? I reminded Dad that when his father died and my wife and I were living in Brooklyn, he didn't call me with the news until after the services so I wouldn't even be tempted to spend the money to fly down. By God if anybody in this family is going to make a big deal out of dying. That's the idea, at any rate, but I have the feeling this defiance might have a counterproductive effect. After all, Dad was the one who lobbied to make this drive out to Stamford. Homeward one last time, perhaps, for him, and for me, too, for that matter. I'll have no good reason for ever going back, although I might.

From the cemetery you can see the highest structures in town: the Methodist church, the water tower, and the largest and most handsome of several three-story brick mansions, on sale at the time for $125,000. It needs gardening and general maintenance; the beautiful paneling and cabinetry and stained glass are in mint condition. There's no way that anything taller than these structures will ever be built here, although everyone believes that Stamford and the surrounding communities will maintain their present population, or close to it, for the foreseeable future. Wal-Mart also thinks so, and they must have demographers on their full-time staff.

Driving south out of town toward Anson and then on to Abilene, thirty-eight miles away, we passed the grandstands of the Texas Cowboy Reunion, with the rickety-looking facility in the process of renovation, and a few miles farther on turned west on Farm-to-Market 92 to Tuxedo, with the accent on the first syllable. TUX-edo, TEX-as, is on the map but not in the index, and the sign doesn't state the population, so I don't know what that is. Minimal, certainly. What the sign did say was ONCE A TOWN—1907—NOW A FARMING COMMUNITY. This land west of Stamford is perfectly flat as far as the eye can see, although it starts bouncing again fairly soon, in every direction, and loses its worth for cotton. Exactly here, it's great cotton country, Dad assured me, and it looked as if it would be great for anything. Less than ten miles west of that hardscrabble Stamford Cemetery, these furrowed fields were that deep, deep brown that signifies several feet of rich soil. Given enough water, you could grow a tropical forest here.

My granddad Henry was a cotton ginner, among other things, and he put in a long stint at the gin in Tuxedo, owned by the same man who owned the one in Avoca, now ransacked for parts and fallen to the ground. We were headed toward the Tuxedo gin to see if it was still in business, although the last cotton would have been ginned in December. Thirty-five years earlier, Henry often took me to work, where I was impressed by the infernal racket made by the machinery as it stripped the fiber from the hull. Granddad knew which machines he could reach a hand into and pull out a wad for inspection, and which he couldn't. Men were always being injured in those cotton gins. If OSHA has made radical and beneficial changes in any industry, I hope this is the one. Fifty or sixty years ago, these gins were belt-driven by steam power. Dad remembers when one of them broke during a run and slapped my grandfather across the head, breaking his neck; Henry wore a make-do brace for weeks, and could just as easily have been killed. That era didn't feature workmen's compensation, either. I remember the aftermath of another accident, when Granddad sat around mournfully in a cast after one of the huge dollops of lead used to weigh the bales gave way and crushed his foot. While he was recuperating (as at all other times) he survived on black coffee, bacon burned black, white bread, and cigar smoke. Doctor after doctor had warned him about his diet, but he didn't listen until a little Jewish doctor from Germany—my sister-in-law's uncle—somehow got through to him in Houston. He quit smoking overnight, to everyone's amazement, and thereafter would eat the occasional string bean. In the chest of drawers in his bedroom in Stamford, they found a box of very stale cigars.

My grandfather liked it out in this country for the same reason I do: there aren't too many trees. One reason he didn't appreciate trees was that he wanted to see where he was going, and he had good reason to feel this way. In addition to the cotton ginning, he sold Studebakers, and at that time, the mid-fifties, the Golden Hawk was one of the fastest assembly-line automobiles sold in the United States. Henry convinced his grandchildren that he personally had to test-drive every car he sold in order to make certain it achieved the promised speed— 140 miles per hour, as I recall in my imagination, but 120 is more like it, according to hobbyists. I fell for this tease, naturally. Hell, I fell for everything. I fell for it when my father said he was building the doghouse because Texaco required every employee to have one. I fell for it hard when I begged for a set of snare drums for Christmas one year and the big boxes behind the tree turned out to be luggage for my frequent visits to my grandparents in Stamford and Ozona.

"Do you know how fast a hundred and forty miles per hour is?" Henry asked us grandkids rhetorically. I remember the evening vividly. He then held his right hand next to his right eye, splayed apart those hardworking, stubby fingers, and said, "The telephone poles are only *this far* apart."

· · ·

The two cars parked by the office indicated that the Tuxedo gin was indeed still a going concern. We introduced ourselves to Betty McDougal, office manager for six years after showing up as an accountant without a day's experience in the business. A question here, a question there, and pretty soon the Bryans had a small-world story to carry away: as a high school student, Betty worked with Corene, my grandmother, at Webb's Department Store, after my grandmother moved on from the Strauss store across the square. She had given Betty a pair of pillowcases for her wedding in 1964, which Betty still had.

In the winter Betty has the office to herself, with just one ginner keeping things maintained in the gin. In this part of Texas, gins run from October through the end of the year. My grandfather would sometimes finish the season "up north," then move down to the Gulf Coast and run one of the gins there; the 320 miles between Stamford and Edna, say, make a great deal of difference in the growing season. I walked across the pavement to the gin itself, a metal structure somewhat larger than a basketball court with a ceiling three stories high, the whole space fairly jammed with giant machines. The technology has changed very little in the thirty-five years since I had last stepped foot in here. A crew of eleven men is standard. In the old days, many of those workers were technically illegal, but not anymore. The gins are the first place the federals look for citizenship or for the green card, so they almost always find it. During the season, work proceeds as long as there is cotton to gin and the machines don't break down. Optimal output is twelve to fifteen bales an hour, each bale weighing five hundred pounds. In 1995, the Tuxedo operation had ginned 3,200 bales, Betty told us. Not a great year, by any means, but better than the following one, a record-low 1,100 bales—a disaster. A good season is 5,000 or even 6,000 bales, and the bad and the good can follow hard on one another: 1,300 bales in 1980, 8,500 the following year. The dry-land farms around here yield anywhere from a disastrous one fifth of a bale per acre—not enough to harvest so they plow it under—to one and a half bales on an exceptional farm in a glorious year. After fifteen minutes of Betty's explanation, which rivaled in complexity the accounting on Joe Gonzalez' paycheck from his milk cooperative in New Mexico, I decided that the farmer's bottom-line ginning cost will be $30 to $40 per bale, including the credit for the cottonseed, which is sold by the gin for its useful oil. He will sell the bale for about $300.

Back on Highway 277, Dad and I drove south through Anson, past its disappointing county courthouse, and into another landscape altogether. Dad gestured toward this terrain and challenged me to spot the difference. That was easy enough: not much farming here, but plenty of scrub brush and oak. Precisely, he said, and this sandy, unfarmable soil is known as shinnery or sand shinnery. This particular belt is four or five miles wide and stretches for miles along the length of the rich North Texas farmland. There are pockets of shinnery elsewhere, and all of it sells for peanuts.

In Abilene we bunked at the Motel 6. Despite Dad's doubts, I assured him the place was trustworthy and conveniently located to both the Wes-T-Go Truck Stop, our dinner destination, and to the airport from where he'd leave for Houston in the morning. In the so-called lobby—considerably smaller than the rooms themselves, to give you an idea—a woman dressed in American Indian garb and wearing a pair of huge eyeglasses was presenting a small crystal to our hostess Flora Sherman, the aspiring memoirist I mentioned several chapters back. This self-professed minister had dug up and purified this crystal herself, she assured Flora; it would make her wishes come true. Flora's face was a mask not of indifference, exactly, though it was definitely noncommittal as she graciously thanked her customer for the gift. After the woman departed with her room key, I said to Flora, "You never know," and she said, "Not in this business." Of course, I already knew her feelings on that subject. When I emerged from the office and handed my father his room key, the minister's traveling companion—an interesting-looking guy with long, gray hair and a leather hat and a leather jacket—was throwing a stick into the pecan tree on the other side of the parking lot, trying with occasional success to knock down some of the nuts. This struck me as behavior akin to the habit of my father and his golfing buddies, who troll for balls along the perimeter of the lakes at the Willowwisp Country

Club; mention to these guys that you need to buy a sleeve of balls and they look at you funny.

The minister was waiting patiently in a stretched-out pickup, the window rolled down. Passing by, I asked in my best offhand manner, "What's your church affiliation?"

She shot me a look before replying, "M.S.S.A."

I blinked.

"Ministry of Spiritual Self-Awareness."

"What kind of dog is that?" I countered, nodding at this great-looking dog riding on the front seat.

"Scottish Highlander."

As I thought: Bob Sundown's breed. And suddenly this woman didn't seem too friendly. I couldn't see her bestowing one of those beneficial crystals on me anytime soon, so I wished her good-afternoon and walked off to see whether Dad approved of his ground-floor, west-facing room. He pronounced it okay, and since we still had some leftover Pearls, I iced them down and two hours later we finished them off while admiring the brilliant sunset through the window, listening to the roaring lullaby of the diesel tractors on I-20. The thing is, however, I couldn't look at that sunset as a perfect backdrop for this magical moment, because in Stamford I'd been amazed to learn that even this part of Texas has what locals think of as a significant air pollution problem. The bearer of this disconcerting news was David Ballard, my mother's cousin, who had joined my father and me for lunch at the Cliff House.

A retired veterinarian, David was an aviator, too, starting in 1968. Not half a dozen years later, he assured us, the pollution was much worse. You don't really notice it until you get in the air above it. The main culprit is Mexico, over the horizon to the southwest. Across the border from Big Bend National Park, two coal-fired power plants pump 250,000 tons of sulfur dioxide annually into the air. On many days, that park all but disappears, and most of the year they're breathing this same stuff in Abilene and Stamford, almost three hundred miles to the northeast. But the good news—taking a longer historical viewpoint—is that the tremendous dust storms that plagued this part of the state, the southern edge of the Dust Bowl during the Depression, have finally abated. The stories about these storms are not fantastical. I remember one myself from the mid-1950s, when my family lived in the last of the three houses in San Angelo. On that otherwise clear afternoon, we saw the dark brown line low on the horizon to the northwest. My brother was playing Little League baseball, and my mother and I raced to the field to pick him up. When the storm struck, darkness descended. Everyone in the restaurant in Stamford remembered the omnipresent dust in this area in those days, even in the absence of such storms. "Unbearable" was David Ballard's assessment. The dust can still be bad, though nothing like it was.

Sipping his beer at the Motel 6, my father changed the subject. He told me that of all the thirty-four years he had worked for Texaco, he totally enjoyed only the four as a land man out in the field. The higher he rose in the company—pretty high—the more isolated he became from that work he truly savored. He didn't say this in so many words; I surmised it. He did say that most people don't really enjoy their work, so he doesn't feel rooked. I agree with that premise and take it a step further, theorizing, in my darker moments, that all the inherently worthless jobs, even if sometimes enjoyable, are just as bad for the soul and the society. I have in my hand a favorite article from *The New York Times* about the new shape (rounded corners) and the new logo ("uninhibited and irreverent") and the major new advertising campaign for Doritos, including half-time sponsorship of the Super Bowl. The idea is to create "excitement" for the "spirit and personality" of the venerable snack chip. Many bright people are involved in the effort, and for the most part they'll be smiling and laughing because the $50 million campaign will work, sales will spike, and bonuses be awarded, perhaps some industry prizes, too. This charade and millions like it are the price we pay for the way we live now, as I see it. But with his dark memories and optimistic outlook, my dad would never go along with that gloomy and self-important assessment, and why should he.

The Texas Company was a heavy-drinking company in the earlier years of my father's career. In the sales department, almost everybody drank. You had to, practically, and a lot, but at least you were driving a company car. Most of my parents' friends were Texaco people, and a few of them drank way too much. This was back when bourbon and scotch were the norm. On summer weekends the party got going at eight o'clock and the steaks weren't served until ten-thirty or eleven. At the beach one night, a friend and I hid on the floorboard of the backseat while his falling-down father drove that car around looking for us, swerving and cussing. My father allowed that he hadn't enjoyed that aspect of corporate culture in the fifties and at least this much has changed for the better in the last thirty years.

Back then, drinking was in but divorce was out. I have many divorced friends, my parents very few. "What did people do instead?" I asked my father, assuming that both of us agreed the verities of human nature hadn't changed much in the intervening years.

"Tough it out."

Okay, fair enough.

"Would you change anything in your life?"

"Not really." Regarding work, his only real option had been to strike off on his own in real estate, but it's hard to do that with the security of a good salary in hand and with a family to support. "And very few do it," he made certain I understood.

I replied, "Well, I wouldn't be doing this"—this particularly itinerant kind of book, certainly—"if we had children. We wouldn't have moved those fifteen times."

"I'm sure not," he said. Then he wanted to know if our "goal" was to get back to New York City. Almost every time we talk on the phone and absolutely every time we get together, he asks me something like this. Such vagrancy as I've exhibited concerns him, and in the motel room he resisted my joking invocation of the genetic or Lamarckian explanations, so I just said I didn't know. I'm bad on goals, by predisposition and, now, by conviction. Events culminating in the white-light episode in Dallas were the clincher. Would I change much about the way *I've* gone about things? Not really. I do wonder what would have happened if we'd bought a small place in Manhattan in the seventies, when they were declaring the city dead and practically giving nice co-ops away.

At the Wes-T-Go Truck Stop that night, we must have waited twenty minutes for Dad's fried chicken—a good sign, because that's how long it should take. I'd been bragging about the restaurant for two days and was gratified when the crisp pieces won his approval. The ministerial couple from the motel walked by our table on the way to their own. The old fart gave us a wink and a nod, but his wifely companion, the M.S.S.A. pastor, pointedly stared down through the Plexiglas at the salad bar.

Driving to the airport the following morning, Dad was mainly silent, and so was I. Shaking hands before he walked out to the plane, he quickly averted his eyes and reminded me one last time, "Now, don't put much about me and your mother in this book."

CHAPTER 18

The offices and courtroom of Justice of the Peace Samuel Matta, Precinct 1, Place 2, Taylor County, Texas, are in the basement of one of the two courthouses in Abilene. State trooper John Murphy needed to check with an agent of that court on some minor matter, and I tagged along. After dropping my father at the airport, I had decided to hang around town for a couple of days, and setting up this second tour of duty with John, months after the first one, had been easy enough. So it's simply not true that government bureaucracies are inherently unresponsive.

John knew these courthouse functionaries extremely well, because the JP is the court of first resort in Texas. It's where traffic violations are adjudicated or, more likely, settled at the last minute. While we were there that morning, in fact, a young man of earnest disposition decided he had no choice but to plead out on his undeserved speeding violation once Judge

Matta told him he wouldn't grant a postponement of his trial just because the youth was scheduled to take a school exam within the hour. He should've done something about this conflict earlier. Now he listened as the judge dictated the terms of surrender—how much he had to pay in court costs and by what date he had to complete the defensive driving course. Given the guy's lackadaisical relationship with the Gregorian calendar, Judge Matta emphasized that this was the date by which the course must be *completed*, not just started. The sullen defendant felt aggrieved and poorly served by the injustice of it all, while the rest of us watched with silent amusement. But the fellow brightened when he learned that the required course was offered at his school, Abilene Christian University. Something about this student's emotional affect seemed to me slightly akilter. When I mentioned this to John Murphy in the hallway, he promptly observed that quite a few of the local Christian college students acted that way. All the tensions created by all that deep thinking about unearthly matters, we concluded.

That morning John dispensed some speeding tickets and warnings—about fifty-fifty—and in the afternoon we returned to the courthouse for the trial of the man who claimed that the state had no authority to issue traffic citations—specifically, the citation issued by trooper Kevin Massey for driving a motorcycle eighty in a fifty-five zone. Word had spread among the troopers that some kind of militia, maybe Posse Comitatus itself, was a growing presence in the Midland-Odessa area to the west. This man, a guard at the local state prison, might be the vanguard of an impending incursion into the Abilene region—and this was two months before the Oklahoma City bombing.

Samuel Matta's basement courtroom is a utilitarian affair with the exception of the six juror seats, which are mounted on swiveling pedestals. The defendant was dressed in a sharp suit, pink shirt and coordinated tie, and his motorcycle boots. On the defense table in front of him was a large blue law book. He had a crewcut and sat stiffly erect staring straight ahead at the wall. I have to admit, looking at the defender, knowing something of the story, I wondered whether all of us had passed through an unseen metal-detector. This was a man with smoldering emotions. His name? Let's settle for James Adams.

Judge Matta entered through the side door to his private chambers and we all rose. Invited to address the court, James posed an arcane Sixth Amendment question, and in the course of the judge's answer I learned that the JP is not a court of record, at least in Texas. No court reporter is present. If this defendant wished to be so tried, he'd have to concede round one this afternoon and then take his appeal to the county court of law, where he could have all the official records he desired.

Next, James wanted the flags removed on grounds that this court had no jurisdiction. He drew manifold distinctions between common law, equity law, maritime law, and criminal law, though his point was unclear to me. John Murphy and I exchanged raised eyebrows. Judge Matta listened with a straight face and said, That's all well and good, but how do you plead? When James refused to enter a plea on those same jurisdictional grounds, Matta stated that he was quite comfortable with his own reading of his court's jurisdiction as set forth in assorted laws and constitutions, so, one last time, How do you plead? The defendant resumed his filibuster until the judge threatened him with contempt of court. James sat down, and Judge Matta entered a Not Guilty plea for him.

I liked this judge. In Texas, JPs are elected officials and seldom lawyers: Matta came out of law enforcement; Abilene's other JP had been a TV weatherman. They handle an array of matters, mainly misdemeanors handed out by the police and arraignments that might end up in higher venues. They see and hear a little bit of everything. For the most part, they're not dealing with whiz-bang prosecutors or defense attorneys. They need to be hands-on, with a sense of humor to accompany their sense of justice, but they need to keep the straight face, too. Judge Matta gave the impression of possessing all of these qualities, and, indeed, John Murphy told me after the trial that he was, among the state troopers, a favorite of the local judges.

After that preliminary skirmish, the judge invited prosecuting attorney Gary Oren to present his case, and Oren called trooper Kevin Massey to the stand. Massey outlined the circumstances of the alleged violation, then led the court step by step through the quality-control procedures exercised by all DPS troopers over their radar equipment. James Adams and I were the only ones present who didn't know this testimony by rote. After twelve years' service, Judge Matta must have heard this legal boilerplate hundreds of times. I was intrigued by the description of the two little tuning forks used, supposedly, at the beginning of each tour of duty to check the calibration of the radar. The vibrations of one simulate a car—or motorcycle—traveling thirty-five miles per hour, the other a speed of sixty-five. I glanced at John Murphy, who was sitting next to me. Neither he nor Martin Hernandez had told me anything about these tuning forks. Later, John gave me a demonstration, and his unit checked out perfectly.

When it was his turn with the witness, the defendant challenged Massey's account of some of the details of their meeting out on the highway. For one thing, James didn't remember keeping his hands in his pockets in the initial stages of the episode, the specific behavior that had provoked the trooper to order him to take his hands out of his pockets and place them on the patrol car. At one point in this exchange, prosecutor Oren objected that the defendant was arguing his own case rather than eliciting testimony from the witness. Sustained, and Matta then advised James that he could do all the arguing he wanted when the time came, but not now. The defendant then returned to matters of jurisdiction, challenging the state's authority to issue traffic violations because it lacks the authority even to *establish* speed limits in the first place. Citing further distinctions between various kinds of law, he concluded that this case comes under criminal law and asked trooper Massey where in the penal code it says anything about speeding.

On the stand, Kevin Massey cited *Vernon's Civil Statutes*. James reiterated his point about criminal versus civil jurisdiction. During the ensuing discussion I learned that a driver, when stopped for a traffic violation, is technically under arrest until he has signed the ticket and been "released" by the peace officer. In short, you can't just walk away, and refusal to sign is cause for arrest. But if this is criminal law, James continued, where is the damaged party, as required by criminal actions?

How the hell should trooper Massey know, I wondered, and why was prosecutor Oren sitting silently through this courtroom charade? In fact, at one point another kibitzing state trooper rifled quickly through his *Vernon's* and leaned forward to hand it to Oren, opened to the germane citation (6701-D, John Murphy whispered).

The defendant moved for a mistrial. The judge declined the invitation and said, "I'm not here to train you." James continued his argumentative questioning, and finally Gary Oren objected. Matta sustained the point and added, "This court will not be put on the stand and become the defendant. You're welcome to take that argument to the Supreme Court or the Court of Appeals." Matta furthermore emphasized that this was a real, official *trial*, not "an O.J. Simpson–like pretrial *hearing*. So don't give me any more of this other stuff about jurisdiction. All I want to know is whether you're guilty of speeding."

The courtroom burst into applause. Not really, but the judge had won us over to his point of view. And I quit worrying about the metal detectors. James Adams no longer seemed threatening; "lost" would be more like it.

Did the defendant have anything else by way of defense?

No, your honor.

Did the defense rest?

I guess so, your honor.

Prosecutor Oren then gave a thirty-second summation, James offered none at all, Judge Matta found him guilty, assessed a fine of $100 plus court costs, and then explained that an appeal to the county court of law would require a $200 bond. In an aside, he informed the defendant that he would have been more impressed if his arguments hadn't seemed to be some kind of political statement masquerading as legal argument. When James tried to convince him that this was a serious legal challenge, Judge Matta said, "I don't think so."

A few months later, I called Judge Matta's office to inquire what had happened in the matter of *Taylor County v. James Adams* and was told that the defendant had neither filed an appeal nor paid his fine and court costs. Therefore a *capias profine* warrant for his arrest had been issued. I waited a few months and called back and got the same answer. I concluded that Adams wasn't being actively sought, but should he ever be detained for another violation and punched into the computer on a "10-29," he'd be handcuffed on the spot.

Naturally, John Murphy and I ate lunch that afternoon at the Wes-T-Go Truck Stop, and I finally met Ken Black, the restaurant manager. A couple of days later, Ken and I sat down to discuss the business. Since he draws his workers from the same pool denigrated so vehemently by Bob Popplewell, whose rattlesnake ranch is about eighty miles east, I asked about the help. Ken is somewhat happier with his situation. When it comes to finding and keeping good employees he does quite a bit better than the turnover average in the service industry—an astounding four hundred percent annually. "We don't *get* the cream of the crop. We try to *form them* into the cream of the crop. There's a lot of my people I didn't think would ever work out, but they're still here." That's when I hazarded a guess that members of the House of Yahweh would make great employees, and I began an explanation of this local cult, about which I'd heard from a motel clerk. Key point in the group's doctrines, as explained in ten densely argued pages in one publication: Abilene, Texas, is on the same latitude—thirty-two degrees north—as Jerusalem, Israel. The motel clerk didn't tell me, and maybe didn't even know, that founder Yisrayl Hawkins was born in Oklahoma with the legal first name of Buffalo Bill, which he understandably changed after entering the religious arena in Odessa.

Ken knew all about the House. A woman from the Yahweh group—a stripper prior to her conversion, according to Ken—had been on staff until she began objecting to serving pork. She didn't even want to scrape the dishes on which another waitress had served the bacon. This was against her religion, she had told Ken, who then told her that it was against *his* religion that it was against *her* religion to serve bacon to their *mutual* customers. So she went elsewhere for employment. However, other House of Yahweh members still come into the restaurant once or twice a week. "Real nice people," Ken concluded, while pointing out that, in general, large church groups are the worst when it comes to thievery. When a bus-load from a church pulls up at the convenience store out by the gas pumps, he puts an extra man inside to watch those Christian kids. They're the worst. (At the rattlesnake ranch, it's the undergraduates Bob Popplewell has to watch closely; here, it's the Christians. You could wonder what's going on in this country, or you could conclude that kids are kids.)

Like many men and women in and around Abilene, Ken put in his twenty years of military service while based at Dyess and stayed in the area upon retirement. This flat land either weaves a spell on you or it doesn't; for some, the biblical lati-tude is a factor as well. When I asked Ken how civilian life compares with the military, he replied quickly in the vernacu-lar. "Well, I don't have to sleep in no tents! I don't have to cook outside!" Then again, his career in food services had been an accident. Ken had planned to go to electronics school before he met with the Air Force recruiter in 1967. This con artist told him, "Hey, don't spend your money. We'll guaran-tee computers in the Air Force."

But after basic training, the verdict was, "Food services."

"Wait a minute," Ken had protested. "That's *wrong*. I'm supposed to be working with computers."

"No. No you're not. Says here you're in food services."

And so he was, for twenty years. Mostly based in Texas, Ken sometimes flew around the world providing personalized food services for a four-star general. On February 1, 1988, he retired. On February 2, he started work at the Wes-T-Go be-cause the ex-colonel who was managing the restaurant knew Ken from when he'd accompanied the general to Guam, where the ex-colonel had been based—the seamless web once again. And this goes double for the truck-stop business, because every trucker knows every other trucker, thanks to the CB radio. "Word of mouth here will make you or break you," Ken said. "Sometimes you want to tell a guy to hit the road, but you can't do that or they're on their CB telling everyone else not to shop here because we've got a bad-ass manager. And you can't have an unfriendly waitress in a truck stop. A lot of stuff the drivers will tell you, you've got to let roll right off your shoulders."

And not just the drivers. The waitresses have to deal with the likes of Jim Halsel, too. Jim's famous for his ability to grab rattlesnakes bare-handed and not get bitten, which is the key, of course. I met the man known locally, regionally, and nationally as Snake Man at this very truck stop, where he'd once worked as a mechanic and often dropped by for coffee. At some point in our lengthy encounter, just as Jim was confessing that he might have lost a little of his speed and dexterity, our waitress passed by with the coffee and made a crack I couldn't hear but Jim did, and he taunted her in a nanosecond. "Trip or stumble and see how damn slow and old I am. I'll mount you 'fore you hit the floor." He giggled. "Nail you like a lightning bolt." He glanced at me. "Keep tellin' 'em, if they trip, stumble, or fall, don't worry about it. I'm gonna give 'em a soft place to land. They keep their distance."

In return, the waitress just laughed. As Ken Black was saying, if you can't handle hardball repartee, you don't last in the truck-stop-waitressing trade.

"Attitude is everything," Ken continued. "I can teach anybody anything but attitude. But someone unfriendly would never stay anyway. The other girls would run 'em off. Or they'll quit, because they know they're not wanted here by the other employees. I try to tell my waitresses—everybody—to treat these people like they're your family. We want 'em to feel like they're home."

Ken suspects that some of his waitresses make more than he does, counting their tips, and he knows they make more than the assistant managers. But when I asked one of the women working the counter if she averaged fifteen percent, she said, "Gosh no." Ten percent? "Maybe." So I don't know. Then again, even ten percent of the thousand meals the restaurant serves on a good day is a considerable sum to divvy up.

"The waitresses will say that they don't want to do this the rest of their lives, but then they do it. They understand they're going to be lower-middle-class. They like it here," Ken said, then paused. "But they're also buying lottery tickets." So is everyone else who stops for food and fuel. Wes-T-Go will sell

$3,000 worth on the day of a big payoff, $500 on all others. Of course, this place is famous from Dallas to Midland-Odessa, a 350-mile stretch of I-20, and truckers spread the word all over the country. The place is clean. Marlboros sell for $1.69. The tortilla chips are home-fried. The salsa is prepared from scratch. The refried beans don't come from the can. The pancake batter includes real buttermilk. The pies are fresh out of the oven. The salad bar comes straight from the garden. The fried chicken, as noted during my father's visit, takes the full twenty minutes. Counting the convenience store out by the gasoline pumps, the truckers' office by the diesel pumps, and the restaurant, Wes-T-Go daily pours between three hundred and five hundred gallons of coffee. That figure confounded me as much as the one for toilet paper sold by Bruce Bollinger to the Mobil Mini-Mart in Seligman, Arizona, but at least this number has an explanation: all the thermoses filled to the brim by truckers.

"We have about five cooks who can do anything back there," Ken told me, and with some pride. "Most have been here for anywhere from nine to fourteen years. We make everything. That's why we're so good." Ken estimates that only twenty percent of his volume derives from truckers. Several locals, like the elderly couple who had just shuffled in from their brown pickup, eat here three meals a day, seven days a week. An old man who actually *lives* in his blue pickup eats here often, with Thanksgiving dinner on the house. The guy had worked at Dyess, was rifted out—downsized—by a budget cut, was too old to get a job anywhere else, and now scraped by on a small remittance supplemented by collecting bottles and cans. A very nice man, Ken said, just *real* poor.

Another regular was sitting at the counter at Wes-T-Go on November 8, 1988, when he saw the B-1 bomber from Dyess crash on the other side of the interstate; first on the scene, he loaded two of the four crew members into his pickup. His name is Walter Gilstrap, and when I met him he told me this story. I looked it up later in *The New York Times*, where Walter is quoted as saying, "They hugged me and I hugged them, and two of them asked me to call their wives." From this stretch of I-20, you can see Dyess's bristling antennae and satellite dishes to the immediate south; if the wind's blowing from the north, you can pull over and watch the famous planes take off or land directly over your head on training missions. As my wife accurately pointed out, the B-1 looks like a paper airplane.

Anyway, this is one of the best restaurants in Abilene, period, Ken Black states without equivocation. "When a new restaurant opens in town," he reported, "our business goes down. Two weeks later, it's back up." Sunday buffet? Always packed, as it is before and after the big high school football games up and down the interstate and on Saturday nights after the stock car races, in which Ken sometimes runs his own modified 350 Chevy. The only slack time is the early morning shift, two to seven a.m.

Libbye Cleaver, one of Ken's assistant managers, slid in next to him in the booth. The House of Yahweh? Sure, Libbye knew about it, since they have a church in Little Rock, where she'd lived before moving here about a year earlier, to help take care of her mother in Abilene. She was shocked at the wages, after making $500 to $600 a week waitressing in Little Rock. Ken nodded his head and said, "Everyone around here starts at minimum wage. Don't expect to make six or seven dollars an hour." But that's what service stores have to pay in Dallas, I told him, according to a timely story in the *Morning News*. "LOW-WAGE LABOR POOL DRYING UP," the headline read. Some franchise chains have management positions whose only job is to steal the more efficient hourly employees from other franchise chains; when these burglars find a candidate, they slip him or her a note. Jobs paying $6.50 can go begging in Dallas, and $7 will be hard to fill. In Abilene, they could auction off such jobs, with heavy bidding driving the number down.

Libbye had also been wary of working in a truck stop, even though Ken had a management opening for the ten p.m. to six a.m. slot. No way, no thank you, Libbye thought, but what was her real-world choice? After signing on with Ken, she got a better offer from The Kettle, whose salary Ken couldn't match. But a few months later, she was back at Wes-T-Go. "Really, I should have stayed here," Libbye told me while glancing at her boss, who took the opportunity to kid her about this misjudgment. Then Ken told me, "Denny's also took some employees from Wes-T-Go. But they came back, too."

"I don't call anyone here 'employee,' " Libbye continued. "I call them 'the people I work with.' Everyone is treated the same here." Echoing Ken's earlier statement, she added, "You have to be a 'people person.' The day you're not, you've got to go out the door. I had three people tell me the other night this is the cleanest truck stop and the nicest personnel they've ever seen."

Libbye asked Ken if he'd told me the story about the wallet. No? Well, Ken explained, a young girl had turned in a wallet found in the women's restroom. When Ken had gone through it looking for identification so he could contact the owner, he discovered a set of explicit pictures of the owner herself; he knew this because the face in these photographs matched the face on the driver's license. The woman was from El Paso.

"Now, when we mail the wallet to her without those pictures," Libbye asked rhetorically, "will she have the nerve to call back and ask where they were?"

Ken and I looked at each other. Our consensus was, no, she wouldn't have the nerve. Libbye agreed. Then Ken trotted out one of his all-time favorite stories. "This lady came in to buy some cigarettes while I was giving the cashier a break. The girl wanted two packs of cigarettes. She was with a guy. I gave them to her and asked if there would be anything else, and she said, 'Yeah, how about a hug? Today's my birthday.' She looked to be in her midthirties, but I said, 'Oh, how old are you? About twenty-five?' And she lifted up her blouse and she said, 'Do *these* look like they're twenty-five?' There was nothing on under there, nothing and I'm . . . whatever. I'm fumbling with the money. I'm glad it wasn't her anniversary! I don't know what she would have showed me then."

Shots had been fired a couple of times in Ken's seven years at the truck stop—"because the guy didn't like the soup or something," as he put it with a laugh. But, generally, the truckers are the least of his problems, most of which accompany the drunks off the highway. Ken has no patience with these birds.

Any aggravation at all and he alerts the state troopers and that drunk is history. Hitchhikers can also be a nuisance, but if they sit down, order, eat, pay, pee, and leave, that's fine, no matter how many ear, lip, nose, and belly-button rings they might wear. Start pestering drivers for a ride, however, then you're off the property. "I hate to say this," Ken added, "but even people who solicit with the little key chains—the deaf—we have to move them on, too, because that irritates people. That's all the time. They're cruising through, trying to pick up five or ten bucks. We have people come in trying to sell perfume. We get all kinds of stuff. And I don't care what you say, people do react to a full moon. It's true. Even our employees. If you don't believe it, come to a truck stop on a full-moon night."

Is the scene here at Wes-T-Go a fair slice of humanity? Libbye and Ken believe it is. What's more, they exclaimed practically in unison, "It's different every day!" That's one of the great things about the job—but not great enough, as it turned out, in Libbye's case. A few months later, she took a few days off to visit family in Arkansas, left some clothes in the locker, and never returned. Probably moved back to Little Rock, Ken figured, nor was he surprised. Even with an annual turnover far below the industry norm, he'd been watching them come and go for seven years now.

CHAPTER 19

"Snake Man" Jim Halsel is a blue-ribbon, world-class talker, a colorful guy with a colorful trade who will benefit greatly from the upcoming world in which every book comes out on CD-ROM instead. Hell, he's already been featured on several TV shows about rattlesnakes. That's how them L.A. Guns knew about him, from the National Geographic Special. One day Jim had been over to the Merkel Truck Stop, eight miles west of the Wes-T-Go and a competitor of sorts, but laughably inferior. But anyway, there Jim was when the rock group pulled up in their touring bus. Telling me the story while sitting at the horseshoe-shaped counter near the Wes-T-Go's front door and drinking their rocket-fuel coffee, Jim couldn't at first recall the exact name of these rockers. Guns 'n' Roses? Guns of August? L.A. Law? We went through all the options before the right one came to him. I'd never heard of the group. Jim continued, winking and grinning, "They crawled off that bus of theirs and they was macho as hell, hair down to here, dressed out in their tight leather and everything. Well, someone pointed me out to 'em. First I thought they'd heard us—me and a bunch of guys were remarkin' about how cute them L.A. Guns were. Didn't know whether to fuck 'em or fight 'em! Thought we were gonna have to fight our way out of there! But they'd seen me on TV and said, 'Are you the Snake Man?'

" 'Yeah.'

" 'We seen you on TV and wanted to know if you have any snakes on your truck. Saw your truck settin' out there. We'd like to see some.'

"By now the manager and all the waitresses come out to watch. I said, 'How many you want to see?'

" 'Oh, a bunch of 'em. We're gonna take pictures.'

"*Okay*. I commenced to throwin' these six-foot rattlesnakes at their feet and you never heard the likes of such squealin' in your life. You'd have sworn you were in some woman's *sorority* house. Them long-haired hippie suckers! They was cuttin' trails, man. Just a squealin'. Some of 'em even on top of the damn gas pumps. So they had all the picture-takin' they wanted—*from a distance*."

Celebrities: Christ, they're everywhere, even out here. Ken Black had already told me about the time Garth Brooks had come into the Wes-T-Go by himself at 3:30 a.m., incognito. The biggest celebrity I saw with my own eyes on my interstate travels was back at Dealey Plaza, where one afternoon the wailing of massed sirens approached from downtown. Looking east, I saw that Elm Street had been cleared, and two motorcycle cops soon arrived at the plaza as a vanguard and blocked all traffic. Word spread that Al Gore was in town to deliver a speech about fatherhood. This must be Al Gore, roaring up to visit Dealey Plaza! If so, he'd be the first high-ranking government official to do so.* The visitor was indeed the veep but his

---

*You sometimes hear that Teddy Kennedy once paid a private, nighttime visit to the Sixth Floor Museum. This is not true, according to the senator's office. A couple of members of what's known within the Kennedy establishment as "the next generation" have visited Dealey Plaza. That's all.

limousine rolled through at thirty miles an hour without even slowing down, surrounded by dozens of motorcycle cops—to all appearances, as many or more cops than had protected the president's limousine in 1963. Through the tinted windows of the limo I could see Gore, seated alone in the expansive backseat and craning his neck to look up at the schoolbook depository, maybe up at the grassy knoll. Then he was gone. The entire episode took less than a minute, maybe only thirty seconds, but the plaza remained charged with the residual excitement and buzz created in this society by only one phenomenon that I know of, and by the particularly eerie vibrations set off by the appearance of this particular category of celebrity at this particular category of celebrity site.

Bob Popplewell also had his own celebrity stories—two, in fact, both featuring snakes, of course. He was the snake wrangler on *Natural Born Killers* (his wife Phyllis had a couple of unpleasant encounters on the set with the notorious Oliver Stone), and he also sold the skins to *Maverick* (the snake that frightens Mel Gibson's horse is a $100,000 robot; the leading man wouldn't go near a real one). When the snake rancher related these tales, I recalled his stories about tourists who like to "prick" the snakes, and his ideas about the dynamic of "transference" in that odd relationship. Logically enough, I inquired whether something similar might account for our complex infatuation with our celebrities, whom we worship in some way, but whose almost inevitable acts of self-destruction we seem to enjoy rather than deplore—maybe because we fear and resent them and their hold on our imaginations. Like with the snakes. But Bob shrugged. Along with me, he's stumped by this whole subject.

Jim Halsel is no jock-sniffer; he just enjoys gloating about the day he put one over on them hippie, broke-dick suckers. On the other hand, with Jim you can't always tell where the storytelling leaves off and the horseplay begins. Here's a guy who revels in his reputation and probably isn't above embellishing a few of the details of his exploits. Although he's about as crude and vulgar as a fellow can be, I also suspect he's got a big heart behind the crusty demeanor. And after a while, who cares if what Jim claims is true down to the last snake? When I met him at the Wes-T-Go, he was wearing a baseball cap that read NO MUFF TOO TOUGH and was, to my eye, a dead ringer for a weathered Kevin Costner. He proceeded to inform me that the area radiating for one hundred miles in every direction holds by far the greatest concentration of rattlesnakes in the world. Many of the houses here are built on piers, thus providing snakes with fine nesting sites: cool in the summer, warm in the winter. The snakes live under most of these houses, but go out at night and return home before dawn, so the homeowner may have gobs of snakes without knowing about them until one fine early morning when the lady of the house sees one dozing beside the back porch and immediately calls 911, and then the sheriff comes over. In the meantime, though, the snake has slid back under the house, so the sheriff calls Snake Man, who tells this lady she can either live with this snake and, probably, many more, or retain his services to assure a snake-free environment, or just move out of this particular house— which has happened, when the possibility of waking up with a snake in bed is just too much. Jim charges a minimum of $250 *plus* he gets to keep the snakes. He told me he once pulled 385 rattlesnakes from beneath one house, the smallest of them three and a half feet, and I believe him. I must report, however, that Bob Popplewell says that every town out here has its own renowned snake man, and that catching rattlesnakes bare-handed isn't nearly as difficult as one wants to believe.

When one of the managers on the diesel fuel side of the Wes-T-Go business passed the lunch counter, he and Jim exchanged formulaic insults. Not that long before, Jim had chased this man across the parking lot with a six-footer. Another time, back when Jim was a mechanic here, a supervisor who'd been giving him some lip was working in a small wire enclosure in the shop. Jim fetched a snake, tossed it in, and closed the gate. All hell broke loose in the shop, naturally— and in the restaurant, as Jim again doubled over with laughter. Another time he placed a slider in the cooks' locker.

Should Jim pull this in-your-face or at-your-feet stunt on you, the only guaranteed key to survival is not to move. Freeze:

it's that simple. "If you move, he's gonna bite you," Jim told me. "Don't move. I don't care if he's laying on top of your foot. He's gonna rare up, be half-cocked, just like a pistol. Now, you take a pistol and pull the hammer back one click, you can't squeeze that trigger. It won't fire. A snake's the same way. He comes up, he's in the warning position. If you watch real close before he strikes, he'll make *one more* backward movement, then he's on his way. But if you don't move, he won't go to that full cock. He's gonna stay rared up, but he'll back away from you."

Snake Man nodded out the window to the parking lot and told me about the state troopers and deputy sheriffs who asked him what to do if they stopped someone on the highway and walked up on a snake—a very possible occurrence. "I took those three highway patrol and two deputy sheriffs and put 'em right there in a circle. And I had my truck pulled up right there. Five-and-a-half-footer, *that* big around, I throw'd it right in the damn middle of 'em! Right there! And you could hear every one of 'em, sucking up." He gave his wheezy little laugh, *he-he-he-he*.

"Did they stay still?"

"You ain't a-kiddin'. You couldn't of knocked 'em off that sidewalk if you'd used one of them trucks out there. They looked like a bunch of fenceposts. That snake was ready to nail 'em if they moved. Finally, I stepped back out of the circle and gave the snake an exit. He backed out and crawled across the parking lot. I went out and got him and put him in the truck and said to those guys, 'See there, you can do a lot of things you don't think you can do *when you have to.*' Don't move. Remain still. Remember, he's just as afraid of you as you are of him. He's gonna back away. *If you let him.* But if you move, you've threatened him. He's gonna defend hisself, just like a dog sleeping out by the door. Let the dog lie there. Don't bother him."

In disputes between snakes and men, Jim Halsel is always on the side of the reptiles.

I asked how he got into this trade in the first place. He said, "Over in Vietnam, I just developed a 'didn't give a flying shit' attitude about nothin'. If you get killed today, so? If you make it, great. I was 101st Airborne, demolitions expert for 'em. Which was bad nervous. You was a nervous wreck *constantly*. So you develop that attitude. When I come back, I *still had* the attitude. Far as that goes, still got it. If I get bit, tough. Shoulda been more careful. Anyway, I got in the pest control business and got to doing termites. They'd call you out on a termite inspection and I'd be crawling around under there and shit there'd be *gobs of snakes*. I was findin' more houses with snakes than termites. Well, shit. I got to checkin' and there wasn't a soul that did snakes. So I was doing termites *and* snakes. Still do some, but me and the other pest control companies have an understanding. They don't mess with my damn snakes and I ain't gonna mess with their termites. I've tried to get 'em to go under a house. Hell no. There ain't enough money."

I know the feeling. "What about the first time?"

"The first time," he conceded, "you're nervous as hell."

"How do you do it? What's the secret?"

"Be fast and don't miss. And *don't be afraid*. Respect 'em, but don't be afraid."

I tried again. "How, *exactly*, do you catch a rattlesnake?"

He reminded me that the snake must make that *second* short cock before striking. "That's when I grab him," he said. "Don't give him a chance to come forward. I've been doing it thirty years, haven't been bit yet." He knocks on the lunch counter. "Grab his head itself. Anything else and he'll turn on you and he's gotcha. You can get him just below the head and he can take and turn that head and bite you."

I had observed such behavior at Bob Popplewell's place, and those heads didn't even have bodies. I had Jim's own quickness and dexterity demonstrated to my satisfaction in the parking lot, where he performed all sorts of coin tricks and challenges, grabbing the quarter out of my hand before I had moved a muscle, that kind of thing. In any game like that, Snake Man will make you look as slow as Christmas. I beat him once, then realized from the glint in his eye that I had been set up. Is this quickness something you learn or something you're born with? "About half and half," Jim answered. "The older the snake, the better chance you stand. If I was ever to get bit, I want a seven-foot rattler to tear my ass up. Bite the hell out of me, I don't care. But I don't want no foot-or-below bitin' me."

I asked how this could be.

"It's like that coffee. Your baby rattlers, they stay with their mother for two years. Now you can imagine, a baby rattler's head's about the size of that nail. Now how in hell's he going to catch a mouse and swallow it? He cain't. He's got to be at least two years old. So he either eats what's rejuvenated by his mother, or bugs."

Regurgitated, I believe.

"So his venom is *stored*. Just like that coffee there. Leave it for two hours and come back and drink it. It'll throw you through that damn window. You cain't do it. The longer it's stored, the stronger it is. That's the whole purpose of that venom."

Jim told me about the box of about two hundred six-foot rattlesnakes he had at the house and into which he chucked a large wharf rat he'd picked up somewhere, just to see what would happen. "This was one mean bastard." He chuckled. "The snakes thought they were gonna eat, but *the hell they did*. They got the worst ass-whupping they ever got. That rat was all over that box, like taking one of them kids' Super Balls and bouncing it off the walls *whew whew whew whew*. That's the way that rat was—all *over* that damn box. And every time he passed by they'd nail him, and every time they'd nail him he'd turn and grab 'em by the damned head. There goes another snake. He was killing my snakes! *He-he-he-he.* I took a long stick and beat that damn rat to death."

Talking with Jim, I noticed that several truckers sitting nearby were letting their delicious food get cold. Jim's subject and delivery do command attention; he favored us with one last story for the road. "I was under a house putting in a sewer line and had a black widow crawl in and bite me on the inside of my ear. If you can imagine somebody taking a poker out of the fire and white-hot jamming it in your ear, that's what it felt like. Head swelled out to *here*. Had to have it drained every day. Have a *high respect* for them spiders. I can see the snake, but I can't see that damn spider. And a needle, well, I spent most of three and a half years in a hospital getting stuck constantly for this bad hand. It has metal in it now. Back when I was younger I was in a motorcycle wreck. Ruby Oswald—Lee Harvey Oswald's mother—was my nurse. This was before 1963. So I'm terrified of needles. Doctors do not give me shots. I'm either gonna black out or *stomp your ass*, one of the two. Me and one doctor went to a damn hospital *together*, me to get a tooth out and him to get his jaw wired. I had told him, 'Don't come at me with that damn needle.' Evidently he didn't believe me. This was over in Odessa. He said he never touched me with that needle, but I could *feel* that needle, now. In my mind I could feel that needle, and I just come across with a right, and that metal hand hit him just so. It was an accident, but I broke his jaw. That doctor took me to court. Trying to sue me. The only reason he couldn't is his nurse was standin' there and testified that I did prewarn him. The dentists in Abilene, they know. They don't give me no shots. They *gas*. If they don't want to gas, just take the damn tooth and be done with it. Don't come at me with no needle."

Done deal, Snake Man, as long as you promise not to come at me with no rattler.

Of all the gubernatorial candidates I have known, Royce Owens stands out. He worked with Snake Man Jim Halsel before going into politics, but he didn't quit the snakes in order to run for governor. He quit when his son divorced and left his two kids with Royce and his wife, Nina, for a period of time. Neither grandparent wanted boxes of snakes in the yard.

Jim had told me about his former associate. I located Royce through the phone book, and the following noon we took our seats in the booth at the Wes-T-Go. The former candidate and incumbent custodian at nearby Tye Elementary School wore a black knit shirt and a Texaco cap and a wry grin and said right off, "I took more chances maybe even than Jim does. But I don't take *too big* of chances. One day I was on my back and he was on his stomach, and we couldn't turn over. He was looking down on the ground, and I was looking up on the cinder blocks. That makes your hair stand up and your adrenaline flow. I understand not many people would do that."

Royce considers himself different from his fellow Texans in many ways. "I'm more tolerant, more forgiving," he assured me. Take the subject of divorce, about which I asked Royce at some point because I was beginning to believe that calamity was particularly rife in these parts. Almost everyone I met seemed to have a divorce in the past. Of the nine troopers in Martin Hernandez' and John Murphy's squad, five were divorced; of the ten troopers in the other squad working out of Abilene, five. The veteran Max Shaw told me that he always urged young troopers *to have other friends*, to get beyond the world of law enforcement, to beware the tendency to see the world and people in black and white, with themselves pitted against everyone else. Otherwise, all the sewage backs right up into the marriage. Royce agreed that this plumbing analogy seemed apt and applicable, and not just with troopers.

"Are you married?" he asked me.

"Twenty-three years."

"Don't you feel you've forgiven a lot and a lot and a lot?"

"I don't feel that I have, but I feel that I would."

"You have, but you may not realize it. Hasn't your wife forgiven?"

"Yes."

"Well, with a lot of these young kids, one time and that's it. 'I don't like you anymore, you drink the wrong Pepsi. We're getting a divorce.' *Incompatibility.* I think they ought to change that law to where it's as hard to get married as it is to get divorced."

Royce would change many things about society and its laws. That's why he ran for governor of Texas in 1990, the campaign in which Democrat Ann Richards beat Republican Clayton Williams, thanks in large part to Williams's remark that sometimes rape is like bad weather, if it's inevitable you might as well lie there and enjoy it. He actually said this to a group of *reporters* during a storm that wiped out some kind of hunt. So he shot himself in the foot instead, and still almost won. In some states that statement would have meant instant de facto disqualification, but not in Texas. Royce shook his head in dismay. Williams was the candidate who beat him in the Republican primary, after Royce had put twenty-two thousand miles on his Ford Festiva in about two months. Part of this was vacation time from the elementary school; otherwise, he'd finish work, drive four hundred miles to Houston for a speech, then drive back to Merkel that same night. He spoke twice at the Dallas Country Club, receiving a polite and positive reception there and everywhere else.

However, he's not necessarily fooled by polite receptions. "Just to show you how people are," he told me, "I had thirty— maybe thirty-two, I forget the exact number—come up to me and look me right in the eye and say, 'I voted for you.' However, only four votes were recorded for me in Merkel." He grinned. "Maybe they voted for me *in their hearts*."

Royce is proud of the nice write-up he received in Molly Ivins's syndicated column, where she declared him the clear winner among the Republicans in the last of a series of debates. "No question about it," Molly wrote, "if Royce X. Owens had $6 million of his own money to spend, he'd be the heavy favorite for the Republican nomination right now. . . . Put Royce X. Owens on a horse in a series of ads bathed in golden light, and you would have one helluva fine gubernatorial candidate."

The only caveat: she misspelled the name "Merkle," Royce's hometown.

With $6 million Royce might have been an opponent for Clayton Williams to reckon with, but I personally don't believe that even such a fortune could have saved the custodian from Merkel from some of his more far-out positions. In fact, the longer we talked at Wes-T-Go, the more I believed he'd chosen the wrong party affiliation. While agreeing I had a point, he didn't seem unduly bothered by running a Republican campaign calling for *fewer* prisons, among other counterrevolutionary planks.

Regarding prisons, Royce said, "I can say honestly people don't care about jobs in the state of Texas. I can say that they would rather have more prisons than jobs. Everybody needs to be treated fair. Everybody needs a job. And you can't make it on $4.25 an hour and raise a family. Well, how can you create jobs? Certainly not by building prisons and putting people in 'em. We have two prisons here, one county jail, and they want to build another one. People are hung up on this. I can *cure* this."

Royce's sensible solution: make the *jurors* pay for long prison terms. That would cure them of the habit. This proposal, as the candidate outlined it for me, is a little rough around the edges, perhaps, but cogent in its essence. Nevertheless, as I told Royce, "This is not an idea whose time has come."

"I realize this," he replied. "But it's practical. People are vengeful. My problem is I don't hate people."

AIDS was a subject on which Royce's ideas were even less likely to strike a responsive chord with the electorate, much less with the Republican subset. Read the following remarks with the understanding that the candidate was speaking with the greatest irony: "AIDS is a *positive* thing, and a lot of people can't see this. Take Magic Johnson and Pee Wee Herman. If your son could be only one or the other, which would you pick for him? Magic. Nine out of ten people will pick Magic Johnson. Now, he's got AIDS, he shook the president's hand, he made the Dream Team, he played all over the world, he came back and got a $14 million contract. And what about Pee Wee Herman? They took his show off the air. They condemned him. But you tell me which one was practicing safe sex? That's right. So now tell me what Americans want."

"That's a little quirky, Royce."

"I understand that. But you take masturbating. How many people have you seen raping at the same time? But of course people get on my case about this."

In Vietnam, Royce could have relaxed in the relatively safe position of personnel sergeant but volunteered as well for an assortment of infantry and helicopter assignments, including door gunner. Life on the edge, and it's the same with politics. Where's the next edge, I asked, and he replied, "I don't know.

Something might come up. A good friend wants me to go to Alaska. He has a tour-guide thing. Takes you on a vacation, six, seven days, twenty-five hundred bucks. He owns his own boat. He's been up there for ten years. I would quit my job here."

"What would your wife say?"

He hesitated, then said softly, "I've got a good wife. Whatever I'm for. We've got a good marriage . . . let's see . . . about forty-one years."

I met Nina that evening because Royce invited me out to the house for dinner and chess. She did indeed seem to be a good wife and a good cook—baked chicken, mashed potatoes, vegetables, salad—and Royce a good husband. They live in a small house in this little town west of Abilene, a home crowded with stuff and the air sometimes heavy with cigarette smoke. Nina, who doesn't play, disappeared when Royce broke out the chess board and pieces. I'd heard that he was some kind of national champion; he's not, but he's a damn good chess player who could probably get his rating up to 1,800, conceivably 1,900, if he worked on his game and spent less time organizing tournaments. So he believes. On a good day, he can give a 2,000 player—that's very strong—plenty to think about. A few weeks earlier, Royce had beaten just such a guy from Lubbock, a veteran who had played more tournament chess over the past two years than anyone in the United States yet decided against a second game against the man from Merkel. Royce favors the English Opening in order to slow things down. Is hell with his knights. Will trade his bishop for *your* knight at just about every opportunity. Does not mind the black pieces. All in all, I felt fortunate to catch him napping in a couple of speed games, but he was frequently distracted by the numbers coming in on television. This was election night, 1994, and Royce had predicted that Ann Richards would be re-elected over George Bush, Jr. By ten o'clock, we knew better. By eleven o'clock, the Republicans had triumphed everywhere and I had bid Royce and Nina a nevertheless hearty farewell. By midnight, I was sound asleep in my motel, fairly content in the conviction that life does indeed go on and that the

Democrats deserved it, in Texas, at least, where Ann, perhaps ready to move on and make some money after decades in state politics, had run a weak campaign. With Royce's fresh heart for the good fight, if not with his platform, she might have prevailed.

CHAPTER 20

At the front desk of the "Y" in Abilene, directly across from the reproduction of the famous painting of Jesus Christ by Warner Sallman, I asked the nice lady where I might find a really good cup of coffee, postswim, not the standard issue at the Wes-T-Go. I had in mind some cappuccino. I did. I'll admit I craved a cup. The lady replied that Furr's sometimes had excellent coffee.

"Furr's?"

"Yes, the cafeteria over on Alameda Street."

Instead, I drove to the Mall in Abilene, which is, in fact, the only mall in Abilene, on the south side of town, where I was surprised and delighted to find the Cappuccino Cove, a nifty kiosk on the broad central boulevard of this air-conditioned emporium. The first afternoon I walked up, the *barista* was polishing his machinery at one end of the horseshoe oval that seated eight customers on stools. The stools were empty at the time; midweek, midafternoon, the whole mall was virtually empty. I immediately engaged this man in conversation and discovered that the *barista* was the owner as well. Bill Bedford is his name, aviation navigation his former game, although it went into sudden-death overtime in Vietnam one day when the tail of his C-130 cargo plane grazed a small shack at the end of the runway at Kontum, north of Pleiku, and everyone on board, including Bill, was lucky that a deep and wide ravine was just beyond. The plane lunged down into that airspace before getting a second wind and roaring away on a vital mission. In another action years later, the triumphant Persian Gulf campaign, Bill had mustered for commander's call at the base in Saudi Arabia when he overheard the operations officer telling some other fliers about an incredible incident in 'Nam twenty years earlier, when the C-130 immediately in front of his plane had grazed a small shack at the end of the runway at Kontum, and *the same thing* had then happened to this officer's own warplane. "I was in the first plane!" Bill had shouted across the squad room. Then, at Camp Smith on Oahu, an officer told Bill a wartime story about two C-130s nipping their tails on the same small shack at the end of a runway north of Pleiku. Bill's plane again! Small world!

He retired after finishing out his military years in Abilene at Dyess, partly because he felt recent cutbacks in funding were hurting morale. He then took lessons in a Cessna until he realized that flying, in and of itself, was no longer that big a thrill, and that to graduate to the genuinely thrilling planes would require more time and training than he felt he was willing to give the sport, so he had quit and opened this Cove about a year before I walked up and began quizzing him about the temperature of the steamed milk (175 degrees), and was it whole or two percent (the latter). He pointed out the certificate verifying that Cappuccino Cove was voted best coffee in Abilene by the local *Reporter*. When I pointed out the consolation prize awarded the Olive Garden, Bill sneered, "They make it in bulk and store it in a thermos."

He studied his craft and trained in Dallas and then experimented with various roasts with a company in Tyler, Texas, in the piney woods east of Dallas, and the hard work showed. His espresso blend is a shrewd mix of Colombian and Costa Rican beans, intentionally quite close in taste to Lavazza Super Crema. Bill is convinced that $2 for an espresso beverage is a sizable expenditure for the basic Abilenian. Nevertheless, business was acceptable; not great, but getting better as he slowly built a base of return customers. One of these walked up and admitted he'd never heard of "this kind of coffee" until Bill had opened for business, but now he was hooked on latte with one or another of the various Torani flavors. Probably three fourths of Bill's customers request a Torani flavor. At his urging, I tried the popular hazelnut. Totally unacceptable. No longer real coffee. Otherwise, Bill served me a really nice cappuccino, not quite as astringent as the famous Starbucks brew, closer to the lighter, more winy taste delivered by the Java Trading Co., for example. Very satisfying mood elevation.

Despite acceptable trade, Bill was thinking about pulling up stakes and setting up in a town of similar size farther north. Even San Angelo, a slightly smaller town than Abilene about ninety miles to the southwest, has better coffee, Bill assured me. Up in the panhandle, Amarillo (on I-40) has better coffee. Lubbock (the southern terminus of I-27) has better coffee.* Part of the problem, I learned later, is Abilene's three private, nominally Christian colleges, whose zealous and successful efforts to keep out state colleges had inadvertently also kept down the market for sophisticated, secular coffee. Abilene Christian (Church of Christ), Hardin-Simmons (Southern Baptist), and McMurry (Methodist) had even blocked other college programs on the Dyess base.

I researched the allegation about the veto wielded by the three Christian colleges, which is precisely the kind of folklore that sometimes contains a kernel of truth. In Texas, the first place to look for the answer on such a matter is the State Constitution. Just the index to that document is almost as long as the entire United States Constitution, and the actual text is a closely printed fifty-six pages. While the constitution creates a

---

* As it turned out, Bill would sell the Cove and open a restaurant in downtown Abilene.

Hospital District for Hidalgo County and abolishes the one for Lamar County, I looked in vain for anything about higher education in Taylor County. I turned next to the legislative record and learned that in the early 1970s, State Senator Grant Jones had indeed successfully engineered legislation whose rationale was undoubtedly high-flown, but whose main purpose was to bar the development of inexpensive state colleges in Abilene. The actual bill was cleverly crafted to avoid naming any town specifically; it achieved its goal with a "population bracket" so restrictive that only Abilene fit the parameters.

Eventually, however, the citizens of Taylor County chafed at this deprivation, and a study confirmed a profound need for affordable higher education—tuition at the three private schools runs about $7,000; at nearby Angelo State in San Angelo, $1,500; at Cisco Junior College, under $1,000—and finally, in 1991, the restriction was erased from the books. The Chamber of Commerce immediately organized a victory party at the Abilene Country Club at which the chairperson of the Higher Education Committee in the State House of Representatives was expected to rise and announce the impending arrival of a state campus. Instead, Wilhelmina Delco rose and announced that no such campus was foreseeable due to a lack of funding and the unwillingness of existing state colleges to share the current, shrinking budget.

In the end, Abilene had to settle for a branch campus of Cisco Junior College, set up in the old Wal-Mart: discount education in a minimum-wage town.

Saturday night at the Mall in Abilene: with high school youths flirting everywhere and Luby's featuring spicy grilled alligator for $4.10, Bill Bedford turned the Cappuccino Cove over to Wendy, whose mother was there, too, because this was just about the only opportunity she had to spend time with her daughter, who in fact was enrolled at Cisco Junior College. Maybe Wendy's mother also showed up to keep an eye on the social situation, because a man had been leaving Wendy huge tips including, one evening, $20 for a single hazelnut latte.

Wendy had finally convinced him that this wasn't appropriate, and he hadn't been spotted around the kiosk for a while. In his wake came speculation that this benefactor was none other than Jack Grimm, the local oilman involved in plans to raise the *Titanic* who had also developed a reputation for bestowing large sums on deserving individuals.

Wendy and her mother knew about me, the guy who'd been talking with Bill for the book about the interstates and all that. "Have you been published?" Mom asked. When I graciously presented my bona fides and mentioned some gratuitous ghostwriting, a young man by the name of Chris, seated on the other side of the horseshoe, took the cue to tell us about the time his grandmother's television had suddenly turned itself off, green smoke pouring into the living room, and the two of them had laid their respective heads on a pair of Bibles lying on the coffee table until the smoke had cleared about an hour later. My jaw dropped: Chris was off and running with his ghost story before Wendy's mother had been able to inform him what "ghostwriting" means. Unfazed by this new information, he segued into a supernatural episode involving his grandmother's bed, after she'd moved out of the haunted house. And the family has a photograph of yet a third ghost!

I couldn't decide whether Chris was teasing us, but I don't believe he was. Then I learned that he'd worked for Bill Bedford right here at the Cove before, Bill told me later, a series of work-wise misunderstandings came between them. In Bill's version, Chris had spontaneously awarded a customer such a deep discount on coffee paraphernalia that no profit remained for the owner; and another time confusion arose between Bill's military time of 1300 hours, when he wanted Chris to report for duty the following afternoon, and Chris's usual starting time of 3:30 p.m. The two numbers are similar; you can see how Chris might have failed to focus on the subtle distinction. At any rate, he showed up two and a half hours late and was sent home eight hours early. Do we have here the classic conflict between the stern prior-generation boss and one of today's relatively laid-back youthful employees? On this I will interpret no more forever. Regarding books, Chris had no choice but to agree with everyone else kibitzing at the Cove that evening. "Yeah, they're dying," he acknowledged sadly. Wendy admitted that she used to read dozens and dozens of books in elementary school; now, none at all.

Kids. What can you say? But the saving grace of this media-besotted generation is supposedly the fact that they really know their liquor. They're hyper-hip, we're reassured; all that quick-cutting on MTV has really honed their interpretive skills. You can't fool them. Maybe you can't, but maybe you won't have to, they seem so disengaged. Chris even walked out on *Pulp Fiction*, failing to see the point of it all. A man and his wife then joined our impromptu party and ordered a pair of laced beverages, the popular German chocolate mocha, a confection of hazelnut, caramel, coconut, chocolate, and even espresso. They were en route to the adjacent cineplex, so I asked if *Pulp Fiction* was their selection. No, because they were Christians.

The following Monday morning, Bill Bedford and I shared a good laugh about my report of the previous evening. He also got a kick out of the ghostwriting contretemps, wagging his head despondently. And he loved the line I'd received from one of the mall walkers. The doors of the mall are opened early in the morning to accommodate the many exercisers who find the climate-controlled conditions to their liking. This happened to be a cool, clear morning, perfect for alfresco walking, and the major city park isn't far away, but I counted well over fifty men and women marching briskly through the place. Including every alcove and cul-de-sac, their track is three quarters of a mile long. Four laps, three miles: the standard workout for members of the Heart and Sole Walking Club. But I had to rework the math because when I asked one guy about the distance, he replied, "Six eighths of a mile."

Bill and I laughed hard when I repeated this line. "No, no," he gasped between heaves, "I'm not sure that's right. I think it's twelve sixteenths!"

On my way to the adult video and bookstore in Merkel, the would-be governor's hometown, I stopped for dinner at the

Merkel Restaurant, where I knew the owners. Marion Shelton had taken over the restaurant and adjacent motel after her husband had died some years back, and she ran a tight ship. Maybe this was in the genes—Scandinavian—and the geography—Minnesotan, originally. Marion is the first to agree that Texans are friendlier than either Scandinavians or Minnesotans; she realizes her face doesn't necessarily light up with pleasure when greeting every customer. As a former teacher in suburban, middle-class Minneapolis, she had had no acquaintance with small-town, West Texas interstate mores in which the kids smoke and almost everyone else either works for the minimum wage or is divorced, or both. Still, the flat place had grown on her, as had its people.

Though her establishment is on the service road south of I-20, it caters primarily to the local populace and to workers stationed here temporarily. However, this is not a no-tell motel. Any drug dealer or flagrant prostitute would last about five minutes in Marion Shelton's domain. Next door is what appears to be a former restaurant with red aluminum siding, now the Christian Life "Full Gospel" Church, the phrase denoting a rigorous approach to the inerrancy of Scripture. The town of Merkel (population 2,469) is the kind of town in the kind of country in which any kind of building might be pressed into service as a sanctuary.

Marion's son Gary is the chef and heir apparent. While Ken Black swears that almost nothing comes out of a can at the Wes-T-Go, Gary's incredible yeast rolls with the texture of cotton candy are just about the only item he even prepares beforehand. Order refried beans and Gary refries *your* beans. Order bacon and he fries *your* bacon. Some locals give Gary a head start by calling in their orders. The wait would be worth it, but why wait if you don't have to? For my dinner, Gary prepared a delicious blackened catfish and presented a plateful of the succulent rolls. When I mentioned my next destination, he exclaimed, "Oh, yeah, they've been advertising some special appearance in the Abilene paper all week."

"Really?" I said. In Abilene? Home of all those Christian colleges, and where the best old-time hardware store is Bible Hardware, and not because that's the owner's last name?

"Big ads," Gary assured me.

I thanked the chef for the fine meal, departed, crossed under the interstate, and followed the service road on the other side to the truck stop where the Snake Man put one over on them L.A. Guns. Adults Etc. is directly next door, and not by accident. I probably wouldn't have given the place a second thought except that state trooper John Murphy had mentioned it briefly. Management had called him out to break up a fight between a married couple. The guy had been in the habit of dressing his wife up in miniskirts, a low-cut blouse, and heels, then sending her into the store. He wouldn't permit her to say anything. Apparently he just enjoyed watching the other men watch her, and she played along. But this one evening, apparently, he decided to go further and ordered his wife into one of the private viewing rooms. Now he was pimping for her, John hypothesized, and at this the wife finally rebelled. The couple had been married twenty-three years and were frequent patrons of the store. All in all, John concluded, it was "a sad deal."

So I began trying to reach the owner of Adults Etc. or, failing that, the manager. But nobody who answered the phone wanted to talk about the business. They *could not talk* about the business, they made clear, nor could the second people to whom the first people handed the phone. Slowly but surely, however, after a series of calls placed from motels and the pay phones at the Mall in Abilene and the Wes-T-Go, I insinuated myself into the middle of things and learned that the man I needed to talk to wasn't the man who John thought ran the show—by now he was old news—but rather an individual named Chuck, who in turn was never around. Until this week. No sooner was my father on the plane to Houston than I was on the phone and informed that if I called back in the afternoon, Chuck would be there. Bingo.

Over the phone, I immediately delivered my stock declaration of intent and went out of my way to demonstrate that I was writing about all things great and small regarding the interstates, with no focus at all on the pornography trade, with no particular axe to grind anyway. That's fine, Chuck said, but this store had been the target of assorted pickets, protests, and vandals ever since it opened six years earlier; it didn't really need or desire any publicity, good or bad, that I might provide. I would have to write him a letter at the local post office box, include a résumé of previous publications and a list of my questions, and wait for a reply. He would pass this packet on to the ownership's lawyer, who would, in all likelihood, Chuck admitted, decline to proceed with the deposition.*

On the phone, Chuck seemed like a nice enough guy; he certainly wasn't belligerent. Regarding the pickets who had greeted the store's grand opening, he really didn't have an argument with that activity—he even served them coffee and donuts—because no one is stronger on First Amendment rights than folks in this business.

He was vague, naturally, on the subject of his role in the ownership of Adults Etc., but I somehow inferred that whoever does own the store also owns others elsewhere. I asked Chuck.

"Oh yeah!" he exclaimed, then stopped. "But there you go!"

After declining to answer questions, he caught me red-handed trying to ask one, yet with no hard feelings he invited me out to the store that evening for a special personal appearance by two major stars, Persia and Lexus Locklear, who between six and ten p.m. would be posing for pictures, dancing, and signing autographs. I'll be there, I assured him, and when I called Houston to make sure my father had gotten home with reasonable dispatch—he had—I intrigued my mother with the news that my next interstate assignment required me to drive out to this adult bookstore and meet a couple of famous buxom women. Hipster that she is, Mom got a real kick out of that.

Adults Etc. is a clean, well-lighted place with plenty of parking in the rear. Truckers get ten percent off, and every last customer—men, women, and couples alike—puts on a lackadaisical, walk-in-the-park air. Maybe they actually *feel* this way, and I'm the only one with a stir in the loins as I walk the

---

*As it happened, he not only declined to proceed, but even to answer.

aisles studying all the pictures, books, magazines, and videos of the beast with two backs, sometimes more, and with plentiful mouths as well. I asked one of the ladies at the front counter if Chuck was around, and she pointed him out, standing toward the back near the table where Persia and Lexus Locklear were on display. A big guy with a strong grip, Chuck introduced me to the stars, one pretty, one very pretty, both featuring computer-enhanced graphics, it seemed to me—a turn-off, in my case, although I wouldn't go so far as to say that my loins lost interest entirely. Chuck pointed out the nearby display of the two women's respective best videos. Meanwhile, one of his associates was using an old-fashioned Polaroid camera to take $10 snapshots of customers posing with either star. With one of the shy fellows, Lexus took his hand and placed it on one of her hooters and then went below the belt with her own hand and no one had to say smile.

Chuck showed me the rest of the store and introduced a couple of other employees, of whom there were half a dozen altogether, at least, in a place no larger than a standard 7-Eleven. I was pointedly *not* pumping Chuck for information, but he did freely mention the ownership group's terrific store on I-40 outside Amarillo, four-star all the way, twice the square footage of this one, with viewing rooms featuring color TV, couches, and a coffee table. That's one of the busiest stores in the country. Then a voice over the P.A. system announced that Persia and Lexus would soon return to the dance floor in the little theater off to the side, so we should purchase our tokens now. Chuck assured me these shows would be packed all night. I thought about taking this opportunity to draw some insights about eros and civilization before reluctantly deciding that pandering to our low-end lust was surely unnecessary in a work of this stature. So I said goodbye to Chuck, who was probably snickering to himself about my bashfulness. On my way out, I passed on their way in the most mousy, timid-looking couple I'd ever seen. Other than the obvious truckers, most of the shoppers at Adults Etc.—dozens of them, by the time I left—looked like neighbors and solid citizens, and some of the obvious truckers did, too, but this little man and his sweet wife were even more so: surely they enjoyed nothing so much as the company of their grandchildren. This lady audibly gasped when she saw the first picture, and her husband said, with justified annoyance, "Well, what did you expect?"

The following morning, stopping by the Merkel Restaurant to pick up a piece of Gary Shelton's coconut pie for the road, I was opening the door when an elderly fellow stepped out of his pickup. Because he was wearing a baseball cap that advertised the Hughes Gin in Avoca, Texas, I introduced myself. This was Herbert Meads, and we immediately established that he had attended school in Stamford with my father, although he couldn't place the name. Herbert had also run the cotton gin in Tuxedo before my grandfather Henry got the job, back before anyone had heard of green cards or overtime pay, laissez-faire times that Herbert remembered fondly and at length. Finally we said goodbye and I stepped inside, bought my dessert, bid farewell to the owner and the chef, and returned outside to soldier on in my car.

But not for long. By now, I knew my chosen route between Dallas and the coast as well as I knew the keyboard on my laptop computer. I had bivouacked in quite enough motels and stopped at enough highway restaurants to last me quite a while. I needed new tires. And after all this time in "Tex-as, my Tex-as," I had a hunch that New York City was once again just over the horizon.* By now, however, I was unfazed. I had found consolation in this epigram from Emerson: "People wish to be settled; only as far as they are unsettled is there any hope for them."

That's nothing but good news for my wife and me, and nothing but good news for this culture, too. I agree with odologist John Brinckerhoff Jackson: the future does give every sign of being short on dignity but long on vitality; the interstates, not the back roads, will remain the asphalt and concrete wave of the future. There are worse destinies.

---

*And so it was. My wife and I moved back up in November 1995.

EPILOGUE

Then the phone call from the nursing home finally came: my grandmother Myrtle, the last of her kind, had died in Ozona at the age of ninety-five. The family stayed out at Tom Mitchell's Circle Bar spread, where the Christmas tree bedecked with white lights was suspended by a stout wire directly above the swimming pool. Everyone sitting in the Jacuzzi agreed that this must be in violation of some kind of code, even in Crockett County.

Saturday morning was lovely and warm for the season. In my grandparents' plot at the Cedar Run cemetery, not quite a mile south of the interstate, the two live oaks planted by my grandfather as acorns decades before were now large, handsome specimens. Bailey Post had enjoyed taking his grandsons to admire the fragile seedlings, and I remember how he leaned down to cradle these tiny trees with his large hands with prominent blue veins, just like my own hands, and how he watered them on a finely tuned schedule. He did the same with the trees planted in appropriate places on the otherwise natural landscape of the hillside on which he had lived.

Bailey Post was born in 1896 and died in 1979. Myrtle Post was born in 1898. Now, in 1994, their story was concluded, and therefore part of mine as well. I was surprised more people weren't present for the graveside service until my grandmother's loyal friend Jonesy Williams reminded me that Ms. Post, as she always called her, had outlived not only everyone from her own generation, but almost everyone from the next one, too. Another of her old friends, a rancher's wife, looked around at the graves and said, "A lot of these people are ones she helped in so many ways." Among the floral displays was one from the Myrtle Post Garden Club, named in her honor years ago. I happened to notice the name on the stone in the adjacent plot. MITCHELL, it read. Buried there is Marsha Mitchell, born in 1933, died in 1978. The date seemed about right, so I asked Jonesy Williams, and, indeed, Marsha Mitchell was Tom Mitchell's wife.

The service for Myrtle Post was short and sweet, as my mother had requested. The brief eulogy was delivered by the new Methodist pastor in town, a man who had never really known my grandmother, and he invited us to wonder at the miracle of the Resurrection. I know for a fact that neither my mother, father, wife, brother, sister-in-law, niece, nephew, the vast majority of my friends, nor I myself believe in resurrections. But Grandmother did believe in the Easter story. She was a devout Methodist and as kind and wonderful a lady as ever lived. If there should be a heaven, Myrtle is sitting pretty. If there's not, would she feel cheated? I can't believe it.

For a quick meal before leaving town, the family drove in separate cars to the Café Next Door; the preacher walked in the restaurant shortly after we arrived and everyone nodded from a distance. This café is next door to the Texaco station and convenience store at the main interstate intersection in Ozona. The conglomerate is the handiwork of Joyce Maness and her family. I give Joyce top billing only because I knew her from an earlier visit, and because she's a retired schoolteacher who had been a friend of my grandmother's. Her daughter handles the gas station, her son runs this restaurant, her husband pays the bills for both. He used to run the Texaco station on old 290, the station my grandfather patronized as he drove around town on his hospital errands, including going to the tire store across the street, which doubled as the bus station. That's where we picked up the shipments of blood. Weldon Maness kept that station going for a couple of years after he opened the new one on the interstate, then sold it to the Mexican-American who owns it still. This old station on the old highway still gets most of the old business in town.

The Manesses decided to open the Café Next Door when they realized how often motorists asked while gassing up, "Where's a good place to eat?" Their answer to that question has a high, angled wood ceiling and an expanse of windows providing southern exposure and an appropriate view of the embankment of I-10. That glass must be thick, and the insulation, too, because the restaurant is remarkably quiet, considering. Almost all the noise comes from the bustle inside. After lunch, my wife and I said goodbye to my mother and father and drove around Ozona one last time. Would I ever be back? Maybe not, although I like the town and love the difficult land. But that's the way it goes. Every day of the year, thousands of cars and trucks pass within a mile of the town square. How many of these motorists and truckers know or care anything about this town or the people who live and die here? Few, if any. How many will ever be back this way? Some, not many. The fast highways must be both cause and effect in this regard: easy come, easy go, lots of transience, shallow roots.

ACKNOWLEDGMENTS

Literally hundreds of people have contributed to this book, including many encountered on the interstates but unmentioned in my story. I thank them all for their contributions. To those who are identified and maybe quoted I say, All the thanks in the world. To those who play big roles in the saga, I can honestly say, Without you, there is no *Uneasy Rider*. Everyone, please forgive anything that's wrong.

For the dozens of men and women who helped with my research but aren't mentioned in the story, I have no choice but to resort to the following long list, which unfortunately implies a perfunctoriness of appreciation I certainly don't feel. They were all great: Steve Baker, Helm, Pletcher, & Hogan, Houston; Gary Baumer, Allan McGinty, and Pete Walden, Texas Agriculture Extension Service; Mark Brandenburg, Golden Gate Casino; Marver Brown, Sixth Floor Museum, Dallas; Carlton Carl, office of former congressman John Bryant; Janet

Coleman, Department of Transportation, Washington, D.C.; Nellie Connally, Department of Interior, Washington, D.C.; Mike Cox, Public Information Office, Department of Public Safety, Austin; Leota Cox, Circle Bar Truck Corral, Ozona; David Crane, House Committee on State, Federal, and International Relations, Austin; Dominick Delbalso, Cleveland District Attorney's Office; Derrick—no last name—at the Travis County District Court; Amy Engler, Greyhound Bus Lines; Jim Eskin, Department of Agriculture, Washington, D.C.; Jane Friday and Mario Ortiz, United States Border Patrol, Dallas; Nelson Galloway, John Guerrero, and Martin McLaughlin, Texas Department of Transportation; Roy Hale, Texas Alcoholic Beverage Commission; Jeff Harris, Rand McNally; Tom Kelly, Chamber of Commerce, Williams, Arizona; Paula LaRocque, Dallas *Morning News*; Clark Larson, United States Border Patrol, El Paso; John Misiti, Texaco, Inc.; Deborah Montoya, *New Mexico* magazine; Steve Niswander, Korendyke Transport, Dallas; Keith Olive, Department of Public Safety, Ozona; Lt. Pinon, New Mexico Department of Taxation; Dave Prince, Newell Motor Coaches, the best in the world; Dale Szyndrowski, Distilled Spirits Council of the United States (DISCUS); C.W. Thompson, United States Border Patrol, Marfa, Texas; Bruce Tiffany, Six Flags Over Texas; Maureen Tooley, Herald Publishing Company, Truth or Consequences, New Mexico; Richard Weingroff, chief historian of the Federal Highway Administration (a special thanks here; in his field, Richard's the one); and Richard Wells, Wells Gaming Research.

I relied mostly on people, not books, but two books should be mentioned by way of an abbreviated bibliography: *Discovering the Vernacular Landscape* by John Brinckerhoff Jackson, Yale University Press, 1984; and *Wheels*, Wilfred Owen and Ezra Bowen, editors, Life Science Library, 1967.

Patient and helpful readers of portions of the book were Leslie Clark, Eva Freund, Steve Gaskins, Steve Hanks, Joe Kane, Gaines Post, Kay Rogers, Judy Ryser, Fred Waitzkin, and Wendy Wolf. Gaskins and his wife, Kathy Larson, provided a great place to stay in Minneapolis. That story figures in the book. Gaines and his wife, Jeanie, in California provided much needed R&R along the way, as told; likewise, Kate Correa and Lisa Schwartzberg in New Mexico. Charla and Rich Tindall of San Marino, California, owned the house in Dallas in which my wife and I stayed for most of the period I was working on this book. That story definitely figures into things; I hope the house-sitting trade-off worked as well for them as it did for me. Finally in this category, many thanks to Mary and Bill Henrich, who've housed me several times in several places.

I thank my mother, Wynona, and my father, Bob, for their editorial efforts with the appropriate chapters. My wife, Patty, was terrific, of course, in this capacity and others. Joe Spieler did his usual great agenting job. Editorial assistant Rob Grover was helpful at all times in all matters. Most important of all: my editor, Gary Fisketjon, adamantly steered the book clear of at least one horribly wrong turn, later made the key structural suggestion, and did a tremendous job sharpening the final draft.

THE BEST OF OUTSIDE

The First 20 Years

from the editors of *Outside* magazine

Here the editors of *Outside* have selected over thirty essays that take us around the world from the slums of Haiti to the jungles of Peru, from the peaks of the Himalayas to the beaches of Belize. Among the authors included are: Jon Krakauer, who experiences a deadly week on Everest; Jane Smiley, who recalls an adolescent adventure in fox hunting; and Thomas McGuane, explaining his reasons for hunting.

Nature/Sports/0-375-70313-6

HEART AND BLOOD

Living with Deer in America

by Richard Nelson

Here Richard Nelson explores an elusive and heart-stoppingly beautiful creature that embodies our vanishing wilderness. Yet recently deer have become increasingly abundant—so much so that they threaten to overflow their traditional habitat and wreak havoc in America's suburbs. Nelson tracks his quarry from the coast of Alaska to a game ranch in Texas, visits with animal rights activists on the opening day of hunting season, shows us how deer figure in the world of the Native Americans, and brings us closer to the natural world, and, thus, to our own true selves.

Nature/0-679-73686-7

BAD LAND

An American Romance

In 1909 Congress offered 320-acre tracts of land to anyone bold or foolish enough to stake a claim to them. Drawn by inventive brochures, countless homesteaders went west to make their fortunes. Most failed. In *Bad Land*, Jonathan Raban travels through the unforgiving country that was the scene of their dreams and undoing.

Winner of the National Book Critics Circle Award for Nonfiction
A New York Times *Editors' Choice for Book of the Year*

History/Current Affairs/0-679-75906-9

VINTAGE DEPARTURES

PECKED TO DEATH BY DUCKS
by Tim Cahill

In this grand tour of the earth's remote, exotic, and dismal places, Tim Cahill sleeps with a grizzly bear, witnesses demonic possession in Bali, assesses the cuteness quotient of giant clams in the South Pacific, and survives a run-in with something called the Throne of Doom in Guatemala.

"Tim Cahill [has] the what-the-hell adventuresomeness of a T. E. Lawrence and the humor of a P. J. O'Rourke."

—Condé Nast Traveler

Travel/Adventure/0-679-74929-2

BURY ME STANDING
The Gypsies and Their Journey
by Isabel Fonseca

Fabled, feared, romanticized, and reviled, the Gypsies—or Roma —are among the least understood people on earth. Now a diaspora of twelve million, their culture remains largely obscure. But in Isabel Fonseca they have found an eloquent witness.

"A revelation: a hidden world—at once ignored and secretive, persecuted and unknown—is uncovered in these absorbing pages."

—Salman Rushdie

Current Affairs/Travel/0-679-76743-X

BAD TRIPS
Edited and with an Introduction
by Keath Fraser

From Martin Amis in the air to Peter Matthiessen on a mountaintop, some of the best-known writers of our time recount sometimes harrowing and sometimes exhilarating tales of their most memorable misadventures in travel.

"The only aspect of our travels that is guaranteed to hold an audience is disaster. . . . Nothing is better for survival."

—Martha Gellhorn

Travel/Adventure/0-679-72908-9

FALLING OFF THE MAP
Some Lonely Places of the World
by Pico Iyer

Pico Iyer voyages from the nostalgic elegance of Argentina to the raffish nonchalance of Australia, documents the cruising rites of Icelandic teenagers, gets interrogated by tipsy Cuban police, and attends a screening of Bhutan's first feature film.

"[Iyer] writes the kind of lyrical, flowing prose that could make Des Moines sound beguiling."
—*Los Angeles Times Book Review*
Travel/Adventure/0-679-74612-9

SHOOTING THE BOH
A Woman's Voyage Down the Wildest River in Borneo
by Tracy Johnston

A heroic and entertaining tale about a woman's harrowing ride down the treacherous rapids of the Boh River in central Borneo and through the uncharted realm of middle age.

"Funny, candid, riveting. . . . I enjoyed this book immensely."
—Joe Kane

Travel/Adventure/0-679-74010-4

THE ENDS OF THE EARTH
A Journey to the Frontiers of Anarchy—
from Togo to Turkmenistan, from Iran to Cambodia
by Robert Kaplan

Traveling from West Africa to Southeast Asia to report on a world of disintegrating nation-states, warring nationalities, metastasizing populations, and dwindling resources, Kaplan emerges with a gritty tour de force of political journalism.

History/Current Affairs/0-679-75123-8

A YEAR IN PROVENCE
by Peter Mayle

An "engaging, funny and richly appreciative" (*The New York Times Book Review*) account of an English couple's first year living in Provence, settling in amid the enchanting gardens and equally festive bistros of their new home.

"Stylish, witty, delightfully readable."

—*The Sunday Times* (London)

Travel/0-679-73114-8

CAVE PASSAGES
by Michael Ray Taylor

From a 1,000-foot-deep sinkhole in Mexico (where a seasoned diver drowned while the author watched in horror) to Wyoming's aptly named Great Crawl of Death, Michael Ray Taylor takes readers to some of the world's deepest and most treacherous caves.

"Finally, a well-written book about the glories and dangers of caving."

—Tim Cahill

Travel/Adventure/0-679-78125-0